THE ACADEMIC LIFE

A CARNEGIE FOUNDATION SPECIAL REPORT

The Academic Life

SMALL WORLDS, DIFFERENT WORLDS

BURTON R. CLARK

WITH A FOREWORD BY

ERNEST L. BOYER

THE CARNEGIE FOUNDATION FOR THE

ADVANCEMENT OF TEACHING

5 IVY LANE, PRINCETON, NEW JERSEY 08540

Library of Congress Cataloging-in-Publication Data

Clark, Burton R.
   The academic life.

   (A Carnegie Foundation special report)
   Bibliography: p. 335
   Includes index.
   1. College teachers—United States—History.
2. College teaching—United States—History.
3. Universities and colleges—United States—History.
4. United States—Intellectual life. I. Carnegie
Foundation for the Advancement of Teaching. II. Title.
III. Series.
LB1778.C53 1987   378'.12'0973   87-15068
ISBN 0-931050-31-6
ISBN 0-931050-32-4 (pbk.)

Copies are available from the
PRINCETON UNIVERSITY PRESS
3175 Princeton Pike
Lawrenceville, N.J. 08648

To Philip Neil Clark

1954–1986

I hold every man a debtor to his profession, from which as men do of course seek to receive countenance and profit, so ought they of duty to endeavor themselves, by way of amends, to be a help and an ornament thereunto.

—Francis Bacon, MAXIMS OF THE LAW, WORKS

We want to draw the lesson that nothing is gained by yearning and tarrying alone, and we shall act differently. We shall set to work and meet the "demands of the day," in human relations as well as in our vocation. This, however, is plain and simple, if each finds and obeys the demon who holds the fibers of his very life.

—Max Weber, "SCIENCE AS A VOCATION"

The absolute scholar is in fact a rather uncanny being. . . . A man will invest his sum of living in the study of Sumerian potsherds, in the vertiginous attempt to classify the dung beetles of one corner of New Guinea, in the study of the mating patterns of wood lice, in the biography of a single writer or statesman, in the synthesis of one chemical substance, in the grammar of a dead language. . . . To the utmost scholar, sleep is a puzzle of wasted time, and flesh a piece of torn luggage that the spirit must drag after it. . . . It is indeed a haunting and haunted business.

—George Steiner, "THE CLERIC OF TREASON"

CONTENTS

LIST OF TABLES

ACKNOWLEDGMENTS

THE COMMITMENT to fashion this volume originated in late 1982 when Ernest L. Boyer, President of The Carnegie Foundation for the Advancement of Teaching, agreed to support a national field study of American academics. The ensuing major grant from the Foundation, incorporating funds from the Mellon Foundation, allowed me to mount an extensive research effort that otherwise would not have been possible. I am deeply indebted to Dr. Boyer, the Carnegie Foundation, and the Mellon Foundation for the opportunity they provided.

The magnitude of the investigation required a small staff in which two postdoctoral research associates played a leading role in planning and carrying out the research. Sydney Ann Halpern (1983–1984) and Kenneth Ruscio (1983–1985) made numerous visits to participating universities and colleges to conduct the interviews on which my later writing so much depended. Their efforts were invaluable: their own writings from the study have informed mine. A third research associate, Gary Rhoades, offered insightful criticism from beginning to end. I am much indebted to the contributions of these three young scholars. Over the course of several academic years, six research assistants, all graduate students at the University of California, Los Angeles, were also variously involved. I wish to thank Mitchell Bard, Marie Freeman, Ronald Opp, Ann Hansen, Curtis Shepard, and Betty Glick for work that stretched from field visits to routine tasks that overlooked their intelligence and initiative.

I am also particularly mindful of the necessary contribution to the study made by the several hundred professors and administrators in universities and colleges, disciplinary associations, and other academic locales who agreed to be interviewed. They patiently conversed about our concerns. The openness of American higher education was reflected in the willingness of these respondents to actively enter into our particular pursuit of the truth. It is a pleasure, on behalf of all those in the UCLA research group, to thank those who met us more than halfway when the knock on the office door produced an interviewer equipped with fifteen pages of open-ended questions, a tape recorder, and a smiling request for the appointed hour of time.

Cindy Caloia and the staff of the communications processing center in the UCLA Graduate School of Education helped to prepare numerous drafts of the manuscript over many months. Adele Clark provided the general editing that helped translate some sociologese and educationese into clear English.

A volume on the academic profession in late twentieth-century America written by an academic already three decades beyond the doctorate surely incurs a host of unconscious, as well as a multitude of conscious, intellectual debts. The readily identified sources range from such American observers as Logan Wilson, David Riesman, Clark Kerr, Walter Metzger, and Martin A. Trow—from whom I have learned more than is specifically acknowledged in the following pages—to the growing group of scholars in other countries who have shed light on the academic profession. Particularly instructive have been the writings of a number of British colleagues, especially Lord Eric Ashby, Harold Perkin, A. H. Halsey, Tony Becher, Maurice Kogan, and Graeme Moodie. Like so many others, I have absorbed much about the workings of higher education and science from the late Israeli sociologist, Joseph Ben-David. Most of all I wish to acknowledge the source of my intellectual roots of 30 years ago. Philip Selznick modeled for me a sociological perspective that sheds light on how organizations and other major social units, including professions, fashion distinctive identities that respect competing interests and multiple values. I am indebted to his imagination, insight, and generosity. The way of looking at the world that I acquired from him has served as a general guide in a half-dozen studies of higher education institutions and systems at home and abroad. A perspective wears better than a method.

BURTON R. CLARK
Santa Monica, California
April, 1986

FOREWORD

by Ernest L. Boyer

WE ARE VERY PLEASED that Burton Clark, one of the nation's foremost higher education scholars, has, in this landmark study, focused so perceptively on the condition of the professoriate today. *The Academic Life* examines the teaching and research functions in the academy and contributes richly to the Foundation's long tradition of examining the condition of education in the nation.

One of the unique features of this report is its careful consideration of the diverse settings in which academics work. And we cannot help but be impressed by the ingenious adaptations that have made the professoriate amazingly serviceable at different levels and for different constituencies throughout the 350 years of America's higher education history.

Professor Clark, in his insightful study of the academic life, finds few universal truths, not for lack of effort or perception, but because there are exceptions to virtually every practice considered common. Even the most familiar assumptions about how college faculty members spend their time prove to be contingent on such inconstant factors as the types of institutions where faculty members are employed, the mix of disciplines in which professors teach or study, the ranks they hold on the academic ladder, the opportunities they have to interact with their peers, the level of instruction they offer, and the opportunities they have to participate in campus decision making. We have, in short, a profession consisting of many professions and there is reason for considerable satisfaction in the uniquely American way similarities and differences have been blended.

The condition of the professoriate is not wholly satisfying, however. Professor Clark reports, for example, that the seniority of candidates too often outweighs teaching ability and scholarly merit in deciding who is promoted. Faculty movement between sectors of American higher education is often difficult if not impossible to accomplish. Students, particularly undergraduates, hear a lot about the almost bewildering variety of curricular offerings but, once in the classroom, they often settle for unchallenging monologues followed by routine assignments. To make matters worse, good teachers who spend "too much" time with students too often are regarded by colleagues as men and women with misplaced academic goals.

If there is a key word in Professor Clark's penetrating analysis, it is "hierarchy." The academic profession he describes involves several interlocking ladder systems. How far up the ladder one can proceed often depends on which rung one's foot lands first. For example, there is a hierarchy of institutions, ranging from research universities, which have the greatest prestige, to community colleges, which, from the professional view, often seem to have the least. There is a hierarchy of disciplines, with the "hard" fields like biology and physics at the top and "soft" fields like sociology and education at the bottom. There are hierarchies within institutional faculties that conform to the traditional ranking of full professors at the top and lecturers and instructors at the beginning levels. And where the range in academic ranks is not broad enough, college administrators can raise the ceilings and lower the floors by creating special endowed chairs for faculty stars and a variety of full- and part-time out-of-track positions below the traditional "entry level" for the men and women who meet classes that regular faculty on the tenure ladder have no time for.

There is also a hierarchy of tasks. At some institutions, research is regarded as more prestigious and important than teaching. Almost anywhere it is more prestigious to teach one or two hours a week than it is to teach ten or twelve hours. And at many colleges, those who allow themselves to be recruited into administrative committee service may be charged by their colleagues with wasting time.

Burton Clark also reminds us that the importance of the tasks professors assume changes significantly with the institutional setting. Most obviously, research, which is the surest endeavor to earn credit for a professor at a university, plays a much less significant role for faculty at colleges that concentrate on undergraduate education.

These observations about faculty priorities parallel the findings of an extensive survey of faculty we conducted as a part of our companion study on the undergraduate college. Our faculty survey revealed that less than

xvi

one-third of all faculty members say their interests lie "very heavily in research," or in both teaching and research "but leaning toward research." Although more than 60 percent of the faculty members in the same survey said that they were currently "engaged in scholarly research work" they expected to lead to publication, almost 60 percent had never had a book or monograph published "alone or in collaboration," and about one-third of the faculty in four-year institutions had not had any professional writings published in the last two years.

In the Foundation's report on the undergraduate experience, we observed that "while not all professors are or should be publishing researchers, they, nonetheless, should be first-rate *scholars*. We understand this to mean staying abreast of the profession, knowing the literature in one's fields, and skillfully communicating such information to students." Professor Clark makes the same distinction between research and scholarship when he defines scholarship as "maintaining control of primary material," and research as "finding out something new about a topic or author or field." Both activities are essential. Research, however, will be most successful at those institutions committed to support it with up-to-date, often very expensive, facilities, equipment and specialized staff, while college and university teachers can and should be scholars wherever they are employed.

Too often, we found that universities and colleges give the highest rewards to those faculty members who may not be committed to giving their best effort to the students who pay their tuitions with an expectation that they will be well taught. Although many faculty members sincerely assert their fondness for students and are excited by the satisfaction they derive from teaching well, the academic culture too often holds such enthusiasms in low regard.

One symptom of insufficient regard for teaching is the increasing use of part-time instructors to meet enrollment demands in certain courses. While such teachers may have a good command of the knowledge to be taught, they are rarely regarded as full members of the campus community and are not expected to assume responsibilities or enjoy rewards commensurate with those of full-time academics.

Elevating teachers and teaching to a higher position in the hierarchy of the academic profession, while sustaining and enriching the tradition of scholarship and research, is one of the most urgent priorities confronting higher education. And the greatest responsibility for leadership in that effort probably lies with the nation's research universities. These institutions not only have acquired a reputation, usually unfairly, for undervaluing teaching, they are at the top of the prestige ladder, and they are most likely to be watched and emulated. If they neglect good teaching other institutions are likely to undervalue it as well.

Another persistent theme in Professor Clark's analysis is that authority over faculty behavior is unevenly distributed and often seems remote from the laboratory and classroom. The larger the institution, the more remote from individual faculty members the controlling influence seems to be. In contrast, patterns of organization in which power descends by assignment from trustees to presidents to deans to individual faculty members on down the line are found primarily in small liberal arts colleges. At public institutions, and particularly at two-year colleges, government officials may have extensive authority and control over such matters as salary levels and institutional financing. On these campuses, faculty often have formed unions in order to secure a stronger voice in institutional decision making.

Feelings of remoteness from their own institutions, and feelings of isolation in academic departments that have little interaction with other fields of study, also encourage faculty members to seek company and encouragement from national or even international discipline-oriented societies and associations.

One of the central questions raised by Professor Clark's analysis of the condition of the American faculty is how the centrifugal forces of decreasing authority on the campus and the increasing attraction of external reward and support systems are to be countered. The question is central to the academic enterprise. If students are to be well served by their teachers, their colleges and their universities will have to find ways to exert a much stronger pull than many now do on faculty loyalty and support.

In reflecting on the powerfully significant insights reported by Professor Clark, I was struck by several priorities that may be useful for colleges to consider as they seek to restore vitality in academic life.

First, at every institution, teaching should be valued as the responsibility of every faculty member. At research universities, in particular, good teaching should be considered as important as research as a route to tenure and promotion. The rank of Distinguished Research Professor is already in place at many universities. There should also be the rank of Distinguished Teaching Professor to extend special status and salary incentives to professors who are outstandingly effective in the classroom.

Second, all professors should be first-rate scholars. We understand this to mean staying on the cutting edge of the profession, knowing the literature in one's field, and skillfully communicating such information to students. While not all college teachers can or should strive for publication of their research findings, failure to encourage commitment to scholarship as we have defined it undermines the undergraduate experience regardless of its academic setting.

Third, colleges and universities should work harder at demonstrating the priority of faculty participation. They should reward teaching as a faculty challenge and responsibility. They also should provide more opportunities for faculty members to participate in institutional development. If colleges and universities are successful in such efforts, faculty members may come to regard their institutions as sources of fulfillment as great as seeing one's name in print in the pages of a professional journal or hearing the applause of one's fellow scholars at a professional meeting.

Fourth, a balance must be struck between full- and part-time faculty. No more than 20 percent of the undergraduate faculty should be part-time, and when part-time faculty are used, their employment should be educationally, as well as financially, justified.

Finally, periodic faculty renewal is increasingly essential. Comprehensive plans for professional faculty development need to be developed on all campuses. Sabbatical leaves should be available at all colleges and universities, and funds be appropriated to help teachers develop new ideas and improve their instruction. Exchange lectureships and other such arrangements should be encouraged.

In the search for excellence, colleges and universities cannot ignore the condition of the academic profession. This issue is central to everything the academy is expected to accomplish. We are fortunate, therefore, to have Professor Clark's wonderfully detailed and reflective analysis at a time when the vitality and vision of higher education is being vigorously reaffirmed.

ERNEST L. BOYER
President,
The Carnegie Foundation for
the Advancement of Teaching

INTRODUCTION

THERE CAN BE no doubt that the academic profession is an odd occupation. Composed of many disciplines, its alphabet of specialties stretches from anthropology and astronomy to Western civilization and zoology, encompassing along the way all the natural sciences, social sciences, humanities, and many of the arts. Operating also as the training ground for other professions, its membership includes doctors, lawyers, architects, engineers, and representatives of other advanced crafts. Variety is its name, for it is inevitably a conglomerate of interests in which purposes and tasks steadily divide along lines of subject, clientele, and occupational linkage. And opaqueness is its style, for who can fathom an econometrician when he or she is in full stride, let alone a high-energy physicist, a molecular biologist, an ethnomethodologist newly tutored in semiotics, or an English professor determined to deconstruct literary texts?

This uncommon profession was once relatively simple. In its medieval form, six to eight centuries ago, it embraced only a few fields and a small clientele. But the growth in knowledge that began to accelerate markedly in the nineteenth century and the expansion in student numbers that has been the hallmark of recent decades have led to large institutions and huge national systems that support and require a complex professoriate. Nowhere among the nations of the world has this complexity become greater than in the United States. America has evolved a swollen and diffused academic aggregation whose members now serve not only as the central work force of universities and colleges but also as society's main carriers of the values of science and higher learning. The significance of this profession in American life is hardly in doubt. If individuals cannot get anywhere without some book learning, then the occupations richest in intellectual content move to the center of the stage. It follows that those who seek to understand modern society can hardly know too much about the academic profession; yet inquiry and insight have lagged. Relatively little is known

xxi

about what goes on in the profession's many quarters. What is the quality of workaday life for its varied members? How do they conceive of themselves and their lives? What, if anything, holds them together? How autonomous are these professional workers near the end of the twentieth century, and how much are they subject to bureaucratic dictate? What determines the profession's contemporary strengths and its more glaring weaknesses?

To confront the fundamental issues of this profession in America, we are compelled to adopt a broad organizational approach. American academics are distributed in widely varied institutions as well as in different disciplines, in many kinds of universities, four- and two-year colleges as well as in numerous subjects. The structures and cultures of those diverse settings cry out for our attention; they heavily shape the academic life. It is no longer useful in the United States to speak of "the university" or "the college" as an entity singularly forming "the academic man." As we traverse an extended domain, we find many kinds of academics who are distinguished simultaneously by subject and type of institution. Wisdom, then, begins with the will to disaggregate, seeking to give proper weight to settings that make a difference. As academic labor becomes finely tuned, we must play to a theme of differentiation. We are obliged to compare parts of the higher education system so that we may study the character of the academic division of labor and highlight its significant effects.

History also immediately stakes its claim in our analysis. Academic forms have great staying power: aspects of guild organization have evolved in European higher education over eight centuries; the use of trustees in modern America is rooted in patterns of control laid down in the colonial period. In academia, if anywhere, awareness of historical primacy and sustained evolution informs the present.[1] The contexts and developments of earlier eras have significantly determined the patterns of today and have set the trajectories that extend into the future. As it hones our sense of constancy and change, the long view of history also leads us away from the ups and downs of current events. Critical thought on American education suffers from a momentary mentality that excites proclamations of a crisis each year and a revolution every decade. Administrators and politicians have to work in short time frames: meetings of national associations offer new themes every year. But observers free of the immediate pressures of gathering and spending should seek the steadier tone that history helps to prove. We need to turn, however briefly, to the unique past of American higher education if we wish to deepen our understanding of the unique present and likely future of its core profession.

As we pursue the organizational foundations of academic life, we are also served by cross-national awareness. National contexts produce large differences: the French system of higher education is fundamentally different from the German, the German from the British.[2] By borrowing forms and ideas a century ago from a host of international sources and by evolving along pathways set by its own traditions and political imperatives, the Japanese system now exhibits a unique configuration of public and private institutions, of chaired professors, state officials, and lay trustees. In its extensive decentralization and sharp competition, the American composite of academies and academics is singularly different from other major centers of learning. Especially when compared with Continental Europe, American academic life has taken a fundamentally different shape that includes a different relationship to government and a different form of rank and status. In a companion volume, an international group of experts have explored how national, institutional, and disciplinary contexts shape the academic profession.[3] Conclusions drawn from that effort have helped to establish certain basic features of the American system and its resident profession, whose importance might otherwise have been overlooked or underestimated.

Any study of the academic profession must also confront at the outset the pros and cons of viewing this particular occupation as a profession that has many similarities to other professions. Taken in the large, it clearly can be placed among professionalized occupations as yet another major form of collective action that simultaneously grants and limits freedom as it attempts to link gain to responsibility. For a half-century, arguments have waxed about how to define a profession, variously emphasizing expertise, training, certification, self-determination, normative controls, and altruistic service.[4] Analysis of the many professions—preeminently medicine and law—has moved through stages that have ranged from blissful acclaim that they are the best hope of mankind to scornful condemnation of their domineering and exploitative ways.[5] A recent reasonable conceptualization of a profession that moves beyond the passing polemics reduces multitudinous listings of attributes to three—the collegial, the cognitive, and the moral. It defines a profession as "an occupation that regulates itself through systematic, regulated training and collegial discipline; that has a base in technical, specialized knowledge; and that has a service rather than profit orientation enshrined in its code of ethics."[6] Knowledge-based expertise is central: a hallmark in itself, it serves both as the principal source of authority and as a basis for pathways of training, certification, and career. Ambitious occupations attempting to climb the ladder of professionalism soon realize they must claim a firm foundation in special knowledge. That base allows them to seek not only the rewards of higher status and more power but also to make collegial and moral gains: "professionalism is also a kind of solidarity, a source of meaning in work, and a system of regulating belief in modern societies."[7]

From a distance, the academic occupation clearly fits the scholarly and commonplace conceptions of profession. Its specialized knowledge is front and center; collegial and moral components can be readily observed. But general definitions and discussions do not take us very far; they leave us suspended at a level that overlooks too much that is important. Increasingly a holding company for diverging groups, the academic profession is so radically subdivided by workplace and subject that it entails a qualitative leap in complexity. As we move from the mind's eye of myth and cant, and from the neatness of summarizing terms, we even find that meaningful boundaries no longer exist in parts of American academic life to separate an academic estate from the rest of society. In the pursuit of academic professionalism, there is every reason in contemporary America to seek the character of "the many" inside "the one," to emphasize divergence, to view the profession as something other than isomorphic in its underlying tendencies. Its logic may well be the very opposite of the logic of the professional iron cage.[8]

The account of the American academic profession offered in the central chapters of this book is based on research undertaken between 1983 and 1985. Conceived as an intensive and largely qualitative exercise, the UCLA Study of the Academic Profession drew mainly upon recorded interviews with about 170 faculty members located in six fields of study in six major types of institutions (Appendix A). The fields were physics, biology, political science, English, business, and medicine. The institutions ranged from leading research universities to community colleges. Supplementary discussions held with presidents, deans, union representatives, and others extended the interview base to over 230 taped conversations. We promised anonymity to individuals and camouflage for institutions within sectors. The primary sessions with faculty members in sixteen institutions—public and private—spread throughout the country averaged about one and one-half hours. They provided rich verbatim faculty responses to questions about the nature of their work, their involvement in their disciplines and institutions, the beliefs they held about their own profession, their forms of authority and sense of power, their career patterns and opportunities, their participation in academic networks outside their own departments or professional schools, and other related matters. Seeking fullness of response, the recorded interviews were guided rather than tightly preformed. Here was a chance to listen to academics in their own modes of expression, to hear their own explanations of complex interactions and issues, and then to sum interpretively to isolate general patterns, with only minimal advanced standardization and virtually no quantitative analysis. The field research sought richness, intensity, and connectedness.

In one- and two-week visits to the sixteen institutions, the interviewers also gathered information about faculty from records and documents. In a minor but often insightful way, they picked up clues on institutional cultures and faculty styles. To spend a week in a leading ivy-draped private liberal arts college located in a pastoral setting and then a short time later to walk the cement-block hallways of a downtown public community college is in itself a revealing experience. Excursions were also made to the national headquarters of a half-dozen disciplinary associations to interview their leaders and gather information from their records. Additional interviews with disciplinary leaders were carried out at a few national meetings. Together with the existing research literature, these secondary forays importantly supplemented what we learned in the primary interviews.

The UCLA research group also had early access to the national survey of 5,000 academics carried out by The Carnegie Foundation for the Advancement of Teaching in the Spring of 1984 (Appendix A). Based on a mail questionnaire containing hundreds of questions, this important survey followed up on the earlier 1969 and 1975 Carnegie surveys. It offered statistical data that, as evident in the central chapters, proved useful on a number of issues.

Thus the mid-1980s investigation that underlies this book sought out academics in several ways; particularly it attempted to combine intensive interview with the results of extensive survey—the qualitative with the quantitative. However, throughout this volume I have relied mainly on the interviews, preferring to stress what we learned from hundreds of hours of focused conversations. By giving voice to professors' own accounts of their academic doings and thoughts, the interviews flesh out meanings that often remain ambiguous or hidden in the statistical results of surveys where, on broad issues, individuals have only the chance to offer hypothetical responses to prescribed scenarios. No one method of social inquiry is ideal. The approach of open-ended field interviewing on which I rely is deficient in its inability to demonstrate representativeness and in its loose control of bias in deciding what will be reported. But it is better to suffer the slings of such selection than the sorrows of superficial responses that inhere when respondents answer mail questionnaires by simply checking boxes or circling numbers opposite prepared answers, unable to explain what they individually mean, or to say what is really uppermost in their minds. Analysis based on recorded conversations gives respondents a fuller, more intense role. I have quoted them extensively.

Part I sets forth the historical and systemic foundations of the academic profession in America. Beginning with the small colleges of the colonial period, an array of institutions evolved at an increasing pace in the nineteenth and twentieth centuries to distribute American academics in diverse settings. The immense variety of universities and colleges is uniquely American; the contemporary distribution scatters professors all over the map in contexts that variously define their profession (Chapter I). But the institutional scatteration was only one of two major forms of growth and dispersion. The other form lay in the changing nature of knowledge itself. Beginning in the nineteenth century, general subjects gave birth to a host of specialized disciplines, new subjects generously imported from the outside were rapidly dignified, and one subject after another greatly extended its boundaries. More widely than elsewhere in the world, academics became distributed on the axis of knowledge: a contemporary grasp of how American academics are defined by specialty requires an endless canvass that is only roughly depicted by ordinary classifications of subjects (Chapter II).

In both institutional location and disciplinary affiliation, the emerging imprint of the profession has spelled diversity, a break-up that accelerated under the shift from elite to mass admission that has typified American higher education in the twentieth century. This double differentiation has been driven to its present extreme form by an intense institutional competition for scholars and students within a national system huge in size and radically decentralized under private and public forms of control. The competition has led to rankings, turning institutions and sectors into hierarchies of status that deeply affect academic life. With no one in charge, the system as a whole struggles with the advantages and disadvantages of competitive disorder and unplanned hierarchy (Chapter III). An odd stage is set for a profession.

Part II pursues dimensions of academic professionalism in five chapters that draw directly on the 1983–1985 research. In the beginning there is work—the daily duties and practices of the academic life. Toil is sorted into different combinations of research, teaching, and ancillary assignments. In Chapter IV we observe radically different arrangements, from virtual think-tank settings at the top of the institutional hierarchy in such resource-rich fields as physics and biology to virtual secondary school conditions at the bottom, where general teaching in introductory courses suppresses specialization. I explore in universities and comprehensive colleges the bifurcation between the underestimated domain of professional schools (medicine alone is a huge, complex operation) and the letters and science departments that have long been the source of professional and popular imagery of the academic. The faultlines are many, with the crucial divide occurring between research-driven contexts and those given over almost fully to teaching. In arranging work, differentiation is clearly in the saddle.

The diverse configurations of tasks naturally drive apart the identifications of academics and fracture their beliefs. In Chapter V professors tell us of their sense of solidarity with their disciplines and professional fields. Since meanings vary with workplace, much occupational consciousness is also tied to type of institution. A community college teacher is virtually compelled to see academic life differently from the scholar in a leading liberal arts college or a university. The problem then arises whether some broad professional ideologies may in part bridge the divergent settings, perhaps offering a triumph of mind over matter. But shared ideals, it seems, have at best a modest effect. The routes of cultural integration lie less in unities of commonness than in overlapping meanings among narrow specialisms.

After work and culture, authority cannot be far behind.[9] Many observers of the academic profession—and of professions in general—place control as the central issue. Who decides what will be done in core areas of professional concern—the professor, the administrator, the trustee, the state official, the student consumer? What is the extent of professional autonomy and self-determination? Chapter VI specifies the disciplinary and institutional bases of academic authority, highlighting those that virtually guarantee professional dominance (even in the face of strengthened bureaucracy and increased state intervention), and contrasting the settings in which professional autonomy gives way to clientele demands and managerialism. In this fractured profession control varies widely. Authoritative participation is decisively shaped by the base of dependence. When that base shifts from peers to students and administrators, a sense of powerlessness gives rise to the unionization response.

Chapter VII examines the career lines of American academic life, extending the picture of a complex division of labor offered in the earlier chapters. Seen as a critical fourth dimension of professionalism, the career is a flow of assignments and statuses that, at its best, leads to a sense of achievement and meaningful participation. But the career patterns are segmented and complicated. There are many poorly guarded entrances into this loosely coupled profession. During training, careers become sharply defined along disciplinary lines. During placement, they branch into the various institutional sectors. Numerous faultlines appear: between research careers and teaching careers; between the academic and the clinical; between the permanent and the temporary; and between the full-time and the part-time. The recent growth of temporary and part-time academics means new marginalities in the profession, careers that are qualitatively apart from traditional patterns and standard imagery. Yet even at the margin we find academics turning to the intrinsic rewards of the academic life for satisfaction and solace.

Chapter VIII pursues academics as they reach beyond their own departments and professional schools to associate with others in their fields. Formal and quasi-formal ties proliferate in bewildering configurations of specialties, disciplines, and multidisciplinary interests, which often subdivide geographically in catchments that vary from metropolitan areas to the international scene. Academics back and fill between generalist and specialist meetings. They weave webs of informal, virtually invisible, ties around precise common interests. Tocqueville's famous comments about the propensity of Americans to form associations apply several times over, since in no other sector of American life do autonomous individuals and groups, standing outside the unities of the national state, have more reason to seek out others of their kind for exchange of information, support, personal advancement, and acclaim. The sense of solidarity is served, but in limited circles. Paralleling the symbolic linkages highlighted in the earlier analysis of academic culture, the associational integration of the profession is a product of incremental connections across an extremely pluralistic landscape.

The concluding comments of Chapter IX begin with the historical transformation of the academic profession into a modern third moment in which the weak amateurism of the first phase and the somewhat integrated professionalism of a second period have given way to a quantum leap in diffusion, diversity, and separation. We need to understand that the cancer ward of the medical school hospital is as much a part of academia as the renaissance studies component of the department of English. We need to face the simple fact that the remedial work of the open-door community college commands a faculty larger than the professoriate of all the private liberal arts colleges. Grasping the sheer magnitude of the differentiation and the tangledness of the academic domain is a necessary step in the triumph of realism over romanticism in understanding American academic life. Central to the shaping of the tangled web is the interaction between profession and organization that steadily becomes more complicated. The disciplinary imperatives of the profession are forces to which every type of university and college must accommodate. In turn, organizational mandates variously liberate and constrain professional impulses as they mix the two core tasks of research and teaching in qualitatively different combinations. In one setting professional dominance is heavy; in another it gives way to a virtual deprofessionalization. Closely correlated with professional control is the relative strength of peers and students as the primary audience.

Three judgments on the logic of the academic profession in America follow. Foremost is the hegemony of subjects. The force of expanding knowledge is intrinsic, changing the profession from within its most basic units. Everywhere, here and abroad, the academic business is significantly knowledge-driven. In America, competition and hierarchy extend and deepen the effects of organizing work, belief, authority, career, and association around a nonprofit pursuit of bundles of knowledge. Second, the dual commitments of academics to subjects and institutions greatly strengthens centrifugal forces in the profession. Its instincts run counter to the standardizing isomorphism that more unitary professions may possess. Whatever integration is present comes mainly from pluralist patterns of multiple membership and overlap in subjects and interests.

Last, the very nature of research and teaching as human activities promote the tendency for academic life to remain, for some, a calling. Disciplinary fields become absorbing lifelong assignments for many scholars, fashioning intrinsic rewards that capture imagination and anchor commitment. We can identify where this capacity runs strong and where it runs down, the latter threatening the benefits accruing from academic professionalism. In the more favored locations academics still find a virtual religion in upholding intellectual integrity. The devotion to knowledge not only survives but has great power. When appropriately supported in universities and colleges, this professional devotion possesses many lives.

PART ONE

The Foundations of the Academic Profession

CHAPTER I

The Evolution of Institutions

But, I ask, by whom were these institutions founded, and endowed, by legislative or by individual benevolence? The answer is, almost universally, by individual benevolence. And whence came that individual benevolence? The answer is equally obvious, it came from the religious. . . . The colleges in this country are, in truth, almost strictly the property of the religious sects.

—FRANCIS WAYLAND, DISCOURSE AT BROWN UNIVERSITY (1835)

I have before me the report of the commissioner of education for 1880. According to that report, there were 389, or say, in round numbers, 400 institutions, calling themselves colleges or universities, in our country! . . . The fact is sufficient. The whole earth could hardly support such a number of first-class institutions. The curse of mediocrity must be upon them, to swarm in such numbers. They must be a cloud of mosquitoes, instead of eagles as they profess.

—HENRY A. ROWLAND, ''A PLEA FOR PURE SCIENCE'' (1883)

THE AMERICAN ACADEMIC profession was launched with hardly a professor in sight or even an academic administrator to help out. The first center of academic work in the American colonies began with the inspiration of John Harvard and a small band of fellow Congregationalists, loyal sons of the church, who judged in 1636, only some fifteen years after the landing at Plymouth, that the salvation of their denomination and colony required a collective effort christened a college, however small it might be, however pale an imitation of the subcolleges of Oxford and Cambridge. In this new place parsons would rule as self-appointed overseers who would designate a cleric as president. They would assemble each year two or three, or even four or five, resident tutors to instruct and supervise several dozen, perhaps even fifty, young charges.

Among the "young inexperienced tutors waiting for a pulpit,"[1] there were no dominating masters, no chaired professors, no pretenses to a self-defining professoriate. With the trustees, the elders of the church and state, fully able to decide what would be taught and who would teach it—and how much the tutors would be paid and how they would live—the instructional staff were hired hands.

How things were to change in the following three and a half centuries! One "poor colledge in the wilderness" became 3,000 enterprises, some of them with student bodies in excess of 50,000. Small groups of temporary tutors became huge aggregates of tenured professional experts whose knowledge conveyed power. Profound change in the institutional foundations, starting slowly at first, accelerated markedly in the defining decades of the nineteenth century. As institutions grew more numerous, they diversified, proceeding by addition rather than by substitution. New types grew up alongside older sectors, widening the array of academic locales. Once established, the various sectors showed a powerful capacity to project themselves into the future, shaping the character of newer forms with their own precepts. As new academic work built upon the old, the past flowed steadily into the present. Still today, after all the massive shifting in the weight of different types of universities and colleges that has taken place since the last half of the nineteenth century, profoundly redirecting the faculty, we can discern the imprint of ideas and forms that became embedded in the first two centuries. No radical disjunctures, no revolutions, cast off the old, leaving a clean field for the new. Strung between the dead and the living were institutional forms that refused to die. And no one had the power to order their demise whenever they appeared inefficient or otherwise fell from favor.

THE DEVELOPMENT OF DIVERSITY

The American colonies were hardly an appropriate setting for an autonomous profession. Lilliputian colleges were all they could support. It took half a century before William and Mary (1693) and Yale (1701) followed the establishment of Harvard College. Only six other colleges succeeded them before the Revolutionary War, all erected in a sparsely populated territory devoid of old cities, a medieval heritage, and substantial resources. These early efforts needed only a handful of men to teach a small set of prescribed courses, in a type of institution that was to evolve into what we now call the private liberal arts college. This general type had its roots in England, where clusters of colleges composed Oxford and Cambridge, but the distinctive American pattern was to be the single college operating in isolation, preferably in a pastoral setting. Begun by various religious groups, the colonial colleges took the legal form of chartered corporations functioning under the control of a group of overseers, drawn from outside the academic life, who represented the denomination or the government of the colony or both.[2] Their control blended the private and the public: the modern private-public distinction was not sharply drawn until the nineteenth century, especially when, in its later decades, great personal fortunes and well-to-do alumni became an attractive source of support for institutions able and willing to venture the private route.[3] The president of Harvard long received some salary from the Massachusetts General Court, and the governor of Massachusetts presided over the Harvard Board of Overseers until 1865.

But the small "old-time" college that was to dominate American higher education until after the Civil War established an important genetic imprint in the form of ultimate control by a board of laymen, a form later transferred to institutions fully funded by states, where trustees or regents were then charged with representing the public interest. With the trustees of the early colleges free to select a teaching staff as they pleased, organization clearly came about from the top down. Composed of local notables, the controlling boards were physically and psychologically close to "their" staffs; they were able and usually inclined to shape the decisions of those they hired and to check their behavior for deviation. Beginning with the first designated president of Harvard, who espoused a heresy by refusing to have his fourth child baptized, college presidents were fired for interpretations of religious doctrine that differed from trustee orthodoxy. Tutors had even less occasion for autonomous thought and action. Moving on to the ministry or to other occupations after a temporary assignment of a few years—they perhaps completed a master's degree along the way—they had good reasons to do as they were told and get on with it. This pattern of sponsorship by local interests and direct control by external figures differed significantly from the main European forms of organization that were to be influential internationally. There, faculty (and sometimes students) had early banded together in guilds, attempted to govern themselves through collegial principles, and maneuvered as best they could against the somewhat removed officials of state and church who ruled larger jurisdictions.[4] In the American colonies there could be no academic guilds.

The private and local features of the colonial colleges were also destined to have lasting effects. Although some of them were related to state-level government in their early decades, they were even then significantly independent of government if compared to Continental institutions and to later American public institutions directly financed by individual states. Being private was critical to the explosive growth that took place in the first half of the nineteenth century: any group could have a go at establishing a small college. With the American population expanding behind a westward-moving frontier at a time of a great religious revival, small communities and religious groups strewed colleges across the landscape in a chaotic fashion, particularly in the western reaches of the eastern and southern states and in the new territories that now make up the midwestern and border states. A first generation of nine colleges from the colonial period was joined by a second generation of an additional thirty-six between 1789 and 1830 and a third generation of one hundred thirty-six more between 1830 and 1865.[5] The assemblage of small colleges rapidly took on the appearance of what a later critic, desiring to build major universities, called a cloud of mosquitoes. Since good intentions and high hopes readily outran the resources available to many founding groups, that swarm experienced much infant mortality as well as a high birthrate. Of the more than 500 attempts to found colleges that were chartered by individual states between 1800 and 1860, only a minority, according to one classic analysis, got underway and survived to the end of the century.[6]

But in this Darwinian struggle, the college form was gradually strengthened. Over a period of 150 to 200 years, between 1650 and the early 1800s, the control mechanism of a board that managed the endowment, property, and affairs of an institution possessing the legal status of a charitable trust became unalterably fixed in the American system. Then, as commerce and industry produced considerable private wealth in the last half of the nineteenth century, the colleges moved to become fully private. They were able gradually to turn to support from individuals and families, seeking bequests for endowment and buildings that, together with tuition fees, provided a private financial base. Businessmen also gradually replaced ministers on many controlling boards, attenuating the influence of churches at the same time the colleges were shedding any lingering connections with state officials. By 1900 the crowd of small private colleges, grown to nearly nine hundred, was distributed throughout the country. The heaviest concentrations were in New England, the Middle Atlantic States, and the Midwest; the lightest were on the West Coast. Truly independent from all public authorities, small in scale, and centered on work leading only to a bachelor's degree, the private college set the terms for much of what followed it.

Notable among those terms was the phenomenon of the loyal alumnus. Deeply romanticized during the nineteenth century as the American model of voluntary support of higher education, the small college, set apart in the countryside or in a small town, developed the capacity to elicit uncommon loyalty from graduates, students, and staff. Hardly to be seen as organizations, the colleges could operate as intensive communities in which young people spent four critical years in places that were highly conscious of their own struggle and achievement. The small colleges could be, and often were, emotional hothouses that turned graduates into persons filled with fond memories and institutional devotion. In the last half of the twentieth century, it is well-known that many small private colleges have developed rich symbolic lives that hook graduates to them, often for a lifetime. This instinct to develop organization sagas has deep roots. No former student has ever more emotionally staked the claim of his or her own college—and others of its kind—than did Daniel Webster, class of 1801, when he defended the independence of Dartmouth College from state control before the United States Supreme Court in the famous case of

1819. (See Vignette One.) In a five-hour brief in which he pulled out all the stops, Webster—according to legend—had himself, Chief Justice John Marshall, and others in tears. Early on, the small American college could make strong men cry.

The university came late to the United States, long after the first European universities in Bologna, Paris, and Oxford had undergone centuries of development, decline, and renewal. The first university to be established as such, Johns Hopkins, did not arrive until 1876. Other institutions were slowly evolving from "college" to "university": Yale developed graduate work in the 1850s and awarded the first American Ph.D. in 1861, and Harvard established a graduate department in the 1870s.[7] Other private colleges—Princeton, Columbia, Brown, Cornell—soon followed, making up a sector of private universities that, joined by Stanford and Chicago in the early 1890s, was well in place by the turn of the century. It was during this period that presidential leadership came into its own, beginning with the long reign of Charles W. Eliot at Harvard (1869–1909) and the time in office of such renowned entrepreneurs as Daniel Coit Gilman at Johns Hopkins, William Rainey Harper at Chicago, and David S. Jordan at Stanford. These figures were models of the "captain of erudition," the swashbuckling leader who vigorously solicited money, recruited faculty, assembled an administrative staff, and proclaimed the greatness of his institution. As they waxed, so did authority move from the board of trustees to the president and his staff. And the competitive dynamism of American higher education, already endemic among the colleges, leaped forward when the autonomous universities, influenced by the German emphasis on research, set out to become great research universities. What they competed for was leading scientists and scholars.

At the same time, public universities were emerging. The earliest ones, established in North Carolina, Georgia, Tennessee, and Vermont, dated from before 1800. But it was not until after the Civil War and toward the end of the century that state universities (and what were often initially state colleges of "agriculture and mechanical arts") developed as an awesome form, aided in many cases by the resources offered to the states by the federal government through the famous land grant legislation of the 1862 Morrill Act. Strong first in the Midwest, most of these public institutions spoke of serving the sons and daughters of the average man, the

8

VIGNETTE ONE
DANIEL WEBSTER AND THE SAGA OF
DARTMOUTH COLLEGE

This, Sir, is my case! It is the case, not merely of that humble institution, it is the case of every College in the land. It is more. It is the case of every Eleemosynary Institution throughout our country—of all those great charities founded by the piety of our ancestors to alleviate human misery, and scatter blessings along the pathway of life. It is more! It is, in some sense, the case of every man among us who has property of which he may be stripped, for the question is simply this: Shall our State Legislatures be allowed to take *that* which is not their own, to turn it from its original use, and apply it to such ends or purposes as they, in their discretion, see fit!

Sir, you may destroy this little Institution; it is weak; it is in your hands! I know it is one of the lesser lights in the literary horizon of our country. You may put it out. But, if you do so, you must carry through your work! You must extinguish, one after another, all those greater lights of science which, for more than a century, have thrown their radiance over our land!

It is, Sir, as I have said, a small College. And yet, *there are those who love it*—.

Sir, I know not how others may feel (glancing at the opponents of the College before him), but, for myself, when I see my alma mater surrounded, like Caesar in the senate house, by those who are reiterating stab after stab, I would not, for this right hand, have her turn to me, and say, *Et tu quoque mi fili! And thou too, my son!*[20]

SOURCE: "Daniel Webster Argues the Dartmouth Case, 1819," in *American Higher Education: A Documentary History*, edited by Richard Hofstadter and Wilson Smith, Volume I, pp. 212–213. Copyright 1961 by The University of Chicago. All rights reserved.

farmer and the mechanic, thereby assuming populist overtones that contrasted with the ostensible elitist qualities of the private universities concentrated in the eastern part of the country.[8] Linked to popular support, they admitted high school graduates on a relatively unselective basis and oriented the undergraduate part of the institution to consumer demands and occupational requirements of the home state. Like the comprehensive secondary school, they tended to promise something for everyone: agriculture, forestry, engineering, even home economics for "girls" destined to become "homemakers." An open-door philosophy came early to modern American higher education.

But, like their private counterparts, the American public universities married the new emphasis on specialized research and advanced training to the old commitment to liberal education by augmenting undergraduate colleges with graduate and professional schools. The formal graduate tier—an important American invention—became a place for systematic advanced training. Providing for graduate students became the way professors in departments could shift their teaching away from the more elementary courses offered to undergraduates and toward courses more closely linked to research and the cutting edges of scholarship. Here was the mechanism that would most aid the coming to power of the cosmopolitan research scholar. But no institution, public or private, could afford to let go of the undergraduate tier. Johns Hopkins tried, but could not. There was too much well-grounded legitimacy in the heritage of the liberal arts: the popular imagery of college was fixed on undergraduates; their numbers were needed on the income side of the ledger for tuition or state allocation. Competition, henceforth, would not only be sharp but Janus-like. As noted by Joseph Ben-David, "While competition for scientists and scholars compelled the universities to establish graduate schools, competition for students compelled them to maintain their liberal arts programs."[9] For faculty, this was to mean henceforth a latent competition between peers and students as the audience of first resort.

The state universities in particular had to develop a hybrid character that would position them to both look up and down, and in and out, as they related to faculty and students and attempted to link a wide range of vocational fields to the natural sciences, social sciences, and the humanities. The University of Michigan, for example, had to garner support from its state legislature primarily on the basis of what it did for Michigan undergraduate students and for the economy and culture of the home state, but it developed national and international standing by providing attractive conditions at the graduate level in a range of disciplines and professional schools for research-minded faculty and students. Even more than in the private universities, a separate administrative staff had to be assembled for the purposes of development and coordination, headed by a president whose delegated powers steadily broadened and intensified. The early decades of "the age of the university" saw the growth of bureaucratic administration, not in the national Capitol, nor primarily among educational overseers in the state house, but locally, right there on campus amid faculty and students.[10] Henceforth, in the big business of American complex universities, trustees were to recede while administrators moved forward. And a major growth in faculty had begun. What had been a national professoriate of 11,000 in 1880 multiplied three times in three decades to 36,000 in 1910 (Table 1).

Alongside the private college, the private university, and the state university, other types of institutions were now emerging. Most important before 1900 was a separate set of public colleges established to train teachers[11]—a considerable separation of teacher education from the embrace of universities that was later to bedevil the professionalization of schoolteaching. First known as normal schools, and closely associated with the school structures of the individual states, these enterprises initially gave a few years of training, mostly of secondary school level, to prospective elementary school teachers. After the turn of the century, the institutions in this category also undertook the preparation of teachers and administrators for secondary schools, gradually gained the right to give the bachelor's degree, and took on the name of "teachers college"—a promotion from "normal school." By the 1940s these institutions were evolving beyond teacher training programs into their current form of public comprehensive colleges whose undergraduate scope is virtually as wide as that of the university but with fewer esoteric, scholarly specialties and more occupational ones. Growing rapidly after World War II, many of these colleges subsequently acquired the title of *state college university*, or simply *state university*. They today typically operate with a moderate degree of selectivity as part of a division of labor in which the more established public

TABLE 1

GROWTH OF INSTITUTIONS AND FACULTY
1870–1980

YEAR	INSTITUTIONS[a]	FACULTY[b]
1870	563	5,553
1880	811	11,522
1890	998	15,809
1900	977	23,868
1910	951	36,480
1920	1,041	48,615
1930	1,409	82,386
1940	1,708	146,929
1950	1,851	246,722
1960	2,008	380,554
1970	2,528	573,000
1980	3,150	846,000

[a] Prior to 1980, excludes branch campuses.
[b] Total number of different individuals (not reduced to full-time equivalent). Beginning in 1960, data are for the first term of the academic year.

NOTE: Beginning in 1960, includes Alaska and Hawaii.

SOURCE: U.S. Department of Education, National Center for Education Statistics. *Digest of Education Statistics: 1982* (Washington, D.C.: 1983), pp. 105, 107.

universities have become more selective. Their evolution has left many of them with a muddled institutional character—neither teachers college nor full-fledged universities—that complicates the identities and satisfactions of professors who serve in them.

Still other groups of institutions developed. Among them were the public and private engineering colleges and universities, now headed in prestige by the Massachusetts Institute of Technology (MIT), opened for instruction in 1865, and the California Institute of Technology ("Cal Tech"), founded in 1920. Because the right to sponsor institutions has been so dispersed in private as well as in public hands, many kinds of specialized postsecondary institutions have emerged. A bewildering array of accredited theological, art, and detached professional schools were created, which gave courses toward a bachelor's or a postbaccalaureate degree. By the third quarter of the twentieth century it was to become impossible to define with any clarity where higher education began and ended among institutions that claimed to offer postsecondary instruction. An unbounded institutional base, as we later see in detail, has helped lead to an unbuttoned academic profession.

Contributing in a major way to the extension of the institutional base is the recent startling development of an American "short-cycle" unit first known as the junior college. Accepting a role that limits its collegiate attention to the first two years, this type of institution also invested in one- and two-year terminal vocational programs. The two-year colleges developed under private auspices as well as under public control, but the public sector became the main site, particularly as the more comprehensive "community college" concept took hold. With some 70 public ones in place by 1920, the two-year college movement developed a momentum that led to over 175 institutions in 1950 and more than 250 by 1940, establishing a major organizational base, particularly in California, for rapid proliferation and expansion in the era of mass higher education that followed World War II. Swelling to 1,000 institutions by the early 1970s, this sector became the truly open-door part of the American system, a filter that allowed other sectors to become more selective, even as the system as a whole took all comers. It also became an important locale for adult education, developing a comprehensive coverage of clientele greater than that of the comprehensive high school and moving institutions toward the posture of an adult community center. The impact of this latter-day sector on the American professoriate has been grossly underestimated; its imposing size alone warrants much attention and analysis.

All of these sectors that were deeply entrenched in American higher education by the middle of the twentieth century contained important differences. The private sectors, with only one-fifth of the students and one-fourth of the faculty, remained enormously varied, even as they gradually

13

gave way numerically to the public sectors. Private universities are divided into a number of important subtypes: the research-centered university, highest in prestige and national in orientation—Chicago, Columbia, Yale; the secular urban-service university, lower in prestige and more local in orientation—Boston University, New York University, the University of Cincinnati; and the Catholic municipal university, usually standing well down the prestige hierarchy and oriented both to locality and Catholicism—the University of Portland, University of Dayton, Seton Hall University, St. John's University. Private colleges have continued to exhibit even greater variation: the secular, elite liberal arts college able to compete for students with the top universities—Swarthmore, Reed, Amherst; the above-average institution that may still maintain a modest religious connection—St. Olaf, Baldwin-Wallace, Westminster; and the rear-guard place that may have to struggle to gain or retain accreditation and is sometimes still dominated by a denominational board or a president—Oral Roberts, Rio Grande, and Bob Jones. Some institutions found at the tail end of the academic procession, inferior to the best high schools, are, as put by David Riesman, "colleges only by the grace of semantic generosity."[12] Just in itself, the private sphere has something for everyone, including numerous locales in which "academic freedom" has no meaning for faculty.

Similarly, within each type of public institution—university, state college, community college—dispersed control has produced a wide range in the mixture of purpose, program, and academic quality. Among the leading public campuses of the states, the University of Mississippi offers a qualitatively different environment for research and teaching than the University of California, San Diego. Among the four- and five-year state colleges, a good share of which have lobbied their way to gaining the title of university, Western Kentucky University differs extensively from Brooklyn College or San Francisco State University. Suburban Foothill Community College in Los Altos, California is an academic showpiece differing radically from Chicago Loop College or Los Angeles City College, downtown community colleges that operate with more than 20,000 students, most of them poor and belonging to a minority, who will never make their way beyond a few months or a year of training. Within as well as among the sectors, formal quality control ranges downward to virtually zero. Among others, young athletes have shown that it is possible to enter major public or private universities with test scores and achievement records that place them in the lowest 5 percent of the population.

The institutional evolution of the American system, in interaction with disciplinary and system characteristics specified in Chapters II and III, has profoundly shaped the professoriate. In the long view of 1636 to 1980, the position and power of faculty have been enormously strengthened. As long as the system was dominated by small colleges devoted to a fixed common curriculum, the faculties by modern standards remained extremely weak. Top-down organization meant that if trustees chose to have their hired hands toe the line in religious doctrine as well as in personal deportment they could do so, right down to the proverbial number of angels dancing on the head of a pin. If the trustees wished to have somebody run the college for them, then it was the man *they* selected to be president who himself could be fired from year to year. But the growing complexity of college organization in the nineteenth century gradually abridged the reign of the trustees. The university form insisted on a shift in prestige and power. As it became the great center of academic specialization, it also became the place for the avant-garde of all the emerging specialties we trace in Chapter II. Its substitution of the elective system for a fixed curriculum played to the new specialized interests of the faculty—teach what you wish—even as it offered a cafeteria of choice to the students—take the courses you want. Amateurs could no longer supervise directly the complex organizations emerging before their eyes. Power moved to the president and to what staff he chose to help him in his administrative rounds: registrar, business officer, admissions officer, dean of faculty, dean of students, secretary to the board of trustees, and on, ad infinitum, in a stream that was to make professors groan. The era of 1880–1930 is now recognized as a period of strong presidents, a high point of administrative control. But behind the development of administrative power there lay a gathering thrust of professional power, led by the new type of professor, rooted in research, whose recognized talent gave him individual bargaining power.

Thus, faculty authority had been truly slow in developing, its forms forged largely in the late nineteenth and twentieth centuries, not within the context of a formal governmental system, as in Europe, but within the setting of the established powers of local trustees and administrators.

What changed within the local hierarchies to give influence to faculty was their gathering control of knowledge brought about by research-driven specialization. Once the research ethic was in the driver's seat, there could no longer be a common curriculum taught by men of general learning whose responsibility in the first instance would be the moral character of the young. When the universities sought the rewards of research, they also moved toward a modern profession of academics in which self-government would be strengthened. They created settings in which professors would acquire primacy in determining the precise nature of their own work—what they would teach and what they would research—and would have more than a passing influence, subject by subject and classroom by classroom, in determining who they served. The academic guild came late to American higher education, but come it did, and on the back of fragmenting bundles of knowledge that allowed "teachers" to become "professors" by acquiring the authority of arcane knowledge.

But the shift from trustees to presidents to faculties did not play evenly across the increasingly diverse sectors of institutions. The teachers colleges and especially the community colleges marched to different drummers. They took on twentieth-century bureaucratic forms that contained much managerialism, often influenced decisively by the administrative style of elementary and secondary education and state departments of education. Their teachers were not to have the persuasive powers of research at their disposal. When unionization came to American higher education in the 1960s and 1970s, it marched through their doors as a response to their sense of weak self-government vis-à-vis administrators, trustees, politicians, and the laity. Their situation contrasted sharply with what was increasingly found in the research universities and the leading private colleges, in which personal and collegial privileges were worked out and institutionalized in the workings of the department, the senate, the academic committee, and the national academic association. Professors who acquired great renown by means of their research and scholarship became the leaders in the associations that were established to strengthen the hands of academics along disciplinary lines. When the American Association of University Professors (AAUP) was formally initiated in 1915 as an all-inclusive body—"industry wide" rather than craft-centered—leadership came from high in the institutional hierarchy: John Dewey, E.R.A.

16

Seligman, and Franklin Giddings from Columbia; Roscoe Pound from Harvard; Richard T. Ely from Wisconsin; and Arthur O. Lovejoy from Johns Hopkins.[13]

THE CONTEMPORARY DIVISION
OF THE PROFESSION

In the late 1970s and early 1980s some 700,000 to 850,000 academics are spread among the more than 3,000 institutions that appear in formal classifications. As a rough first cut, about one-fourth to one-third are in universities, another third are located in four- and five-year colleges, and, surprisingly, nearly one-third are to be found in two-year colleges. About 75 percent are in public institutions, 25 percent in private ones. But a three- or even six-fold grouping of 3,000 universities and colleges in the American system is clearly too limited. Various classifications have in recent years sought to discriminate better among types of institutions; the well-known Carnegie classifications of 1973 and 1976 have been particularly informative and revealing.[14] Drawing upon the 1976 effort, Table 2 maps American higher education by number of institutions and student enrollment in eleven types of institutions that become twenty-two when public and private institutions are separated. Similar national data on faculty are not available, but the student proportions are broadly indicative of faculty distributions. Working from, but going beyond, this statistical picture of broad contours we can note a half-dozen simple but nevertheless critical features of the institutional foundations:

1. Among the universities, approximately one-half are classified as "doctoral-granting" or "service" rather than "research." The doctoral-granting group contains private universities that turn out few Ph.D.'s, have little endowment, and do relatively little research: for example, Northeastern University in Massachusetts, Marquette University in Wisconsin, and the University of Denver in Colorado; and public institutions that similarly award only a few doctorates each year and lack substantial research funds: for example, Ball State University in Indiana, Idaho State University, and East Texas State University. The imagery of American universities—and of university academic life—set by the top ten, twenty, or even top fifty universities is inappropriate for American universities as

17

INSTITUTIONS AND ENROLLMENTS IN AMERICAN HIGHER EDUCATION, BY TYPE OF INSTITUTION, 1976

TYPE OF INSTITUTION	NUMBER OF INSTITUTIONS				ENROLLMENT (IN THOUSANDS)				
	TOTAL	PRIVATE	PUBLIC	PERCENT PUBLIC	TOTAL	PRIVATE	PUBLIC	PERCENT PUBLIC	PERCENT OF TOTAL
TOTAL	3,074	1,608	1,466	48	11,164	2,414	8,750	78	100
DOCTORATE-GRANTING INSTITUTIONS	184	65	119	65	3,062	673	2,389	78	27
Research universities I	51	22	29	57	1,144	278	866	76	10
Research universities II	47	14	33	70	803	125	678	84	7
Doctorate-granting universities I	56	18	38	68	805	200	605	75	7
Doctorate-granting universities II	30	11	19	63	304	70	234	77	3
COMPREHENSIVE UNIVERSITIES COLLEGES I	594	240	354	60	3,170	797	2,373	75	28
Comprehensive universities and colleges I	381	131	250	66	2,627	571	2,056	78	23
Comprehensive universities and colleges II	213	109	104	49	542	225	317	59	5
LIBERAL ARTS COLLEGES	583	572	11	20	531	511	20	4	5
Liberal arts colleges I	123	123	0	0	154	154	0	0	1
Liberal arts colleges II	460	449	11	2	377	358	19	5	4
TWO-YEAR INSTITUTIONS	1,147	238	909	79	3,978	153	3,825	96	36
SPECIALIZED INSTITUTIONS	560	490	70	12	416	278	138	33	4

SOURCE: The Carnegie Foundation for the Advancement of Teaching. *A Classification of Institutions of Higher Education, revised edition* (Berkeley, Cal., 1976), p. xii.

a whole. The membership of the American Association of Universities (AAU), a self-selecting group of top universities that numbered fifty-one in 1985, leaves out over one hundred and thirty other universities that range "down" in type and quality to places that are universities in name only. The lives of professors, even just within the university category, are likely to vary considerably.

2. Among the top universities, private ones loom large. With much stability over the last four decades, six or seven of the top ten rated universities have been private (Harvard, Stanford, Yale, Princeton, Chicago, Columbia, and Cornell), with three or four public institutions (University of California, Berkeley, University of Michigan, University of Wisconsin, and University of California, Los Angeles) variously interspersed.[15] The Massachusetts Institute of Technology (MIT) and the California Institute of Technology ("Cal Tech") have also come to rank extremely high as top quality private institutions that are increasingly comprehensive in nature. Professors in all private institutions number about one-fourth of all professors; in the leading universities, though, they are well over one-half. Thus, the private foundations of the profession are much stronger in those sectors that do the most research, produce the most Ph.D.'s, and have the highest status. The strong private underpinning among leading universities particularly helps to maintain distance from the embrace of government, despite the very large increase in federal financing since World War II.

3. Among the six hundred universities and colleges grouped under the vague label of "comprehensive universities and colleges"—institutions with numerous vocational as well as liberal arts programs, and offering no higher than the master's degree—professors are distributed in both public and private institutions. In this confusing category appear many state colleges (Fort Lewis College in Colorado, Trenton State College in New Jersey, Albany State College in Georgia) and numerous private institutions that are neither traditional universities granting doctorates, nor campuses centered on liberal arts (Pepperdine University in California, University of Bridgeport in Connecticut, DePaul University in Illinois). There is much movement in and out of this sprawling family. Liberal arts colleges become typed as comprehensive colleges when they take on more vocational programs. Institutions happily move out of this category "up" into university

status when they begin to give doctoral degrees and garner more research money. This institutional zone has been a somewhat uncomfortable one for professors; one's academy is neither a true university nor a four-year liberal arts college, but an unsure hybrid often seeking to change its spots.

4. The liberal arts colleges, numbering about six hundred in 1976, have only about 5 percent of total students and not much more than that of all the faculty. They therefore count numerically for very little in the profession at large; community college personnel bulk at least four times larger. But symbolically and objectively, professors in these colleges are more influential than their numbers would indicate. Their settings are at the core of the romantic tradition that has a powerful hold on the American image of undergraduate education. The top fifty liberal arts colleges are serious competitors for the best universities, public and private, in attracting talented students; clearly this is so for Swarthmore, Williams, and Smith in the East; Carlton, Oberlin, and Earlham in the Midwest; and Reed, Mills, and the Pomona-Claremont complex in the West.

Table 2 strikingly reveals that no public campuses qualify as leading four-year colleges, a telling commentary on the ingrained inability of state systems as wealthy as those of California and New York to participate in the institutional form that most sturdily underpins liberal education. Efforts to fashion public campuses around a liberal education focus, selectively drawing high-quality students and deliberately remaining small, have floundered under the imperatives of state systems that have required them to become larger, more broadly focused, and more similar to flagship models. Such public deviants are generally exposed to processes of re-socialization that bring them back into the fold.[16]

5. The community colleges are an enormous set of well over one thousand institutions that handle over one-third of all students. As of 1976, 80 percent of them were public institutions that absorbed over 95 percent of the students (in this category). The public community colleges have been *the* growth industry in the great post-1960 expansion, willy-nilly turning this sector into a primary foundation of the professoriate. Any type of workplace that plays host to one-fourth or one-third of the members of a profession surely has major impact on that profession. And this setting is the one that differentiates most sharply from other institutional locations.

20

Could there be a separate academic occupation here, one not far from schoolteaching in its general character?

6. Another five hundred to six hundred institutions, in 1976, fell into a miscellaneous category of "specialized institutions" that contains theological seminaries, schools of art, music, and design, business schools, engineering schools, and even military institutes. These special-purpose institutions are all accredited. Within their midst we find such substantial institutions as the University of California's medical school in San Francisco, the Hartford Graduate Center in Connecticut, and the Baruch College branch of the City University of New York. Although the Carnegie classification can be readily rearranged to depict a general hierarchy of institutions by simply moving the leading liberal arts colleges up several notches, its major types contain many twists and turns, not least in a bottom category that contains the Juilliard School of Music.

Even the most comprehensive classifications of institutions in American higher education must be seen as rough and ready. There is no one best way to define the boundaries of depicted types; in all schemes, odd bedfellows appear in most of the categories. And, behind all efforts to classify, no national office has the authority and capacity to command uniform, exact reporting. Discretion abounds when institutions are asked to provide faculty data, even more than when they furnish the facts of student enrollment.

Notoriously slippery is the definition of a liberal arts college. One insightful effort to assess whether "the liberal arts" had become "an endangered species" used a simple three-fold classification of liberal arts colleges, comprehensive institutions, and specialized professional-technical colleges, locating institutions by degrees awarded in various fields of study.[17] Institutions awarding 80 percent or more of their degrees in the academic fields were reasonably classified as having a liberal arts emphasis. It turned out that only three out of four of the institutions classified as "liberal arts I" schools in the Carnegie classification were liberal arts schools as defined by this earned-degree approach. More striking, only one in five of the institutions classified as liberal arts II still appear in the liberal arts category. The earned degree data came from 1971–1972, that is, before the heavy swing of the 1970s toward vocational fields. In short, hundreds of schools

21

called themselves liberal arts colleges when they were already significantly invested in vocational programs.

Beyond all these many confusing types of universities and colleges there are innumerable postsecondary institutions that fall outside the accredited lists. There are, for example, several hundred known four-year colleges that fall below the line of accreditation. Some "new" institutions that appear in successive formal lists are then simply born-again institutions that have moved across the accreditation threshold. In addition, proprietary business and vocational schools that do not purport to give college credit are free to start up as small businesses: a mid-1970 estimate noted 7,000 to 8,000 such institutions.[18] And adult education, much of it of an unknown educational level, is dispersed in the United States among schools, colleges, churches, libraries, museums, trade unions, and classrooms in the military and industry. There are no locational limits. But the normal definition of the professoriate extends no further than to the accredited institutions. We confine our attention to them.

Fashioned out of a long, uncontrolled evolution, the institutional base also exhibits much restless shifting. Since in every decade some institutions leave the official domain, while others arrive or shift their ecological niche, analysts have had to learn not only to compute birthrates and deathrates but also to probe for emigration and immigration. The study cited above that classified institutions in three general types showed that between 1972 and 1981, 449 institutions were "new," 207 had "failed," *and* 592 institutions had moved from one category to another. For change in a single decade, the data are striking, not least in the huge amount of internal migration. The imbalances in the migratory exchanges reveal what happened to liberal arts colleges in a decade of rising vocationalism: "net migration was by far the major factor accounting for attrition in the liberal arts program category, with 11 institutions changing from a liberal arts emphasis for every net failure of a liberal arts school."[19] In short, institutional mobility is high, with attrition within any category more likely to result from emigration than from death. In the 1970s the liberal arts became the impoverished area that pushed institutions toward emigration. Comprehensive colleges and specialized professional programs became the attractive areas toward which institutions moved in order to recover their health.

22

It is enormously compelling in the American system to sort professors by their institutional locations. More than anywhere else in the world, their employment base is diversified. We have to search among types of settings if we wish to become better informed about academic life. And the settings are dynamic. With no national mandates to hold institutions in a planned alignment, with fifty state systems variously structured, and with fifteen hundred private institutions proceeding largely under their own initiative, the evolution of the professoriate's institutional setting has an unplanned logic born of the system itself. And the largely unguided institutional development is but half the story, for we have yet to turn to the dynamics of the disciplines. In Chapters II and III we explore further how the peculiar American structure of higher education powerfully scatters professors, places them in the hands of market forces, and makes professional self-government subject to the whims of local settings. The context is an open, self-evolving system.

CHAPTER II

The Elaboration of Disciplines

The field of research only opens wider and wider as we advance, and our minds are lost in wonder and astonishment at the grandeur and beauty unfolded before us. Shall we help in this grand work, or not? Shall our country do its share, or shall it still live in the almshouse of the world?

> —HENRY A. ROWLAND, ''A PLEA FOR PURE SCIENCE'' (1883)

It is necessary, therefore, to ask: what distinctive characteristics of nineteenth century knowledge impelled its creators and custodians to turn their particular competencies into professions? The obvious answer is specialization.

> —JOHN HIGHAM, ''THE MATRIX OF SPECIALIZATION (1979)''

The "Idea of a University" was a village with its priests. The "Idea of a Modern University" was a town—a one-industry town—with its intellectual oligarchy. "The Idea of a Multiversity" is a city of infinite variety.

> —CLARK KERR, *THE USES OF THE UNIVERSITY* (1963)

T HERE IS NO MORE stunning fact about the academic profession anywhere in the world than the simple one that academics are possessed by disciplines, fields of study, even as they are located in institutions. With the growth of specialization in the last century, the discipline has become everywhere an imposing, if not dominating, force in the working lives of the vast majority of academics. Organized around individual subjects, the disciplines have their own histories and trajectories, their own habits and practices. Going concerns in their own right, they also couple their members to national and international groups of scholars and researchers. As they promote affiliations that slash across institutions, they turn "locals" into "cosmopolitans."[1] Professors are never the same after they have tasted the delights of subject specialties that join them to far-flung peers.

The duality of enterprise and discipline is inherent in modern higher education. The academic sphere must have organized ways of bringing together savants and learners. It must also relate scholars to one another within specialties. The disciplinary tendency is as much "in the nature of things" as the institutional linkage. It was there in the beginning some eight centuries ago in rudimentary form in the faculties of Western universities that trained lawyers, physicians, theologians, and even notaries.[2] This type of organization was strongly suppressed, but never eliminated, in the American colonial colleges when academics were largely confined to teaching a common classical curriculum. Modern concentration on the disciplines flowered first in Europe when the nineteenth-century German university launched the age of academic specialization. From the 1870s onward, it became an American preoccupation, laying a faculty base that was to diversify to an extreme degree after World War II. Under special conditions of the American system, the development of institutional sectors and the elaboration of disciplines fed upon one another. The result has been that in America more than anywhere else the professional identities of academics have been distributed in a wide array of disciplinary vessels.

THE EVOLUTION OF A DISCIPLINARY BASE

In the evolution of the American academic profession to its contemporary huge size and extreme specialization we can observe two primary forms of growth, one "substantive," the other "reactive."[3] *Substantive growth* is the increase in faculty that stems from the absorption of new subject matter. It is produced largely by the ways in which academics and their supporting institutions generate and accommodate knowledge. It is largely professor-driven, but it is also encouraged or restrained by the incentives set for academics by their institutional and disciplinary contexts. *Reactive growth* is the increase in faculty that follows from heightened clientele demand. An increase in faculty trails behind an increase in students. This second form of growth is a well-known phenomenon, one widely perceived as the basic force driving expansion and realigning fields. But much of the growth and diversification of the American system, particularly in the late nineteenth and early twentieth centuries, came from the substantive form, an absorption of new subjects by academics and their host systems. As identified by Walter Metzger, four processes drive this fascinating form of professional development.

Substantive Growth

PARTURITION   Throughout the long, slow evolution of the small band of colonial colleges, and well into the days of "the antebellum college" in the first half of the nineteenth century, academics were hired mainly to teach a small set of compulsory courses centered on classical languages, moral philosophy, mathematics, and a little natural science. Faculty members were still relatively homogeneous. They shared some common knowledge, were thrown together in a common didactic cause, and, typically, were proficient in Greek and Latin. Indeed, in the seventeenth and eighteenth centuries, educated people could be interested simultaneously in mathematics, the sciences, literature, philosophy, music, and the fine arts. Students of the history of mathematics have pointed out that "the year Leibniz' first work on the differential calculus appeared in the *Acta Eruditorium* (1684), the journal also carried articles on theology, archeology, linguistics, philosophy, and the anatomy of snakes."[4] But the common bonds of these small, tight communities were already being loosened in the early decades of the nineteenth century. Such early colleges as Harvard, Yale, Columbia, and Pennsylvania led the way into a wider range of offerings. New subjects were born out of the more inclusive, established ones, which were becoming swollen from the ingestion of new material. In particular, new academic sciences issued from natural philosophy and natural history. As an academic subject, chemistry was in place by 1820, soon followed by astronomy, physics, and biology.

By twentieth-century standards, the new fields were extremely small, with only a few books and a few professors. From detailed examination of student notebooks, faculty reports, college publications, and textbooks in fifteen ante-bellum colleges, Stanley M. Guralnick concluded:

> Where the whole of mathematics and science instruction within the American college curriculum of 1800, for instance, had been contained in two books (and those of doubtful quality), that of

27

1825 was taught from no less than four, and that of 1850 from a minimum of ten. Where scientific subjects had commonly engaged one professor per school in 1800, by 1830 there were usually two, and by 1860 four, with occasional instances of scientists making up over half of an individual college's faculty. [There was] a tenfold increase in the total number of science professors recruited from 1828 to 1860. . . .[5]

Notably, the pre-Civil War evolution gave the scientific fields an academic base *before* the coming of the universities. It changed the very meaning of classical education, making "classical" synonymous with a spread of liberal arts fields that included the scientific ones.[6] And the momentum of academic specialization was early embedded in the institutional structure, even if its scale was insignificant by later university standards. By the 1860s, in their prescribed curriculum, students at the leading private colleges were introduced to botany, chemistry, astronomy, geology, and physics.

After the middle of the century, at an accelerating pace, parturition continued. Biology delivered genetics and microbiology and then cross-fertilized with bordering sciences to produce biochemistry and biophysics. In the social sciences, parturition came later and in a more confusing fashion. But the mother subject, moral philosophy, gave birth in the 1860s and 1870s first to political economy and then to political science. The first field, renamed economics, in turn took only a decade to eject a new one called sociology. The emergence of the academic social sciences was driven by the infusion of such new knowledge as the works of Darwin and Spencer. The volume of factual findings and alternative perspectives could not be contained within the vessels of the traditional, general subjects.

PROGRAM AFFILIATION By 1860, one-fifth of the American colleges that offered only a bachelor's degree were doing something more than providing a liberal arts education. A trend to "college-plus" was already underway, with colleges of general learning developing programs to train for the learned professions of medicine, law, and divinity—in effect, developing professional schools that conferred first-level degrees. Such professional programs, themselves new subjects, in turn aided the process of parturition. (Chemistry's early birth, for example, was hastened by its role in the training of physicians.) This process of affiliation soon spread beyond the boundaries of the several learned professions, extending its reach after 1880 to many semiprofessions and would-be professions. In came the fields that followed in the footsteps of medicine: dentistry, pharmacy, veterinary medicine, and nursing. Such claimants as social work, journalism, education, and various subfields of engineering became part of the academic family, even if some of them were to become "minor professions" placed down past the salt in the status hierarchy of the fields. The professor of history had been joined by the professor of social work.

The American professions, as we know them today, took shape in the 1880s and 1890s. It was then that "higher education and the professions were brought close together again. New professional schools attached to universities were started, old ones prospered, and even some of the proprietary schools linked up with liberal arts colleges. Equally important, the undergraduate college course increasingly became a preliminary to professional study."[7]

Growth by program affiliation became central in the long-run adaptiveness of American higher education. In his valuable analysis of the rise of the professions in the United States, Robert H. Wiebe has stressed the central contribution made by an open-door mentality on the part of American universities toward occupations that sought professional standing. "Considering the potential of the universities for frustration," he noted, "it was extremely important that higher education permissively, even indiscriminately, welcomed each of the new groups in turn." With the emergence of the modern graduate level of instruction in the 1870s, the universities served as "outposts of professional selfconsciousness," even in some cases "frankly preparing young men for professions that as yet did not exist." By 1900 the universities "held an unquestioned power to legitimize, for no new profession felt complete—or scientific—without its distinct academic curriculum." Acting as "centers for philosophizing and propagandizing," the universities "inculcated apprentices with the proper values and goals."[8] The institutions of higher education, proactive as much as reactive—and generous to a fault—played a crucial role in almost all the professional movements that were producing a new urban middle class in the United States.

29

DIGNIFICATION   Interacting with parturition and especially with affiliation was a process in which the poor reputation that kept a subject out
of the academy was somehow converted into a credible one that sufficed to
gain its admittance. Modern languages were a classic case. In the few old-
time colleges of the seventeenth century, the only good academic language
was a dead one. English was dignified in the first half of the eighteenth century, French in the second half. The first American professorship in modern languages at Harvard in 1819 gave legitimacy to the task of teaching
students how to read and speak foreign languages, with German later to
become a favorite among those heading for the prominent universities of
Germany for advanced instruction and apprenticeships in research. Technology became a second major case. A general field long regarded at home
and abroad as too practical to deserve a place among academic subjects, it
had a belated but definite entry. Applied science and engineering began to
appear in some private colleges and in the state universities in the late
1840s.

Considerably through dignification, substantive growth in the professoriate—and higher education generally—simply ran amok after 1880:
"Not only were the techniques of pursuits aspiring to be professions readily granted the benefit of any doubt, but the knack of the kitchen, the ath-
letic field, the military parade-ground, the concert hall, the art studio, and
the business office—competencies once too lowly to be noticed—were
raised to the stature of academic fields."[9] Hence music, physical education,
and even "military science." By the turn of the century, virtually any subject was a candidate for academic legitimation. If "boys" were to be trained
vocationally for the farm and the factory, then some "girls" were to have
the opportunity to take bachelor's degrees in "domestic science" or "home
economics"—diplomas that would indicate serious college-level training
in the skills of housekeeping.

DISPERSION   Substantive growth also took place through a process in
which an academic subject spreads itself imperialistically far beyond its initial boundaries. History is the prototype, a subject always taught in
American colleges but one that served at the outset as a supplement to the
classics (Greek and Roman antiquities) and theology (ecclesiastical history). It thereby was limited largely to the time before the fall of Rome or

30

to materials Biblical and sacred. From the 1880s onward, history exploded in coverage, extending its research and teaching first to modern Western societies, including the American, then to some Eastern cultures, and, by the turn of the century, embracing the entire world in time and territory. By similarly widening its scope, anthropology also became an important field, at once scientific and romantic, which was able to take the student to the far corners of the earth as well as back in time before recorded history.

Many were the fields that would grow steadily by spreading substantive boundaries. Economics gradually found out that economic behavior was everywhere, in public and nonprofit as well as in private sectors, in the actions of universities and museums as well as those of business firms. Sociology slowly spread itself in the twentieth century as a field that can study any aspect of society—the cinema, sports, crime, and religion, as well as class, race, and power. As a "perspective," each of the social sciences learned that it could poach at will.

Primarily through these processes of substantive growth, the American effort in higher education became extremely eclectic, far more so than in Britain, France, Germany, and elsewhere. Walter Metzger contends that diversification did not merely affect the system: it defined it. University and college catalogs thickened, and equity among disciplines and specialties was formally promoted by alphabetical listings of subjects and numerical orderings of courses, even if some subjects were more equal than others. By 1900, let alone recent decades, there were few if any centerpieces around which to group the curriculum and anchor a resident profession. Overwhelmed by wave after wave of specialists—the Ph.D. was "an octopus" whose tentacles reached into every academic corner—the proponents of general education and liberal education had already lost the main battle. They were to fight on in the twentieth century, rushing forth time and again under the banner of "the cultivated man" from their remaining redoubts in the liberal arts colleges and in the undergraduate colleges of some universities, particularly the leading private ones. But the die had been cast. As the American professoriate became a profession of ever-widening scope and steadily increasing specialization, it moved from its early inflexibility to a state of permanent extreme plasticity. It absorbed subjects and then absorbed still more. There was hardly any body of knowledge that was beneath it.

31

The Conditions of Liberation

Behind this radical enlargement and extreme democratization of subjects, we can discern an array of liberating conditions. One was secularization. Even in the antebellum decades, the hold of religion was loosening:

> . . . if science had not yet triumphed, neither did theology reign. At the beginning of the nineteenth century, there existed neither an excessive devotion to the classics nor a desire to teach theology. . . . By the time that Yale abolished its faculty orthodoxy test in 1831, the secularization of the northeastern colleges was fairly complete. And classics, too, occupied an increasingly diminished role in the curriculum.[10]

After 1850, one college after another was reducing, if not cutting entirely, its ties to a religious past. After 1875 the universities, new and old, were largely a secular lot: to take on a religious commitment, as did Catholic institutions, was to play the university game with one hand tied behind the back. By the end of the nineteenth century, the great bulk of new faculty recruits were coming from secular foreign and domestic institutions. Hence the confines of religious doctrines were gradually stripped away, leaving scholars and scientists free to think as they pleased—or to find their dogmas in science, politics, or other secular spheres.

Another major force was the gradual shift in all leading and ambitious institutions from teaching to research. Where teaching once had been the only task that counted, it became an activity whose rewards could be made subsidiary to those of research. The universities that took hold in just four decades after 1870 became dominant over the small colleges that had held the stage for over two centuries. By 1910 some two dozen major private and public universities—most were members of the Association of American Universities (AAU)—were where leading academics assembled. With this ascendance, the interest in research became an overriding imperative. Teaching might remain the activity that consumed most of a professor's time: undergraduate instruction was too essential to the welfare of the university or college to be sacrificed to the interests of research. But a pronounced disparity in teaching loads was developing. Already in 1908 a survey by The Carnegie Foundation for the Advancement of Teaching found university faculties averaging eight to ten hours of teaching a week in non-laboratory subjects, while their counterparts in liberal arts colleges were in the classroom about fifteen to eighteen hours.[11] Universities steadily built research time into faculty work. And in the balance between research and teaching time, the universities became systematically differentiated. The more prestigious ones required light teaching, the others, heavier burdens. By 1920 the expectations were six to eight hours per week for the one, ten to twelve for the other. To require no more than six to eight hours of teaching became "a mark of first class practice."[12] As the universities sought to provide time and resources for professors to do research, the efforts to create and reformulate knowledge became deeply engrained.

Secularization and the growing institutional commitment to research were general conditions in the late nineteenth and early twentieth centuries that American professors might have shared with their European counterparts. Uniquely American, however, was the special leverage for enlargement and diversification that came from the invention of the graduate level as a second major tier in the ladder of grades. This postbachelor level gradually absorbed the major professional areas of study, alongside advanced programs in the basic disciplines.[13] This separate sphere for advanced degrees—the master's, the doctorate, and the special degrees of the professional schools—gave the American structure a strong vertical thrust in the systematic preparation of disciplinary specialists and professional experts. In Europe, students pursued medicine or law directly upon entering higher education. In the United States, they had first to spend four years in the undergraduate zone of general education and rudimentary exploration of fields. In Europe, students pursued advanced work in a basic discipline beyond the first degree without the benefit of much formal course work, essentially staying on in the shop of the chaired professor, to do some research and perhaps engage in some teaching. In the United States, students entered structured programs of graduate work in departments, with sequences of courses, formal requirements for entry and exit, and lectures along with seminars. Hence, at the higher level, professors occupied themselves with systematic teaching as well as research. Although the undergraduate part of their work necessarily had to center on beginning and intermediate materials, the graduate level gave them more room to turn to individual specialties while treating income-producing students as research apprentices and proto-peers. In short, the graduate school became a special institutional space for expanding and diversifying the substantive contents of higher education.

This was the nearest thing to a revolution in American higher education.[14] Actually an evolution over many decades, and hence without the dramatic impact of a true revolution, the development of the graduate school level of the American hybrid university markedly changed the conditions of the professoriate. Alexandra Oleson and John Voss noted in *The Organization of Knowledge in Modern America, 1860–1920*, that the American graduate schools

> were not teacher-training institutions or normal schools; rather, their distinctive purpose was to develop productive scholars and scientists. If American graduate training provided the incentive to undertake research, college and university teaching afforded the opportunity. In this setting, the concept of what professors should be was transformed: they assumed a new identity as specialists aware of the inherent obligation of the scholar to advance as well as disseminate learning.[15]

The many graduate schools were soon deep in M.A.'s and Ph.D.'s: students enrolled at the graduate level rose from fewer than 50 in 1870 to nearly 6,000 by the turn of the century. Where the universities had conferred only 1 advanced degree in 1870, they awarded over 1,500 master's and nearly 400 doctoral degrees in 1900 (Table 3). The ratio of advanced to first degrees was to steadily improve: in 1880 and 1900 master's and doctoral degrees combined, compared to the output of bachelor's, were one to fourteen; in 1920, one to ten; in 1950, one to seven; and in 1980, one to three.

The long-run returns from the graduate school output to an expanding academic labor market were to be immense: "By 1920, the spread of higher education and the identification of the college teacher with scholarship—in theory if not always in fact—provided America with a reservoir of manpower for research far larger than that of any European country."[16] Professionalism in the modern sense of esoteric knowledge in the hands of full-time experts had descended upon the professoriate.

Also powerfully American in encouraging the substantive growth of the professoriate were new tools that became dear to its heart: the department

TABLE 3

GROWTH OF CONFERRED DEGREES, 1870–1980

YEAR	BACHELOR'S DEGREE[a]	MASTER'S DEGREE[b]	DOCTORAL DEGREE
1870	9,371	0	1
1880	12,896	879	54
1890	15,539	1,015	149
1900	27,410	1,583	382
1910	37,199	2,113	443
1920	48,622	4,279	615
1930	122,484	14,969	2,299
1940	186,500	26,731	3,290
1950	432,058	58,183	6,420
1960	392,440	74,435	9,829
1970	827,234	208,291	29,866
1980	999,548	298,081	32,615

[a] Bachelor's and first professional.
[b] Master's except first professional. Beginning in 1970, includes all master's degrees.

SOURCE: U.S. Department of Education, National Center for Education Statistics. *Digest of Educational Statistics: 1982* (Washington, D.C.: 1983), p. 105.

and the professional association. Walter Metzger has stressed that "between 1870 and 1900 practically every subject in the academic curriculum was fitted out with new or refurbished external organization—a 'learned' or 'disciplinary' association, national in membership and specialized in scope; and with a new or modified internal organization—in a department of instruction as the building block of most academic administrations. These were more than formal rearrangements of the campus workforce: they testified to and tightened the hold of specialization in academic life."[17]

One macro and external, the other micro and internal, the association and the department became powerful organizational instruments. One pulled together a discipline across all local boundaries; the other served to support small clusters of disciplinarians at the operating levels of institutions. In the rearranging of American academic life, the emergence of departments was a critical step. They turned faculty members knowledgeable in subjects into "resident agencies for far-flung disciplines"; they became "the means by which control over academic appointments, which had already [by 1900] shifted in many institutions from the governing board to the president, would shift again (especially in the major universities) to faculty members in their disciplinary formations."[18] Henceforth, the department would be the unit where discipline and institution converged, an operating component in which academics might be subject to the strain of trying to serve two masters, but, more important, would find that two sources of support enhanced their power. The duality could be turned to good advantage.

The emergence of disciplinary associations tracks well the proliferation of subjects and specialties. Among the associations extant in 1985, only 2, each generalist in character, were founded before 1800: the American Philosophical Society in 1743 and the American Academy of Arts and Sciences in 1780 (Table 4). Only another 10—among them the American Statistical Association (1839), the American Association for the Advancement of Science (1848), and the American Geographical Society (1852)—were founded between 1800 and 1880. The takeoff occurred during the last two decades of the nineteenth century, when more than 25 associations formed along modern disciplinary lines. These included the Modern Language Association of America (1883), the American Historical Association (1884), the American Economic Association (1885), the American Society of Zoologists (1890), and the American Physical Society (1899). In steadily increasing numbers, 43 associations were formed between 1900 and 1919, 58 in the next two decades, 77 between 1940 and 1959, and 150 in the quarter-century between 1960 and 1985.

By the latter period, associations had become finely honed, springing up to support and to honor such esoteric interests as one might find in the Virginia Woolf Society, the Tissue Culture Association, the Society for the Anthropology of Visual Communication, and the Society for Nursing His-

TABLE 4

NATIONAL DISCIPLINARY ASSOCIATIONS, 1985, BY PERIOD IN WHICH FOUNDED

PERIOD	NUMBER	PERCENTAGE OF 1985 ASSOCIATIONS
PRE–1800	2	1
1800–1819	0	0
1820–1839	1	0
1840–1859	5	1
1860–1879	4	1
1880–1899	27	7
1900–1919	43	12
1920–1939	58	16
1940–1959	77	21
1960–1985	<u>150</u>	<u>41</u>
TOTAL	367	100

NOTE: A similar analysis up to 1966 may be found in Harland G. Bloland, *Higher Education Associations in a Decentralized System* (Berkeley, Cal.: Center for Research and Development in Higher Education, University of California, 1969). The analysis shown here, updating the findings to 1985, was made by Ronald Opp, UCLA graduate student. See Appendix B for a listing of the disciplinary associations.

SOURCE: Disciplinary associations for which dates of origin are available in the *Encyclopedia of Associations: 1985*, Katherine Gruber, ed. (Detroit: Gale Research Co., 1985). Four additional associations did not report founding dates.

tory. Notably, 90 percent of the 1985 associations have been formed in the twentieth century, with over 60 percent since 1940. How many small attempts died along the way is unknown, but the number must have been sizable, especially in the 1960s and 1970s. As instruments of subject aggrandizement, the associations offer formal groupings that perforce lead on to still other associations as their subjects split into still more specialties. For over a century, they have provided yet another powerful condition and force for the ascendance of the disciplinary point of view.

THE CONTEMPORARY DISTRIBUTION OF FACULTY

Amid the contemporary clutter of academic subjects, we can, by clumping or splitting as we please, identify several dozen major disciplines or isolate several hundred specialties. A typical breakdown of the primary disciplines and professional areas lists more than thirty fields, each a profession in its own right, equipped with the cognitive, collegial, and moral components that are the benchmarks of professionalism. Table 5 depicts the array of disciplinary professions by grouping fields in six broad clusters. Most impressive is the sheer diversity of subjects: physics and social work, philosophy and business administration, history and engineering, botany, and law. A host of major interdisciplinary programs, offering bachelor's degrees, master's degrees, and sometimes doctoral degrees, is not shown. With a new one appearing to develop every year in the last two decades, combinations of subjects press for resources and departmental nationhood: in the social sciences, as an example, such new interests as policy studies, urban studies, environmental studies, women's studies, ethnic studies, Afro-American studies, and Asian American studies abound.

Notable is the sheer size to which the major fields have grown. Mathematicians and statisticians number over 30,000, chemists over 18,000. In the social sciences, psychology contains approximately 25,000 professors, economics 15,000. In the humanities, English is a primary field that teaches large numbers of undergraduates: its ranks, totaling perhaps as many as 50,000 to 60,000 full-time and part-time, are many times larger than the total professoriate in some small countries abroad (there are 11,000 academics in all of Sweden). We know that professional school faculties are now substantial, even if they are difficult to count: numerous appointments, especially in medical schools, are variously temporary, clinical, and part-time. Combining all the "hard" and "soft" professional fields (Table 5), their ranks now approximate one-half of all professors. As rough estimates, another 20 percent are in the sciences, and the remaining 30 per-

TABLE 5

DISCIPLINARY DISTRIBUTION OF FACULTY

DISCIPLINE OR PROFESSIONAL AREA	PERCENT OF PROFESSORIATE*	DISCIPLINE OR PROFESSIONAL AREA	PERCENT OF PROFESSORIATE*
PHYSICAL SCIENCES	13	BIOLOGICAL SCIENCES	7
Mathematics and Statistics		Biology	
Chemistry		Physiology and Anatomy	
Physics		Bacteriology, Molecular Virology, and Microbiology	
Earth Sciences		Biochemistry	
General/Other		Zoology	
		Botany	
		General/Other	
SOCIAL SCIENCES	13	HUMANITIES	17
Psychology		English Language and Literature	
Sociology		Foreign Language and Literature**	
Economics		History	
Political Science		Philosophy	
Anthropology and Archaeology		Other	
Geography			
General/Other			
"HARD" PROFESSIONAL	20	"SOFT" PROFESSIONAL	30
Engineering and Industrial Arts		Education	
Agriculture and Forestry		Business, Commerce, and Management	
Medicine		Arts	

39

TABLE 5 (*cont.*)

DISCIPLINARY DISTRIBUTION OF FACULTY

DISCIPLINE OR PROFESSIONAL AREA	PERCENT OF PROFESSORIATE*	DISCIPLINE OR PROFESSIONAL AREA	PERCENT OF PROFESSORIATE*
Nursing		Physical and Health Education	
Dentistry		Home Economics	
Other Health Fields		Law	
Architecture and Design		Journalism	
Vocational and Technical		Religion and Theology	
		Social Work	
		Library Science	

* These broad estimates are based on the percentage of faculty who appeared in these fields in the sample of faculty used in the 1984 Carnegie national faculty survey. Since the survey undersampled part-time faculty and did not include some 500 specialized colleges, the above figures particularly underestimate the share of faculty in disciplines that use many part-timers (English, business) and the professional-field faculty in specialized colleges.

Because national data on faculty are poor in dependability and noncomparable from one agency or study to the next, I have refrained from specifying percentages for all the specific fields.

** "Foreign language and literature"—widely used in classifications—subdivides into a number of language departments, e.g., French, German, Italian, Slavic, Spanish.

cent divide about equally between the social sciences and the humanities (history is a field that can be classified either way). Numerically large as individual fields are English, mathematics and statistics, and biology, in the letters and sciences half of the professoriate, and engineering, business, education, and medicine in the professional school half.

Among the major fields, the explosive growth of knowledge in the biological sciences in the 1960s and 1970s has now made biology *the* case of subspecialization. It is a field in which five or more subfields may achieve separate departmental standing within a single university: at UCLA departments of biology, microbiology, microbiology and immunology, biomathematics, and biochemistry exist; molecular biology, a large interdepartmental program, also offers the Ph.D. A department of biology may list over thirty fields—from animal behavior to photosynthesis to neurobiology—in which graduate students may specialize in taking the Ph.D.[19] Another theoretically mature discipline, physics (still generally assembled in one department) also possesses a wide range of imposing subfields that grant the Ph.D. They include elementary particles, nuclear physics, plasma and astrophysics, solid state physics, acoustics, and spectroscopy. Still further subdivisions exist. For example, elementary particle physicists separate into the two camps of cosmic ray physicists, who study natural particles, and high-energy physicists, who use accelerators. And so for chemistry, with such major specialties as organic, inorganic, and physical. Bridging these principal disciplines in part are the recognized specialties of biophysics and biochemistry.

Of course, such intense internal specialization is not the province of the sciences alone. Historians group themselves within departments in such major clusters as American history and European history. As they embrace the globe in time and space and obtain more faculty positions in departments, they create such groupings as ancient history, Japanese history, the history of science, and the history of religions. Within the clusters, individuals frequently specialize locally as one-of-a-kind experts: they might, for example, cover the history of the American West or that of nineteenth-century France. In the leading institutions, academic labor becomes evermore finely tuned in the social sciences, the humanities, and even the arts (Egyptian art history is one example) as well as in the physical and life sciences.

In turn, the professional schools carry on the permutation of subjects. The study of education is a soft, immature subject principally based in departments and schools of education; in the 1980s it already entails a dozen or more subspecialties ranging from "early childhood" and "special education" to "school administration" and the "economics of education." The enormous organizational unit called the medical school houses an enormous array of specialties in research as well as fields needed for the preparation of doctors. Its formal demarcations are a lesson in specialization: psychiatry and neurosurgery; pediatrics and internal medicine; anesthesiology and public health, which is also increasingly disassociating as a professional school in itself. Major medical schools are the size of Pentagons (see Vignette Two), with an intensity of activity not to be imagined in humanities departments. Virtually in themselves, American medical schools are living proof that academia is now endless.

THE PROFESSORIAL MATRIX

In these first two chapters, we have seen how, near the end of the twentieth century, the American professoriate is distributed in a gargantuan aggregate of over 3,000 universities and colleges, and how, in turn, it is also dispersed in a disarray of subjects. The two lines of affiliation intersect to form an enormously complex matrix in which niches are defined for individuals by their dual memberships in institutions and subjects. To pin down professors by both specific institution and specific discipline would require a scheme containing over 3,000 rows to represent institutions and 100 or even 200 or more columns to depict major disciplinary specialties and formal professional school segments. Left to the imagination, this ultimate accounting would appropriately portray the colossal scope, the virtually ungraspable complexity, of the modern-day operating framework of the American professoriate upon which its very existence depends. All usable numbers and other reductions of data on types of disciplines and sectors of institutions are but a crude representation of these tens of thousands of locations in the institutional-disciplinary matrix.

But, for the purposes of analysis, some limiting categories must be used: in Part Two, we work with six fields in six types of institutions. As we do so, patterns soon emerge. For example, simple statistics pinpointing where

VIGNETTE TWO
A PENTAGON OF MODERN MEDICINE

The 800-bed UCLA Center for the Health Sciences, the medical center . . . fills thirty-five acres of the university campus. . . . When the center was built in 1954, it was designed to combine treatment with teaching and research, a triple role that was unique at the time. Laboratories and classrooms integrated with inpatient wards on the same floor was unprecedented. Because the emphasis was on academics, patients were selected on a value-for-teaching basis. That is still somewhat true today, although there is greater emphasis on community health needs than in the past.

It began modestly enough: a $23 million, six-story, 600,000-square-foot building. In twenty-five years, however, it has quadrupled in size. Now it is a $110 million, ten-story, 2,400,000-square-foot conglomerate of modern science. The Pentagon supposedly has slightly more available space, but with about twenty miles of corridors—no one seems to know exactly how many—the medical center is larger. In addition to the original hospital, medicine and nursing schools, and laboratories, there are now a complete emergency medical center, extensive outpatient clinics, the Marian Davies Children's Clinic, the Jules Stein Eye Institute, schools of dentistry and public health, a neuropsychiatric institute, the Charles E. Reed Neurological Research Center, a brain research institute, the Jerry Lewis Neuromuscular Research Center, the Jonsson Cancer Center, and a biomedical cyclotron. In 1980 the center admitted more than 26,000 patients, treated almost 56,000 emergency cases, and had operating costs of $130 million on gross revenues of $132 million. About 1,800,000 clinical laboratory procedures were performed, more than 11,000 operations were done, and nearly 12,500 babies were delivered. And the scientific enterprise of the center's doctors and researchers was underwritten by grants of more than $130 million. Only three universities received more. Modern medicine is a big business.

SOURCE: From *Life and Death on 10 West* by Eric Lax. Copyright 1984 by Eric Lax. Reprinted by permission of Times Books, a Division of Random House, Inc.

various disciplinarians are located among the types of institutions indicate there are "upward-tilting" and "downward-tilting" fields in the professorial matrix—areas of professorial and student commitment that weigh heavily in research universities at one extreme and in lesser four-year colleges and, especially, community colleges at the other. Biology is upward-tilting: as sampled in the 1984 faculty survey, biologists number about 7 percent of all academics; but they are over 12 percent of the faculty in the top research universities and only 5 percent in the community colleges. Medicine looms large in the universities, there possessing over 10 percent of the faculty. The "health" fields—with dentistry, nursing, and other specialties joining medicine—become at least 20 percent in the universities. When "health" is joined to "biological sciences," the involved professoriate totals a third or more of the university campus.

In sharp contrast, English is a downward-tilting discipline: its preponderant jobs are well down the line. Among all professors, those in English approximate 8 percent; in leading research universities, they are only about 3 percent; but in less selective liberal arts colleges they constitute about 12 percent and in community colleges about 14 percent—or one in seven of the total faculty. Business is also distributed among all types of institutions—in clear contrast to medicine. Professors in this applied area number about 5 percent of all faculty members, but only about 3 percent of those in the leading universities. They are significantly more represented in the lesser "doctorate-granting" (essentially nonresearch universities) as well as in the community colleges, at over 7 percent.

Scatteration defines the professoriate in late twentieth-century America. And, field by field, the dispersion is very uneven. As homes for the professoriate, the various types of institutions do not recapitulate one another—on even the simplest matters. They offer different worlds.

44

CHAPTER III

The Open System

Thus a clean break—psychological, social, and economic—had to be made, and a new life started. But England was not the country where to do it . . . her society was too homogenous and solid, her opportunities . . . too narrow. . . . Thus the United States appeared as the sole country where, perhaps, an attempt would be successful to carry out the threefold transition: as a human being, an intellectual, and a political scholar.

—FRANZ NEUMANN, *THE CULTURAL MIGRATION* (1953)

This has been a system which placed a premium on innovations, and has been open to a great variety of social pressures. . . . Innovation became a pervasive tendency of the American university system, as in the similarly competitive German one during the 19th century, but in contrast to the German case this innovativeness has not been limited to pure nonutilitarian science and scholarship, but has been extended to applied and professional fields too.

—JOSEPH BEN-DAVID AND AWRAHAM ZLOCZOWER, ''UNIVERSITIES AND ACADEMIC SYSTEMS IN MODERN SOCIETIES'' (1962)

SOME NATIONAL SYSTEMS of higher education change more rapidly than others, driven forward by dynamics we only dimly comprehend. In the last half of the twentieth century, the huge American array of institutions and disciplines has been unparalleled in its restless proliferation. Nowhere else do we find so many institutions crisscrossing so many specialties in an array that steadily widens. We observe a peculiarly open and adaptive system that at once makes some professors very vulnerable to external demands and equips others with uncommon professional autonomy. What drives this academic matrix? What gives the American system a distinctively dynamic cast? Complex answers must necessarily be based on two interacting conditions: extreme competitiveness in the context of institutional hierarchy.

THE CONDITION OF COMPETITIVE DISORDER

From the beginning, the American system of higher education was destined to generate a competitive struggle that often would be brutally harsh. Neither in 1636 at the founding of Harvard, nor in 1787 when the colonies were constitutionally assembled as one nation, nor in 1876 when Johns Hopkins became the first new university, and not even in the bureaucratic late-twentieth century has there been a national ministry or a royal commission or a dominating private elite to plan jurisdictions, distribute funds, and otherwise define a formal order. There was not to be an official formation. Instead, the energizing imprint of the system became the very opposite: To each his own, and the devil take the hindmost. Dissenters and reformers learned by the beginning of the eighteenth century, in this sector as well as in other parts of American society, that it was simpler to set out on one's own than to remake an established place where power was in the hands of others: "the dissidents who disliked Harvard, Yale, or William and Mary did not in most cases try to transform them, as English dissidents did Oxford and Cambridge during this same era. Instead, they set up their own competitive colleges to serve new purposes, many of which had not previously been regarded as appropriate for a college."[1] In the language of modern political economy, those who wanted to improve things were positioned *and* conditioned to choose "exit" over "voice."

And who could stand in the way? Although the earliest colleges were for a time close to the governments of the individual colonies, to the point of being territorial monopolies, the supporting polities were never unified and, at any rate, saw controls recede after 1800. College incorporation laws, already haphazardly varied, were eased. After the Dartmouth College decision in 1819, when Daniel Webster so eloquently added to the myth of the independent college, such colleges had a legal basis for independent existence, considerably free from state supervision.[2] In the religious revival of the early nineteenth century, the many denominations and sects that dotted the landscape sharply competed with one another in establishing colleges that would bring in converts. Behind the westward-moving frontier, towns and local land speculators set out to woo colleges as good investments. Regulatory government virtually moved out of the picture, turning the development of the system over to a competitive open market. For example, when Antioch College was established in the 1850s by members of the Christian Church, a Protestant sect, in a town in the southwest corner of Ohio that outbid other towns by pledging twenty acres of land, $30,000, and "life-giving water," the state of Ohio already had twenty-six colleges, all small and all sectarian.[3] By no stretch of any planning imagination did Ohio need a twenty-seventh. But the system already moved to a different logic.

In this strange academic market, there were no one or two flagship institutions, such as Oxford and Cambridge in Britain, or the Sorbonne in France, or, still later, the Universities of Tokyo and Kyoto in Japan, whose power and prestige would allow them to sit astride the system. Professors could no more control the system than could politicians and bureaucrats. If there were to be any order, it would have to emerge out of competitive disorder, largely through imitation and voluntary adoption of successful patterns. In this setting, colleges could and did multiply in the hundreds, as we have seen, scattering the professoriate in approximately 500 institutions by 1870 and 1,000 by 1900. Henry A. Rowland's depiction of the system in the 1880s as a veritable "cloud of mosquitoes" was entirely appropriate.[4]

In the face of unbridled competition, neither eager colleges nor ambitious professors could afford to be inert. Colleges competing for professors as well as for students had to manufacture and highlight competitive advantages, claiming they had a better brand of education than anyone else and then seeking to back the claim with attractive posts for faculty and interesting curricula for students. A new institution could powerfully concentrate the mind of an older one upon making competitive adjustments, as the new Johns Hopkins did to the old Harvard, causing the latter's most famous president to smile kindly upon research-minded professors who otherwise might depart for Baltimore. Charles W. Eliot was slow to rank faculty research equal to teaching. As late as 1898 he "outraged a Harvard professor by suggesting as reasons for not promoting George Santayana that he did not 'lay bricks or write school books.' " But meanwhile, he had been instructed to think differently by Johns Hopkins, whose opening in the mid-1870s "promptly redirected Eliot's thinking on the nature of university faculties. Johns Hopkins offered Harvard professors larger salaries and lighter and more advanced teaching assignments"—a threat that Eliot had to counter, and did, by raising salaries, strengthening the graduate school, and acknowledging that, in his words, "the most influential professors are those who have creative or inventive capacity, and themselves contribute to the progress of knowledge and art."[5]

For institutions determined to be first-class universities, the ante for a competitive financial base was steadily raised. Some of the new private universities came up with funds that were simply astonishing. The initial bequest of $3,500,000 for Johns Hopkins in the 1870s matched the endowment that had taken Harvard two and a half centuries to amass. Ten to fifteen years later, Stanford and Chicago started up with handsome gifts of 24 and 30 million dollars, respectively, that allowed them from the outset to pull faculty talent from elsewhere and to offer a diversified curriculum. By 1910 university and college endowments had swelled to the huge sum of over $300,000,000, with 40 percent of that amount in the hands of eleven private universities.[6] Thus, in the three decades from 1880 to 1910, without planning, the cloud of mosquitoes had given birth to a set of major centers of research and scholarship that could become internationally competitive.

These major concentrations of resources were often exemplars of institutional initiative where the captain of erudition had convinced a captain of industry that together they could assemble the best faculty money could buy. Modesty was hardly the name of the game. With private-sector institutions setting the competitive pace, newly ambitious public universities followed suit by turning to their own state governments for levels of support that would allow them to measure up as significant institutions. They soon developed their own powerful modes of institution-building. Whether in Michigan or Wisconsin or Minnesota or later in California, they had to seem as good or better than the "elite" private universities in assembling faculty talent—or else, they pointed out, they would sit as poor cousins that would shame their states. Soon the leading public university in one state had to be better than counterparts in neighboring states. Positioned to appeal to the pride of an entire population of a state, public institutions learned that their own graduates could be cultivated as lifelong supporters.

The competition was to have no limits. Privately controlled institutions competed with one another on various axes: universities with universities, colleges with colleges, even universities and colleges against each other. Private and public competed. Public institutions not only countered each other across state lines, they took up sharp rivalries within states. Radically subdued in nearly all other leading national systems, the competitive fever became so deeply engrained in the American system that in the late twentieth century we find, for example, Michigan State University squaring off against the University of Michigan, and the University of California at Los Angeles, even within a formally unified state university system, ambitiously driving itself toward a capacity and a reputation that would match that of the University of California campus in Berkeley. The context and the struggle always insist on local pride. Everywhere, faculty, administrators, students, and alumni can be found driving their automobiles across the country as well as to the local market with bumper stickers that proudly identify them as part of a particular academic enterprise that might otherwise be distinguished by its anonymity. Far distanced academically from a Harvard, we find students and faculty proudly loyal to a campus. And a truly committed campus president or chancellor is not above riding in the backseat of an open convertible in whatever major parade can be found at home or abroad to wave to the crowd and otherwise bring the truth of institutional prowess to the power of the populace.

It was inevitable that a competitive open system would dictate a turn to big-time sports. Since no other national system of higher education has done so, the sports connection is a particularly revealing feature. The leading private universities, preeminently Yale, fathered college football in the 1870s in the form of seemingly harmless intercollegiate contests that might channel youthful energies away from intracampus aggressiveness, making the life of professors and administrators a little less dangerous.[7] But the football rivalries rapidly acquired a dynamic of their own: better teams, with better coaches, games before larger crowds that paid more money to fill larger, more costly stadiums. Even by 1905 the contests had become so out-of-hand, with coaches using "tramp athletes" who freely moved around as nominal students, that the President of the United States,

49

Theodore Roosevelt, felt impelled to call football coaches to the White House and otherwise insist that someone clean up the mess. But nothing was to stop this dynamic throughout the twentieth century. After midcentury, the Ivy League institutions might engage in a modest deemphasis of intercollegiate sports, but they still found significant reason to maintain such contests. And elsewhere, with only an exception here and there—the University of Chicago was one—the reasons were compelling to go for the big time. State universities in particular have developed sports as a gigantic add-on, a function that they cannot do without even if they cannot effectively control it. As a trend not played out a century after it began, the expansion of college sports is a good marker for the dynamics of competition in American higher education generally.

The impulse of institutions in this type of system to buy faculty, expand the student body, and diversify the curricula, well in place by the turn of the century, provided a favorable base for the prodigious reactive growth that has taken place in the twentieth century. As common schooling spread upward grade by grade from the elementary level, and the American upper secondary system became far easier for young people to navigate than secondary schooling in other countries, the proliferating and growing universities and colleges sought students by competitively dangling vocational attractions, along with offering the much-praised benefits of liberal education. They rode the tide of swollen outputs from mass secondary education and, in the aggregate, swung from elite to mass in the proportions of the secondary school graduates they admitted. From a base of 4 percent of the age group at the turn of the century, growth led to 12 percent in 1930, 15 percent in 1940 (a figure not reached in many European countries until 1970 and still not exceeded in Great Britain), 20 percent in 1950, 25 percent in 1960, 40 percent in 1970 and 50 percent in 1980. With the expansion of the community colleges in the 1960s providing the ultimate in open access—admission for all, of any age, without regard to academic qualification—the system had arrived at a universal stage where, on academic grounds, 100 percent of the population over eighteen could be admitted. Willy-nilly, with hardly a thought, American professors developed a potential clientele as broad as that of doctors and morticians. The system's reaction to pressures to admit more students simply extended the gluttonous inclinations of a permissive profession whose form had been cast by substantive growth: ingest and then ingest some more; live and let live; there is room for everything and everybody.

The institutional market in American higher education gradually came under some state guidance, especially in the years following the expansion of the 1960s. By the 1980s master plans and mechanisms of formal coordination are found everywhere among the states. State officials seek to specify jurisdictions, reduce overlap, and eliminate institutional redundancies. But the competitive imprint has not been eradicated. Private institutions are still largely driven by their individual imperatives. As they seek to build, so do they compete. Public universities and colleges retain an impressive capacity to itch on their own. They press for autonomy around their engrained capacity to hire their own personnel and significantly shape their own programs. If they find state guidance not to their liking, they wiggle out from under the master plans and state requirements as best they can. And with public control always divided among fifty states, with the national government more in the background than up front, "state coordination" ends up as much on the side of interstate rivalry and competition as in the service of an imposed order.

As the day follows the night, this unique arrangement of higher education radically disperses initiative. For so many institutions, it is somewhere among their own trustees, administrators, and faculty that the will and the way must be found to finance the enterprise at a desired level, to establish its character, and to develop a viable niche among other institutions. The imperatives of self-enhancement have been steadily enlarged in the post-World War II decades, as public institutions have learned how to more fully diversify their support by reaching to private sources—alumni, foundations, business firms, wealthy individuals—while the private ones augment their financial base by extracting support from public quarters, particularly from the many departments of the national government whose interests bear on higher education. For major public and private institutions alike, the financial base is a potpourri of sources: grants and contracts, mainly from governmental agencies but also from industrial firms; student income, from tuition and fees; investment income, from endowment; gifts for current use, from private donors; medical services, when a university operates a hospital; and, for the public institution, an institutional allocation from the state.

As initiative leads to a widening of the financial sources, so does it feed autonomy. Homer D. Babbidge and Robert Rosenzweig appropriately pointed out, in the early 1960s, that "a workable twentieth century definition of institutional autonomy [is] the absence of dependence upon a single or narrow base of support."[8] The conditions of the American system, emphasizing institutional initiative, push institutions away from the singular base. Realistic, dependable autonomy is the freedom not to have any single outside source of support impose policy, a large truth in late twentieth-century higher education that institutions in unitary national systems elsewhere have begun to grasp under the poundings of sometimes hostile regimes.

The dynamics of competitive disorder are clearly rooted in the system's radical decentralization of control. Nowhere else in higher education is there anything approaching a structure in which authority is divided among fifty major public segments and, at the same time, distributed among 1,500 private authorities. Internationally, public national control is the dominant mode, as in France, Italy, Spain, and the many small advanced countries of Western Europe. Among the major countries that remain formally federal, public authority in higher education is divided among a handful to a dozen provinces (essentially six in Australia, eleven in Canada, and in the Federal Republic of Germany), with the national government having a prominent role in Australia and Germany. Notably, these important federal nations all have weak to nonexistent private sectors: in Australia and Canada, as in the United Kingdom, what was once private has become legally or de facto public as public subsidies replaced endowments and tuition. West Germany finds it painful in the mid-1980s to create even one or two private academic enterprises. Among the major democratic powers, only Japan comes even close to the American dispersion of control in private hands with over 700 private institutions handling 80 percent of the students, four times the American proportion. Regions and municipalities are also sponsoring public authorities. But the Japanese national government, through ministerial channels, has long been the primary supporter of the leading public universities, beginning with the University of Tokyo, in a pattern of prestige that placed them normatively and functionally astride the whole system; and beginning in the 1970s, the national government has sought to guide the private institutions while contributing financially to them. The control of the American system is exceptional.

But then we have only to compare higher education with elementary and secondary education in the United States to see that decentralization of control alone cannot account for the condition of competitive disorder and all that it means for the academic profession. Also operating under an extreme version of federalism, the lower levels have not differentiated their institutional forms nor placed operating units in sharp competition. In the late nineteenth and early twentieth centuries, the public comprehensive school drove out public specialized schools, whether academic, vocational, or in the arts.[9] In most parts of the country, private education was also pushed to the periphery. Thus the public comprehensive school became the one best way. School districts composed themselves by assigning these standardized units to territorial catchments.

The contrast could hardly be sharper: Old forms shaped new ones in the higher education system but did not drive them out. When the university became a dominating form, the small colleges went on multiplying in number and even in subtypes, as leagues developed for Catholic colleges, Lutheran colleges, and Quaker colleges, secular colleges first-rank and secular colleges second- and third-rank. The universities soon became quite different from one another. Neither the universities nor the liberal arts colleges stood in the way of the normal school-teachers college-state college evolution. Instead, professors in the established sectors rejoiced rather than wept when they realized that the task of educating teachers had been taken up by others.[10] And while some state universities at first opposed two-year colleges not under their control, fearing greater competition for students and a weakening of their own enrollment base, others, as in California, welcomed the "junior" colleges as part of an institutional division of labor that would free them to concentrate on research and advanced work and to enhance the quality of their pool of students.

Why should secondary and elementary education have strained to dedifferentiate while higher education was so impelled to diversify? The lower levels were strongly affected by the gradually strengthened American belief in the value of the "common school" as a necessary tool for social integration and nation-building in an immigrant society. Spreading upward from the elementary school, the ideology of the common school cap-

53

tured all the secondary grades. Mandatory schooling also provided school districts with captive clienteles, making it relatively simple to grant individual public schools the security of neighborhood monopolies. As schools became noncompetitive as well as similar in character, they lost the need and the rationale to be individually distinctive. Critically, they were also much less driven by the processes of substantive growth that turned professors into self-enhancing groups of experts spinning off in every direction and riding to power on the backs of disciplines. The professionalization projects became astonishingly different, centering in the one case on similar duties in a common unit and in the other on specialization and diversification. In the schools the professionals were "teachers," similar and equal. In higher education they were "professors," dissimilar and—not to worry—unequal.

Logically, the fractured setting of the professoriate might seem less favorable than the shared footing of the teachers to the development of a profession. But, instead, school teaching in America has become at best a semiprofession vulnerable to decline. What has counted in the professionalization projects is the underlying tasks and the institutional and disciplinary foundations. Simpler subjects at the lower levels are a major constraint. Institutional commonness has proved a major obstacle. In this perspective we begin to see why the historic diversity of disciplines and institutions in American higher education is so critical to the overall welfare of academics. The system could become mass without all segments of the professoriate becoming common. The more favored parts have given "the profession" some power to shape a system that in its open competitive way might otherwise entirely follow other dictates.

The sheer scale of American higher education should also be taken into account if we want to understand its competitive disorder. The system's huge, ungainly size boggles the minds of observers from other countries, especially the smaller ones, and keeps Americans from understanding what is going on. We confront not only 3,000 institutions, 12 million students, and a professoriate, full-time and part-time, in the order of 700,000 to 800,000, but a financial outlay, in 1985, that approached 100 billion dollars. In this outsized system, 10 percent errors or misrepresentations in the collection and comprehension of data are in the range of 300 institutions, 1 million students, 75,000 professors, and 10 billion dollars! In itself, sheer

54

size constitutes a potent fragmenting force. In a crowd of over 700,000 academics, with hundreds of thousands of bordering administrators and auxiliary staff, anonymity must necessarily abound. In a continent-spanning country huge size also has a geographic component that extends social distance. How often in the course of a year do the paths of academics in Albany or Baltimore normally cross those of "colleagues" in Oshkosh, Wisconsin, let alone in Pullman, Washington, or Biloxi, Mississippi? If American academics are to be in touch with one another, regional and national associations become compelling.

Simple cross-national comparisons establish quantitative differences in size that surely become quantitative in their effects. Small Sweden, population 8 million, operated a higher education sector in the order of forty institutions, 180,000 students, and 11,000 academics in the early 1980s—the latter numbering less than one-fiftieth of the American ranks. Similarly, Norway, Finland, Denmark, the Netherlands, and Belgium have very compact systems. The major countries of Western Europe are many times larger, but remain considerably smaller than the United States: the Federal Republic of Germany had about 250 institutions, 1,250,000 students, and 125,000 academic staff; France, 350 institutions, 1,000,000 students, and 60,000 in its academic estate, including the *grandes écoles* faculty and the full-time researchers in the "academy" sector as well as the universities and technological institutes; and Britain, the least expanded of the three, had its academic world divided into about 450 relatively small institutions that serve 800,000 full-time and part-time students and were staffed by approximately 120,000 faculty.[11] Hence these major international centers of learning possess a professoriate, broadly defined, that is one-fifth or less the size of the American aggregation. Remarkably, the United States has virtually as many faculty members as Britain has students. Even in Japan, a truly massive system of higher education with over 1,000 institutions and 2 million students, the ranks of academics swell to approximate only a fourth of the American number. And Japanese higher education is far less developed at the graduate level, conferring, in 1982, only 15,000 master's degrees compared to 300,000 in the United States, and only 4,000 Ph.D.'s compared to over 32,000.[12] Enormous in all respects, the American system is, comparatively, weighted toward the highest levels of education and training, an outcome of the creation of the graduate second tier a century ago.

A substantial amount of choice is also natural in a system that is large, open, and competitive. Compared to higher education in the United Kingdom, France, the Federal Republic of Germany, and other systems generally, the basic structure offers students innumerable options and second chances. Open access is a staggering feature when seen against a backdrop of systems where, even after two decades of "democratization," those deemed qualified to enter top out at a third or less of the relevant youth age group (and at much less for older adults), as in France and the Federal Republic of Germany; or even at one in six or seven, as in the United Kingdom in the mid-1980s, where public-sector cuts in governmental expenditures and a faculty obsession with quality may reduce the numbers still further.[13] The American system also offers prospective students high mobility among institutions: Sector boundaries are permeable; standardized units of credit can be carried from one institution to another; and transferring is encouraged by the way the state systems structure higher education. In short, students have repeated opportunities, now and later, to negotiate sufficient credit for a bachelor's degree and the more advanced certificates.

Most important for our purposes is simply that, on an international scale, the system, even in bad times, remains the land of job opportunity for faculty. Since at least 1940, the balance of trade in brains among countries has favored the United States as the great importer. Relatively tight systems in which senior posts remain scarce commodities and research funds are not readily available to younger academics lose talent to the American professoriate. The irony is surpassing: National systems operating on a relatively elite basis, with top positions for only a few, cannot necessarily attract and hold talent, while a chaotic uncontrolled open system, mass in its totality, provides opportunities for that talent.[14] For such major European systems as the United Kingdom, France, Italy, and the Federal Republic of Germany, let alone their small neighbors, the capacity to absorb talent in comparison to the United States, especially in the sciences, cuts at the very heart of national advance.

The classic case involving Great Britain and the United States came about at the time of the migration of European intellectuals and scientists from Continental Europe during the Fascist era. Britain was commonly the first stop, the preferred destination. But the British system could not absorb the emigré scholars, no matter how eminent or promising in talent: "of the refugee physicists who came initially to Britain, lack of *permanent* employment opportunities eventually encouraged a majority to move on elsewhere, mainly to America. Many more were too discouraged by the limited job prospects to come to Britain at all."[15] American higher education could and did absorb them, at Duke, Cornell, Rochester, Princeton, Notre Dame, the California Institute of Technology, and elsewhere at ambitious second-rank universities as well as among the top ten research universities. And even small colleges got into the act, for scientists and non-scientists alike:

> At Sweet Briar, in Virginia, a German woman, Hilde Stücklen, was the chairman of the physics department for thirteen years; in Winston-Salem, North Carolina, the distinguished Italian biologist Camillo Artom has engaged in research since 1939; the Austrian composer Ernst Kanitz taught at Winthrop College at Rock Hill, and Erskine College at Due West, both in South Carolina. . . . No state of the Union has been entirely without intellectual immigrants.[16]

For Britain a golden opportunity was missed: "Gosh, what they could have gotten at that time for nothing," an involved scientist, Victor Weisskopf, later noted.[17] Or as Paul K. Hoch said:

> One effect of the differential absorption and integration of refugee physicists was to be . . . the decisive shift of the main centers of world physics from Europe toward the United States. Great Britain, primarily because of the more static nature of its university base, and more exclusive orientation toward conditioning an educated elite, was only able to profit from the migration of refugee physicists to a lesser extent, losing many of the most eminent practitioners to the U.S. . . .[18]

For want of some openness and flexibility in its system of higher education, Britain remained on the wrong end of a "sea change" in the location of scientists and intellectuals.[19] The matter is deeply structural. Four decades later, in the 1980s, the interchange of academic and intellectual talent between Europe, including Britain, and the United States still has a westward flow. The capacity of an open system and a loosely integrated professoriate to adapt and to absorb has offered significant advantages in the shifting of talent among major centers of learning.

Within the American system, faculty choice is naturally much more problematic for the vast majority who labor without the benefit of a major research reputation. In a weak job market, as it was in the late 1970s and early 1980s, many are treated badly, thrust, as temporary and part-time employees, into a proletarian position. But, in contrast to national systems that are less differentiated and less competitive, the system provides an array of institutional niches toward which academics can differentially wend their way. Employment slots are not so much all or nothing as they are in systems with only one, two, or three sectors, each operating as a separate compartment. Instead, particularly in bad times, academics slide from preferred to less-preferred institutions: for example, from first jobs in research universities to ones in service universities to yet others in state colleges or in the lesser private colleges, and, finally, to join the growing number of Ph.D.'s who teach in two-year colleges. But in bad as well as good times, professors do not make their way to individual campuses by means of formal national screenings. They and institutions have to choose each other. And for institutions striving to be better staffed, the faculty becomes the item, the critical resource, that best ensures a virtuous circle of more prestige, more money, and better students. Trustees and administrators need many things for effective institution-building, including, generally, a good football team. What they need most in meeting the competition is to recruit and maintain a faculty perceived as first-rate.

In a particularly disordered national system, competition among universities and colleges is what guarantees their seriousness.

THE CONDITION OF HIERARCHY

Differentiation and competition have led to extensive hierarchy. Instead of sitting side by side in a passive horizontal arrangement governed by a parity of esteem, the major institutional sectors have evolved a vertical ranking that, first of all, is rooted in tasks and jurisdictions.[20] No matter how much it may wish to be otherwise, the two-year college is junior, restricted, in the grade structure, to the work of the freshman and sopho-more years and the awarding of a two-year degree. Extending several more years up the ladder and offering bachelor's and master's degrees, the state college and the private liberal arts college occupy a higher operational niche. At the top, leading universities now stretch beyond the Ph.D. into semicertified postdoctoral training. It is a quite objective matter that, for matriculated students on the move, the feeder sequences run strongly from the two-year college to the four-year college and the university, and from the four-year college to the university, making clear for all to see that there is a vertical differentiation based on institutional location in the lad-der of education. In contrast to other national systems, in which a small number of sectors have watertight boundaries, with little or no transfer-ring of students and their credits, this aspect of hierarchy is systemic in American higher education.

It only takes the perceived value of graduation to turn the hierarchy of sequence into a powerful hierarchy of prestige. Where are graduates placed in the labor force? How are life chances enhanced or diminished? With graduates proceeding directly to different levels of occupational prestige—secretary in one case, engineer in another, doctor in a third—prestige is virtually transferred automatically from the occupational world to the pre-paratory institutions. Always a powerful coin in the academic realm, much of the use and abuse of prestige is lodged in the general rankings that both academics and the laity make when they think about different kinds of uni-versities and colleges. They can hardly avoid coming to terms with repu-tations, institution by institution, let alone sector by sector, as they think about contributing money, or enrolling a son or daughter, or signing on as faculty. Unofficially, but with powerful effects, universities and colleges are seen as high, medium, or low in quality. With each passing decade, published rankings appear more frequently, and are widely noted in news-papers as well as used by institutions and professors to assert superiority or to argue for greater support in the quest for higher status.[21] Sectors also overlap: Leading liberal arts colleges are seen from within and without the profession as "better" than mediocre universities. With search for prestige omnipresent, even colleges located in the lower rungs of the educational sequence find it useful to stress that, as quality institutions, they can help students gain access to the better institutions at the higher levels.

Such hierarchies are an affront to democratic instincts. They produce large numbers of have-nots, leading in the American case, to hundreds of thousands of professors developing a sense of relative deprivation as they judge their own successes against that of others who are simply positioned by the system to be better off. In the extreme a sharply peaked institutional hierarchy can isolate several institutions in elite positions and block out all others. But then at the other extreme, a flat nonhierarchical arrangement eliminates the incentives for institutions to strive hard to better themselves. It is in the moderately steep structures of prestige in a competitive setting that we find both the openness and the incentives for institutional improvement. Even as it makes climbing difficult, the hierarchy provides grounds for hope. Institutions are permitted and encouraged to compete for better personnel; hence scholars, particularly younger ones, can flow from one institution to another in search of better conditions of work. Institutions can attempt to shift their clienteles toward the higher quality inputs of their reputed betters. The whole wild business of competition in American higher education may begin with survival, but above that threshold it is a struggle to first maintain status and then to enhance it. With no monetary profit marker by which to judge success, prestige is the required coin. To have more of it is to live better at higher rungs in one's own league and in the system at large.

The importance of status hierarchies in promoting competence has long been stressed by "best-science" advocates. Science requires some concentration of talent and resources. It can hardly be promoted by scattering talent and funds equally across a large number of institutions and programs. France in the West, and the Communist nations in general, have sought to strengthen science by investing in a separate research structure, taking a national academy approach. But if best science, or best scholarship more broadly, is to have supportive locations within higher education itself, there must be some concentrations within and especially among institutions, thereby introducing distinctions. The problem then is to couple the resulting hierarchy with some openness, pluralism, and peer review. This combination is what Henry A. Rowland was after when he attempted to specify in the 1880s what should be done to improve the science of physics in the United States. If the American system was going to replace the "cloud of mosquitoes" with a few forms that would compare with the great academic centers found in Europe—they provided "models of all that is considered excellent" and thereby stimulated physicists to their "highest effort"—there would have to be some concentration of talent in a few first-class universities.[22] The resulting status pyramid would be commanded at the top by a scientific elite but hopefully open to talent at the bottom. Critical would be pluralism at all levels of the hierarchy, with groups of physicists divided along lines of specialty, training, and geography and having access to many journals and granting agencies. Before, and especially after, World War II, the American system did indeed evolve in this direction.

Institutional hierarchy can operate as a form of quality control. The status structure apportions respect and rewards on grounds of perceived competence, utilizing both public opinion and peer assessment. A hierarchy can concentrate resources efficiently for the implementation of such expensive tasks as the training of bureaucratic elites and the manning of major research laboratories. The problem is always how to preserve high standards and at the same time to allow for institutional and individual mobility. If the hierachy is reasonably open—not fixed by the more the more, the less the less—it generates the process of academic drift in which institutions of lesser status seek to make themselves over in the image of institutions of higher standing. Drift is toward "better" as that is operationally exhibited in top institutions. Despite its often-criticized effects in homogenizing a system, drift is a standards-serving process.

Thus, despite all the problems of invidious distinction that it brings, institutional hierarchy is a way of inducing hundreds of thousands of quasi-autonomous professors and institutional administrators to work hard. For one's self, one's department, one's institution, and one's class of institutions, hierarchy hooks interests to chariots of ambition. It involves a most curious combination of professional assessment and market competition in which the merit principle is written large. Especially in a large, open, and competitive system of higher education, hierarchical differentiation and the merit principle may be inseparable.[23] The distinctive strength of the whole American enterprise in higher education may well be that its competitive hierarchy—so hostile to the confines of central planning—introduces both incentives and spaces for spontaneity that encourage innovation and the pursuit of quality.

Critical for understanding the nature of the academic profession across the full range of institutions is the way that hierarchy affects the openness of the American system. Open to what and to whom? Open primarily to substantive growth, the self-elaboration of fields of knowledge, or to reactive growth, the expansion and shifts that follow consumer demand? At the top—as we see in full detail in Part Two—there is a realm of research and peer judgment in which professional responsiveness is primary to the growth in knowledge. At the bottom we confront a realm of teaching and student attendance in which responsiveness faces toward consumer demand. Perhaps we get "not what we deserve but what consumers demand and professionals are willing to supply,"[24] with location in the hierarchy decisively affecting the relative influence of consumers and professionals. Academics dictate more at higher ranks, consumers more at the bottom. As we grasp the great differences that attach to location in the institutional hierarchy, we are able to understand better why a vast open system of higher education can be so much a creature of consumer demand and, at the same time, a place where some academic professionals, individually and in small clusters, have unparalleled control over their working lives.

THE SYSTEM AND THE PROFESSORIATE

Relatively unregulated, the American system of higher education is the extreme case among advanced systems of weak guidance by government. From the adoption of boards of trustees to the pastoral provision of trees and lawns, the historical evolution of institutions carried habits from the private realm to the public sectors. As private-sector norms became central to the character of the system, coordination was provided more by the market than by state authority. When formal state systems developed, they were laid down over institutions conditioned by the engrained privateness of the system at large. For the professoriate, the effect was profound: It was bred outside of central government.

Europeans generally do not think of faculty members and allied researchers as a profession largely because academics are so intimately a part of the state. They are funded, employed, and given status as one or more "corps" rooted in departments of government and in national civil service.[25] Institutions of higher education are parts of an embracing formal structure officially topped by one or more ministries. The state and the ac-

62

ademic estate are all the more indivisible when the universities traditionally have prepared their best graduates to enter the top categories of the national civil service or for leading roles in the national political structure. It was in Britain and America that a profession developed on a more independent footing, and although British academics have moved rapidly since the mid-1960s toward the embrace of the national state, American professors have not.[26] They have been strongly anchored against the tides of twentieth-century nationalization by both the strength of private institutions and the splintering of public control inherent in a radical federalism. The result has been an unplanned grant of extraterritoriality to the profession, an occupation much less firmly in the grip of government than found elsewhere among major counterparts. Distance from government is the central difference between an academic estate in Europe and the academic profession in the United States. The historical development of the American system has given modern-day academics a relatively strong capacity to maneuver vis-à-vis government.

In comparative perspective, American academics also have a relatively strong capacity to maneuver in and among institutions. Nothing stands out more sharply in cross-national comprehension of the behavior of universities and colleges than the high degree of entrepreneurship and competitive spirit of American institutions. The system will not leave the institutions alone: They are enterprising because they have to be. And in their individual efforts at institution-building and status-raising they are considerably dependent on the attraction and retention of faculty talent: sharply at the top, where the ideals and images of academics are mainly formed, moderately at the middle levels of academic standing, and least where institutions survive on the poorest cut of academic talent.

Egged on by a compulsive, competitive search for talent in an unregulated system, the academic disciplines, through substantive and reactive growth, have become impressively large, specialized, and self-amplifying. In an increasingly professionalized society permeated with conditions that make everyone dependent on experts, the many proliferating academic disciplines have become authoritative communities of expertise. Physics, chemistry, and biology; economics, psychology, and anthropology; history, English, and classics—each has become the epitome of esoteric knowledge in the hands of an organized community of practitioners. As the system forced institutions to compete, and institutions sought specialized professors as the critical resource, so were the disciplines strengthened in the anatomy of the system and in the individual institution. To know the score in modern American higher education is to be acutely aware of how much the system is discipline-driven as well as market-driven.

The interaction of system and professoriate has also led to crucial organizational arrangements. Central has been the making of the department as the place where disciplinarians nest in their local setting to do the work of research and teaching and whatever other duties they take on. The department becomes the basic unit of organization because it is where the imperatives of the discipline and the institution converge. It is a different vessel for academic labor than is the chair unit so common around the world, operating to diffuse status and power from the one academic to the many, enhancing collegial authority at the expense of personal dominion. The department also differs sharply from the college unit of organization, that interdisciplinary, undergraduate-centered form modeled for the world in the colleges of Oxford and Cambridge and so much admired by American academics seeking to strengthen the education of undergraduates. Unabashedly committed to the single discipline, the department provides a supporting environment for master specialists and their apprentices at whatever cost to the integrated learning of neophytes. And it is particularly the power of disciplines behind departments that diminishes managerial hierarchy inside academic organizations. The tendency of professionalism to flatten bureaucratic hierarchies, now noticeable in business organizations and public bureaus as they switch to greater use of human capital and the resources of knowledge, has long had its strongest expression in the academic world.

Just so, the voice of professors is enhanced. They use the department as a tool to mediate between the realities of a particular university context and the demands and desires of their own discipline.[27] This powerful instrument has been relatively democratic in its internal operation, "inexorably pressured to treat all members on an equitable basis":[28] Administrative heads rotate; each member has the opportunity that others possess to engage in autonomous teaching and research; all have access to whatever supports are available in the form of teaching assistants, research assistants, research funds, and sabbatical leaves. Forming the base of the structure of faculty power, the department has undergirded the development of a dual authority structure within universities and colleges that on the campus at large takes the form of a major faculty collectivity, usually the academic senate, counterposed to the administration. The department is the local rock on which the power of voice is based in academia, the organized base for the capacity of academics to exercise influence within the organization to which they belong and to branch out into larger circles.

Also clear is the vast enhancement of professional mobility that the interaction of system and profession has promoted. Market power, we may call it, a power that comes from the capacity to enter a system and particularly to move around within it. In discussing physics as a profession, Gerald Holton has noted the remarkably heterogeneous social background of persons engaged in some collaborative research. He pointed to this feature as perhaps the most important factor "in explaining the growth of science in our time. Nowhere else can one find a better *experimental* verification of the general worth of the democratic doctrine, which is often uttered but rarely tested seriously. Social and geographic mobility in a field of work, as in society itself, is the essential prerequisite for a full exploitation of individual talent."[29] The opening of the American academic profession to individuals of diverse social backgrounds took place largely after World War II, with considerable long-standing unevenness among fields of study.[30] However late it came, and however retarded the entry has been for women and some minorities, the general competitive openness of the system, with so many restless institutions and disciplines, has been a lever that opened doors to talent. Equally remarkable for the self-enhancing nature of the system has been the high degree of internal mobility, with the capacity of academics to choose and to move enhanced by the competitive bidding for talent that has loomed large for over a century among the many institutions that are esteemed or have the ambition to be.

Thus the historic pattern of interaction in this particular national system has given much power to the experts. But professional leverage was not extended to all. Many were left weak, stranded on the periphery. Professors were distributed in institutions, far from leading research universities, that marched to different drummers, arranging work in different packages, shaping beliefs to the realities of different contexts, establishing different environments of authority, and segmenting academic careers in different types. In Part Two we trace these dimensions of academic professionalism as they twist and turn through the labyrinths of the modern American academic world. As we do so, we shall at times see a veritable rose garden. But benefits have costs, and we shall also see weeds and ungainly graftings and worry along with others about possible mounting deficiencies of the American academic profession. There is much to attract the eye and to praise, and so much from which sensitive souls want to shrink. Most of all there is the strong possibility that the academic profession in America must exist in disarray. In a supporting system so large and so loosely coupled, with no one in charge, the problems of unity and order are enormous. Threatening to leave it in pieces, the system rips at the fabric of the profession. The very nature of the national system is the very root of the problem of having *an* academic profession capable of effective performance.

Given the complexities of its host system, and the variations thereby introduced in it, the American academic profession, if taken in the singular, also becomes a fountain of contradictions. It is elite, but it is mass. It dances to the tune of research, but most of its members only teach. It is full of peer controls, but it is susceptible to consumer pressures. It has high prestige—yet it does not. And on and on: Any assertion of a single mode can elicit an appropriate counterargument. Analysis must necessarily seek the pathways of differentiation, grasping that the singular is really always plural, with dissimilar, even opposing, components leading off in different directions. In Part Two we follow the trails of difference.

*The Dimensions
of Academic Professionalism*

CHAPTER IV

The Imperatives of Academic Work

The conservation and advancement of the higher learning involves two lines of work, distinct but closely bound together: (a) scientific and scholarly inquiry, and (b) the instruction of students. The former of these is primary and indispensable.

> —THORSTEIN VEBLEN, *THE HIGHER LEARNING IN AMERICA* (1918)

Nowhere does the contrast between the lesser college or university and the major university come out more markedly than in the performance and evaluation of the research function.

> —LOGAN WILSON, *THE ACADEMIC MAN* (1942)

Being a college professor is the closest thing to being an entrepreneur in terms of controlling your own destiny, but you get a salary while you are doing it.

> —BUSINESS PROFESSOR, RESEARCH UNIVERSITY (1984)

THE LONG-RUN TRENDS described earlier leave no doubt about the changing nature of the academic profession in the United States. Each decade since the mid-nineteenth century has seen the profession grow larger and more heterogeneous. Substantive and reactive growth combined explosively after World War II to push it into new subjects and into the hands of new clienteles. But although the general trend of differentiation is clear, its composition is clouded. Academics themselves find it difficult to comprehend what academic life is like in its many corners. Even within the confines of a single large campus, much of what fellow workers do is beyond ordinary informal observation. The daily rounds of the professor of classics do not lead to the corridors of the management school, where the strange ways of this neighboring tribe could be observed. The medical school anesthesiologist has no reason, in the normal course of affairs, to become acquainted with the working life of a political

69

scientist expert in voting behavior, let alone that of a scholar immersed for all time in Dante. Mutual ignorance then also multiplies across the types of institutions. It is virtually impossible for a research scientist running a major laboratory at a leading university to know or even imagine what academic work is like for a professional colleague who teaches mainly introductory courses in a struggling rural private college or who devotes nearly all efforts to first-year students in an urban community college. Complexity blocks direct comprehension in higher education as clearly as it does elsewhere in society. Inquiry is required: We are compelled to go out into the field to ask questions, observe, and probe written records so that we can reveal what otherwise will remain obscure.

We begin with the essence of academic work. What is it that academics actually do? We know that teaching is the nearest thing to a common activity, but it is a task that varies greatly in nature and allotted time, shading off for some into a minor role. Research, the other principal activity, also differs immensely in kind and commitment. It serves as the primary basis for prestige in the many disciplines—and in the profession as a whole—and is bound to play a substantial role in major universities. When he portrayed inquiry as the "primary and indispensable" line of work in "the conservation and advancement of the higher learning" six decades ago, Thorstein Veblen clearly had grasped an imperative of American higher education.[1] But many settings in the American system not only change the nature of research but seek to eliminate it entirely. In addition, by choice or necessity, professors spread themselves beyond these two major tasks. They advise students, even, in some locales, formally counsel them. They administer: individually, as heads of specializations, departments, divisions, colleges, and senates; and collectively, in bodies and innumerable committees where one-person-one-vote decision making attests to the vitality of collegial authority. They consult. They serve in professional associations. They sometimes expend their energies quite widely.[2]

Professors in the American system, whether young or old, junior or senior, are also likely to find their activities merging in a seamless blend. In our field interviews they even argued that their activities cannot be separated, that the one is often the other: that research is teaching, often at its best, when apprentices work side by side at the bench with the master; that teaching is research, when efforts to transmit knowledge in the classroom

70

and instructional laboratory generate new insights or reformulate problems and concepts. The blending of activities includes informal conversations with colleagues in the hallway, lonely hours of thought while grading examinations and papers, and one-to-one mentoring when advising students on courses and careers. In quite different institutional and disciplinary settings we find professors moving in many different directions, even during a single hour of work, with the telephone an instrument of frequent distraction: In the course of a week they typically must shift among a plethora of duties. Responsibilities also shift for many from one semester to another; some teach heavily in one and little in the next. One academic year may be different from another, especially for those entitled to sabbatical leaves. Virtually all change gears between "the academic year"—in fact, it is only eight or nine months—and the summer. The seamless, and often shifting, blend of activities turns any formal accounting of time into a charade, a game that professors sometimes have to play with legislators and administrators who believe, or must pretend they believe, that occasional hazy estimates of hours and proportions of time offer accountability on how much professors work and how they allocate effort.

The blend of activities includes a blurring of home and office. Professors can be notoriously difficult to find at their listed workplace. Much of what they do is similar to a craft pursued in a cottage industry: It can be carried and done at home. Even an anatomy professor in a medical school told us that "when I want to do something important, I go home. Nobody calls me at home, and there is no one there, and I go there for a particular purpose and I do it." And a young woman in the English department of a leading private college that prides itself on devoted teaching indicated how essential it was to steal away:

> I've found there is time for research if you're smart, and one thing I've learned is that I take one day a week and mark it in my calendar, I just mark it off. I go home and I unplug my phone and I work on my research. If anybody asks me to have a meeting that day, I will come out with my calendar and say, "Oh, I'm sorry, I'm booked for the day."

Thinking is difficult in a busy office. Consequently, many professors work their way toward schedules of work and conditions of space and quiet that allow them to stay home some of the time, whether to prepare a lecture, write an article, call a colleague, or just do nothing while a good thought is supposedly percolating.

A professor who is generally at a desk in an academic office may also appear to be a monument of indifference, even casual laziness, while actually in concentrated pursuit of daily work. A mathematician may fiddle with coffee cups, scraps of paper, well-chewed pencils, and stubs of chalk while working out sequences of symbols that only a few in the same craft can follow. Discretion in the control of time and the performance of duties is a remarkable feature of the profession, particularly in research universities and leading four-year colleges. Where this discretion is strongest, employees are not really employees. Instead, they are staff members who "are available for consulting, to engage in research activities . . . , to lecture off-campus, or to work in the library or in their own gardens—as long as they fulfill their teaching duties. . . ."[3] There is much "maneuvering time," as a community college teacher called it, in all the institutional settings, even as its amount and character varies. This feature of academic work can be much envied by professionals in other fields who are much better paid. The physician, for example, beginning a daily round of tightly scheduled hospital and office appointments at 7:00 or 8:00 in the morning.

How then can we best grasp the "work load" of academics? Professors, administrators, and trustees alike nearly always define it as the amount of time spent in classroom teaching—"the teaching load." The reason is clear: Teaching is an institutional obligation for which hours can be specified. While other activities are carried out in free time, teaching is done in constrained time. Proposals to add more required courses or shift from a three-quarter to a two-semester academic year are immediately examined by professors for possible bearing on "faculty work load," which is immediately translated as the "teaching load." Professors are as sharply aware of this as are workers concerned about a thirty- or forty-hour week. "Research load," on the contrary, is not part of the vocabulary. Research time may be mandated in the long run, where it is required for retention and promotion, but in the here and now it is not a formal duty. It is done in the time freed from teaching.

Thus, for professors concerned about saving hours for research, time spent teaching is time diverted. It may be mandated, but it steals time away

72

from something more basic and is seen as more of a burden; more time for research is not. Time spent on administration, we may note, is widely viewed as wasted, often not even regarded as a legitimate demand. Thus, especially in settings where incentives for research are strong, professors will lighten their work load by holding down the number of hours earmarked for the classroom. The fixation on teaching time as the definition of load speaks volumes about the conflicting duties, incentives, and preferences found in the American professoriate.

THE INSTITUTIONAL DEFINITION OF WORK

The many sectors that define the institutional diversity of American higher education also define a remarkable diversity in tasks and conditions of work. Part of an engrained division of labor within the professoriate, these differences are relatively stable. Any significant changes occur over decades.

Teaching Load and Research Time

Various national surveys have offered estimates of the average teaching load of American academics ranging from seven to ten hours a week. But such estimates are virtually devoid of meaning, and they obscure the reality of great differences: Some professors teach two hours a week, others fifteen to twenty, and still others cluster at such modes as six, nine, and twelve. In close analysis of data gathered in the first (1969) Carnegie survey of faculty, Martin Trow and Oliver Fulton showed convincingly that "teaching loads may vary from a norm of as little as three courses *per year* in the 'academic' departments of high-quality universities to five or six courses *per term* at junior colleges." Additionally, by covering part of their own salaries out of research grants, faculty in the leading universities can obtain "released time" that lightens their minimal load even further. Translated into hours, the enormous differences in institutional requirements have meant that "less than one-fifth of those at high-quality universities spent over nine hours per week in class, compared with four-fifths at junior colleges."[4] These observers appropriately concluded that the as-

73

signment of teaching loads is a primary mechanism whereby an extreme differentiation of higher education is encouraged and effected.

The 1984 Carnegie survey did not ask professors for a single estimate of their weekly teaching load; instead, it inquired separately about their undergraduate and graduate teaching. But a similar story of great differences can be readily seen. Using the nine basic Carnegie categories of institutions, we see in Table 6 that only about one in twenty faculty members in the leading research universities was teaching undergraduates more than eleven hours a week compared with three out of four in the two-year colleges; about one-third of the Research University I faculty were not teaching undergraduates at all in a given semester or term compared with a tiny minority so reporting in the community colleges—staff members who apparently were otherwise occupied in counseling or administration. Two-thirds of the faculty in the leading universities were teaching undergraduates less than four hours a week or not at all. (Their involvement at the graduate level is shown in Appendix C.) Between the two extremes, the figures run smoothly in order up and down the institutional types, the exception being that fewer faculty in the better liberal arts colleges teach larger loads than do faculty in the comprehensive four- and five-year institutions.

Although appearing precise because they come in the guise of numbers, the results of answers to questions posed in national surveys should be taken for the general patterns they suggest. Slight changes in the wording of questions often change the specific results; the meanings of questions may vary from one setting to another; and, in academic surveys, there generally is much biased sampling, for example, clinical faculty, temporary faculty, and part-time faculty are routinely understated in the faculty rosters of institutions from which samples are drawn. Thus, even teaching-time data need to be treated broadly. In the general pattern that dependably emerges, we can estimate that loads center in the range of four to six hours a week in leading universities (research universities I and II), nine to twelve hours in lesser universities, comprehensive colleges, and liberal arts colleges, and fifteen hours in two-year colleges. Beyond all doubt, teaching loads increase significantly as the institutional contexts shift from research universities to nonresearch universities and comprehensive colleges; they moderate among the better private liberal arts colleges; they increase again in the lower ranking private colleges; and they

74

TABLE 6

WORK LOAD: TIME SPENT ON TEACHING
UNDERGRADUATE COURSES, BY TYPE OF INSTITUTION

TYPE OF INSTITUTION	HOURS PER WEEK				
	NONE	1–4	5–10	11–20	OVER 20
	(PERCENT OF FACULTY)				
RESEARCH UNIVERSITIES I	31	35	28	6	0
RESEARCH UNIVERSITIES II	19	35	33	11	2
DOCTORAL-GRANTING UNIVERSITIES I	14	27	40	18	1
DOCTORAL-GRANTING UNIVERSITIES II	13	17	42	38	2
COMPREHENSIVE UNIVERSITIES AND COLLEGES I	8	13	41	36	2
COMPREHENSIVE UNIVERSITIES AND COLLEGES II	5	13	42	38	2
LIBERAL ARTS COLLEGES I	3	9	53	32	3
LIBERAL ARTS COLLEGES II	4	14	36	43	3
TWO-YEAR COLLEGES AND INSTITUTIONS	3	9	13	65	10
ALL INSTITUTIONS	11	18	32	35	4

Total respondents, 4,731

QUESTION: "During the Spring term, how many hours per week on the average are you spending in each of the following activities? . . . A formal classroom instruction in undergraduate courses."

SOURCE: The Carnegie Foundation for the Advancement of Teaching, 1984 Faculty Survey.

peak significantly higher in community colleges. Nothing is plainer or more consequential in the arrangement of American academic life.

The level of instruction extends differences in the nature of teaching loads. Beginning classes are typically lecture courses, with relatively large numbers of students per class. Intermediate classes of the upper division of undergraduate years are also largely carried out by lectures, but with smaller numbers, and some take the form of seminars. Advanced classes at the graduate level entail small numbers of students and shift still further into seminar-discussion formats and laboratory research settings. For all institutions taken together, approximately one-half of the faculty teach only undergraduates, another one-third teach both undergraduates and graduates, and about one in ten teach entirely at the graduate level (Table 7). In the leading research universities, far fewer concentrate entirely at the undergraduate level, with one-half working at both levels and one-quarter teaching only graduates. (The survey understates professional school faculty, who are for the most part limited to graduate instruction.) Many senior professors in letters and science departments concentrate their efforts largely if not entirely at the most advanced level, along with all those teaching in professional schools that have only graduate level programs. Then, too, in the universities, such onerous duties as grading frequently can be shifted to teaching assistants. When we asked a physics professor in a leading university about "issues of how you do your grading," he replied that he never had to worry about such matters because "I never grade. My graduate students do the grading."

In contrast, the loads for professors in liberal arts colleges are almost completely undergraduate-centered. For two-year college instructors, teaching loads are in introductory courses, since they teach only freshmen and sophomores among matriculated students and mainly first-year students at that: Each cohort is decimated after the first year as students drop out, complete one-year programs, or transfer early to a four-year college or university.[5] Again, there is a predictable gradient between the extremes, except for the interesting case of the "liberal arts colleges II," where one in five professors claims some graduate level teaching. Colleges in this category, as noted in Chapter I, are prone to add graduate programs in one form or another, becoming more comprehensive by level as well as by field as they adjust to student demand and otherwise try to pay their bills.

The main reciprocal for teaching load, of course, is research time. In the broad picture of the national survey, one-third of the faculty in the leading universities report spending more than twenty hours a week in research, with one-half indicating ten hours or more (Table 8). As we move down through the sectors, research time decreases markedly, except in the lead-

TABLE 7

WORK LOAD: TEACHING AT UNDERGRADUATE AND GRADUATE LEVELS, BY TYPE OF INSTITUTION

TYPE OF INSTITUTION	LEVELS OF INSTRUCTION			
	ENTIRELY UNDERGRADUATE	BOTH LEVELS	ENTIRELY GRADUATE	NOT TEACHING
	(PERCENT OF FACULTY)			
RESEARCH UNIVERSITIES I	16	56	23	5
RESEARCH UNIVERSITIES II	28	54	14	4
DOCTORAL-GRANTING UNIVERSITIES I	31	57	9	3
DOCTORAL-GRANTING UNIVERSITIES II	39	52	6	3
COMPREHENSIVE UNIVERSITIES AND COLLEGES I	52	38	7	3
COMPREHENSIVE UNIVERSITIES AND COLLEGES II	65	30	3	2
LIBERAL ARTS COLLEGES I	94	4	1	1
LIBERAL ARTS COLLEGES II	79	14	5	2
TWO-YEAR COLLEGES AND INSTITUTIONS	94	2	1	3
ALL INSTITUTIONS	56	33	8	3

Total respondents, 4,932

QUESTION: "Are your teaching responsibilities this academic year . . . (1) Entirely undergraduate (2) Some undergraduate, some graduate (3) Entirely graduate (4) Not teaching this year?"

SOURCE: The Carnegie Foundation for the Advancement of Teaching, 1984 Faculty Survey.

TABLE 8

RESEARCH TIME, BY TYPE OF INSTITUTION

TYPE OF INSTITUTION	HOURS PER WEEK SPENT IN RESEARCH				
	NONE	1–4	5–10	11–20	OVER 20
	(PERCENT OF FACULTY)				
RESEARCH UNIVERSITIES I	7	13	22	25	33
RESEARCH UNIVERSITIES II	9	14	27	26	24
DOCTORAL-GRANTING UNIVERSITIES I	11	23	30	19	17
DOCTORAL-GRANTING UNIVERSITIES II	10	37	27	14	12
COMPREHENSIVE UNIVERSITIES AND COLLEGES I	22	32	28	12	6
COMPREHENSIVE UNIVERSITIES AND COLLEGES II	26	32	24	12	6
LIBERAL ARTS COLLEGES I	17	30	30	18	5
LIBERAL ARTS COLLEGES II	42	39	13	5	1
TWO-YEAR COLLEGES AND INSTITUTIONS	46	33	15	5	1
ALL INSTITUTIONS	23	27	23	15	12

Total respondents, 4,426

QUESTION: "During the Spring term, how many hours per week on the average are you spending in each of the following activities . . . Research?"

SOURCE: The Carnegie Foundation for the Advancement of Teaching, 1984 Faculty Survey.

ing liberal arts colleges, where a moderate number of hours in the classroom and relatively small class enrollments serve to release time and energy for some research and scholarship. Instructors in the less selective liberal arts and community colleges have little or no time for research: Four out of five of their faculties claim four hours a week or less, with something approaching one-half reporting no time at all spent on research.

The very nature of research can vary by institutional setting. From the field interviews and the national survey, Kenneth Ruscio has drawn essentially a "little science—big science" distinction between the character of research typically carried out in leading liberal arts colleges and in leading research universities.[6] Research in the small-college setting depends less on outside financial support, particularly from the major donor, the federal government. Fewer than one in ten in the faculty has any money at all for research from federal agencies compared to one-third in second-level research universities and over one-half in the leading universities. Small-college research is less formally organized, with few, if any, research assistants and no "post-docs" to compose a research team. It is, therefore, individually more flexible. It is also typically more "horizontal" than research in the university, more often spread across neighboring subfields and even across several disciplines. It is justified by faculty in part as an investment in future as well as in current students. The members of an economics department in a leading liberal arts college, feeling burdened by teaching and advising responsibilities that kept them from doing research, creatively set aside one day a week for "future students." By conducting research, they maintained, they would acquire the knowledge, skills, and sense of involvement and competence necessary to teach later generations effectively.

Behind the numbers that reveal similarities and differences in the time devoted to research lie all kinds of significant differences in what is done in that time. The differences in the institutional contexts of research are likely to become even greater in the future, as the advanced research favored by funding agencies becomes more expensive, more tied to sophisticated equipment, and more frequently housed in major academic units devoted to research, at the same time that the small colleges attempt to fashion a liberal arts college model of research and scholarship. There are many definitions of research among types of institutions.

Beyond the two basic lines of work—formal instruction and inquiry—there is a plethora of other activities, such as administration, preparation for teaching, informal advising, formal counseling, outside consulting, outside professional practice, and participation in professional associations in which professors up and down the institutional line are variously engaged. Here the categories and the data are particularly fuzzy, hard for respondents to clarify and for observers to interpret. "Administration" is an interesting case in point since it bears on the issue central to unionization of whether professors in their individual rounds and in their collective responsibilities are "managers" or "workers." Survey results show little variation across types of institutions. The vast majority of faculty members in all kinds of institutions report spending some time on administration (Table 9). However, the seamless blend of activities makes it difficult for respondents and analysts alike not only to clearly identify what administration is but to separate it cleanly from teaching and research. To supervise a small team of teaching assistants in a large lecture class or a group of research assistants in a laboratory is to select appropriate personnel, arrange for their employment, monitor their interaction, and direct their work week-by-week. But such supervision is usually counted in professorial minds as teaching or research. Administration is thus likely to be underreported rather than overclaimed. And the individual assessment of time spent on administration does not tell us about the collective actions of faculty senates and committees on student admission and evaluation, the curriculum, and faculty policies and practices. A few faculty members, elected or appointed, spend substantial time in such rounds, with the general understanding that they represent the others. From individual office to faculty senate, faculty "administration" is an enormously varied line of work.

Similarly, the national survey shows little variation among the remaining forms of academic effort. In time given to preparation for teaching, university professors, who supposedly shirk such work, seem as much or as little involved as community college teachers (Appendix C). In time reportedly given to "professional practice," university professors caught up in the survey are not noticeably different as a general class than the staffs in all the other types of institutions. Similarly, in "advising and counseling students," large differences do not appear. These inherently ambiguous categories of activity, even more difficult than teaching or research to pin down, undoubtedly have different contents in different settings.

In the allocation of faculty time, then, what we can take primarily from the national survey is the immense variation by type of institution for the two core tasks of instruction and inquiry. The variation is so extensive that any stated averages for the system at large obscure more than they reveal. Standard comments about "the American professor" as one who engages

80

TABLE 9

HOURS SPENT ON ADMINISTRATION, BY TYPE OF INSTITUTION

TYPE OF INSTITUTION	NONE	HOURS PER WEEK			
		1–4	5–10	11–20	OVER 20
		(PERCENT OF FACULTY)			
RESEARCH UNIVERSITIES I	9	45	29	9	8
RESEARCH UNIVERSITIES II	10	47	26	11	6
DOCTORAL-GRANTING UNIVERSITIES I	10	47	28	8	7
DOCTORAL-GRANTING UNIVERSITIES II	13	44	29	10	4
COMPREHENSIVE UNIVERSITIES AND COLLEGES I	12	45	28	8	8
COMPREHENSIVE UNIVERSITIES AND COLLEGES II	9	50	26	7	8
LIBERAL ARTS COLLEGES I	10	43	34	7	6
LIBERAL ARTS COLLEGES II	9	51	27	9	4
TWO-YEAR COLLEGES AND INSTITUTIONS	16	51	25	5	3
ALL INSTITUTIONS	12	47	27	8	6

Total respondents, 4,685

QUESTION: "During the Spring term, how many hours per week on the average are you spending in each of the following acitvities? . . . d. Administration (departmental or institutional including committee work)?"

SOURCE: The Carnegie Foundation for the Advancement of Teaching, 1984 Faculty Survey.

in both teaching and research are false: Nearly all members of the professoriate teach, but only a minority are significantly involved in research. And the gross differences in these core activities captured in national surveys are but the beginning of an understanding of the extent of the variation.

The Zest for Research

The impression that professors in universities are put upon by the burdens of "publish or perish" turned out in our interviews to be largely a myth. It does not take into account the intrinsic rewards of critical thought and inquiry that lend considerable zest to the lives of so many professors in the leading universities, in the minor ones too, and even in the liberal arts colleges. This is not surprising. Socialization in graduate schools places many neophytes in close contact with professors who are dedicating their lives to research or scholarship, who appear to never look at the clock to find out whether it is time to stop working, who stay with their thoughts or experiments at whatever price to their personalities and home lives. As we shall explore further in Chapter VII, for some the quest to be a scientist or a scholar started long before graduate school. The early infatuation that becomes lifelong was expressed by a physicist at a leading university:

> There is no substitute for dealing with the things that we deal with. I mean I'm just as crazy about that as I was when I was 14 or 15 years old. . . . I knew I had this inclination, I just never thought I would do it. And it's the only way.

And, in a second case:

> Oh, I couldn't do anything else. . . . if anybody can be fulfilled, whatever one means by that . . . if you want to solve problems or do anything original or creative, then it's one of the few places that it can be done, and if you don't succeed with the opportunities I've had—which weren't as good as some, but were great—then it's just my fault. So I'd say if I had it to do over again, there are a few things I would do differently, but I sure would be a professor again.

In many instances, doing research is necessary to preserve one's self-image as a scientist *and* to project an appropriate model for students. A biologist in a leading liberal arts college explained that:

> If you are not doing research you really are only masquerading as a scientist, I think. That is my own prejudice: Technically, you won't keep up; and I have seen plenty of horror stories of people

who haven't kept up as soon as they stop doing research. . . . [And] part of your teaching is directing student research and really serving as an example to students who ultimately want to become biologists. If you aren't doing anything, you don't provide that example. You are just somebody who lectures to them and stuffs their heads with information, but you don't serve as a model. I think [that] in the humanities it is more the model thing that is important.

Research is also an extremely open activity in which professors develop individual directions of effort and styles of operations within whatever blend they have worked out among research, teaching, advising, administering, and consulting. A young professor in a business school expressed clearly how he combines research and consulting:

Some of my research in recent years has come out of some of the consulting, finding practical problems that have been left to be solved and writing a thought piece that would lead up to some research ideas as a result. . . .

It is very closely related to the feeling one gets in teaching, in that one takes some abstract concepts and sees if they'll fly. But in the classroom the judgment of whether it flies translates into students saying, "Yes, this was entertaining." With executives, it turns into "Yes, this is useful." So it's a different measure.

In this definition, consulting can serve research even better than does teaching, thereby giving an academic rationale to an outside activity that also serves material interests. From the same professor: "I have a family, two kids. Consulting was a necessity rather than an 'extra.' "

When we later analyze academic careers (Chapter VII), we observe the precarious situation of younger academics in the 1980s in certain fields in certain institutional sectors, thereby tying discontent to well-structured sources that deprofessionalize virtually all they touch. If, in contrast, we want to know how good things can be for some young faculty members, even in so-called hard times in American academia, the above-quoted assistant professor serves in a top business school that encourages its faculty to group their teaching loads in two academic quarters, leaving the third, along with the summer months, free for research. This was no secret. To compete for the very best talent, the school openly specified in its recruitment correspondence and advertisements that one-half of each year would be completely free from teaching. The school also guaranteed summer research stipends that would significantly enhance annual income. Professors' notions of what was "necessary," rather than "extra," were thereby inflated. In this pocket of affluence—a leading management school in a leading university—no traces of economic depression were to be found. Morale could hardly be higher, for here was a major field that had suffered from lack of academic respect and now found that its day in the sun had come.

Across some 170 intensive interviews, we encountered remarkably little resentment about "publish or perish," with complaints issuing mainly in four- and five-year colleges, where some professors felt left behind as the institution attempted to evolve from college to university. In the 1984 faculty survey, as well as in our interviews, professors in the research-dominated sectors were a relatively satisfied lot. They receive the highest rewards of prestige and salary, grounds alone for self-satisfaction. But more idealistic and intrinsic reasons are also relevant: Research professors like to do research. They learn to like it in graduate schools, if not before; they learn to like it on the job. The pleasures of inquiry (or scholarship) are found in the humanities and the social sciences as well as in the physical and biological sciences: and, it turns out, in institutions well down the hierarchy as well as in the universities that operate as national centers of excellence. A fair number of professors are capable of keeping two thoughts in mind at the same time: They have the goal of being a scholar as well as being a teacher. A professor of English in a nondistinguished university explained:

> My primary goal when I came here was to be an outstanding teacher. I didn't want to be just competent; I wanted to be an outstanding teacher. The other goal that I set for myself was my goal as a scholar, and that was to write well. I wanted people to read what I had to say about Joyce and say that "he writes well on Joyce." To read someone who writes well and to write well on someone who writes well is, I think, a goal that I set for myself.

A physicist in the same institution told us that "if I wake up at two o'clock in the morning and I can't sleep, I may be thinking about physics, and where do you put that in your statistical report?" When asked what an

84

ideal arrangement of duties would be for him, he replied, "Just give me a job in a research institute and tell me to do research all day." Further down the institutional line, in a public comprehensive college not long out of its teachers college days, a professor of English came on strong:

> I am thoroughly immersed in my discipline, which is English literature. I am of the view that a person teaching in higher education is by definition an active, functioning publishing scholar. This feeds the teaching, this maintains the enthusiasm, this keeps the juices flowing. I am quite frankly appalled by the lack of professional activity, especially publication, that so many in the academic world are, in my judgment, guilty of. They are not doing their job. I don't quite understand how they distinguish themselves from high school teachers or community college teachers. . . . I really don't understand how one can function in the academic setting without being engaged in some research.

Thus, an interest in research seeps well down the institutional line. Whether for extrinsic or intrinsic reasons, the attraction stays alive even in settings where heavy teaching loads and limited resources sharply limit the possibilities of inquiry. When academics were asked in the 1984 survey, "Do your interests lie primarily in teaching or in research?" and were given the four categories of response shown in Table 10, only those in lower liberal arts colleges and community colleges broke away from the rest of the professoriate in having little interest in research; even in those locales a third or so of the faculty claimed *some* interest in research. In the intensive teaching environments of the leading liberal arts colleges, as many as one out of four faculty reported leaning toward a primary research interest and seven out of ten claimed a research interest as well as a teaching commitment. Research is hard to keep out. Faculties want it; most institutions either want it or have to allow for it. Making allowance for research, even encouraging it, remains "a mark of first-class practice." The more things change, the more they remain the same.

The Community College Difference

In comparison with all the other types of colleges and universities, even the minor public and private four-year colleges that are closest to it in nature, the community college has become a qualitatively different world of work.

TABLE 10

PRIMARY INTEREST IN TEACHING OR RESEARCH, BY TYPE OF INSTITUTION

TYPE OF INSTITUTION	HEAVILY IN RESEARCH	BOTH: TOWARD RESEARCH	BOTH: TOWARD TEACHING	HEAVILY IN TEACHING
	(PERCENT OF FACULTY)			
RESEARCH UNIVERSITIES I	16	49	23	12
RESEARCH UNIVERSITIES II	15	40	27	18
DOCTORAL-GRANTING UNIVERSITIES I	8	34	36	22
DOCTORAL-GRANTING UNIVERSITIES II	6	18	45	31
COMPREHENSIVE UNIVERSITIES AND COLLEGES I	3	22	34	41
COMPREHENSIVE UNIVERSITIES AND COLLEGES II	3	22	35	40
LIBERAL ARTS COLLEGES I	4	22	44	30
LIBERAL ARTS COLLEGES II	1	9	27	63
TWO-YEAR COLLEGES AND INSTITUTIONS	1	7	23	69
ALL INSTITUTIONS	6	24	30	40

Total respondents, 2,896

QUESTION: ''Do your interests lie primarily in teaching or in research? . . . (1) Very heavily in research (2) In both, but leaning toward research (3) In both, but leaning toward teaching (4) Very heavily in teaching.''

SOURCE: The Carnegie Foundation for the Advancement of Teaching, 1984 Faculty Survey.

Here institutional mandates most completely dominate disciplinary incentives. The reasons are manifold. Classroom hours are high, in the range of thirteen to sixteen, and student loads per class are heavy. Community college teachers in letters and science fields spend virtually all their time covering broad subjects at the introductory level, first in their own major field of training and then in bordering fields. The college becomes a place for generalists rather than disciplinary specialists. As a result, community colleges have long attempted not to hire the "over-qualified" Ph.D., having learned from experience that those who confuse the two-year setting with the four-year college, or especially the university, will be at best out of place and at worst troublemakers. During the 1950s, less than 10 percent of two-year college instructors held the doctorate, with as many as 25 percent having only a bachelor's degree or less. Then and now, the master's degree is the typical preparation. In the 1970s, the proportion having the doctorate increased to about 15 percent;[7] in the 1984 faculty survey the figure had risen to about 20 percent. Those holding the doctorate are but part of a total faculty that includes instructors of occupational subjects whose certification is mainly based on experience within the trades they teach.

Community college teachers have been increasingly inundated with clienteles other than freshmen students who come on directly from high school full of hope, often in spite of prior poor achievement, that they will transfer later to a four-year institution or university. They also have to serve terminal students preoccupied with vocational programs, who often outnumber the transfer-minded ones. Most important, many community colleges, in recent years, have virtually turned themselves into community centers, places for any and all adult education, with nonmatriculated enrollees heavily outnumbering the matriculated student body. In the early 1980s the mean age of community college students had climbed to twenty-nine years.[8] Faculty members face a large floating clientele who gain entry easily and who leave just as effortlessly. "Students" may come for a single class in photography. They may enroll in auto repair courses and stay just long enough to learn to repair the defects in their own cars, which brought them to the class in the first place: After "the ignition system" has been covered in a lecture-demonstration, those who had ignition trouble disappear. "Enrollments" are then a sometime thing, especially difficult to comprehend when head-count financing by states or local districts encourages administrators to blur all internal distinctions between one type of student and another.

On top of all this, community college teachers have had to shoulder the heaviest burden of remedial work. American high schools graduate students without regard to achievement—reading at ninth-grade level or doing mathematics at the seventh-grade level—who then flow without hindrance into "open door" or "open access" colleges. Curricula have been adjusted downward: "By 1980, 90 percent of the enrollment in community college liberal arts classes was in courses for which there was no prerequisite; one-third of the enrollment in mathematics classes was in courses in which the content was less than algebra and three out of eight students taking English classes were in remedial sections."[9] The requirements for reading and writing have fallen. Intensive research in one representative community college showed that students were expected to read very little. Even in textbooks, they read not for content or ideas but only for the minimal amount of information needed to pass quick-score examinations.[10] A nationwide survey showed that students were required to write papers in only one in four humanities classes, one in ten science classes. Less than half of the liberal arts teachers gave essay examinations.[11] The transfer curriculum had become essentially "grade 13 plus remedial."[12]

The community college difference, then, rests not only on the truncating of the grades that limits instructors to the first two years of postsecondary education, transfer and terminal, but also on the diffusion of character that has followed from institutions becoming community centers and remedial schools. The context calls for a faculty that can be readily adjusted to rapidly changing consumer desires. Regular full-time instructors must frequently spread themselves across subjects and times of the day. Irregular part-time faculty are needed badly. The trend toward part-time assignments, a critical matter examined in Chapter VII, runs strongest in the community colleges. By 1980, over one-half (56 percent) of the community college instructors in the country had become part-timers.[13] Part-time work in the community college cum community center represents the extreme point in the attenuation of both disciplinary and institutional connections, leaving the academic worker relatively rootless.

We can draw a main conclusion about the evolution of teaching loads in the long course of the twentieth century. Do American professors now teach more, or less, than they did at the turn of the century? The answer is they do both. Their loads have become more extensively differentiated in a wider set of institutions. In the 1908–1920 data reported in Chapter II, we learned that university professors taught somewhat less than counterparts in four-year colleges; *and* that the more noted the university the lighter the load, with six to eight hours taken, by 1920, as the mark of "first-class practice." Three-quarters of a century later, first-class practice in the universities has been to reduce teaching loads to something like four to six, and often two to four hours. Leading liberal arts colleges have reduced loads to nine or less. Professors in the other private four-year colleges and the huge public four-year college sector constitute a major mode at twelve hours. Most important, the tremendous growth of the two-year colleges has shifted one-quarter to one-third of the total professoriate to loads of fifteen and higher. And, at one extreme, teaching time is time with selected advanced students; at the other, it is time with unselected entrants, many of whom must first be brought up to "postsecondary" work. Diversification of teaching loads and tasks is a fundamental aspect of the institutional differentiation of the higher education system. It is also a primary component of the meaning of hierarchy.

THE DISCIPLINARY SPECIFICATION OF WORK

Before setting out to interview professors, we knew that their teaching as well as their research would vary from one field to another. After all, physics is physics and English literature is English literature, and never the twain shall meet. Earlier research had effectively shown large differences in the duties and cultures of disciplines, to the point where one could speak of an epistemological determination of work.[14] But we were surprised by how much teaching, let alone research, turned out to be a varied activity. Especially within the universities, departmental and individual combinations of duties are highly *un*standardized. It is to be expected in these settings that professors will have relatively light teaching loads, a modest amount of contact with undergraduates, graduate teaching, and much "free time" for research. But even in such simple matters as time in the classroom in the course of a year, the dispersion is great. The academic tribes semi-isolated in the numerous departments and professional schools often make their own collective arrangements that are then individually

89

reshaped. Here, field interviews tease out information that is difficult for national surveys to reach. In one leading university, professors in four liberal arts fields drew the differences, largely unknown to them, as they discussed their teaching loads:

Associate Professor of biology: I teach two quarters out of the year. I have my own immunology course [in the] fall quarter. Fifty percent of my time is involved in the lecture hours and student contact hours, et cetera. In the spring I coordinate a large class which I only teach about the first third—about seventeen lectures—but I'm the coordinator, so I put in a lot of time also. I would say probably about 50 percent also.

This biology professor is free from teaching at least one-half of each year; when she is on call, she teaches one course during one academic quarter and shares the teaching of another course during another quarter. Beyond her normal schedule, along with all her colleagues in the letters and science departments, she is also entitled to sabbatical leaves that approximate one-sixth of her time over the years.

Professor of physics: Well, teaching is a complicated thing; it depends on what you call teaching. When I'm talking to my graduate students, it often is somewhere on the border between teaching and research. I can't break that down for you so easily. Actual teaching of my courses? I actually have classroom contact of three hours a week. I guess I spend three hours for every hour of teaching, preparing. That's probably an overestimate. It's probably two hours for every hour of teaching. The standard teaching load [in his department] is one course per quarter. There are a lot of activities that I have to take care of involving teaching. I don't grade the papers, but I oversee students who grade the papers.
[The formal teaching is] more graduate than undergraduate, but I try to teach an undergraduate course each year. . . . I rarely, if I can avoid it, teach medical students, and I haven't had much experience teaching undergraduate science majors . . . more than likely, if I teach undergraduates, it would be for the liberal arts majors, physics for poets.

This physicist apparently teaches all three quarters of the academic year, one course at a time, and generally at the graduate level. Like his colleague

90

in biology, he has to coordinate or manage a little while engaged in teaching, serving as overseer for teaching assistants who grade papers. When he teaches undergraduates, maybe once a year, he prefers a class for liberal arts majors ("physics for poets") than for science majors, and he is generally able to negotiate for himself a teaching schedule that keeps him away from that dreaded breed known as medical students.

> *Professor of political science*: [The load is] four courses a year spread over three quarters. This year, I'm doing fifty-fifty [graduate/undergraduate breakdown]. That is not untypical . . . there is not a lot of teaching load pressures. Nobody is saying you have to teach 500 students to pull your oar. . . . Probably 40 percent of my working time is spent teaching and preparing, and so forth, although sometimes that is hard to keep separate from research because the preparation often involves similar activities. Probably 50 percent of my time is spent on research and 10 percent on departmental and university committee activities.

This social scientist has a significantly heavier formal teaching load, now up to four courses a year instead of the two or three in the sciences, and may spend half of that load with undergraduates. He is a full professor: The load of an assistant professor would typically tilt more toward undergraduates, especially in state universities with their large undergraduate enrollments. But this political scientist still manages one-half of his time for research—at the maximum, in a two-course quarter, he is not teaching more than six hours a week—and is pleased that no one in his part of the university is pressured to teach hundreds of students.

> *Professor of English*: Classroom teaching, probably about 60 percent. I am in charge of the undergraduate program in the English department, so I would say I spend far more time now in counseling responsibilities. I am also serving as a general advisor to freshmen. That is a responsibility you are asked to accept maybe once every ten years. Therefore, at the moment I would say maybe 15 percent of my time goes to that kind of activity. . . . The standard teaching load for our department is five courses a year. That is by the quarter system. I teach everything from very large undergraduate lecture courses [with] three or four hundred people in the course . . . down to the other kind of course which

I am doing this quarter, which is a small seminar limited to fifteen in Renaissance lyric.

Our humanities man at this first-line institution is much more involved in teaching: his formal course load is double that of his colleagues in biology and physics, and he sees hundreds of undergraduates in large lecture courses, along with seminar clusters of graduate students in such an esoteric specialty as "Renaissance lyric."

This professor of English also called our attention to a rotation of major tasks in which a good share of the members in a department take turns, performing such roles as "general advisor to freshmen" or "being in charge of the undergraduate program." Such duties are often seen as dirty work, a burden to be shifted from one to another in the name of fairness, unless one or two individuals turn up who like that kind of thing. For a given faculty member, the blend of duties changes significantly from one semester to the next, one year to the next.

How much time did the humanities man reckon he had for research?

In an academic quarter it would be the balance, about 10 percent. One's research is done during summer vacations and on sabbatical leaves. During a regular quarter it is simply impossible to do any serious research if you are doing the rest of the job properly.

And he drew for us an important distinction, spelling out the meaning of "scholarship":

I want to make a distinction between research and scholarship. I think, in the humanities, scholarship is terribly, terribly important. Scholarship, as I define it, consists principally of control of primary materials. Research, on the contrary, is essentially devoted to finding out something new about your topic, or your author or field. I don't think that has the same importance in the humanities as it does in the sciences, and I think the humanists do themselves a disservice by trying to behave like scientists and in placing this tremendous emphasis on novelty. . . . What the search for novelty can produce in the study of an author like Shakespeare is increasingly aberrant, idiosyncratic. . . . I would like to have more time to sit down and read books—not critical books but primary texts.

92

Thus, even in a major university, a professor in the humanities reports that time beyond teaching and other institutional duties is scarce, especially between September and June in the normal academic year. And scholarship, he tells us, should be distinguished from research: free time in the evenings or in the summer months or on sabbatical leaves—or some of the time spent in preparing lectures and seminar materials—ought to be devoted to gaining greater "control of primary materials," rather than given over to developing one more original interpretation of what, for example, Jane Austin really meant. Such scholarship is even more intimately blended with teaching than are research, administration, and consulting.

Clearly, teaching loads and research time can vary markedly across the fields found in a university. The disciplinary "specs" for academic jobs are systematically different, based apparently on the level of resources made available for research as well as on the relative emphasis that fields place on it. The more resource-rich the field, like modern physics and biology, the greater the time apportioned for research and the less for teaching. The more the value placed on new knowledge, the greater the time apportioned for research. The humanities, in a long steady slide, have become relatively resource-poor. Their faculty members are also more involved in the general education courses required of undergraduates. Thus, even in the best of places, institutions that overall are well-off, professors in the humanities, compared to the sciences, teach more and do more of it at the undergraduate level.

The Professional School Difference

Among all the subject matter differences that divide the professoriate, none are larger in the latter decades of the twentieth century than the sometimes gaping divide between professional schools and "the basic disciplines." In the system-at-large, we noted some hiving off of special-purpose institutions. The last category in the Carnegie classification of institutions gathered up some 560 detached medical schools, technological and engineering colleges, theological seminaries, teachers colleges, art schools, and so on, which offered more professional than liberal arts courses and were more specialized than comprehensive. Here "professionals" are largely isolated from letters and science "academics," who in turn are protected from whatever pressures the norms and practices of the professional schools might bring to bear. University and four-year college academics in general need take little note of a detached aggregation that exists in a residual category of institutional odds and ends.

But what cannot be overlooked because of their immediacy are the schools of the major and minor professions that exist as parts of universities and comprehensive colleges. These schools cover medicine, law, engineering, business management, education, nursing, dentistry, veterinary medicine, architecture and urban planning, social work, public health, librarianship, agriculture, music and dance, theatre arts—to name only the more common ones, with other occupations lined up at the university entrance and struggling to get a toe in the door one way or the other. Professional school locales that represent and train directly for an outside occupation now bulk large in the academic profession, despite the widespread tendency to shunt them to one side in research analyses as well as in common conceptions of the university and the academic profession.[15] They are fundamentally different academic units. To explore their effects upon the profession, our study pursued the two fields of medicine and business. We concentrated mainly on medicine because of its sheer magnitude in the modern American university and its extreme differentiation of academic roles. Medicine is at the cutting edge of changes in the professoriate that are wrought by professional school subjects and commitments.

While different professional fields give rise to quite different types of professional schools, what the schools have in common that separates them from nearly all the letters and science departments is the effort to combine practical and academic missions. They begin with the necessity to face, Janus-like, in two opposite directions. A young assistant professor in a management school plunged right in:

> I mentioned schizophrenia before—one of the problems in my particular field is that it's not enough to keep abreast of the academic journals. You have two constituencies. You have the academic brethren, and life would be a lot easier if that were the only constituency we had. When I went into academics, I thought, "Gee, if I could only be a sociologist and go live in an ivory tower, I'd be very happy." I think I would be, but the other constituency is the practicing managers. That covers our research, too. Usu-

ally, we have some kind of results of whatever thing we're testing, whether it's financial performance or . . . it's got to be grounded in something useful to managers. It means that not only am I reading academic journals, I am also reading the business press. You have to stay current with what's going on, so there is a current events component to it, which makes life very inefficient from an academic standpoint.

A similar tension, we note in passing, is found in schools of education that must constantly attempt to become more scholarly, in order to achieve and maintain legitimacy in the university family, while also involving themselves directly in the improvement of educational practice. The first means research and publication, the second means time spent in the teacher education laboratory, the university elementary "lab school," the local school district, or the office of the state superintendent of public instruction.

Professional schools vacillate between these two poles. A school of education may have struggled relentlessly throughout the 1970s to become a place of serious research and scholarship, under a virtual mandate from the campus administration and the academic brethren, year by year, academic appointment by academic appointment, to be respectable according to the letters and science norms of the campus. But then, in the 1980s, its administration and faculty attempt to swing the character of the school toward practice under pressure to do something to improve the schools. In turn, a medical school may edge for a number of years toward the academic norms of the university in order to strengthen its position within the university itself. It goes "academic." But then, in a subsequent period, its inherent duality pushes and pulls it toward practice, then to obey the norms of the outside practicing profession, it goes to "patient care." Throughout most of the twentieth century, American medical schools have tended to go academic. But under the increasingly powerful thrust of a high-cost "health industry," they have moved in recent years into the overwhelming problems of effectively operating huge medical organizations.[16] The academic side of a medical school may prefer the next appointment to be another biologist doing basic research, or even a historian or sociologist of medicine. But those in charge of a major teaching hospital, with its innumerable operating rooms and patient-care wings, are likely to find another anesthesiologist to be the more compelling need.

Professional schools stretch the academic system by differentiating and proliferating the roles of faculty-level personnel: into both clinical and scholarly, part-time and full-time, nontenured and tenured, and outside-based and inside-committed. In modern medical schools the divisions are virtually endless, with extreme differentiation occurring as a structural response to an extreme complexity of tasks. Basic to the fragmentation of academic work in medical schools is the simple fact that vocational training in medicine actually takes place under the aegis of the university:

> University training programs in business, engineering, and law transmit the intellectual bases of professional practice. Entrants acquire practical skills after formal training in the early years of their careers. In medicine, not only is clinical training a legal prerequisite for practice, but much applied training takes place within institutions of higher education. Medical colleges, and other health training schools modeled after them, are the only professional schools in which students, trainees, and faculty routinely engage in hands-on professional practice.

For the purposes of this hands-on training, universities must have "teaching hospitals": "of the 127 medical schools in the United States today [1984], 65 own their own hospitals, and the majority of others control the management of one or more hospitals."

Thus, all that a hospital engages in, a university undertakes. And whatever "the health care industry" does—group practice, prepaid public and private medical plans, health maintenance organizations (HMOs), and so on—will sharply affect the medical segment of the university. Most important for the professoriate, there must be such clinical departments as surgery, radiology, and internal medicine, along with such basic science departments as anatomy, physiology, and biochemistry. The latter may be similar in character to departments in the letters and science segment of the campus, but the clinical units cannot be. They staff and manage hospitals and teach in the context of professional practice. As much a part of a hospital as a medical school, clinical departments are together the strongest structure in all of higher education for expressing an orientation toward practice within a contextual duality of the academic and the the practical. They have a distinctively different set of tasks.

Around those tasks, roles and time schedules proliferate in a host of nontraditional ways that center on the vagaries of medical practice. Individual faculty members have substantial patient-care responsibilities; hence they must make hospital rounds and work within the confines of a hospital's scheduling of patients. Indispensability becomes defined by patient care: You cannot run the shop without anesthesiologists, even if all on the local staff never publish a single article among them. Faculties have developed their own forms of group practice: Fiscal and administrative units called faculty practice plans (FPPs) handle physician billings and redistribute the income to specific clinical departments and to the medical school as a whole. The departments, in turn, use the largest portion of their share to pay faculty salaries. Here, academic work produces direct income: in a pooled fashion, patient fees and insurance plans pay salaries. In interviews conducted in our study, heads of departments of medicine indicated that those FPP funds constituted one-third or more of their income.

Combined with research funds, patient-care revenues have brought entire clinical departments into the stressful situation of drawing two-thirds or more of faculty salaries from "soft money," that is, not from regular institutional allocation. This puts clinical faculty under substantial pressure to generate their own income. Vicious circles can be readily entered. As Sydney Ann Halpern observed from the fieldwork:

> If a young faculty member does not succeed in acquiring research funding quickly—or if an older faculty member fails to maintain external funding—the department head may load on clinical duties that would make future research and grant activity close to impossible. Assistant professors with heavy patient-care duties are likely to have great difficulty publishing enough to obtain academic tenure. . . . A number of respondents in the study volunteered the opinion that life in clinical departments was more tension ridden and less rewarding than it was in previous decades.

New types of physicians whose competencies center in patient care have then had to be added. Clinical skills rather than research and scholarship become the preeminent criteria. "Academics" become full-time clinicians, splitting off from the researchers. There has had to be increased role differentiation, since, at the same time, there has been no attenuation in the top schools in the value placed on research. Hence dual appointment sys-

97

tems are likely; for example, a line that offers the possibility of tenure and one that does not. Irregular slots—"adjunct" professors—are sorely needed. Then, some can vote in faculty meetings and some cannot, especially in academic senates and all-campus committees. Some are eligible for sabbatical leaves but others are not.

Data collected by the Association of American Medical Colleges (AAMC) shows the trend. "In 1975, 58 percent of American medical schools reported they had non-tenure-accruing appointments with separate titles. By 1983, 77 percent were using non-tenure-track posts in clinical departments, 73 percent in basic science departments. During the latter year, 43 percent of American medical schools indicated that more than one-quarter of their faculties were in non-tenure-track appointments." Tenure guarantees little to academic physicians, since institutional funds provide only a fraction of faculty salaries within clinical departments. The income for funding the positions has to be generated by the incumbents themselves, from the two sources of patient-care revenues and research grants. Again, the trend is predictable: By 1983, 40 percent of the medical schools indicated that tenure guaranteed a position but no income, and in another 22 percent that tenure assured only a portion of salary. Academic medicine is a place where tenure is up for grabs, seen increasingly by deans and the professors themselves as irrelevant, far too costly, and a source of invidious distinction. It is out of such varied and changing settings of academic work that the meaning of tenure becomes substantially eroded, much to the dismay of the brethren in the basic disciplines.

The last word comes down from the dean of a leading medical school:

> Medical schools are becoming more like big corporations. That's what they are. We have the health care business, the industry right in the middle of the university. . . . The kinds of controls that a dean can exert are largely economic and managerial rather than moral or related to a vision of academic life. . . . [In the future] it will be much more difficult to see the academic health center as a place for the creation of knowledge for its own sake.

THE PARADOX OF ACADEMIC WORK

The greatest paradox of academic work in modern America is that most professors teach most of the time, and large proportions of them teach all the time, but teaching is not the activity most rewarded by the academic profession nor most valued by the system at large. Trustees and administrators in one sector after another praise teaching and reward research. Professors themselves do the one and acclaim the other: "Although the overwhelming majority of academics perform little or no significant research . . . they still consider [in survey after survey] the most meritorious effort to be contributions to the discipline."[17] Call it a paradox, a dilemma, a contradiction, or what you will, the gap between duty and reward is generally voiced as a problem that people of good will should be able to solve. It is seen as a grand irrationality, one that can be laid at the foot of stupidity or cupidity. *If* professors would only stop chasing the holy grail of scholarly prestige upon which they set their eyes in graduate school, they could better do their work, paying more attention to students. *If* institutions would only settle for all-teaching niches in the ecology of the system, they would not constantly compromise their capacity to teach by letting professors direct their energies elsewhere, "fleeing" the classroom and even the campus a good share of the time. Despite protestations that teaching is research and research is teaching—a cogent self-analysis in some settings—professors themselves constantly sense that the one activity does indeed draw time and energy from the other. They talk about this tension and wonder about its resolution. Surely someone, the cry goes, should begin to set things right by first dampening the power of research rewards and by weakening the dominance of graduate school professors. The paradox really indicates that things are broken and should be fixed.

But it cannot be otherwise in the modern American system of higher education. The paradox is fixed by the conditions of competition and hierarchy that underlie the long-run logic of an enormously large, heavily differentiated, open system of higher education. The system cannot be simultaneously elite and mass without considerable differentiation. Esoteric activities do not go hand-in-hand with open-door clienteles: Attentiveness to students of average and below-average ability erodes the conditions for best science and high scholarship. As work activities are distributed among sectors, the resulting hierarchy of prestige sets in motion the "upward" competitive clamoring of professors and institutions. Teaching institutions remain all-teaching at the price of remaining in the middle and lower reaches of the hierarchy. They ascend in status as they lighten teaching loads to free time for research and scholarship. Leading liberal arts colleges emphasize teaching, but they reduce teaching loads to nine hours a week or less, with small classes, and require that a good share, if not all, of the faculty publish or otherwise assume a scholarly posture. For established universities and would-be universities, it is even more true in 1985 than it was in 1900 or 1920 or 1940 that "the mark of first-class practice" is the provision of considerable time for research, preferably up to 50 percent or more. This is the way the system operates. Statesmen bent on major repairs soon find that their categorical imperatives, couched in the "musts" and "shoulds" of the rhetoric of reform, stumble over an inability to state "how" the incentives that so decisively affect the behavior of institutions and professors might be changed.

The paradox has its own rationality. The work of teaching is quite necessary. It maintains the system, first of all by appeasing essential clienteles and by paying the bills. It is also a great source of intrinsic satisfaction, as we later see, producing an intense commitment from many academics up and down the hierarchy. But the work of research is also quite necessary, and increasingly so. It develops the system, first by appeasing the disciplines and rewarding disciplinarians for advancing knowledge and technique. Further, when a system of higher education only teaches, it risks becoming profoundly obsolete. Academic work is then likely to become a standardized repetition and expansion of already existing "goods and services."[18] Growth becomes mainly reactive, with institutions and professors trailing passively behind expanding student demand. There is then nothing new under the sun: Physics and biology and political science and English are handled as fixed bodies of knowledge. If the academic profession then swells its ranks, it simply repackages the old work for mass production. In and of its own operations, the system would, by modern standards, bog down.

What keeps modern systems of higher education dynamic are the conditions and incentives that promote the developmental effects of research and scholarship. To grasp this point is to understand the twentieth-century advantages of American postsecondary education. It is a classic "muddle of oddments."[19] In the matrix of sectors and disciplines that supports academic work, some segments are virtually monopolized by the imperatives of teaching. We have seen the nature of academic duties and responsibilities in those sectors—preeminently the community colleges—where

100

teaching is the sine qua non. As teaching becomes everything, the institution becomes client-driven. But there are other types of institutions that are either driven by or importantly shaped by the imperatives of research. We have highlighted the nature of academic work in their midst, especially in the letters and science departments of the universities and in the academic side of the professional schools. The overall structure then mandates a restless search for the new research finding, the critical reformulation, the original synthesis that will inform anew a discipline or a specialty. The system is then more professor-driven; disciplines are more in the driver's seat.

The prestige hierarchy dictates that the research imperative propel the system. The values of inquiry, which are transmitted in the graduate schools of the universities, percolate down the line. Individual professors and their institutions ascend in the hierarchy to any substantial degree by investing in research and offering some new results. If the lower reaches of the hierarchy exhibit an unparalleled massive commitment to open-access teaching, the commanding heights insist on an intense commitment to research.

That many varieties of research and teaching exist side by side without interfering sharply with one another is a testament to the benefits of differentiation. Huge size has helped by providing space and freedom for contrary efforts, which in small systems must squeeze against and confront one another. Decentralized control has been virtually a necessary ingredient: No centralized public system can plan so much differentiation and make it work. Under these conditions, American academics have come to accept that a greatly muddled differentiation is a normal course of affairs, that it is natural and perhaps even good for the professoriate to be assigned to such radically different places of work. Or, if not good, that one can still maneuver to personal and institutional advantage by publishing that noteworthy article or book that elicits an offer from a better place or by nudging one's institution from an unwanted to a more desirable niche.

With all of its necessary inefficiencies and impracticalities, research drives academic organizations into an opaque maze of professional nonlinear forms. If the academic profession only taught, counseled, and administered, then the commandments of twentieth-century bureaucracy could more fully take over. Professing would be closer to schoolteaching, suffering many of the indignities of that "minor profession" in modern America.[20] It is research, as a task and as a basis for status, that makes the difference. It becomes the flywheel of the motor of professional development as it connects the motivations of hundreds of thousands of academics to the ideals of scientific and scholarly progress.

The minority of academics who are actively engaged in research lead the profession in all important respects. Their work mystifies the profession, generates its modern myths, and throws up its heroes. To have the research demon by the tail can also be a lifelong pleasure, involving a sense of craftsmanship, originality, and success. When asked what characteristics of a piece of research he most values, a leading physicist responded:

> I guess the thing that I value the most—because anyone can reach it by caring—is craftsmanship. And it means what it means in any field. And the other thing I value is bringing things together in a new way. I think of myself as able to solve problems extremely well. I haven't invented a theory like Einstein did, for example, but on the other hand, I can solve some problems that no one else has been able to do. And I get them right. I'm very jealous of my reputation of being correct when I say something. And so I think that solving problems correctly in a craftsmanlike way is the thing that I think characterizes my work. And there is a lot of originality to it too . . . but one doesn't think of it explicitly. I mean you can't think of it . . . like, I think this morning I'll be original. . . . You just can't think of it that way. I just see things my way and solve it. I've been able to do that a few times. And that's why I get grants.

THE ENDLESS VARIETY

Individual quotes and statistical summaries alike steadily underestimate the varieties of academic work, with one person speaking for a thousand others but only telling the story he or she knows and a few numbers standing for the experiences of a vast multitude. To describe briefly and analyze clearly, more has to be omitted than can be brought in, causing any account to err toward order, straightening up the muddle of oddments. This dilemma of research, present in much modern social inquiry, takes extreme form in efforts to understand a realm where a high premium is put on divergent thinking and action. As Tony Becher and Maurice Kogan observed in a study of British higher education: "Where most social institutions require their members to adopt convergent values and practices, universities—and to a growing extent, polytechnics and colleges—put a premium on creative divergence."[21] Professors are literally paid to think otherwise: to be original in research; to add personal interpretation and flair in teaching; to be the wise consultant who brings novel solutions; to be a self-confessed critic of the ills of society, one and all. Professors are wired to give individual opinions. They speak separately.

But amid the babble of disciplinary tongues and the welter of individual voices, some large similarities permit the broad statements we have fashioned here. Institutional sectors divide academic work into major patterns. At one extreme we find the discipline-focused setting of the research university, intensifying at the top into veritable think-tank atmospheres; and, at the other, the school setting of the community colleges, shading at the bottom into the work of lower grades. In between, there is a luxuriant growth of minor universities, comprehensive public colleges, liberal arts private colleges, and specialized institutions that all shape academic work somewhat differently. Disciplines and professional studies also divide work in significant patterns. The sciences teach less and do more research; the humanists teach more and do less research, preeminently at the highest levels of the hierarchy. As we descend the hierarchy, the disciplines matter less, and they finally even out in settings where institutional requirements triumph. Within the sectors that contain major professional studies, academic work is molded in practical as well as in scholarly forms, with parts of the professional schools, notably medicine, offering a setting of professional practice that in no way can be confused with the obligations of the letters and sciences departments. The cancer ward cannot be mistaken for the wing of the English department that houses the study of Renaissance lyric. In the realities of money and staffing, the first is as much a part of the modern academic profession as the second, even if traditional perceptions still place literature front and center and hide the treatment of cancer in the backrooms of the mind.

Thus, even when we are able analytically to reduce endless variety to a few major patterns, staggering differences are apparent. The forces of fragmentation run strongest in the academic profession in the arrangements for work. Academics may possibly arrange authority so that it serves to structure some uniformities; they may possibly share some thoughts that symbolically produce a common cause. But their work divides them: The profession overall then consists of fundamentally different sets of responsibilities. Notably, the close linkage between inquiry and teaching on which Thorstein Veblen and so many others before and after him have insisted—"distinct but closely bound together"—has been shattered. In the structuring of the profession's work, the one becomes the many.

CHAPTER V

The Enclosures of Culture

Whenever some group of people have a bit of common life with a modicum of isolation from other people, a common corner in society, common problems and perhaps a couple of common enemies, there culture grows. . . . All of us, if we have a sense of solidarity with some occupation, are in some measure members of a community of fate. We are also by the same token participants in a subculture.

> —EVERETT CHERRINGTON HUGHES, *STUDENTS'*
> *CULTURE AND PERSPECTIVES* (1961)

I am really living in a world that is quite different from the one the mainstream professionals live in. . . . At this institution, a second-ranking institution, we are primarily dealing with teachers, not researchers. Those people do a good job of teaching, but I don't consider them doing things that are really interesting.

> —STATE COLLEGE PROFESSOR, 1984
> INTERVIEW

IF THE SETTINGS of work are so endlessly varied, what do we make of diversity and unity in the cultural life of the academic profession? The academic culture is probably fragmented into a thousand and one parts defined by the crosscut of many disciplines in many types of institutions. There is ample reason to suspect that a professor of business in a public community college has little sense of a "community of fate" with an English professor in a leading private liberal arts college. Yet, it is also plausible that academic professionals might find common cause in certain wider interests and in some broad principles of academic conduct even if they work in quite different sites and under radically varying conditions. An interpretation could conceivably emphasize either fragmentation or integration. Moving from one to the other, I shall first affirm the soundness of the view that academic beliefs proliferate endlessly, fragmented by specialism, and then argue that the many specialties of academia overlap to produce a much larger cultural network.

Three concepts—belief, commitment, and interest—help to point the way in exploring academic culture. To believe in what one is doing is something quite different from simply doing it. And belief leads straight to commitment: "Whoever embraces a belief, accepts a commitment. . . . Certainly no one can be said truly to believe in anything unless he is prepared to commit himself on the strength of his belief."[1] From belief may come commitment to principles that create common interests on a large scale. Writing about forms of democracy, Jane J. Mansbridge distinguished three forms of interest: *self-regarding*, a preference for purely personal gain that we often portray as selfish; *other-regarding*, in which we make the good of another individual or group our own; and *ideal-regarding*, in which one's own good is identified with the realization of some principle.[2] Academics may believe in the academic life because of direct personal payoff, such as the achievement of tenured job security; or because it advances the interests of a larger group—a department or an institution; or because it seems to support a broad principle—scientific progress or enriching the literary culture. Other-regarding interests connect persons to each other; ideal interests bind the individual to general principles that orient action.

Organizational and professional ideologies encourage such linkages. The doctor is defined as serving a medical group, hospital, and profession, while contributing to the nation's health and furthering medical ideals. The lawyer is readily portrayed as serving the bar and justice. The professor can be powerfully motivated, and his work richly justified, by academic ideologies that portray him as a loyal contributor to a discipline as well as to an institution, a professional who thereby educates the young, promotes science and scholarship, and enriches the intellectual heritage of mankind. Effective professional ideologies temper, if not tame, self-regarding interests, while also legitimating them, by connecting them to the more altruistic types. Medical doctors do not always attempt to maximize their income or their dominance over nurses and other hospital personnel because the ideals of patient care point the way to something more than the most narrow self-regard. When they do seek to maximize profit and power, they are able to rationalize their posture in their own eyes in the name of first-class

106

medical practice. Or, as put in a deeply cynical fashion by a professor of English we interviewed who got off on a discussion of law as an alternative career, one that "need not be a dishonorable profession": "75 percent of the time you are going to be helping one scoundrel bilk or evade another scoundrel and perhaps 25 percent of the time you are doing something that is in some minute way serving what you might call justice." Such tempering and legitimating are important in the academic life, for here as much as anywhere, individualism and narrow self-interest, richly rewarded, strain against the commonalities of community and principle.

What beliefs and commitments shall we seek? At the outset we need to explore whether American academic professionals identify with their institutions and their disciplines and whether these two primary lines of affiliation work together or in opposition. The long-standing distinction between "locals" and "cosmopolitans" suggests they are antithetical. Do leading scholars who, in the popular stereotype, keep their bags packed and have one foot out the door, identify with their institutional locations as homes or hostels? Do locally oriented teachers, especially in small colleges and in community colleges, drop out of the cultures of their disciplines? Are there academics who identify with neither their institutions nor their disciplines? To grasp the cultural side of academic professionalism, we ought to start with the immediate frameworks that daily shape academic life.[3] Academic culture, particularly in America, grows mainly in the diverse settings of work identified in earlier chapters. We quote professors extensively in this chapter, mainly according to institutional locations that provide the principal lines of division.

This emphasis on immediate setting is different from that often taken by observers of academic attitudes and values who set to work to find correlates and determinants in the social background and external ties of academics. Political preferences that come from external commitments and from an overlay of political parties and politically defined academic unions have at best a minor role, especially in comparison with academics elsewhere.[4] In other than a few small sectors, religious beliefs have been similarly relegated to a weak position.[5] By the time young academics are committed to a discipline and embedded in an institutional setting, the beliefs and identities they import from their social-class background also fade. Sociologists who concentrate on characteristics imported into the academic

107

profession by individual members from their personal background and prior experiences have been essentially looking at the least important components of academic culture. After extensive analysis of surveys of faculty attitudes and values, Everett Carll Ladd, Jr. and Seymour Martin Lipset concluded that the discipline is the major factor differentiating the political views of the faculty: From most liberal to most conservative are the social sciences, the humanities, the life sciences, the physical sciences, and engineering and business.[6] Status within the profession also differentiates: High-status individuals tend to be more liberal. Individual status is of course closely intertwined with the status of institutional sectors: High-status members of national academies come almost entirely from leading research institutions.

Ladd and Lipset found that a basic source of faculty liberalism—the professoriate is more liberal than the general population—is a commitment to research. Attached to this commitment is an ethos of skepticism that translates into a critical attitude toward society as well as toward academic materials. This questioning in turn encourages reformist attitudes and values, especially for those whose subjects involve culture and society rather than physical matter and biological characteristics. Ipso facto, nonresearch sectors reduce this ethos; the clinical parts of professional schools are less supportive of it.

Thus, even for those who want to concentrate on political commitments and on other items of secondary importance in understanding the culture of the profession, the places with which to start in American academia are not father's income or mother's education or church in which one was raised but immediate disciplinary and institutional locations. To comprehend the divisions of the profession, it is more important to know that individuals are physicists, biologists, political scientists, or English professors, or that they are in a medical school or a business school, than it is to know that they are young or old, Protestant, Jewish, or Catholic, registered as a Republican or Democrat—or, increasingly, black or white, female or male. Similarly, it is most important to know whether individuals teach in community colleges or in small leading liberal arts colleges or in research universities.[7] Discipline and sector are intrinsic, deeply structured into the system.

Beyond institutional and disciplinary cultures lies the problematic general culture of the profession at large. Here we must enter a thicket of thought where the entanglements of myth and cant leave few clear pathways. In the fieldwork of the study we probed for idealized versions of "academic man," eliciting stories that enriched our understanding of what academics at their best would like to be. We also sought to clarify whether dispersed academics see themselves as part of a single profession or might otherwise be symbolically linked. Are there some near-common bases for respect? Might there yet be some principles to which most academics remain committed? Where deeply rooted, those bases and principles may give the professoriate a veritable religion, one founded in commitments to knowledge, inquiry, intellectual integrity, and quality. And in those commitments we might well find important sources of satisfaction and morale in faculty careers, a topic pursued further in Chapter VII.

A concluding estimate of the symbolic integration of the profession pursues a thesis, an antithesis, and a resolution. In the thesis we view academia as a cultural network of differentiated groups; in the antithesis as a common commitment to overarching principles; and in the resolution as an institutional framework for both resolving conflicting interests and advancing common ones. Culturally, as well as structurally, the many and the one coexist, necessitating movement among modes of thought that illuminate a configuration of contradictions.

IDENTIFICATION WITH INSTITUTION AND DISCIPLINE

What became most striking in our exploration of the identifications of professors in leading universities is how much the disciplinary strength of their institutions is basic to the value they place upon them. What they perceive and what they like is the "first-rateness" that is defined by the canons of scholarship and research. In answer to the open-ended question, "What is it that you value the most about [your institution]?" respondents in the universities declared it was the stimulation of high quality and cosmopolitan atmosphere:

> *Professor of physics*: I think what I value the most is the presence of the large number and diverse collection of scientists who are

constantly doing things which I find stimulating. . . . It would be very hard to be bored.

Professor of biology: I think it's breadth of interest. It is a large university, and it has a lot of extremely good departments. . . . There are a lot of fascinating, interesting people here, and I think that is an important thing, too.

Professor of political science: What I value most is the intellectual level of the faculty and the graduate students. . . . Good graduate students are very important to me personally and always have been, and having colleagues that are smart is important. . . . A lot of people would say the research climate or the research resources are excellent, but I think the main research resources are not computers and things like that—material things—but the intellectual levels of one's colleagues and graduate students and the time available. . . . We only have to teach two courses [a semester], and that is a tremendous research resource.

Professor of English: One, it is a good school, and I have seen it from a number of perspectives. . . . I think it is a first-rate university, and I think a youngster can come here, pick and choose courses, pick and choose instructors, and probably get for the dollar the best undergraduate education in the country. We have a fine library, and we have excellent teachers here, and we have first-rate scholars.

In the universities, professors are also likely to look at the whole institution through the lenses of their own unit, especially if they are in a professional school:

(*What do you value the most about [the institution]?*) Medical school respondent: The whole university or just the school? (*Well, if the school is what you value most, but looking at [the whole institution]?*) That is a good question, and I don't know if I ever thought about the whole institution. I have inferred about the institution from the school. I don't know if I can answer that, I am not sure. [When I was being recruited], I was more impressed with the school here [than alternative possibilities] and thought that the quality of the university was good, and nothing has happened to change my mind about the quality of the university.

110

Size and complexity surely are at work here. In the universities, large size gives even the acute internal observer so much to comprehend. And the operational autonomy of departments and, particularly, the major professional schools leads professors toward inferring the whole from the part. The major operating units then function as symbolic links between the individual and the institution.

When we asked professors in the leading universities what they did not like, the answers were much more idiosyncratic: "Hummmm! I suppose its distance from some of the major cultural centers of America and Europe"; or, "I haven't really thought about that. I don't think there is really anything significant I would change"; or, "Its immense size and the lack of ability to really get to know very many of the students"; or, "Each department is so strong within its discipline that it hues very closely to normal science in that discipline, and they are not quite so strong that they place a high premium on innovation and departing from the norm"; or, "Football! Because it is so incredibly pervasive. You can't get away from it"; or, "The same thing is true of this university that is true of every university, and that is that bookkeepers frequently run the place, and that is usually because somebody doesn't insist on things being otherwise, so that you have to practice Jefferson's eternal vigilance on that issue"; or, over in the business school, "I would take the accounting area [of the school] and ship it out! . . . I guess the thing that causes me to go home at night with my stomach churning is probably the fact that I heard that accounting has gotten another slot, or finance or marketing, and here we sit twiddling our thumbs, and what the hell is the problem." Parking even came up once or twice. But, as one professor put it, "These things are relatively small compared with the good things, good colleagues, and a sense of community."

Academics in the leading universities find much with which to identify. The whole institution may be incredibly large and complex, a loose conglomerate of departments and schools, but its professors are proud of its quality. They think they experience quality directly in their own departments and in neighboring units, and they infer it indirectly from global reputation. Disciplinary and institutional cultures converge in a fundamental way, since a strong institutional symbolic thrust incorporates the combined strengths of departments, which are significant representatives of disciplines and their cultures. This combination produces a favored site, one in which professors taste the delights of the academic big city, the bustling metropolis full of interesting developments.

A second favored site, one much smaller, more intimate, and tailored to undergraduate teaching, is the leading private four-year college. Here the imagery is more pastoral, even bucolic, as a portrait is painted of genuine academic community:

> *Professor of physics*: I guess the primary advantage is that, in many ways, it is a very enjoyable setting. I mean setting in a broad sense. The students are—the students we get in physics—a delight to work with. . . . The students that I see are just wonderful, and I enjoy tremendously working with them. It is a very friendly place. The administration is basically good-hearted and friendly. The faculty is basically good-hearted and friendly. The particular area—look out the bay windows—is a lovely place to work in many ways.

Such a small community can make some professors feel surprisingly free, even less constrained than colleagues in the universities:

> *Professor of English*: I can't put it in a word, but I think that it is one of the least constraining environments I know of. . . . There is not much emphasis on any particular kind of uniformity here in the way the courses are taught and in the way one conducts one's professional life. There is not, compared at least to other places, the sort of publish or perish mentality. . . . One's relations with colleagues and students it seems to me are left very much to one's own tastes, style, and choice. I think that that, for me, has been the great thing.

> *Professor of biology*: It is a better form of life. I am from Boston, which is very congested. I was thinking—I met a friend who was a graduate student with me who went to [a leading university] and has been a professor there at the medical school for twelve or fifteen years and who has now come to a position at [a very distinguished] medical school . . . so he has really made it and done fabulously well. He was here visiting, and I was feeling rather depressed, but he was pointing out that he would trade places with me in a minute; and I was thinking that if I had an offer from Harvard right now I wouldn't be able to take it. . . . I wouldn't want to live there, for instance, and I also think I would have trouble changing to the different kind of environment. . . .

112

There is no pressure to publish here, for instance, and as a result I have published a lot.

At a time when jobs in the humanities, good or bad, have been scarce for a decade, a young person teaching in an English department in a leading private college even has cause to think he or she has been ushered into Shangri-La, right down to having sensible colleagues:

> *Professor of English*: I can't tell you how lucky I am to have a [tenure track] job like this: It's like a miracle, in my field. . . . There's a lot of emphasis on teaching and a lot of good teaching. I like that because teaching is my real vocation. I mean, I feel most strongly about that. . . . The students are good, I have an office to myself. It's a wonderful office, the campus is beautiful, and I love [the state]. My colleagues are fantastic. . . . The people in this department are sane, which in an English department is not always the case.

In many interviews at leading liberal arts colleges, one could almost hear the ghost of Daniel Webster intoning that it is "a small college but yet there are those who love it."[8] These institutions retain the capacity to appear as academic communities in their overall integration and symbolic unity. Yet individual academics may still feel very free in them. As in research universities, but on different grounds, there is much with which to identify and from which to draw pleasure.

When we move from these centers of strong identification to other types of institutions, the positive evaluations lessen. In second- and third-tier universities, institutions of "some stature," answers to "What do you value most about your institution?" frequently grew short, as if there were little to talk about, often resulting in one-word replies and cryptic phrases: "Location"; or, "The environment" (*The physical environment?*) "Yes"; or, "I guess they don't bother me very much. That is not a very positive thing to say but. . . ." Sometimes respondents began with an affirmative comment and then moved quickly to worrying at some length about the negative:

> *Professor of medicine*: [What is most valuable is] the institution's ability to recognize effective teaching and to reward it to some extent. That is changing—I am saying on the one hand that that

113

is true but on the other hand it is changing every day. . . . Five years from now there will be less rewards for teaching and more reward for research effort. . . . I don't know that we will ever be a major research institution for a lot of reasons. One, that the school, and the university, is well entrenched in tradition with a long history of academics [that are not] related to research. That has got to be overcome, it is not an easy thing to do. We also are in the middle of nowhere. We are an isolated university of some stature, some size, but, unfortunately, we are not on the mainstream of any place. As a result of that, then, you don't have the kind of input [you should have] from the major resource centers like NIH and other funding institutions. I think that is a weakness. [Also] we are not expected to be the primary research institution for this state. Thus, to try and achieve that would compete seriously with other major research institutions within the state that already have recognition for that purpose.

A professor of English in a lesser university expressed pleasure that he was able to leave another institution that was not "a strong degree institution" [at the Ph.D. level], and that he did not have to go off to smaller institutions where "it would have been very difficult for me to publish." Instead, he was able to come to an institution that at least "gave me an opportunity to prove myself as both a teacher and a scholar." But when asked what he valued least about his institution, he presented the muddled imagery that often inheres at the second and third levels of the American institutional hierarchy:

I think the most difficult thing about being at an institution like [this one] is that it has a difficult time coming to terms with itself. I think the more established institutions with strong academic backgrounds don't have the problem that an institution that pretty much is in the middle range of higher educational institutions around the country [does]. I'm not saying that [this university] is a bad institution but it certainly doesn't have the quality students, the quality faculty, the quality programs of the University of Chicago, Harvard, Yale. So I think the university has trouble coming to terms with itself as an institution. When it talks about standards, what sort of standards? When it talks about practicality, how practical does it have to be? How much does it want to sacrifice [of] the tradition of higher education?

114

. . . Often you don't really have a clear idea of what the university is setting as its goals, as its standards. An institution like [this one] is more vulnerable to rapid changes, to fads, to vogues within education. . . . [It] doesn't have a strong sense of tradition. . . .

The effects of incoherent institutional character upon faculty culture appear even more strongly among professors in comprehensive colleges, particularly the public ones. Academics in second-tier universities at least can feel they are in institutions "of some stature." But in the four- and five-year comprehensive institutions, they are not even sure of that. Typically, the college was a teachers college in the not-too-distant past, putting tradition on a bleak footing, and has evolved into a mixed state where it is no longer just an "education school" but neither is it a university. As one respondent explained: "the orientation here is what they call *multipurpose institution*. This has been an education school, and it doesn't have good emphasis on the liberal arts, you know. And also, being a state college, sometimes I find the emphasis is on numbers and not on the quality of education." The curriculum is broadly spread across many applied fields as well as the letters and science disciplines, placing many professors in a posture of service, working less within the confines of their own disciplines and more in undergraduate classrooms filled with students from a variety of fields: "They expect us to teach big classes where enrollments are high, like in American government and political science, but they don't pay much attention in terms of teaching more specialized courses." Respondents frequently refer to an administrative "they" who are able to allocate subjects and decide loads.

In the teachers college turned state college, the newer faculty also have a distinct sense of being different from their older colleagues:

You can make a comparison of the faculty who came to [the] college before the seventies and those who came in the seventies and those who are coming now. You will find the difference, I think, in that most of the Ph.D.'s came in the seventies and now . . . and those who are not Ph.D.'s came in the fifties and the sixties, and I think that in the seventies a lot of good people have come who have an interest in scholarly things.

Clearly, faculty have a sense, as they did in the less prestigious universities, but now even more strongly, that the institution over all "has not come to terms with itself."

With inchoate institutional character operating, with heavy teaching loads suppressing research and its rewards, what then do the faculty value most?

> It has to be the students. I enjoy the students. I try to enter the classroom environment with a spirit of enthusiasm. I have been told that I do, and I take great pride in that.
>
> I think the thing that is most valuable, if there is anything, is the relationship with the students. A lot of students, in some ways, are almost naive. They tend to be more open and noncritical than I think you would find at other places. It makes working with them easier in a way. . . . Comparing it to [an urban university], for instance. Some of the students were downright hostile. I have seen students walk out of classes while the person is lecturing. I don't think that would happen here.

With a little luck, colleagues can be friendly:

> One thing I like here is that people are not bossy. I like my colleagues. They are nice, and they don't like to order you or boss you around.

And occasionally geographic location tops the list, even offered sometimes as a reason to live in New Jersey: "It is located between New York and Washington . . . and has some advantages for me logistically."

Professors in the comprehensive colleges indicated that they experience a relatively weak institutional culture, one that does not stand strongly on its own. But then neither are the cultures of the individual disciplinary departments particularly strong, since research and scholarship are not primary and are not heavily rewarded. Thus, a general dilution of both institutional and disciplinary identifications occurs. Respondents turn to specific comments about their own students and their own colleagues, to perhaps a general friendliness, and to geographic location. The thinning may finally appear as a virtual total absence of an institutional self:

116

(*What is it about [state college] that you value the most?*) Ken, could you give me some notion of what you are driving at? (*What's its strength in your eyes?*) What's its strength. (*I can think of another way I can ask you.*) I guess—what's it's strength? [Pause] Can you give me an illustration of some place that you're thinking of—that perhaps I can, are you speaking of, for example, research? Is that the strength? No, that's not a strength here. Are you speaking of teaching? (*What about it is it that you like?*)

and, on the fourth try, the professor found an answer in the pleasure of dealing with students who are "not great" but "good" and "bright-eyed and innocent and willing to deal honestly with you."

But, even when the institutional self is weak, and the rewards of the discipline are largely out of reach, in their discretionary time professors can maneuver into rewarding postures, for example, that of social activist. A state college professor explained that "my whole reason for getting into this profession has to do with the discretionary time involved, which I can use on community activities and research, which is interlocked." The research part had not worked out: "Part of my improper socialization was that I failed to get excited by these [academic] questions at an earlier stage. . . . I have written some articles that were not published. . . . I have been basically a failure as far as the conventional definition of success in the profession is concerned." But then this leaves all the more time for community activities: "I belong to seventy public interest groups of various kinds, subscribe to a half dozen sources of information; I give to a half dozen to a dozen political candidates every year; I am the editor of a regional exchange for [an environmental magazine] . . . and in the [environmental organization] I have about five positions."

This activist was so involved outside his college that his central tension was not between "my teaching and my outside political activities" because "I have to do my teaching," but "within my citizen activities because there are so many different things that I could be doing." As citizen/activist, he was very thankful that "even though you have a heavy teaching load," being a professor "gives you far more discretionary time than just about any other occupation." And all "teachers" need not be full-fledged "academics": "As a teacher I should not necessarily be an academic. I should be an academic much of the time, but to be an academic all of the time makes a poor teacher." The activist is involved in the real world and can bring real issues back to the classroom. But, then, as a closing twist, there is still the dream of what might have been if early "socialization" had put his feet on the regular academic path. "I still wistfully dream on occasion about holding a position in a major university. I think I would welcome the pressure to write articles and publish, if I had the ability to do it. But I won't do it, it is too late now. I am old and set." So, it could have been better for this state college professor, but his rewarding commitment to activism fills well the space in the academic role left after twelve hours of classroom teaching. There could hardly be a better demonstration of the lures of "maneuvering time" and how the academic role can be variously filled.

In the community colleges, the identifications of faculty with the institution reach the high point of student-centeredness. The pleasures have to lie in teaching in a setting that is distinctly opposed to disciplinary definitions of quality and excellence. Time and again in the interviews, the community college teachers pointed with pride to the task of working with poorly prepared students who pour in through the open door. In the following five examples, they explicitly—sometimes even favorably—compared their situation with what they think exists in large universities and colleges:

> I think we are a teaching college. We are a practical teaching college. We serve our community and we serve the children, the students in our community, and give them a good, basic, strong education. We educate them. We are not sitting here on our high horses looking to publish.

> I think its strength is dedication to its students, really. I have a number of friends who are at [a university] and the pressure there is on individual publications, individual research; here, it's just teaching.

> I really do like to teach, and this place allows me to teach. It doesn't bog me down with having to turn out papers. Before I came here, I told you I was at [a minor university] for five years, and the pressure to publish there was very, very great, and I knew that if I stayed there I would have to publish, and the people who do do publishing there really don't have time for their

118

students. They are in their labs, and if students come in they are a pain in the neck. Here we know that we are here to teach, and this place allows you to do that.

Well, I enjoy teaching, and I like the character and uniqueness of the students here. . . . (*What makes them unique?*) Well, they're unique demographically, I think. As a friend of mine said, "[This college] is probably the new Ellis Island of the United States." I think we have the biggest ethnic mixture of probably any community college in the country.

A variety of things. The people, colleagues as well as students. We've got a wonderful diversity of students here, all sorts of cultures and backgrounds—and the other thing is, at this level, the closeness between faculty and students that you really don't get, I don't think, at the universities.

A professor who had taught in a community college for twenty-two years saw the place as an institution where he could be a "useful eccentric" relating to students who are academically eccentric:

I love the fact that I can be as unstructured and exploratory as I like. I am considered a useful eccentric here, not threatening. . . . There are very interesting students around. . . . Here we take people off the street and perhaps give them some time to grow—state colleges and universities have strict entrance requirements [and] cannot admit eccentric people as far as grades and so on. . . . This is a fascinating place. Here we are like a whale taking a lot of plankton in and some of it is nourishing.

But, personal eccentricity, and being part of an institutional whale, can wear thin:

Eccentricity becomes old very quickly, it is always shallow, and it is almost always personal, and if there is not intellectual content it becomes wow and golly and gee. . . . Sometimes I get tired of eccentricity: We would love to have a purely academic class to teach, be able to study an area that is limited in scope and more in depth. I'm tired of introductory and exploratory classes in breadth—all of English literature in one semester. . . . [Criticizes the English department at a nearby university] Having said

119

all that, I would give my eye teeth to be in the English department at [the university].

Just so, the equity values ("open door," "open access") so strongly emphasized in the community college sector have a payoff in faculty culture. There is an anchoring ideology that promotes identification, one more powerful than that found in the middle-of-the-hierarchy institutions, especially in the comprehensive colleges, where there is no doctrine of equal clarity and power. Even in complex educational institutions, it is useful to be either fish or fowl. At the same time, there are limits to the pleasures to be derived from teaching only introductory courses, *and* from relating incessantly to an unselective array of students of all ages and levels of achievement and ability. In the overall institutional hierarchy, with its emphasis on quality and selection, the community college ideology can play only a subsidiary role. It helps to rationalize the lives of community college instructors, but in the value climate of the profession overall it is at best a secondary value system. The limitations cannot be missed: "It would be nice to be able to teach upper division classes."

The interviews quoted above and in the previous chapter amply testify to the power of disciplinary identifications in research universities and to the attenuation of such beliefs and interests when professors are placed in nonresearch settings. Two respondents in a comprehensive public institution typified "modest involvement" in disciplines. When asked how involved he was in "the affairs of your discipline and subfield," one respondent's mind first turned to "within the department and within my classes?" Asked by the interviewer to turn to the larger picture, he replied: "I would say I am moderately involved. I follow some of the journals, and that would be my involvement." He did not belong to any professional associations—"No, I am not a joiner"; he had been to professional meetings only to recruit—"I did not attend the meetings [the substantive sessions]; we had a busy schedule interviewing." His principal professional group is "within the department." The second respondent noted that he was not as involved in his discipline "as I am with this university and with this department. I don't have a lot of professional activities." But he thought it was important to have a division of commitment in departments in which someone would have "that kind of contact. We just have two or three other

120

people who are very active in the discipline, and it seems like, in the department, we all have a function to perform since you can't do everything. Mine has been primarily the university."

These comments point to a possible advantage of the betwixt-and-between nature of the middle-hierarchy colleges: There is not one controlling definition of the faculty role, as we observed at the two extremes, but, instead, alternative, if confusing, commitments, with some faculty trying to be "active in the discipline" while others retain a local orientation. The battle for the soul of such colleges becomes in large part the issue of how much of the one or of the other. Incentives and rewards shift from teaching toward research in the drift toward full university stature; or in the opposite direction, especially in times of economic turndown, when the institutional need to attract and please undergraduate students becomes the administrative leverage for more hours in the classroom and an increased ratio of students to teachers.

In contrast to these mild cases of disciplinary involvement, we listen to the depth of excitement elicited by a professor of physics at a leading university when he was asked what it was about "doing physics" that gave him the most pleasure:

> That's actually the best thing of it all—it's to be good enough to be a part of it. Even if you're not the best, and you don't do quite as well as you thought. To be good enough to be a part of it, and to be thought about when people think about getting together and having a meeting and doing this. I mean, that's the most fun of everything . . . I can't even share that with my wife! There is nobody you can share that with except somebody who had done it . . . that's why my grant is important. I just couldn't see them otherwise. I cannot pay for these things out of my pocket. I don't have that kind of money. And if they ever cut my travel off, boy, I'm telling you. . . . I guess you asked if there was any reason why I'd leave academia. I would be desperate then. I'd sell something. Start spending my own money—because I'm not missing that. It's not worth it.
>
> You know, just talking about it makes me want to get on the phone and arrange a trip! That's something that cannot be done by anybody else in other fields. I mean I can go anywhere I want to go! I just get on the phone and say, "I'm going to happen to

be there"—which is just a story. I'm just going to go! "Now you come up with some money and I'll pay the difference out of my grant . . . and you know we're going to go out some place and drink a bottle of wine that night, and I'm going to give you a great talk. . . ."

And you know, there is nothing in the world that will touch it! I mean I hear about all these high rollers and their things, but they don't have any interest to me. They don't know what it is to match wits with people whose wits are worth matching! . . . But, anyway, I like the profession, I guess, and all complaints are very small compared with that. So that's my loyalty. . . . It's that culture that helps. That's the definition of it. That's the whole thing.

Maneuvering time here is of a very high order, with the professor a walking expression of salaried entrepreneurship. And shining through the remarks is the confidence, even the arrogance, displayed in the culture of physicists. At the top of the stairs, academic life exudes cosmopolitan excitement. In one's specialty, according to the view from there, one runs with the best.

THE CULTURE OF THE PROFESSION

Another rich and revealing part of the field interviews was a section of six questions that sought to explore academic values. Four questions asked about collegiality, academic freedom, violations of academic norms, and the emerging problems of cooperative research involving universities and private industrial firms. Two more open-ended questions asked about outstanding academics and common values. Answers to these questions, often long and discursive, set out a small number of beliefs that came up over and over again, across institutions and disciplines. But, as one might expect, there was also much variation across the institutional sectors, between letters and science fields and professional schools, and among disciplines. Professors rang the themes of productive scholarship and effective teaching; of open inquiry, intellectual integrity, and respect for quality. But, as one respondent put it, such lofty themes may serve as a "low common denominator" on top of which academics place more exacting prescriptions and proscriptions. Some of the most interesting findings can be grouped under the two topics of the idealized academic and the basic ideologies of the profession.

Idealized Types of "Academic Man"

The interviewed professors were asked to "describe someone you consider to be an outstanding academic." As we follow their accounts across institutional settings, and around and among several disciplines, we note how the imagery of the outstanding professor changes.

THE RESEARCH UNIVERSITY   We begin with five professors in different fields in major universities:

> *Professor of biology and chemistry*: An outstanding academic is someone who makes genuine contributions to his or her field in an elegant way, while at the same time is teaching others, passing on that information or the techniques or the approaches, so that it's not just one individual in isolation doing some elegant research but they [sic] are actually training other people as well.

Here is the perfected combination of research and teaching according to the Humboldtian ideal, with research placed front and center, an activity that is individualist, genuine, and even elegant. Teaching trails along as a way of imparting the results of research and thereby bringing others up to the mark. Reducing the isolation of the researcher, it also becomes a more communal act, turning self-regard into other-regard.

> *Professor of physics*: I would be inclined to value most in an academic person his ability to excite and enthuse and to create an environment of exciting science. . . . [Referring to a friend on another campus as model] He doesn't look kindly on people who want him to be on committees and doesn't do it . . . but the authority that he has—first of all, he's an absolutely great physicist who shares his ideas and creates a climate of excitement about physics. He's also somebody who has an enormous ego, but it's the kind of ego that makes you feel good, too. When you're doing physics with him, even the undergraduates—I think it's definitely so for undergraduates—there's just a sense of excite-

123

ment that you and he are the smartest people in the world and you're going to lick this problem.

Here again we find teaching following behind great research, both reflecting "exciting science" and a sense that apprentices as well as masters are "doing" the discipline. From his expertise the master possesses authority. He is also charismatic, seen by others as somewhat larger than life. He can charge up the psychodynamics of the laboratory, the lecture hall, or the seminar by simply walking into the room. His enormous self-regard could possibly make him very selfish. But, lo and behold, his personal egotism stimulates others and increases their confidence in their own ability to solve difficult problems. Self-regard becomes other-enhancing.

> *Professor of English*: I have a good friend who is in history. He has written two absolutely brilliant books. . . . He is probably the finest undergraduate and graduate teacher that I have ever known. I have team taught with him and he takes infinite pains over preparing for the class, he is concerned with the individual students, he is concerned with their writing, and then he interrogates himself after the course, with the help of the student evaluations, with a view to making it even better next time. I have never seen anybody put that much energy into the quality of their teaching. He is tough, he has enormously high standards, he is challenging, he doesn't court popularity, and he is a true intellectual and the students respond to him.

In a third idealized university-type of academic we find the paragon of scholarship and teaching, humanities-style, with "brilliant books" and "enormously high standards," who takes such care in teaching undergraduates as well as graduate students that all respond to him. It only requires a few who even approach the ideal in each department to redeem the humanities part of a university. Together with outstanding scholarly work, they offer more prowess in teaching than is commonly associated with this type of institution.

> *Professor of political science*: Curiosity, taste, and commitment to letting reality speak very loudly so that that becomes the central disciplinary device in one's work. People who I consider to have made landmark contributions are people who are not downed by

124

a particular orthodoxy but, having chosen a problem, look at it from a number of points of view. A commitment to truth.

In the fourth case, a voice from political science, the imagery remains in the domain of "landmark contributions" made by the original thinker driven by curiosity and an unfettered commitment to seek the truth. "Commitment to letting reality speak very loudly so that [it] becomes the central disciplinary device" in academic work expresses well the feeling that research-minded academics possess in their self-asserted "commitment to truth." What comes through is how disciplines serve to regulate academic work, as professors try to inculcate perspectives, concepts, and methods. Underlying the discipline of the disciplines, throughout most of the academic fields, is a belief that the truth must be squeezed from reality.

> *From the business school*: I would like to be an outstanding academic. It is one of the goals I have set for myself, and it is hard to judge whether you have reached those goals given that I make my comparisons on the national level. I would like to be recognized as one of the top five or top ten members of my cohort. . . . That requires outstanding research that gets national exposure.

Our representative business school figure makes explicit what was implicit in the other formulations: In the eyes of university professors, outstanding academics have national stature. Teaching does not give national exposure; rather, "outstanding research" is the chariot to which personal ambition must be hooked. The extrinsic reward is not money but recognition, a form that blends readily with the intrinsic rewards we later emphasize.

THE COMPREHENSIVE COLLEGE As we move to the middle of the institutional hierarchy, the idealization of academics shifts considerably away from research, especially from national renown, and into a profusion of concerns in which teaching is central. Let us listen to five representative answers to the question of an outstanding academic:

> *Professor of biology*: I would say enthusiasm would be important and a person who is in control. Also someone who has a high personal respect for the students. A respectful attitude I would place

awfully high, and a genuine effort to keep up with the field which is easier said than done.

Professor of physical science: Well, steer me along a little if I'm not quite going your way. Number one, he must be good in his area. He must like it and be good. He has to have a background, and he should have gotten it early. Don't stretch it out. Number two, if he's truly an academic, as I would call an academic, he must also have obligations to his students. That is, he must be a teacher. . . . And then of course the last thing, he should have hopefully some ability to play and do his research. I call that play. He should be interested indeed in trying to gain some knowledge or produce some knowledge.

Professor of political science: I think an academic should not be someone who lives and dies in the ivory tower. Personally, I am a sort of pragmatic fellow. I think an academic should teach, write, and do research but he or she should also be involved in some of the practical things within your area of competence.

Professor of English: Active engagement in the profession. . . . You haven't asked me about my teaching. (*Yes, all right.*) I will toot my own horn, I am an excellent teacher. (*How do you account for that—why are you an outstanding teacher?*) Because I am so deeply engaged in my material; I am so enthusiastic about it. I can turn them on. It is my life. I am married, I have a family, fine children, and so forth, but my intellectual life is my study, my work, and that spills over into the classroom.

Professor of business: I guess I will have to go back to one of my old mentors. He was very bright, very sharp intellectually. . . . A lot of interesting research kinds of things. What this person didn't have was a concern for students. I never had a problem with him, but he could be downright cool with people that he didn't think merited his attention. I think the ideal academic would have more of a concern for people and relationships.

The confusion of beliefs that we noticed earlier as characteristic of the middle sectors of the institutional hierarchy, especially in the public four- and five-year colleges but also in the second- and third-level universities, is evident in these idealized portraits. The professor should teach, do research, and also do some practical things. Respect for students would be very important, even a strong obligation to them, but then also he or she

126

should be intellectually very sharp, have a strong academic background, and be capable of doing research. If heavy teaching loads or weak rewards for research or both displace research, the academic must at least somehow keep up with the field, but that "is easier said than done." Outstanding teaching in the local classroom may then possibly be seen as "active engagement in the profession."

In short, belief follows work. The academic job in comprehensive colleges is different from that in universities. Although influenced by university norms, conceptions of the ideal are pulled toward local realities. The location generates a different culture.

THE COMMUNITY COLLEGE What makes an outstanding academic in the eyes of community college instructors? The ideal, to be very student-centered, is told succinctly by two respondents from physics and biology:

> *Professor of physics*: At this level, that's someone who is primarily with [students]. Our goal here is to help students learn. Someone who is able to do that; and that could, of course, happen in a variety of ways.

> *Professor of biology*: They exhibit a caring attitude toward students and other people.

But even in the eyes of those located in the settings that are most remote from the top institutions, the ideal faculty member ought to keep up with his or her discipline:

> *Professor of political science*: A person who has a very strong grasp of the various facets of his discipline, who is constantly updating his knowledge through research and scholarship.

> *Professor of biology*: Somebody who loves the subject, of course, and is able to convey his enthusiasm to other people. . . . Somebody who always keeps current with new developments . . . reads widely, of course, and conveys his knowledge by writing and hopefully does some good research as well.

> *Professor of biology*: Somebody who is active in their field, so that lets a lot of us out. . . . I mean active in the core of one's area—research! (*An outstanding community college teacher?*) One who

127

can get across the idea to the students and, probably more important, excite the student to want to learn and to do the work on his own.

As elsewhere in nonuniversity settings, community college respondents often harkened back to their days in graduate school, pointing to what they liked and disliked in the setting in which they took their training. A political science teacher told us:

The better teacher not only has a good subject background, he is interested in adding to it or keeping up with it. . . . That person must also be interested in students. I have met people who are brilliant in writing books, and so forth, but who didn't like students. I worked for people like that when I was a reader at [a university]. I had a professor who I worked for at one time who told me he hated undergraduates—they are morons. I was an undergraduate, so I really couldn't say anything.

But a professor of business administration had had better experiences:

"When I think back, I had some extremely good teachers, and when I use the word 'teacher,' I think I emphasize what I think's important . . . ability to get students interested in the material, to get them to grasp the material whether it be Shakespeare or art or geology. . . . "(*What does it take?*) Well, I don't really know. Some of it is merely style. . . . I used to have one who used to wear a cape, and he was teaching us five books that he loved, and it was a literature class. And he would get up there and march around the room and it was very theatrical, but it kept everybody involved. And he really seemed to love the material. . . . [In another case] statistics was something I did not look forward to, and this guy was great! He handed out Crackerjacks the first day of class, and we had to pick out the peanuts and get a sample of how many peanuts there were in Crackerjacks boxes, and he was always bringing out examples that everyone could relate to and enjoy. It made statistics a lot of fun. He was clear, he was straightforward, he gave good homework assignments to bring out the points, he was available, he had an extra session during the term where he would say, 'I'm going to have an extra session Friday at 3:00'—and he didn't assign it to a TA [teaching assistant]. He did it himself, which was somewhat unusual."

128

Hence, when we explore idealized types of academics we find a picture similar to what we found when we asked professors what they valued most about their institutions. Sectoral setting cuts deeply. Only those enclosed in strong institutional cultures of major universities are positioned to go all out in deifying the outstanding researcher or scholar. In the more inchoate cultures of the middle-hierarchy institutions, that idealization diffuses into a mélange of features of teaching as well as of research, practical as well as purely academic capacities, and student- as well as peer-orientation. In the two-year college, where the open-door ideology reigns supreme, the idealization of scholarship is diluted even further, largely replaced by a full-throated appreciation of the capacity to stimulate beginning students. Ideals shape practice, but they also adjust to it. They then become realistic.

The Ideologies of the Profession

When academics are asked about the common values of their profession, we can discern some broad ideas to which they turn, even if they are unsure about how far their own conceptions extend to embrace others. They often verbally twist and turn around general terms, sometimes strike a hopeful normative posture of what *should* be the case, and their words often wander as they think first of their own department and discipline, then of their institution overall, and finally fix on the system and profession at large. In this murky area so much depends on what is asked of respondents. The 1984 Carnegie survey, for example, asked faculty to agree or disagree with the statement, "I consider myself an intellectual." In reply, checking one of four boxes that ranged from strong positive to strong dissent, about four out of five agreed, marking either "strongly agree" (28 percent) or "agree with reservations" (50 percent). This level of assent held up well across the types of institutions, climbing slightly higher in the leading universities and colleges and dipping slightly in the lesser liberal arts and community colleges (Appendix D). Hence, defining oneself as an intellectual might be seen as a broad, common value of the professoriate. But the survey responses give no indication of this definition's salience in relation to other beliefs that academics might have. In field interviews, where we asked more open-endedly about common values and idealized

129

academics, this definition was almost never offered. It was not part of the rhetoric that professors themselves now use. Other terms had priority, leaving it entirely to the observer to infer from those proffered comments whether or not academics might still think of themselves as intellectuals.

The 1984 survey, like all others before it, also took respondents at a fast clip through several hundred disjointed queries. At one point, it asked them in succession to agree or disagree with such statements as: "My field is too research oriented"; "I consider myself an intellectual"; "The new developments in my field are not very interesting to me"; "My job is the source of considerable personal strain." To respond, the surveyed professors were reduced to circling numbers that stood for prearranged answers. Particularly in the "subjective" domain of values, the limitations of this approach are legend. The respondents are not able to provide context, to relate one idea to others, and especially to explain what they mean. The "art" of survey analysis needs always the support of field interviewing and other more ethnographic methods that better supply context, show connections, and probe more deeply for meanings. The perfect example comes along when a national survey asks professors directly whether "despite the differences among institutions of higher education, members of the academic profession share a common set of professional values." We learn from the statistical results that about one in six respondents (17 percent) strongly agreed that there were common values, one in two (49 percent) agreed with reservations, one in four (24 percent) disagreed with reservations, and one in ten (10 percent) disagreed strongly (Appendix D). Thus, about one-third were inclined to think the profession had no common values, while two-thirds agreed there were, but only one in six strongly thought so. There was little variation across the types of institutions. But what values might they have in mind?

IN THE SERVICE OF KNOWLEDGE   In the interviews, faculty members turned particularly to such terms as "knowledge," "information," "intellectual curiosity," "searching for answers," "problem solving," and "sophisticated analysis" to point to what they had in common. A professor of biology and chemistry in a research university declared quite simply: "Striving for new understanding. Wanting to excite and impart information to others. It's really why we are here." A professor of business in a

130

second-rank university put it even more succinctly: "Concern with learning new knowledge." They were joined by a host of others in a similar refrain across the full range of institutions and disciplines:

Professor of business, research university: At some base or gut level there must be something common about people who select into academic institutions. There has to be a certain level of intellectual curiosity, regardless of what discipline you are in, as to why organizations behave this way and why is literature written this way and why do atoms combine this way. There has to be a set of values that—a set of beliefs that value answering questions.

Professor of medicine, second-rank university: It is hard to put them in words but I think part of it is the belief that there are unanswered questions that can be answered, that we can do better, that it is fun to ask questions, it is fun to search for answers.

Professor of physics, second-rank university: In basic disciplines the whole idea is to understand, understand general problems of one sort or another. . . . I think understanding is what any kind of research is about. . . . Some people want to understand simply for the sake of understanding, but others want to understand because there is a tremendous payoff, one way or another, that comes out of it.

Professor of political science, comprehensive college: I think that the academic's goal is to understand. The sophistication of our disciplines affects the levels of understanding. . . . As long as people are serious and systematic it does not matter at what level of scientific validity they are working at, it is still an academic and valuable enterprise.

Professor of biology, community college: One value is just knowledge itself . . . knowledge enhancing the quality of life, a person's life.

"Just knowledge itself"—creating it, caring for it, teaching or otherwise transmitting it—proved to be the nearest thing to common ideological ground. "Understanding" is a touchstone, a principle worth serving. When academics think of their profession's service to society, they put the provision of knowledge front and center. It is an end itself, enriching in itself; and it is a broad stream of means for obtaining societal ends.

131

THE NORMS OF ACADEMIC HONESTY Trailing not far behind in the interviews were assertions about intellectual integrity that connect closely to the ideology of knowledge. In the academic lexicon, knowledge must be handled honestly, for otherwise it misinforms and deceives, is no longer valuable in itself and certainly of no use to society. A professor of biology in a second-level university summarized it best:

> I think that there is the absolute value system that calls for intellectual honesty. I see my colleagues coming down on people, and not colleagues here but everywhere, on the question [of] is that person intellectually honest. Are they truly giving us original information, are they truly teaching in a modern and effective way? Intellectual honesty.

A similar refrain was heard in other types of institutions. A professor of physics in a comprehensive college said:

> Openness to new ideas and a sense of fairness, integrity, and honesty—I guess I want to use the word "honesty"—so that you somehow are frank about your own biases. Now, I don't think it is possible to be completely frank about them, but you try to be. Honest with students. Forthright.

The fullness of commitment to intellectual honesty came tumbling out when we asked for "some examples of serious violations of an academic norm." Without prompting from the interviewers, the respondents frequently turned to plagiarism, falsification, and unfair treatment of students as very serious violations, even high crimes. Here were matters that stimulate emotion:

> *Professor of English, research university*: Plagiarism is a gross and obvious violation of intellectual and academic integrity. [Also,] giving a student a poor grade because you dislike him—or giving him a good grade because you like him—would be a violation of integrity.

> *Professor of physics, research university*: The one that I mentioned earlier—stealing people's research ideas—which . . . you know, [for] young scholars . . . their identity is their work, and to steal someone's identity is an unpardonable sin—that's as low

as you get. That's analogous to murder. . . . That violates the sacred academic norm of scholarship, of honest scholarship.

Professor of biology, second-level university: [Academics] should never steal their students' information. I dislike people who get the students to do all the work and then act as if they did it, publication or anything else. That is plagiarism essentially.

Professor of business, comprehensive college: You can't show favoritism to students, and you can't tolerate cheating.

Professor of political science, leading liberal arts college: Surely, saying in writing what you don't think is true would be a violation of an academic norm. Doctoring the evidence, suppressing parts of it—that sort of thing.

Professor of political science, second-rank liberal arts college: [referring to an instance at a nearby university] A good bit of plagiarism was involved and using the work of a graduate student in that process. . . . Like if someone was to take your work and then incorporate it into a work and then get all the glory. I think that is one of the worst things I can think of.

Professor of physics, community college: [The] student-teacher relationship is really a very special sort of thing, and it's, just by its nature, a very unequal sort of thing. The instructor has very great power over the student, and to misuse that power, in any way, is gross violation of the ethics of teaching.

In the concern about integrity in dealing with students we received occasional comments about sexual harassment: "I'd say the first thing I can think of is what's sometimes called sexual harassment. I guess one way to describe it is using one's power of decision-making as a teacher over students to interact with those people in personal ways." And: "The first thing that comes to my mind would be sexual harassment. Those are the kinds of things—putting pressure on the student. Blackmailing them for any reason with their grade."

No one talked about stealing money or running away with the spouse of a colleague or serving ineptly in administration. What matters in the profession is the honest handling of knowledge—honest research, honest teaching, honest advice—and fair treatment of colleagues and students, using established universal criteria rather than particularistic judgment. In the eyes of researchers plagiarism is *the* crime: It is sufficient cause for full withdrawal of respect, even banishment to the Siberia of a lesser institution. You must not steal ideas, that is "unpardonable," even "analogous to murder," for you are doing violence to someone's professional identity. Similarly, the falsification of research findings is a serious crime: One must not doctor the evidence, nor write what one does not think is true. On the teaching side, favoritism is a serious matter. Students must be treated fairly, without regard to personal characteristics. Objective judgment should characterize the relationship of the dominant teacher with the subordinate student, a relationship where the imbalance of power is a temptation to misuse authority.

THE IDEOLOGY OF FREEDOM We confronted professors with the topic of academic freedom by stating that "Academic freedom is important to the profession. What does it mean for you in your work?" In response, we received some strong answers in which personal freedom was portrayed as an extremely attractive aspect of academic life, even, like recognition, serving in lieu of material rewards:

> *Professor of physics, research university*: Academic freedom to me means two things—one is I can work on whatever I feel like. . . . It's a very big contract. It goes one way. You give me tenure, and you're stuck. As long as I'm good. It also means that in the community I can value exactly as I please, as long as I don't break the law. And it shouldn't affect my work. . . . That I can do what I please. If it wasn't for that, I certainly wouldn't work for the salary that I get . . . the game wouldn't be worth playing.

> *Professor of political science, second-level university*: Yes, it is crucial. It means that there is virtually nothing that I cannot research and write on. There should be nothing that I could not say in class unless it was totally irrelevant, unless it was intended to be malicious or illegal. . . . I wouldn't work in an institution where academic freedom was in jeopardy.

> *Professor of biology, second-level university*: It is a sine qua non for the university profession. I think that if a faculty member ever feels that he or she doesn't have academic freedom with respect to expressing views to the administration, to society, to special interest groups, [and] to industry [that] we may as well

134

get out of the university business because this is intrinsic to what the university is. It is free exchange, academic freedom. That is where we serve society, as an unbiased, unfettered judge of what we should be doing in scholarly activity. . . . If you look at history, that is where universities have best served society—in being the voice of society.

Academic freedom was a totem for the vast majority of respondents across disciplines and up and down the line of the institutional hierarchy. But what aspect of freedom, and from whom? In the research university, as we might expect, professors insisted upon freedom in research. They then sometimes pointed to the culprits who knowingly or unknowingly might constrain that freedom:

> *Professor of physics, second-level university*: It means that in my research activity I am absolutely free. I can do whatever I like. In physics, of course, it is not a great problem.

> *Professor of political science, second-rank university*: It [academic freedom] is not basically challenged so I don't think of it very often, but if it was I would be very upset. (*What would be a violation of academic freedom here?*) Censorship of my research.

The danger might come from institutional administration:

> *Professor of physics, second-level university*: If I didn't have that, some dean might come around and say, "Why are you working on the Aharonov-Bohm effect? The problems in nonlinear optics that you were working on were much more useful. You were getting consulting contracts, and things like that, and now you're sitting there working on this crazy problem and coming up with results that nobody really believes." . . . At [a place of previous employment], a dean could come and tell me exactly that and say, "Look, if you don't get back to your own work we'll have to reconsider whether we want to keep you three years down the line," or something like that. That is a real problem.

In a leading university, a professor of biology and chemistry pointed to the way the locus of the problem may shift subtly from the university to funding agencies: "Constraints have been lifted in large part, but generally they still exist in that if you want to do research, then you have to get support for it, and the support really defines the type of research that you can do."

As the institutional setting shifts from research to teaching, the emphasis in academic freedom changes from freedom in research activities to freedom in the classroom:

> *Professor of English, second-rank university*: [It means] I am free to choose my material without any second thoughts about it—without someone looking over my shoulder—free to say what I think to be the truth. In the classroom you don't have to censor your material or censor your thought.

> *Professor of political science, comprehensive college, with prior experience in a developing society*: People are not coming up and dictating what courses you can teach. When I grew up in Pakistan, and I taught there, there were questions of academic freedom and it came down to things like teaching certain things or the way you teach. . . . You don't have that sort of thing here.

> *Professor of physical science, second-rank liberal arts college*: A definition of academic freedom to a scientist is the freedom to discuss in the classroom what the truths of science are . . . the ability to talk about these theories openly and without worrying about any type of repercussions.

> *Professor of business, community college*: I wouldn't consider it appropriate if somebody told me I had to give a certain type of test. . . . Let's say I was giving an essay test and somebody said, "No, you have to give a short answers test." I would consider that a violation of academic freedom.

> *Professor of political science, community college*: I don't think I could survive without it, I really don't. I think as an instructor it's basic . . . interference with this ability that I have in the classroom to reach my students, by either administrators or other instructors, or the community in general, I hold to be a very important basic thing. I've gone to bat for it once or twice. I was the grievance representative . . . for two years . . . so I had occasion to see a wide number of grievances that had been placed against the administration and other instructors. So to me that's very important.

136

We also encountered significant disciplinary differences. Physicists were quite secure: "In physics, Newton's laws are Newton's laws." On grounds of substantial theory and method and an impenetrable vocabulary, biology would also normally be quite secure, but biologists positioned in the mid-1980s in second- and third-level colleges in midwestern and southern states showed some concern about "creationism" as a lay challenge to the scientific theory of evolution. Four biologists explained their concern and reasoned about the nature of academic freedom:

> (*What would be a violation?*) If you were forced to withhold information because of—I am an evolutionary ecologist, if I were forced—this is the edge of the Bible belt—if I was forced to withhold that type of thinking or information, that would certainly be a violation. (*But you feel there is no violation?*) No, none at all.

> In [this state] this [issue] surfaced recently in the question of creationism versus evolution, explanations for why we are here. We, in fact, have a state law requiring the balanced treatment of those two in the public schools. That could easily really repress the political atmosphere that stands in the university. That's where academic freedom would give us some protection. (*Do you feel that it is justified for professors to be teaching creationism in the classroom?*) It is a hard one, isn't it? I would have to say that I would be dead set against it because it is scientifically, in my opinion, untenable. There is no scientific evidence for that kind of approach, whereas there is an incredible amount of evidence for the evolutionary concept. No one will teach [creationism] in biology, not a soul in this department would touch it with a ten foot pole. . . . Freedom, I suppose, is a body of trained individuals in various fields [able] to decide what is legitimate and what is not.

> I should be able . . . to walk into my classroom and talk about the fossil record and not have to invoke Bishop Ussher's calculations of the beginning of creation every time I turn around. (*And you feel you have academic freedom?*) Oh, yes. Nothing in my experience of seven or eight years at the college would give me any reason to doubt that I have academic freedom in the classroom.

> What violates academic freedom is when I am told "you may not" or "you must" teach a certain thing which violates my own perception or philosophy. . . . It may turn out not to be in a big-

ger sense. For instance, if I go in there and I teach creationism as being academically or scientifically sound, and someone says "quit doing that," then they, in a sense, are violating my academic freedom, even though in a larger sense they are not. If someone tells me I must teach it, then that is the same thing. In short, I would not teach it in the first place, but as an example that is one that springs to mind with biology. We are still fighting that war after all these years.

Whatever their concerns in certain states about the politics of creationism, biologists join their colleagues in physics in knowing that they have a sturdy body of scientific knowledge and that therefore the sharper problems of academic freedom are to be found in the social sciences and the humanities, "where the subject material can be so much more variable." A biologist in a community college pointed to a disciplinary difference when he answered, "I really don't know what it means in this department or in my own work. I think the term is usually more applicable to social scientists, where there could be political interference." Our respondents in political science showed considerable sensitivity on this score. One told of going through a bitter loyalty oath fight in the 1960s—"That was a nasty situation, and people recognized it as a nasty situation"—in which his refusal to sign a disclaimer affidavit brought first a withholding of his salary and then his firing, actions soon reversed by a court decision that the law was unconstitutional. Another political scientist pointed to a potential in-house political threat to his academic freedom:

That is a question that hits fairly close to home. It's the ability to think about political and philosophical questions without being harassed for having what might seem to be the wrong opinion, and there has certainly been at least as much harassment from the left of the political spectrum in the field in which I have worked in the last ten or fifteen years as there has been from the right. . . . One of the things that I do in my work is, for instance, to teach in some sense, sympathetically and respectfully, the work of people who argue that some human beings are inferior to others and that slavery, is, in a sense, a defensible social institution. To make those arguments is to make arguments which are profoundly antithetical to the understanding which led to the foundation of this society and certainly to the understanding

138

which is accepted by virtually all people in the society. And to the extent that it becomes or might be difficult to do that, I would feel that my academic freedom was impaired. (*So you feel you have academic freedom?*) Oh, yes. If anything, it's quite the contrary. The problem is that I sometimes feel I could say these incredibly outrageous things and that my students would just yawn and not notice.

The 1980s are not the 1960s! But whatever the mood of state officials, populist groups, and radical students in the period at hand, the ideologies of the professoriate view academic freedom, in all its variant meanings, as a necessary condition for acting with integrity in the service of knowledge. The one concern shades into the other.

In these current expressions we clearly find the norms of science. In his classic 1942 essay on the cultural structure of science, Robert K. Merton noted that "the pursuit and diffusion of knowledge has risen to a leading place if not to the first rank in the scale of cultural values," for society as a whole, as well as for the academy itself, with that pursuit and diffusion coming from "the ways of science." Among those ways Merton saw four central imperatives: "universalism," an impersonal, objective pursuit of knowledge; "communism," an open, "competitive cooperation" in which knowledge becomes common property; "disinterestedness," in which peer scrutiny gives science a public and testable character; and "organized skepticism," a detached examination of beliefs using empirical and logical criteria, which asks if, essentially, they are proven facts.[9] Reflections of these "imperatives," spoken and unspoken, were clearly found in our conversations with faculty members in the various corners of American higher education. But the ideologies of the profession are broader than the norms of science because they have to cover more ground. They have to embrace the many settings in which research is absent or plays second to teaching, as well as the leading universities and colleges—and those second-tier institutions most determined to emulate them—in which research rules the roost. Notably, the ethos of science has little, if anything, to say about students, and for good reason, since professional peers are *the* audience. But academic ideologies have much to say about students, necessarily becoming focused in the lower half of the institutional hierarchy on students as

139

the most important source of recognition and self-respect. How else would nonresearch academics receive symbolic pats on the back?

In the American academy, "science" is joined to "education." It even gives way to it in ethos, as in practice, in the settings of half or more of the professoriate. Science and education steadily take on more diffuse meanings as higher education incorporates more subjects in a wider array of organizational instruments. In four-year and especially two-year colleges, we find classes in cosmetology and elementary school English. In universities, especially in their extension divisions, we find classes devoted to practices of the occult as well as to routine trades, which have nothing to do with the scientific enterprise and the fruits of its research. Academics have adjusted their ideologies accordingly, to rationalize education in all its specific manifestations and to cover the evermore varied ways of inquiry.

SYMBOLIC INTEGRATION

Our exploration of "the academic mind"—centered on the identification of academics with their institutions, disciplines, and profession at large—has shown an abundance of concerns that are not self-interest narrowly conceived. We have seen a profusion of enlightened preferences that exhibit either a strong concern for others or an impressive concern for a principle or both. "Self-regarding" interests are tempered as well as justified by more altruistic "other-regarding" and "ideal-regarding" ones. Intrinsic features have a powerful thrust: A certain amount of dignity inheres in a profession dedicated to "education" at its more advanced levels, "scholarship" in all its historical and contemporary dress, "truth" in its most rational and empirical form, and "knowledge" in its most advanced streams. The profession is richly endowed with supreme fictions upon which academics draw to explain to themselves and others the value of what they are doing.

Yet the diverging work of American academics increasingly differentiates them into narrow groups that in turn generate separate subcultures. The distinct bodies of knowledge and their epistemological bases alone insure distinctive languages and mores. The divergence strains the supreme fictions, turning a broad theology into a disarray of separatist doctrines. Research professors, state college professors, community college professors, liberal arts college professors, technological school professors, theological school professors, art school professors may all, in common, voice certain phrases, but the meanings of the symbols become different as they are reinterpreted and specified to make sense in varied settings. Broad principles remain, but in their influence on behavior they are steadily outweighed by differentiated understandings that are closer to the realities of everyday life. In academia subculturing is a powerful phenomenon. Proceeding in America by type of institution in addition to type of discipline—with innumerable distinctions on each axis—the separation of academic identities follows in the train of the irresistible division of labor.

How then may we best grasp the cultural integration of the profession? Beyond weakening attachment to attenuating broad principles, is there anything left, any linkage that somehow connect the many parts to the whole? What remains is an overlap of memberships and commitments whereby some academics connect to one another as they partake of two or more cultures. Most belong to a subspecialty within a discipline while they belong to the discipline as a whole. Some belong to a discipline and to a multidisciplinary unit, be the latter a professional school (medicine or education), an area studies program (African or Latin American studies), or a problem-centered unit (environmental or urban studies). Some disciplinarians are so serious about their membership in the profession at large that they join appropriate local and national nondisciplinary associations, subscribe to their journals, and go to their meetings. Most important, all employed academics have simultaneous commitments to a field and to a university or college that penetrate and confront the other, reducing the cultural isolation that comes from an overriding commitment to a single interest.

Diana Crane has acutely observed that the social system of science is an appropriate model for how cultural integration may coexist with cultural diversity in a highly differentiated society: "Contemporary science comprises hundreds of distinct specialties, but each specialty has connections, both intellectual and social, with other specialties . . . cultural integration occurs because of overlapping memberships among cultural communities that lead to the dissemination of ideas and values. . . . " What we find are "interlocking cultural communities."[10] This conception of overlapping cultures has been given vivid imagery by Donald T. Campbell: Each narrow academic specialty may be seen as a fish scale overlapping other scales. A comprehensive social science, or any other large domain of knowledge, is then "a continuous texture of narrow specialties." Integration is "a collective product, not embodied within any one scholar. It is achieved through the fact that the multiple narrow specialties overlap and that through this overlap a collective communication, a collective competence and breadth, is achieved."[11] We might think of overlap as a hidden hand, with collective products and relationships issuing from thousands of semiautonomous actions.

Working on the problem of how to strengthen interdisciplinary competence and to unify the behavioral sciences, Campbell has insisted insightfully that efforts to fill gaps between fields by training scholars who have mastered two or more disciplines are doomed to fail. Instead, the realistic way to proceed, one in accord with the ways of the modern academic profession, is to make those organizational inventions that will encourage narrow specialization in the interdisciplinary areas. Ironically, the interdisciplinarian must "remain as narrow, as specialized, as any other scholar." As we master the logic of this perspective, the slogan for reform becomes "collective comprehensiveness through overlapping patterns of unique narrownesses."[12] Overlap of components is the central idea: In Michael Polanyi's terms, there are "chains of overlapping neighborhoods."[13]

As noted earlier, the meanings assigned to such concepts as knowledge, truth, and freedom may vary widely across distant locations in the grand matrix of disciplines and institutions. But those meanings remain very similar in adjacent subcultures, thereby linking academics symbolically, for example, in physical science departments in major universities. Our imagery of cultural overlap is also heightened when we see the academic world stretching from center to periphery in the form of institutional and disciplinary chains. Institutionally, the hard core of academic values in the American professoriate is found in the leading research universities and liberal arts colleges. The first exemplifies modern science and advanced scholarship; the second upholds the much-respected tradition of liberal education for undergraduates. These locales are anchoring points for central values, centers whose cultured influence radiates first to adjacent types of institutions and then in weakening rays to institutional sectors more divorced in character. The top ten universities are a powerful cultural mag-

142

net to the second ten, the top twenty to the top fifty, the recognized universities to the many comprehensive colleges that so dearly want to be recognized as universities. Academic drift—the unguided imitative convergence of universities and colleges upon the most prestigious forms—has an enormous cultural component. Imitation means adopting *their* meanings as *our* meanings, their practices as our practices, thereby diffusing values from a core toward various peripheries. In the American system, the many types of institutions do not operate as watertight compartments but rather overlap one another to the point of heavily confusing the efforts of classifiers to draw lines between them. Dominant points of view readily diffuse across the nominal demarcations.

There is also a core-to-periphery diffusion along disciplinary lines. The core exists in the most prestigious and powerful fields, generally those most scientific among the sciences and would-be sciences, and those most deeply established among the humanities. The influence of the core disciplines radiates through adjacent fields. In the subculture of academe, it is a long way from physics and chemistry to political science and sociology. But, as cultural communities, physics and chemistry overlap with mathematics, which connects to statistics, both of which in turn link importantly to the "hard" social sciences of economics and psychology. They in turn shade into the softer disciplines of political science and sociology, fields that readily shade into the perspectives of history and the humanities. Also, liberal arts fields serve as academic cores for professional schools. The "basic disciplines" continue to define what is scholarly. When we think of the academic profession, we think first of them, often only of them, and the academic sides of the professional schools look to them for guidance and legitimation. When, for example, librarians seek to fashion a major professional school for their field, they acquire some professors who qualify as great quantifiers, ones able to run with the best in creating information systems, and others who stand as literary figures with a full quota of books and critical essays.

At the outset of this chapter, I posed a thesis, antithesis, and resolution in the conceptualization of academic culture. The thesis emphasizes differentiation and fragmentation: The empirical materials have indeed shown widely varying beliefs, primarily across types of institutions and secondarily across areas of study. The antithesis claims that academics have some common commitments to overarching principles. Here the evidence is weaker, perhaps because such commitments are more difficult to pin down, but we did note widespread use of a vocabulary of ultimate values that suggests some symbolic sharing. The resolution points to modern academia as a system powered by diverging interests that may also allow for a collective comprehensiveness. Here the key analytical handle is the idea of integration through cultural overlap. Integration in American academia comes primarily not from similarity of function, nor from common acquired values, nor from united membership in a grand corps. In a powerfully pluralist fashion, it comes from incremental overlap of narrow memberships and specific identities, with disciplines and institutions serving culturally as mediating institutions that tie individuals and small groups into the enclosure of the whole.

This interpretation offers a realistic grasp of the cultural underpinnings of an advanced academic profession and system of higher education. We no longer need to resort to the now hopeless traditional exhortations that academics must get their act together by signing on for the same ideas and practices—in effect, a cry for a return to "the basics," to "a core curriculum," in the ways of the faculty. The realistic approach to cultural integration is to understand linkages among specialists and specialties. Donald T. Campbell is surely correct: We plug gaps between departments and among disciplines by creating additional narrow specialties that fill voids and link to older specialties on either side. This process of inventing specialties goes on all the time—women's studies is a good example—accelerated or retarded by different patterns of campus funding and staffing. Once a new specialty is in place, even in rudimentary form, we can count on its members to create their own subculture that overlaps bordering fields. But gaps between types of institutions may be more difficult to fill: The processes of academic drift shift entire classes of institutions out of unwanted domains as they seek the postures of advantaged institutions, leaving spaces behind them even as they narrow the gaps in front. Anchoring ideologies then become a crucial element. The American system of higher education and the American professoriate could well use stronger sets of beliefs that legitimate and make emotionally satisfying the roles of minor universities, state colleges, and community colleges, beliefs that would stabilize professorial

144

commitment as much as do the doctrines that give major universities and leading liberal arts colleges such substantial legitimacy.

Each academic segment, institutional or disciplinary, needs a rewarding definition. Overlapping justifications then offer an equation in which specialism gives rise to comprehensiveness. Since organic breadth is gone and common academic culture steadily weakens, the only real remaining possibility is overlapping depth. Whatever integration develops in the future, it will be some subtle form of unity in diversity, some slight family ties among the resilient many, with respect for differences and sturdy professional procedures that undergird trust in the choices of others. The American academic profession is put together culturally as well as structurally in the spirit of a federal nation: *E pluribus unum.*

CHAPTER VI

The Grip of Authority

On a question on which I can form no knowledgeable opinion, it costs my intellectual independence nothing to follow more competent opinions. . . . Respect for authority is in no way incompatible with rationalism as long as the authority is rationally grounded.

—EMILE DURKHEIM, ''INDIVIDUALISM AND
THE INTELLECTUALS'' (1898)

You can secure certain formal requirements [in a university], that lectures are given at stated times and that institutions and students are in attendance. But the heart of the matter is beyond all regulation.

—ALFRED NORTH WHITEHEAD,
''UNIVERSITIES AND THEIR FUNCTIONS''
(1928)

What seems good for Old Siwash is determined not by the transient adolescents who constitute the student body (or would constitute it if they were admitted) nor by the vocal alumni but by the tenured adults who give their lives to the place.

—CHRISTOPHER JENCKS AND DAVID RIESMAN,
THE ACADEMIC REVOLUTION (1968)

WHAT WE HAVE LEARNED about the work and beliefs of professors teaches us in detail that academic institutions are unusual forms of collective action whose nature is well highlighted by the metaphor of organized anarchy.[1] With work organized by subject, disciplines that rationally pursue their individual objectives encourage their departmental representatives to turn nominally unitary universities and colleges into confederative gatherings. With beliefs centered in the necessities of autonomy and freedom for individuals and small groups alike, institutions are forced to accommodate to anarchic strains, perhaps even to

147

bend to Alfred North Whitehead's dictum that "the heart of the matter is beyond all regulation." We cannot help but be struck by the virtual right so many academics seem to possess to go their own way, simply assuming they can do largely as they please a good share of the time, all in the name of rational behavior. Indeed, as put concisely by a Swedish scholar, "What behavior is more rational than the pursuit of truth?"[2] Outsiders often readily accept a logic in which the very nature of academic commitments dictates unique professional privilege. By unanimous vote in a 1985 decision, for example, the United States Supreme Court held that lower court judges must show "great respect" for faculty "professional" judgments in academic decisions, noting that "academic freedom thrives not only on the independent and uninhibited exchange of ideas among teachers and students, but also . . . on autonomous decision making by the academy itself."[3]

But what then of governance? Who rules? How do academic groups articulate their interests in contexts where omnipresent administrators and trustees possess many formal powers and ultimate rights of control? How are the interests of others brought to bear to share or contest the authority the faculty is able to master? How is a war of all against all prevented?

Questions of control over workaday life loom large in all professions. Observers and practitioners alike grasp that an occupation is professionalized to the degree that its members have a strong grip on the helm of control: A profession is "distinct from other occupations in that it has been given the right to control its own work."[4] With professionals increasingly located in organizations, instead of operating as solo practitioners autonomously related to clients, control becomes an issue of profession versus bureaucratic organization: medical doctors versus non-M.D. hospital administrators, social workers opposed to managers of welfare agencies, scientists and engineers against management in industrial firms, and, notably, teachers under the sway of school administrators.[5] So, too, for academics in higher education organizations: Self-determination within the immediate administrative framework becomes the heart of the matter. In the academic domain, large claims of self-government free from religious and civic officials echo down eight centuries of history, with roots that antedate the modern national state. Those claims reverberate first, in twen-

148

tieth-century America, against walls of campus administration that were constructed in the long evolution of trustee and managerial powers. Even though in Europe questions of academic authority often appear on the national stage, in the United States, with its radical decentralization and extensive institutional differentiation, they are more localized, appearing largely within the individual campus.

In contests over who runs the shop, academic professionals have been greatly bolstered by the rise of "the scientific estate" to great power in society and specifically in universities and colleges.[6] While first trustees and then administrators worked to construct organizations that could be run from the top down, as we have seen, nineteenth-century professors gradually acquired the status of full-time experts whose possession of arcane knowledge and technique insisted on determination from below. Especially in the scientific fields, subjects have steadily become more powerful, equipping their owners with hard-to-penetrate influence.[7] Here is intellectual property worthy of a strong professional class. Bureaucratic enclosures may grow ever stronger, but, by the very nature of their work activities, professionals in academia are uncommonly equipped to contend with hierarchical controls. Although variously distributed, the means of production remain significantly in their hands.

We begin with the essence of academic authority as it is formed within basic operating units, the departments, and with the relations of those units to their formal superiors. We observe much personalism as well as collegiality, an "I" under the "we," and we soon find ourselves in the tangled underbrush of relationships that run rationally—or irrationally—in circles, forming webs that differ from one department to another. Most important, the environments of academic authority change significantly as we examine different reaches of the institutional hierarchy. The further we move from research universities, strongholds of an entreprenurial professionalism, the more we encounter milieus that restrict professional status and privilege, leading inexorably, where state law permits, to unionization. Across the profession, control is fractured into forms that variously keep open the opportunities for fruitful development of academic work. Central is the relative influence of peers, administrators, and stu-

149

dents in determining the what, when, where, and how of academic practice.

THE BASES OF ACADEMIC AUTHORITY

Professional authority in academia begins with the simple fact that academic subjects serve not only as areas of work and sources of dignity and faith, but also as bases of control. Discipline-based authority that favors the faculty stands over against enterprise-based authority, which is largely allocated in the American system to trustees and administrators; it is also contrary to system-based authority, which forms around the interests of politicians and bureaucrats at broad levels of policy and control and of outside groups able to penetrate these circles.[8] Different levels of the higher education system serve as alternative bases of authority. Faculty influence begins at the lowest level, inside the basic operating units.[9] It is essentially bottom-up in its orientation and diffusion.

Since it forms around specific domains of work, faculty authority is essentially guild-like in nature.[10] The persistence of guild imperatives in academia right up to the present time cannot be explained on grounds of tradition and professional inertia alone: Powerful compulsions are more immediate. Virtually all universities and colleges of any stature in the United States have department meetings that operate by a one-person-one-vote procedure, with the head of the unit customarily serving as a temporary "first among equals" who will soon be rotated out of office. At the operating level the whole way of doing things is decidedly antibureaucratic; authority based on formal office in a hierarchy of command is radically diminished. Particularly significant in the denial of bureaucracy is the widespread use of election from "below" rather than appointment by superiors when department heads are selected; or, if selection remains formally in the hands of a central official, extensive consultation with department members to weigh the acceptability of possible appointees is necessary.

Delicate fictions, ambiguous definitions—and patience—are then in order. At one of the country's leading universities, a political scientist explained the process of selection in his own department:

150

We call the leader of the department "the chair," and we believe that we elect him or her. The deans call the department person we call the chair "the executive head" of the department and know that they select him or her. That system has been in place for about twelve years. So far, in that period of time, the deans have never chosen somebody who was not the choice of the department. . . . I guess there's no question if push came to shove, the deans would have the say. [But] we have a nominating ballot that goes out, where every tenured member's name appears. It's one person, one vote, and if one person gets an absolute majority, then he or she is in effect nominated to the dean.

Clear or unclear, precise or imprecise, that is how *they* do it. And each department may do it differently, arranging its own nominating and voting procedures, with the understanding that the administration has the formal power, the department the primary influence. In the English department at the same leading university, a knowledgeable senior professor traced *their* process in terms that quite naturally slid back and forth between election and appointment, trust and lack of trust:

It is a fabulous system. We [in the department] want to be able to choose the chairman. The dean's office doesn't trust departments to elect their own chair. A compromise was worked out, and we vote for chairman. We list our top three candidates in order of preference; but the only people who see the results of that election are the incumbent chairman and the dean. So we never know whether the person who is actually appointed as chairman was the person we chose! It is marvelous, and it is based on trust, and we assume that if there is an overwhelming amount of support for "x" that maybe the chairman will say that to the dean and the dean will act on that—but it might not happen. He may choose "y" for his own reasons, and if he does there is no way we can find that out. But, it is wonderful!

This English professor went on to point out that beyond the balloting and confidential assessment "the dean talks to us individually." Further, one more step in the formal procedures stipulates that "actually the chairman is appointed by the provost." But: "The dean recommends one name to the provost and the provost always accepts that recommendation."

Deans and provosts have enough to do without deliberately stirring up

151

trouble for themselves—all the more reason to give departments free rein when they apparently know what they are doing. The capital of residual power that administrators possess can then be spent on needy cases; officials then may occasionally act like bosses. A professor at a major university put it bluntly: "Strong departments will elect strong chairmen, and weak departments will elect weak chairmen, and the latter simply cannot be allowed to happen." He reminisced that "when I was dean, if I had a department that was in the habit of electing its chairman, I simply wouldn't let it have an election." Universities and colleges nearly always have formal mechanisms whereby they can place weak, declining, or particularly perplexing departments in temporary receivership, usually in the form of a committee of respected professors from elsewhere on campus, even from elsewhere in the country, who take over the key decisions in the operation of the suspect department, or directly advise the administration on what to do.

But short of these ultimate steps, normal ambiguous procedures allow for many hands to enter the equations of decision, virtually overplaying the game of authority, while, at the same time, authority rolls around loosely. Theodore Caplow and Reece J. McGee noted in the 1950s that universities have "a kind of lawlessness, consisting of vague and incomplete rules and ambiguous and uncodified procedures. . . . Being defined loosely, authority is allowed to roll free and is taken into whatever hands are capable of exercising it." The system is one of "loose-lying power."[11] After a quarter of a century, in which much codification has occurred, their observation still has merit. The higher the standing of a university or a college, the more likely it is to avoid the trappings of strict managerialism. Ambiguity is seen as functional, allowing the administration to adapt to the disaggregated, intense professionalism of the faculty, with everyone then praising the dominance of "community" over bureaucracy.

The authority of academic professionals is generally described as collegial. That it is. But under collegial rights and procedures there also is a less-noticed element of sheer personal control. Professors individually supervise the work of students; their judgments are only minimally circumscribed by bureaucratic rules or collegial norms that would foreclose individual discretion. They individually supervise teaching assistants, research assistants, and auxiliary personnel involved in "their" work. Per-

152

sonal rulership is quite strong in advanced research and teaching; it is certainly found in the supervision of the graduate student in dissertation research. The "mentoring" role of one or two people then takes over from the collective responsibility of the department and the institution. And, to a noticeable degree, personal control extends throughout the institutional hierarchy. It was a community college teacher who first called our attention to "maneuvering time," the considerable flexibility discussed in Chapter IV that academics have to shape their scheduling of activities. Administrators simply cannot oversee all the tasks of a teacher, especially at the postsecondary level, no matter how many rules they set down. Throughout the system academic work is in a certain sense impermeable.[12] It virtually demands some personal control. Up the hierarchy, that element of authority is brought front and center.

The problem of dividing authority between departments and the central administration may well be how to creatively fuse professional and bureaucratic alternatives. But within the basic operating unit, the problem is how to balance the personal and the collegial, the rights and powers of the individual against those of the collectivity. A strong tilt toward the personal produces barons—or, in guild terminology, masters who have complete control over journeymen and apprentices in their individual domains. A strong tilt toward the collegial produces a collective stifling of individual initiative—"That's not the way *we* do it"—and hence an irrational constraint on the performances and creations to which that initiative might lead. It is possible to combine the worst of each, a situation that allows the individual to be irresponsible in a personal domain of control and the collectivity to be full of stifling rigidities at a broader level. Senatorial courtesy and some exchange of favors made it possible in some traditional systems in Continental Europe for guild authority to wind down toward sheer protection of privilege; chairholders were able to act autocratically in fiefdoms to the point of unfair and even corrupt behavior, while coming together as a faculty that under one chair-one vote procedures put a collective stamp of approval on autocratic power. Where incremental reforms could not change chair power fast enough in the 1960s and 1970s to reduce its growing incapacity to rule effectively, the situation became all the more ripe for governmental officials to intervene and for junior faculty and students to organize as countervailing forces, all singling out senior professors as the enemies of democracy, rationality, and change.[13] The introduction of departments or their equivalents then became an important avenue of reform.

Through the interpenetration of collegial and bureaucratic checks, the American system of departments has managed to avoid the propensity of academic guilds to slide toward closed monopolies and the protection of arbitrary behavior. Junior faculty are department members in good standing, able to be as obnoxious as senior colleagues in committee discussions and faculty debates. Individual mentors are not left entirely alone to approve student theses; they are observed by other faculty who serve on dissertation committees and on higher review bodies that keep an eye on quality. Students assess faculty, formally and otherwise, and vote with their feet. Dossiers of achievement and assessments, accumulated on each faculty member, are studied when advancements in rank or salary are under consideration. Evaluations of professors are made at multiple levels rather than at just one, that is, in turn, by an intradepartment committee, a department faculty—all of its members or the senior ones, an ad hoc committee of the senate, the academic dean or vice-chancellor of academic affairs, and perhaps the president's cabinet of a half-dozen central officials. Alumni and donors peer in on the behavior of professors, departments, and schools through the windows of support and participation they have crafted or have been allotted. In the relatively open setting of American campuses, it becomes difficult to hide group weaknesses or to throw a veil of secrecy over miscreant behavior.

Thus, so much personal rule is present that we can see it as a compelling necessity. But it is generally more than balanced—in the realistic perspective of cross-national comparison—by the spreading of power among a number of permanent professors in the department *and* by the all-campus surveillance exercised by professional and administrative bodies. In the American system, the guild inclinations of the professoriate essentially become transformed into departmental authority, making the department *the* building block of faculty hegemony, even as it serves as the main operating component of a bureaucratic structure. One of the more curious creations of professionals in organizations, the academic department is much reviled by all those who want to tame the impulses of specialists. But it is so essential to the work, culture, and authority of American academics

154

that it simply grows stronger with each passing decade. It solves many problems in ways congenial to the self-defined interests of academics. National systems that do not have it seem to evolve toward it in order to tame the more narrow inclinations of individual specialists and to bring collegial principles to the fore.

AUTHORITY ENVIRONMENTS

We have already seen that academic institutions are disposed to disperse authority in a highly complicated manner. In such a simple matter as choosing a department head for three years, not only will procedures vary from one department to the next within a university or college, but deliberations will flow formally and informally in circles over two or three or four levels of organization, only to drag out for many months. Those who have formal rights to make decisions consult extensively with those who have the right to be consulted. Often the making of a decision takes a show of hands or the passing of a ballot. Many persons within a department, and sometimes outside of it, are normally entitled to be involved. Otherwise, they deem collegiality an empty shell and go about its restoration.

Department members also use collective pressure to correct "mistakes." It happened when a business department in a second-tier university sought to force out a head who did not fit: "We had one individual that we recruited [as head], and after eight months the faculty rose up in arms and put enough pressure on the powers-that-be that the individual finally decided that it was best to move on. His human relations were rather Neanderthal."

At the same time, the simplest imperatives of unity and hierarchy dictate some institutionally rooted authority in which central officials participate, generally to consult, negotiate, persuade, and ratify, but sometimes to resolve and even dictate. Accommodation among interests then depends either on general understandings and ground rules accepted by all relevant groups or on the legitimated capacity of one to rule the others. Those general frames—"authority environments"—are set most powerfully in the American context by type of institution.[14] As we explore issues of control up and down the institutional hierarchy, we encounter different official structures that blend with the professional authority of academics to produce fundamentally different political settings.

The Authority Environments of Institutions

Again the extremes are most instructive. The picture at the top in complex research universities is clear. A political scientist explained:

> On the things that count to the faculty, the faculty have a lot of power. The appointments and promotions process is almost entirely within the faculty's hands. . . . The Board of Trustees gets into the process at a point where everything is all settled. If they have ever overturned a decision, I don't know about it in twenty years. Even the provost very seldom overturns the committee decisions. . . . The faculty has an enormous amount to say. They do over curriculum in general. The academic senate committees, on several of which I serve, I think really control the curriculum pretty much totally.

Whether in hiring and reviewing junior faculty, deciding on promotion to tenure and advancement within the senior ranks, changing course offerings and curricular requirements, deciding who will teach which courses, allocating space within departments, or appointing teaching assistants and research assistants, the top academic professionals have, and know they have, decisive roles. They control much decision making at divisional and all-campus levels by means of committees—formally a part of the academic senate or the administration—on which they serve. A biologist at a second-tier university summarized well the picture painted by university respondents:

> The wise thing about this whole university is [its] administration. Authority is delegated down to the people who really have to live with the results of the decision. As a consequence, the faculty doesn't feel that it is being put upon; we feel that we made the decision we have to live with, and it is really very successful.

Such ideas and devices as rank-and-file "participation" and "quality circles," which American business firms have explored in the 1970s and 1980s to increase production by spreading responsibility and decision making,

156

have been operative in universities and colleges for a long time. Department by department, professors look at alternative technologies and decide what is best for their needs. Collectively, they decide on production and distribution, and on whether to innovate or continue with the old. A real gain is then found in a reduced need for the elaborate information systems that are necessary for centralized decision making. Universities can be very lean at the middle and higher levels of formal control over *academic* affairs, leaving the flowering of white-collar bureaucracy largely on the side of "business" affairs—finance, purchasing, accounting, property management, transportation—and such operations as "student personnel services." Compared to the control structures historically modeled by firms and public bureaus, with their top-heavy inclinations, the American university is a bottom-heavy organization par excellence.

Also prominent in institutions of considerable stature is the collegial capture of administrative posts, stretching from the department headship (it is nearly always more of a voice for the collegial group than it is for "management") to the positions of dean, provost, vice-chancellor or vice-president for academic affairs, and chancellor or president. These posts are ordinarily awarded to academics, generally to those from within the ranks who are trusted by their colleagues. One of "us" becomes one of "them." The we/they schism between faculty and administration is then lessened; a division of labor between faculty and administrators is given greater legitimacy; and, critically, in the eyes of professors they are then freed of the burdens of administration and can go about their teaching and research. Professors who turn out to be particularly competent in administration— and even "like that sort of thing"—tend to rise as they are tested in posts at successively higher levels. They may also come back to the campus as the respected scholars who have been off for a few years running a major office in a government agency, professional association, or business firm. Such administrators typically start out with a capital of faculty goodwill; they are intimately familiar with the rights and rituals of personal and collegial controls within faculty rank; and they have shown a capacity to cope with these particular demons.

When we asked a professor of English at a major research university, "Do faculty here have an appropriate amount of power in terms of running the institution?" he drew a picture of a few academics who advance by choice into key administrative posts while the faculty members in general voluntarily withdrew from administration to bear down even more than in the past on the tasks of research and teaching:

> Gosh, that is an interesting question. At one point I would have said, "No." They should have more power, but I am not so sure anymore. I tend to think that they have about as much as they deserve, and the faculty as a whole tend not to exercise the power that they have, which is to say that they don't participate much in college meetings and things of that sort. They don't put much into an effort to use such channels as are available to influence or shape policy at the university. They do, to some extent, through things like the senate assembly and various committees and so on, where they exercise a certain amount of control and do have an input. . . . The history of this institution is that the faculty who want more power than they have, or who deserve more power than they have, tend to move into deanships and vice-presidencies and presidencies. All our major officers . . . are faculty members from this institution who got more involved in administrative work and found they were very good at it and were interested in it more and more and now really run the show.
>
> [Meanwhile,] a lot of people here are much caught up in the need to keep their noses to the grindstone and apply themselves assiduously if they are going to get ahead professionally, and here that means cultivating your scholarly prestige. . . . The natural tendency, I think, is to say I can't be bothered with a lot of time on faculty committees or parliamentary procedures and college meetings and that sort of thing. . . . You really don't care that much about it. What I really need to do is get my book out. . . .

In short, what the university professors report is an accommodation between profession and organization they find congenial. Ideally, they would like to have fuller control; they complain everywhere that there are too many administrators and take critical note of the year-by-year increase in bureaucratic rules; they might even prefer that the trustees go away. But the influence they possess is more than acceptable: They have better things to do than to diffuse their efforts among budgeting, student registration, parking regulations, and the like. A well-tutored, loyal band of trustees can keep the resources flowing; the well-infiltrated administration can talk

158

things up, present to outsiders an image of unitary accountability, and do the myriad things that need doing in a mammoth, complex organization. Professors may then differentially serve on a few committees while concentrating evermore on what they most want to do. The autonomy to exercise personal and collegial control at the department level in the major research universities provides a solid foundation for extending faculty influence up the line. The sway of professional authority is largely as the faculty realistically want it. In these terms we can understand why trustees and administrators do not dictate what will be done in so many areas of decision, despite their ultimate formal powers and steady growth of tools and procedures available for top-down surveillance and supervision.

But, at the other end of the institutional hierarchy the authority environment could hardly be more different. Collegial control is substantially diminished; the bureaucratic framework is much more prominent. This pattern was sharply etched in a community college that was part of a larger community college district. We asked: "How are new faculty chosen for the department?" A professor of biology answered:

> Well, the procedure is rather strict. First, you have to go through the district personnel office. Now, people who want to teach anywhere in the district have to put in an application to the central office. Then, when we have an opening, we have to go to the downtown office and sift through the files, and then we can call five or six people to be interviewed at that time, and we interview them together with the dean of instruction. We choose three and give them priority rankings, and then that has to go to the president of the college for approval.
>
> (*Who has the most influence in those decisions?*) I would say the chairman of the department would have the most influence. (*What's the length of the chairman's term?*) In this department there's only been two chairmen since the founding of the college. I think that was back in 1938 or so . . . (laughter) . . . well over twenty-five years. . . . (*Within the department, how are the hiring decisions made or debated?*) The chairman and two other members of the department compose a hiring committee that goes to the downtown office and also goes to the interviews.
>
> (*What about curricular decisions, how are they made?*) Those are also centralized. One campus cannot offer a course that's not in the catalogue, and in order to get into the catalogue it has to be

159

. . . okayed by other departments of other campuses in the district and also some downtown people. It's very difficult to alter the curriculum in this district. . . . The difficulty of actually putting it through is so daunting that very few new courses ever get introduced.

In this context, centralized bureaucratic procedures abound. For faculty hiring, a district personnel office receives written applications and puts them on file. A department or college that has an opening it wants to fill has to go to the central headquarters and work from the applications that are on record. The imprint is that of school administration: The colleges operate in a fashion similar to elementary and secondary schools, while differing qualitatively from the procedures of universities and most four-year colleges.

Reforms in this type of authority environment commonly involve the replacement of one bureaucratic procedure with another:

When I came in . . . we had a "vertical" system in hiring, where you had to take an examination scored high enough [that got you] a personal interview. Then you were ranked on a basis of one through ten. If any positions opened on any of the . . . campuses, then the first five [candidates] had to have an opportunity to be interviewed on that campus. Now that system was replaced about thirteen years ago with a so-called horizontal system. I think this is partly in response to affirmative action attempts to give minorities a greater voice. . . . What happened was that people who got master's degrees, or otherwise met requirements for the field, filled out applications. These applications were then placed in a central file downtown [and so on, as described in the previous interview above]. Obviously, people who had previously taught on a part-time basis in the discipline were considered by a local campus. Often, people who wanted to transfer [within the district] when they got wind of the opening would make themselves available, and the [union] contract said that these people had to be interviewed because they were within the district.

The respondent went on to specify intradepartment procedures around what "the contract now says." He added, "I think that's generally the way it is. I can verify that by showing you the contract." Collective-bargaining

160

agreements add bureaucratic detail as they seek to specify procedures and rights.

Other community colleges, less bureaucratic in detail, show a similar pattern of managerialism: They give more power to administrators and trustees, and, in public institutions, to higher public officials. In the smallest and best-managed community college we visited, state law even prohibited tenure. When asked about faculty power, a professor replied, "The bottom line is that we don't have any. We're an advisory group. It's time that the administrators here listen to us. . . . The bottom line is, it's their decision." The president concurred: He and other key administrators carefully consulted with faculty members, he reported, but the power to decide rested in their own hands.

As size increases, the hierarchy of control stretches. In a larger public community college: "As we get bigger, you get compartmentalized. You get a bigger hierarchy, more levels of supervision; and we also have the fact that you have to deal with the county government." The close relationship to a branch of government extended the cloak of ambiguity placed over decision making at levels removed from the faculty: "You can use it, you know. If you don't want to give an answer you can say that you have to check back with the county. I worked somewhere else where the answer was you have to call Albany on that one." As buck-passing becomes routine, faculty are more likely to become resentful and inclined to pursue unionization alternatives in order to nail down some rights in contracts and to specify formal procedures that will take place in the sunlight.

Interviews in institutions situated between the extremes of research universities and community colleges demonstrated that as one moves up the status hierarchy, one encounters more professional control, and as one moves down, one observes more administrative dominance and even autocracy. In the best private liberal arts colleges, as in the research universities, a bargain has been struck in which the faculty feel reasonably comfortable with their portion of "shared authority." They are clearly "scholars"—an important base for professional claims—not mere "teachers," a definition that would downgrade them toward the status of organizational employees. They work in institutions esteemed for excellent liberal education—or what remains of it in an age of increasing specialization—with strong tradition coloring the setting. Small size helps to give

161

the college faculty a cohesive sense not obtainable in large universities. Personal relations between administrators and faculty are often close. The small departments may have less power than their large counterparts in the universities, but the faculty can cohesively assert itself, and the administrators cannot buck-pass in a labyrinth of offices nor hide in remote corners.

Not everything is sweetness-and-light, with easy collegiality leading to rapid decision. When discussion swirls around a tenure decision, for example, both faculty and administrators often become irate: Deliberations may be slow and time-consuming; those who cannot make up their minds back and fill; those who begin with closed minds can exercise their sheer stubbornness; those who enjoy campus politics can put their wiles to work. One social scientist outlined some of the cumbersome details of participation in promotion and tenure decisions in a leading liberal arts college where a key faculty committee was elected by the faculty:

> The process begins with the departments. The department makes a recommendation or does not make a recommendation. That goes to an elected faculty committee, and I think that is a very bad idea but there it is. And you can imagine the politics that swirl around that. People get elected to that committee, I would argue, because they are perceived as being permissive in the matter of tenure. . . . The committee says yes. When there's been a positive department recommendation [and] a positive committee recommendation, it is very difficult for the administration to do anything except acquiesce, even if it wanted to.
>
> When you get a split recommendation, when you get a recommendation where the department says no and the person says "I want to put my own case before the faculty committee," the individual goes and puts his case before them and the faculty committee recommends tenure. The president then looks at the department recommendation and the committee recommendation and overrules the faculty committee. Or it has worked the other way, where the department has recommended [yes] and the faculty committee has said no and the administration has said, "Tough decision, close but. . . ." There is, by the way, no governing board involvement . . . it's the faculty and the president and the dean of faculty that are really actors in this.

162

A colleague in the humanities in the same college concurred in this picture of the overall allocation of influence. With respect to tenure, he said, "That's a faculty decision right up to the final stage when it goes to the administration. . . . By the time it gets there, it really, basically, has [become] a faculty decision."

When asked, "In general, do faculty feel pretty content with their say in what goes on?" the social science respondent above displayed the same willingness to have a role for administrators that we noted as widespread in the research universities. The faculty has enough power and a sufficient sense of authority to admit openly to the importance of administrative intervention and power to occasionally overrule:

> I think so . . . it always depends. In any faculty there are winners and losers. And the guys who are winning at a particular time, they don't have any problem at all, and the guys who aren't winning, well—but there is a lot of faculty governance around here. We have *too* much faculty governance at this place! It has taken too much time with too many people. You will get no complaints from me about tyrannizing by the central administration. I wish they would tyrannize a little more.

A natural scientist at the same college joined the refrain of mixed feelings with the often-heard view that faculty members "who would like to spend all of their time running the college" do not have anything better to do. They can be seen as campus politicians, even as "street people" who spend their time gossiping in the hallways:

> What I do know is that the faculty who are most engaged by college governance are the people whose intelligence and opinions I respect the least. They are people with time on their hands very often because they are not doing anything else, so, I don't know, I have mixed feelings. I think we have a reasonably competent administration and for the most part I am happy to let them go ahead and do it, with occasionally keeping an eye on them or harassing them when necessary. I guess I think the faculty is certainly as involved as it needs to be.

The environment of authority in a leading liberal arts college can also appear exceedingly attractive to an academic when he or she knows about

163

the situation in small colleges not so blessed with tradition, resources, and status, where administrator "harassment" can be "Mickey Mouse." Noted a younger professor:

> My parents teach at a small liberal arts college and I'm very much aware that in contrast to many places the faculty here have a great deal of freedom, let's call it; it's not power but freedom. That is, nobody makes you defend your—. You want something Xeroxed? You go Xerox it; nobody asks you why. You want some pencils, take them. . . . There's none of this Mickey Mouse stuff. Nobody calls you in your office to see if you're there. My mother's had that experience. Nobody reprimands you at the faculty meeting because you did this or that, and that's what I mean. There's a very professional atmosphere."

Having unquestioned access to the Xerox machine and the supply cabinet containing pens and pencils may seem trivial to professors in major universities, but for many others such items are a tangible part of the difference between the liberties of "a very professional atmosphere" and one made petty by detailed administrative regulations.

As we shift from the first-rank liberal arts colleges to those of lesser status, the authority environment generally stiffens, making it more difficult to reconcile the contradictions of professional and organizational controls. Faculty members complain more about powerlessness in the face of a remote "it":

> I think that the faculty probably feels a certain amount of powerlessness. The faculty would probably think that the administration has a vast superstructure which doesn't work as hard as we do. It is not even geographically in the same place we are; it is somewhere else on campus doing God-knows-what and it has ultimate authority over our lives. It does all of this like the Wizard of Oz behind a screen and is kind of faceless. I think that is how the faculty regards the administration. . . . [But] it is not total abject powerlessness . . . because it [the faculty-administration relationship] is unionized and everything is done under contract.

164

Thus, even in a relatively small college with a student enrollment of 3,000 the faculty can perceive a substantial hierarchy rearing above them. A second professor remarked:

> Well, you've got . . . the board of trustees and then the president[and] four vice-presidents who report to the president. Under the vice-presidents are various administrative units that they are responsible for, and so, you know, it just reports back up or decisions flow down. And then there are various faculty committees that various administrative officials serve on for advisory purposes. Its a wonderful schematic organizational make-up . . . but I don't think that this facilitates clear understanding of concerns of the various operating units.

Power slides from the collegial group in many ways. For one, the chairmanship becomes a more powerful post, with the incumbent "appointed by the deans and the president of the college" for an indefinite term. Where "the chairman has been chairman since 1966," his own authority is likely to have "the most influence in the hiring and firing of junior faculty." He or she may be a peer but is "more 'peerful' than the others. It doesn't hurt to be friendly to him or her because, after all, he or she is going to make up the list of classes." Also, primacy in tenure and promotion decisions moves out of the department and up the line: "Recommendations are sent from here and appropriate supporting documents, but then the decision lies outside the department in the hands of the committee [an appointed faculty review committee] and the president and the deans." In turn, the faculty committees are seen primarily as advisory to the top officials:

> Most of our committees, it seems to me, are advisory committees. . . . They're doomed to a slow death because you know that even if you talk about something endlessly and come up with your "advice," the academic vice-president or the president can simply do what they wish in the long run. It's nice to have gone through that process and, typically, they do listen to you because they want to keep things mellow, but. . . .

165

The upward shift of authority may then mean either control by a few at the top or at least a strong faculty feeling that "every decision of any moment on this campus is made by two people, and a third in conjunction with one [of the first two]." Requests from central offices may be resented as heavy-handed and inappropriate:

> Would you believe we get a letter every year from the development office asking how much we are going to contribute to the college? Something like 30 percent [of the faculty] contribute enormous amounts. I find that astonishing. I tell them that I contribute every time I come to work. I am sure that is not a popular response. . . .

The public comprehensive colleges also exhibit authority environments in which faculty members are uncomfortable with their lack of self-determination. With respect to hiring decisions, autocracy within departments may be much in evidence:

> All real decisions are made by the chairman. We have the same political situation that the state has; we have the strong governor system. The chairman may make any and all decisions without any further ado from anybody else. In other words, the chairman makes all decisions on promotion, retention, tenure, merit pay, travel money, hiring, you name it, and there is an obligation to consult with the faculty, but there is no obligation to pay any attention to the consultation. . . . It's completely what the chairman says, period. There is no committee that looks at merit raises; there is no hiring committee; there is no tenure committee; there is no whatever. I call it the whispering-in-the-ear method. When it's time for promotion or tenure. we all go whisper in the ear [of the chairman]. . . . That's built into the administrative situation and I don't think it is a wonderful idea. It's not very collegial.

The resulting bitterness is palpable: (*Who would you say then has the most influence on the chairman?*) "Whoever his or her particular friends, cronies, and intimates are." (*How is the chairman selected?*) "We whisper in the dean's ear and then the dean can appoint anybody, including his pet dog, so we have the same deal."

166

Their historic involvement in teacher education also gives many state colleges special problems in sharing authority calmly among faculty as well as between faculty and administration. Their evolution from teachers college to state college gives them for a time an old guard of "educationalists" and a newer faculty of people in letters and science departments, a split that is extended into questions of who staffs and controls the central administration and who has the votes in faculty councils. The annoyance of letters and science professors with professors of education can be found on virtually every campus with a department or school of education; but a relatively permissive attitude of live-and-let-live can abate potential conflict at institutions where education is a minor segment and letters and science tribal leaders feel they are the heart of the institution. The annoyance is much greater when the "disciplinarians" feel they have to wrestle control away from those in education who traditionally were dominant. The old pattern meant that the dean, the academic vice-president, and the president, if chosen from within the institution—a likely practice—came from the department or school of education. Then: "Some of those old establishment folk are still very much around," with professors in the basic disciplines feeling they have to battle hard to dislodge persons who are not capable of intellectual leadership: "The guy was in control here, a very nice man, but an Ed.D.—education establishment—not a hard-nosed academician. . . . He wasn't the sort of person who was going to bring this place to what I hoped it was going to become when I came here in [the early 1960s] with this great commitment for educating the people, the first-generation college students, that are our student body." Accusations still flowed freely in 1964 in this college about arbitrary decisions made ten years before: "He appointed [the dean] unilaterally with board approval and that was it." Pointing to a fellow professor who until recently had been "in the inner sanctum of the education establishment that runs [the college]," a professor in the humanities went on to explode about the college of education: "[He] is now a professor in the foundations of education, whatever the hell they do over there, and that mishmash that goes in all directions, people without disciplines, six characters in search of an author, twelve characters in search of a discipline!" He saw the educationalist old-timers as still "very much a presence here," chairing major committees and making major decisions. They had "seriously hurt this college" by, for

167

example, spawning departments out of the old department of education: "There were people who started that psychology department who were 'ed psych' [educational psychology] people without even Ed.D.'s, and they ended up in there, and they did the 'touchy feelies' during the late sixties and early seventies, and some of them are probably still doing it."

In short, when state-college respondents said to us, "It is a state college, you know," they were referring not to state support and surveillance alone, but to a wide range of internal and intimate issues of control. The imagery meant that "the administration is more dominant," that "the dean or vice-president is probably looked at with more seriousness or fear." It meant in many cases that the chairman dominates other department members. And it sometimes meant that a teachers college legacy still influenced both the distribution of influence among departments and the administrative style of the campus as a whole.

The evolution of such colleges away from a comprehensive college form and toward the promised land of university status, we noted in earlier chapters, has many faculty impulses behind it. High among them is the sense that transformation promises more self-determination. For faculty, it is a deeply professionalizing transition. But the change can readily stall short of full-university standing: Established universities that already occupy the high ground offer resistance, and states attempt to hold the line in a master-plan division of rights and responsibilities among sectors.

The Disciplinary Shaping of Authority

Different disciplines also offer somewhat different authority environments. Their knowledge contents cannot help but shape how departments operate internally, how they relate to other departments, and how they expose themselves to higher-level commands. Departments that operate with well-developed, accepted bodies of knowledge can arrive at a consensus more readily than those confused by ambiguous materials and conflicting perspectives. Decisions on the selection and retention of faculty are more easily made when all members of the department, or a major specialty within it, perceive quality in similar terms of theoretical grasp and methodological competence. A university physicist explained:

I think there's a consensus. I think we know how to recognize it—[high quality work]. Maybe not because we ourselves understand the work, but we do know how to find out. [In] some specialized fields where we don't have anybody actually working, we might have some questions about whether something was as valuable as somebody said it was. It's not hard to find out. If the information doesn't exist within the department, it does exist in the field as a whole. Mistakes on those things happen, but they don't tend to last long.

In contrast, in departments where the knowledge base is vague, disagreement is more likely to prevail: Academics with different understandings of the field fight over courses and appointments. The levels of predictability are different: "University professors in a given scientific field must operate at the level of predictability permitted by the structure of knowledge within the field. Social scientists operate in a much less predictable and therefore more anxious environment than physical scientists."[15] Hence it is not true in the authority structure of a university or college that a department is a department is a department. Attempts to impose the same standards for all departments dictate a uniformity inconsistent with the particular subject matter requirements of specific areas.[16] Substantive differences alone will affect how departments relate to higher levels of organization.

Departments also vary in prestige according to the stature of the disciplines they represent: A department of physics routinely has a much more powerful base of influence than a speech department. And the standing of a department within its own field matters: Those of first rank have a heightened base of acceptance, but those that are undistinguished leave themselves open to the intrusive attention of professors in other departments as well as to deliberate intervention by the administration. The snowballing of influence may be virtuous or vicious: A high-rated department in a prestigious discipline has doubly powerful grounds for autonomous decision making. We asked a professor of physics in a leading research university whether certain departments were more powerful than others:

Oh, yes, chemistry, for a start. . . . They are the strongest and best science department. . . . Their people become administrators. In that sense, you might call them the rulers. (*So from where does their power rise?*) Well, they must have had good quality for a long time. . . . They have produced a number of successful people. . . . They just got stronger over the years. They are pretty highly rated. And they have got some first-rate people. That's just all there is to it. And everybody knows it.

In contrast, a low rated department in a subject lacking prestige is likely to exist on the margin of trust and power, given access only to crumbs left at the far end of the table.

The phenomenon of "the more, the more," in which the powerful become more powerful, occurs also within departments as well as among them. A physicist explained that the powerful have the votes:

(*Who has the most influence in the department around the selection of new tenure-track faculty?*) The group with the largest number of professors. So, I would say solid state experimentalists, and, secondly, the nuclear experimental group, because they have the numbers. (*And they use their numbers to increase their numbers, essentially?*) Yes! And they proceed. When they have a retirement, they perceive that their hallowed strength will be decreasing, and, "Well, we just can't let that happen," and then they get two great candidates and they say, "Well, let's just hire both of them." It's the standard old trick. Whereas [for] the small groups, they say, "Well, you're doing fine—why do you need to get larger?"

Among fields of study, the most extensive differences in authority environments that we observed occur between the "pure" and the "applied," most noticeably between letters and science departments and medical schools. Professional schools have to be somewhat practical; they can hardly ignore the outside profession of which they are a part. As they attempt to bridge to practice, they are likely to become engaged in myriad business details. They are likely to be managerial, with a more hierarchically arranged officialdom. This is especially true in medical schools, where patient care is absorbed in day-to-day operations. Our interviews in med-

170

ical school departments made clear that we were in the presence of a big business. Any questions about how medical school departments were run elicited long answers full of details on "billing and collecting," "budgeting, accounting, and statistical reporting," "fringe benefit management," and coordination on such items as "the clinical contract and medical malpractice." A medical school administrator explained:

> We do the billing and collecting. We do the fringe benefit administration. We do the budgeting and accounting and statistical reporting. Also, we act as liaison with the hospital on certain joint operations, such as the contract for the use of the outpatient clinic, which they staff in their building and we use. So we pay a fee for that, and I'm assisting the negotiations on that and act as liaison for the faculty with the self-insurance program for medical malpractice. Thirdly, on special joint projects, such as if we were to do an HMO [health maintenance organization arrangement] with the hospital, I would be involved with that.

With so much business going on, and so much money involved, formal rules and regulations become much more important than in letters and science units:

> Our by-laws are included in Appendix A of something called "the Rules, Policies, and Procedures of the Division of Health Affairs of the University. . . . Appendix A of that [document] specifically defines the medical faculty practice plan. That indicates how we can spend the money, how we have to budget the income. It spells out the role of the dean in managing the practice plan; it spells out my relationship to the dean; it spells out the fact that we have an advisory committee with people appointed by the dean upon recommendation by the individual department chairs, with one representative per department. Keep in mind that these are clinical departments. The basic science departments [within the medical school] are not represented. . . . The practice plan *is* the doctors. The doctors comprise the practice plan and the . . . administrative office works for the physicians in effect. The function of the practice plan as a whole is just a method of delivering care and billing for service or capitation. . . .

171

Salaries vary across clinical departments, since money comes in according to type and amount of service provided in the hospital part of the medical school: "The pediatricians would tend to generate less money than the neurosurgeons, for example. So there would be less money to put into salaries. That would force an alignment with the national market for academic physicians." And how to divide patient care income is an important, complex matter filled with estimates of overheads and clinical costs and appropriate portions to the medical school as a whole:

> There's a formula that determines how much goes to the medical school trust fund, to be used by the dean for development. The residual of all that goes back to the chair [of the department], and the chair really controls most of that money. (*Can I ask you what percent the dean gets?*) Seven and one-half percent. After the expenses of the administrative office are paid and after the expenses of the clinic operation are paid. . . . (*What is the average overhead?*) About 19 percent for the dean and the administrative office combined. It varies in the clinic, and I don't really have a percentage number for the clinic cost. (*Would it be another 10 or 15?*) Yes. I'd have to calculate that; I just don't have that figure.

In some circumstances, as above, departments get the major share of income they "earn" and then pay their physicians. In others, departments get back a much smaller percentage, for instance, 5 percent, after payment to the academic doctors. But in either case the resource base adds substantially to the authority of headships. Respondents told us that "the department chairs have a substantial amount of say-so over salaries," that there is "substantial flexibility in spending patient income on the part of the chairs." The chair prepares and recommends next year's budget. Once it is approved, then he or she has the authority to spend accordingly, aided by "budget revision mechanisms" that allow income to be diverted from one line item to another during the year. The power of the department head is also enhanced by appointment from above rather than by election by colleagues, and, in many instances, for a long and even indefinite term rather than for the three-year rotation period that has become common in letters and science departments. That power spreads to personnel decisions—from the decisions on areas of specialization for which faculty members will be hired and retained to the individuals actually appointed: "There is discussion [not a formal vote] within the department on the area. Ultimately, the decision is made by the department chairman," and "the recruitment committee decides upon the individuals to invite. The chairman has a big say in which of those individuals will actually be appointed."

When the interviewer exclaimed, "So that's a lot of power," a respondent drew the large picture:

> That is a fundamental difference between medical school departments and departments in nonmedical schools [the rest of the university!]. Traditionally, medical school chairmen have much more power than the chairmen of other departments. (*Even in basic science departments?*) Oh yeah! Our department chairman listens to advice but then makes decisions. I think you could argue that if he started making a lot of decisions that were really unpopular that eventually he would be booted out.

We can conclude that when big money and applied professional practice enter academic units, collegial control diminishes and the power of headships increases. We then see more academic barons as well as more non-academic administrators. Sometimes the head in question is a professor in charge of major research projects and one or more clinics; sometimes it is the head of a department or the dean of the school. In each case, individual power of the chief is increased by the large scale of the resources for which he or she is responsible, together with the control of administrative staff and methods that come with the use of those resources. Thus, to the extent that professional schools move toward the postures of scholarship of the letters and science departments, they tend to evolve the traditional authority environments that characterize those departments. But to the extent they move toward applied work in their own professional field, they move toward nontraditional environments more characteristic of the outside world. Patient care in the medical school is the revealing extreme case, one attended by all the major problems of complex hospital administration.

In the face of those problems the collegial controls of faculty guilds are hardly sufficient. What is added is professional bureaucracy, a managerialism that endows certain professionals with substantial positional authority over other professionals. Headships in letters and science departments may be jobs to be avoided, roles taken on promise of only short terms in

173

office and even finally given away to the good-hearted colleagues who can be prevailed upon to take them. But headships in medical schools and in other professional schools to a lesser degree—are something else. Possessing more authority, they are more serious roles that attract candidates because power is there for the taking. In the structuring of authority as in the arranging of work, "clinical" tasks are different from "academic" endeavors.

However, the differences among fields of study in the authority environments of academics are not as large as the ones we found as we moved up and down the institutional hierarchy. Differences within universities are *continuous* across a wide spectrum of fields: There is some general common understanding of faculty rights and privileges vis-à-vis central administrators and trustees. A similar situation prevails within second-level liberal arts colleges or state colleges or community colleges. The authority environments are more discontinuous across types of institutions: arrangements in the lesser four-year colleges and especially in the community colleges differ qualitatively from those of leading universities. At the extreme of the two-year institution, the local district framework, with its genetic imprint of school trusteeship and administration, makes institutional controls much more powerful than disciplinary influences. Whether academics are in English or physics or business administration has little effect. What matters most in determining their authority is that they are in a community college.

THE UNIONIZATION RESPONSE

It is not difficult to understand why the top of the American academic hierarchy should be vigorously resistant to unionization and the bottom quite vulnerable to it. Aware of their independence and influence, powerfully positioned professors sense they do not need unions. Feeling overpowered by administrators and others, weakly positioned professors sense they do. In roles that are purportedly professional in nature, a sense of self-control stands at the very heart of professionalism. Reversing Lord Acton's famous dictum that power tends to corrupt, and absolute power corrupts absolutely, we observe that, for academics, powerlessness tends to

174

corrupt the sense that one is fully professional, and absolute powerlessness corrupts that sense absolutely. Such corrosion will bring a response.

The attitude at the top was emphatically expressed by a university scientist:

> (*Why do you think there's never been a union [at this university]?*) I don't know. Do you mean a professors' union? (*Yes.*) Professors would hate it. (*Why?*) Because it is an elitist thing to be a professor. You don't really want the kind of decision making that's done by a union. You want to be in a position to say that we don't want this guy because he's not one of the best three people in the field. We don't want somebody telling us that this man has paid his union dues. It's not that kind of thing.

Here, a union would be decidedly unwelcome. Individually and collectively, the faculty feel reasonably secure in relation to administrators and trustees; they are not particularly subject to arbitrary decisions from on high. Such harsh actions as denial of tenure for young faculty come more from peers than from presidents. The situation does not lead to a deep sense of "us" against "them." Tensions with administrators can be handled directly by individuals, or department representatives, or the academic senate and its many committees. Another tool of collective representation is hardly needed, especially if it might come to stress seniority over merit and establish more uniformity by insisting on more rules and regulations.

But the sense of needing a union changes when the individual authority environment is seen as threatening to individual and collective faculty interests. A community college instructor explained:

> If something is going wrong, and someone is coming down on you, and you don't think it is fair, or you want to find out, the union is very supportive and gets good action. I think we all feel it has a place for us, it helps us, it works well in that one against the administration doesn't work, [but] maybe three hundred against the administration speaks a bit louder, and you have someone on your shoulder who can just help you. I think that is the general sentiment.

The feeling that someone may unfairly "come down on you" and that "one against the administration doesn't work" is part of a larger sense—as put by another community college teacher—that "the administration runs the college," with the faculty senate, if one exists, working faithfully "within the range, the limits, that the administration sets up." Then the advantages of unions are taken to outweigh their bad points: "I am not terribly fond of unions. . . . [But] the people that I know [feel] basically that the union is working hard for us and they have gotten us some good things."

The authority environments of many community colleges can cause faculty sentiments to readily harden into a straight management-worker conception drawn from the business world. A professor who had taught in a community college for over twenty-five years saw it that way:

> There has always and forever been an antagonistic relationship between bosses and employees. There has to be. They want to pay as little as possible and make it last as long as possible, and we want to get paid more right now. Management wants to put more back into business so it can expand the business in some kind of future. The present employee wants to have more of the money put into his salary regardless of research and development funds. . . . So there is always and forever antagonism between management and staff.

At the same time, this professor had also been a member of the faculty union for that same long period of time and was not very happy with it and its results:

> (*How has the union affected your working conditions?*) I don't know. I think probably positively but certainly not as much as I would like. I don't know how much worse things would be. I know generally the people who belong to [the union] are people I don't like very much, and whether that makes the union more powerful I don't know. They just brought to us a three and one-half percent raise after three years so at the moment I think I will rejoin the teamsters!

And at the same community college, a physical science professor expressed a continuing discomfort: "Nobody in this department is a member of the

176

union. . . . It somehow doesn't seem to fit. I view myself as a physicist, as a teacher, a professional. . . . We are not the union member types."

When another community college instructor was pressed on why a union was necessary, on "what is it about a community college that requires a union?" he framed the big picture in these words:

> Why does any union take root in any academic area? And the answer to that is because there's been abuses over a long period of time, exploitation of people who are in the profession in one way or another, whether through low wages or little or no fringe benefits, bad working conditions, or some combination of all of those and others that I haven't mentioned. . . . Maybe it's not necessary at this time on a four-year level [or] at a university, I don't know. Maybe one finds oneself satisfied with whatever conditions that exist there and there's no need for organizing collectively against the administration and what they do. But certainly on the community college level, particularly in [this city] where community colleges were part of the K-through-12 system until 1969, and administrators were used to treating instructors as inferiors in many ways. . . . It doesn't seem to be quite the thing to do, if one speaks of collegiality and that sort of thing; but I think collegiality is a two-way street, and it rarely exists, unless on a patronizing basis. . . .

When the authority environments of four-year colleges tilt toward "one-way collegiality," their professors often agree with these two-year college sentiments, but with even more regret and more backing and filling. Beyond the public community college, the public comprehensive college has been the sector most vulnerable to the unionization drive. In one, professors in English, biology, and political science in turn told us:

> I am not sure that I approve of unions. . . . Although I can understand why a union. We are being driven to taking things into our own hands. We are being driven to make militant expressions, but I'm not sure I approve of it. . . . I don't know how often we can be dumped on, you know. We've shown every capacity to take every amount of dumping that anybody can think of without opening our mouths and showing teeth. I don't know how long this will continue.

The second professor indicated that he was a union member, but that "I may be dropping out. I have not been an active member, and [I] don't feel a strong commitment towards it." All the same, the union has been "a good counterforce on occasion to the administration. That is why I joined in the first place. Still, I don't have a union mentality." And with recent improvements in the attitudes of administrators and in campus procedures for decision making, "I am not convinced right now that we need a union, and I greatly fear the consequences of there being organized bargaining procedures for salaries."

The third professor had become staunchly pro-union, prepared to argue that "the union has had an incredibly positive impact on this campus":

> On campus, the union is by far the most active faculty group working toward the improvement of working conditions. The union has been instrumental—now obviously the administration has to be responsive—in putting lighter summer teaching loads on the agenda and getting them, more flexibility in terms of sabbatical leaves, higher promotion raises. A number of very concrete things.

But then he noted how the union had begun to dominate the faculty committee system of the campus: "The union does tend to control university-wide elections. The business college has, as a consequence, not been represented on the budget committee for a few years."

At a second public college we heard a similar refrain voiced by faculty about why a union had come about, with regrets that the collegial had not been sufficiently strong to forestall a turn to the adversarial:

> I am committed to a collegial rather than adversarial relationship between administrators and faculty, but at state colleges very clearly, at least on the Eastern Seaboard and [in] California and the Midwest, the collegial model has clearly declined. . . .

And, from another professor:

> I shudder to think what it would be like if we didn't have the union, given the kinds of situations, or the kind of mentality, to be specific. . . . By mentality I mean the mentality of the admin-

istration. . . . If we did not have a union, things could be much worse.

At a third state college, the faculty were mad at the trustees as well as annoyed with the administrators. Again, deep regrets were expressed:

> (*Is unionization then a necessary evil?*) I don't think it is necessary. I think it is evil. I think there is no call for it if we had the kind of faculty governance that we ought to have, if we were on the order of Harvard, Oxford—any respectable institution. . . . I objected to the notion of having a union. It seems to me it is not the way a college or university ought to be run. I wish it would go away; but some years ago it dawned on me that it is not going to go away, and we are going to have collective negotiations. . . .

What the faculty saw themselves faced with in this instance was an administration that would "make a pronouncement such as you have to have office hours on three days of the week. Now that was taken to negotiation and was settled against them. They cannot require people to do that." Or the administration would quibble over specific procedures for calling in sick, and then for calling in that you are no longer sick, so that a clerk could keep accurate count of sick-leave days. The tendency to issue such orders signified that the administrators thought they were "in charge of the institution" and therefore that "the faculty consists of some privates who are to be ordered around by sergeants and captains." Faculty then judged that it was actually the administration that had "set up an adversary relation."

The faculty saw the trustees as even more arbitrary than the administrators:

> The trustees talk about all sorts of things. They put through requirements for mathematics, for English, one thing after another. . . . Our trustees are doing that all the time. . . . [They] were not consulting the faculty. . . . [And] when it came down to the bargaining table you should have seen their proposal for starting the bargaining. They went back to the Stone Age. They proposed that we be here forty hours a week, that we sign in at 8:00 in the morning and leave at 5:00 in the afternoon. Of course they didn't think about evening classes or anything like that. It was incredible. . . . To me it was really an insult that they even

put out a document of that sort. . . . [They] started out as if they were newly hiring a bunch of crazy people off the streets. It sure didn't set a tone.

These expressed reasons for favoring or opposing unions flesh out the survey findings on faculty attitudes toward collective bargaining. In the 1984 Carnegie survey, faculty in the community colleges and in the lesser comprehensive colleges were much more likely to disagree *strongly* with the assertion that collective bargaining has no place in a college or university: Nearly one in two so reported, compared to one in six in the leading research universities (Table 11). In short, in the settings shown by our interviews in detail as least supportive of collegial relations between faculty and administrators—those most likely to produce faculty outrage over weak authority—faculty leaned toward unionization in the survey to the greatest degree. But even in these settings of relative powerlessness, one in four faculty members tended to agree that collective bargaining had no place in academic institutions; one in two shied away from a strong affirmation of the need to unionize. The interviews richly specified the point that American academics seeking to retain a professional sense and image find unionization not the path of first choice. It becomes first choice in locales adverse to professionalism, where faculty feel that "there's been abuses over a long period of time," where "the administration runs the college." A sense of unprofessional exposure to managerial dictates lies at the heart of the matter.

Not under way until the late 1960s, unionization is a recent phenomenon in American higher education. With only eleven campuses reported as unionized in 1966, the numbers climbed sharply during the next ten years to 160 in 1970 and 430 in 1975.[17] The trend then slowed somewhat, with the number of unionized *campuses* increasing to 830 in 1985. Those campuses were part of about 430 institutions (some multicampus, as, for example, the State University of New York), or approximately one-seventh of all institutions. The unionized units contained nearly 200,000, or one-fourth, of all faculty.[18] Geographically, the unions concentrated in a small number of states that have strong collective bargaining laws, principally in New York, New Jersey, Michigan, Pennsylvania, and California. They have tended to sweep upward from the secondary level, first penetrating

TABLE 11

FACULTY SENTIMENT THAT COLLECTIVE BARGAINING HAS NO PLACE IN HIGHER EDUCATION, BY TYPE OF INSTITUTION

	EXTENT OF AGREEMENT			
TYPE OF INSTITUTION	STRONGLY AGREE	AGREE WITH RESERVATIONS	DISAGREE WITH RESERVATIONS	STRONGLY DISAGREE
	(PERCENT OF FACULTY)			
RESEARCH UNIVERSITIES I	28	25	31	16
RESEARCH UNIVERSITIES II	19	23	33	25
DOCTORAL-GRANTING UNIVERSITIES I	19	25	35	21
DOCTORAL-GRANTING UNIVERSITIES II	13	26	33	28
COMPREHENSIVE UNIVERSITIES AND COLLEGES I	13	20	34	33
COMPREHENSIVE UNIVERSITIES AND COLLEGES II	13	11	31	45
LIBERAL ARTS COLLEGES I	14	21	37	28
LIBERAL ARTS COLLEGES II	10	25	43	22
TWO-YEAR COLLEGES	14	14	28	44
TOTAL	16	20	33	31

Total respondents, 4,889

QUESTION: "Collective bargaining by faculty members has no place in a college or university."

SOURCE: The Carnegie Foundation for the Advancement of Teaching, 1984 Faculty Survey.

the two-year sector and then the four-year sector institutions. They are heavily located in public institutions, only lightly scattered among private ones. The unionization of private institutions suffered major setbacks in two court decisions in 1980 and 1984—the Yeshiva University and Boston University cases—which judged professors to have sufficient influence in important areas of decision making to qualify as managers rather than as workers. In the 1980s counterforces to the unionization drive have clearly asserted themselves, making it likely that certain domains will be hard for unions to penetrate, notably the private sectors and all public institutions in the states where laws restrict rather than facilitate the efforts of unions.

The significant body of research on faculty unions that has accumulated since the early 1970s indicates clearly that unions take different forms according to the authority environments they enter.[19] The more militant ones, closest to the adversarial pole, form where managerial dominance has been strongest. There, the union may readily become more important than the senate or other faculty bodies. The more collegial unions are likely to form where faculty are reasonably satisfied with the way their senate operates on such academic matters as curriculum and selection of colleagues but feel they need an additional tool for collective representation, including lobbying in the state capitol on bread-and-butter issues of salary and workload. Taking a less adversarial posture, such unions attempt to combine the mentality of an "association" with some of the ways of unions. An intense adversarial point of view is restrained by the normal faculty preference for collegiality.

Clearly evident in our field interviews, the collegial preference has the strong bite of status behind it. The further up the institutional hierarchy one goes, the greater the opposition to the adversarial features of unions: The top of the hierarchy is thoroughly nonunion. The top private colleges and universities are seemingly beyond all reach; the top public universities, competing with the private ones, see unions as detrimental to the attraction and retention of leading scholars—all able to bargain for themselves—around whom reputation is anchored and enhanced. Ironically, the leading universities and colleges have relatively liberal faculties, professors who, relative to the general population, look favorably upon unions. There is an opposition between ideological support and academic status.[20] Faculty opinions about unionization are a poor predictor of the

182

propensity to organize.[21] Position takes over from ideology: The interests of those positioned in the uppermost reaches of the system are not favorable to unionization.

The status hierarchy is thus a major barrier to unionization. Unions themselves have been placed in a dilemma of status deprivation: They organize where they can, but as they extend their reach at the lower levels of the hierarchy, they add the imagery of the dispossessed to the reasons why they are largely excluded from the more favored sectors. After two decades of progress, they have become for the most part a phenomenon of the lower hemisphere. Still preferring "soft" but high-status collegiality to "hard" but low-status unionization, faculty in the most prestigious institutions use individual bargaining, departmental influence, and senate hegemony as their principal tools of professional authority.

CONTROL IN A FRACTURED PROFESSION

It is difficult in America near the end of the twentieth century to grasp how the control of academic services operates. No one is in charge. Unitary, centralized systems of higher education can, at least, portray the national government as the supreme covering authority, with academics incorporated in the civic service. But the extraterritoriality of the American professoriate precludes that pretense. Within the profession itself, there are no particular chiefs, nor can we find an interlocking directorate of professors or administrators or trustees, or the three combined, who might exercise a commanding sway. Control is localized in autonomy-seeking, and often competitive, subsets, in disciplines that go their separate ways and institutions that compete. A profession so broken up in its work and culture also generates a disjointed structure of control.

Among the fractured components, various fields exhibit somewhat different combinations of personal, collegial, and managerial controls. The humanities seem to remain closest to an old-fashioned, if dissensual, collegiality; there is little "big business" there. As we move through the social sciences and into the resource-rich sciences, and then still further into professional fields heavily invested in clinical application, the older, preferred forms of academic authority mingle more with the practices of bureaucracy. Major resources must be allocated, attracting the attention of higher officials within and without the system and bringing more administrative detail and hierarchical accountability. Money attracts management; some subjects have more of it than others. "Science administrator" has become a much-used, appropriate term. "Humanities administrator" has not.

Most important is the variation in professional authority produced by the differentiation of types of institutions. The extremes are like day and night: In the most favored locations many professors can virtually write their own tickets; in the least favored we find teachers virtually without any semblance of power. The one approaches the ideal formulated by David Riesman that "a college faculty needs to combine the individualism one associates with artists and free-floating intellectuals with the cooperative-competitive collegiality, not of a submarine crew, but of a research group, a private medical clinic, or the partners in an elite law firm."[22] The other approaches the extreme in which the frustrations of powerlessness corrode all sense of rewarding individualism and rule out the stimulation and comfort of easy collegiality. The one is the home of the "scholar," the other is the bureaucratic assignment of "employee."

Scholars have peers as their primary source of personal and collegial authority. The foundations of professorial influence remain in the individual disciplines, reducing institutional controls. But academic employees have their primary audience in the students they serve. They are more subject to consumerism[23]—and a related managerialism that follows enrollments in the name of expansion, efficiency, retrenchment, and financial exigency. Employees are inherently more expendable than scholars; tenure is eliminated or its protections reduced. They become a secondary work force within the profession. Unionization is frequently their answer, creating a distinctive type of academic authority that seeks to formalize and standardize, to promote system-wide issues and also to move issues to system levels of deliberation.

Professionals have authority readily granted to them to the extent they are special. Rare expertise seemingly brings moral as well as technical authority. But as specialness decreases, authority declines. In the academic profession those who do the most common work have the ground of professional authority cut out from under them. The loss of professional control among full-time academics is greatest among those who teach

184

mostly introductory classes to beginning students in open-access community colleges. We have only to contrast their situation with the specialness of advanced graduate instruction wrapped around state-of-the-art research to grasp that they have shallow grounds for professional control. Type of work goes a long way in academia in determining the extent and form of authority.

The power of specialness offers yet another reason why general education has such an uphill climb in American higher education. Curricula devised by disciplinarians strengthen the select underpinnings of authority by helping to particularize and rarify expertise. In contrast, general education courses weaken subject foundations as they blur special materials into larger units, reducing the experts' claims of specialness. Subjects remain the ultimate base for professorial autonomy: The more arcane the materials, the more powerful the claim to self-determination.[24] Higher education professionals are more favored in this regard than are personnel in elementary and secondary education; and, within higher education itself, the advantage goes to the highest level of advanced work. This is all quite objective, hardly a matter of ideology. Academics who are asked to give up their "narrow interests" and commit themselves to more general curricula can hardly miss sensing the implication for professional status and rewards. They are then soon busy assembling some "distribution requirements" in the name of a broad undergraduate education, politically practicing the art of the possible among varied departmental interests, while leaving full-bodied efforts to construct a general curriculum to the few who still dream of the old days or look to utopian days still to come.

Only the small private colleges possess the conditions that enable academics to push back the power of subject specialty and erect integrated programs for undergraduate liberal education. Around the particular character of the unified, small college, the specialness of close student-teacher relations in a fully residential arrangement, and often the specialness of a selective student body—*and* absent the graduate school—faculties are able to effect a compromise in which the needs of liberal education are reasonably balanced against the pace of research and scholarship. But even in settings most favorable to the maintenance of general curricula, expertise in a discipline and the authority that comes with it have a steadily expanding place. For the individual academic in a leading small college, competence means keeping up with specialized subjects, participating as fully as possible with the specialists who more narrowly and intensely fashion the changing bodies of academic materials. "Scholar" remains the controlling definition, translating decision making into collegial control in a "community" setting.

Underlying the many issues involved in the determination of student access and progress, faculty recruitment and retention, curriculum, and finance, lies the relative influence of peers, bureaucrats, and clients. Sociologists have observed that the social control of expert services may primarily center in professional self-control, governmental-bureaucratic control, or client-consumer control.[25] In American academia, with its pushing back of governmental control and its localization of bureaucrats, the contest comes down primarily to peer-based versus client-based authority, with the latter expressed through organizational management. As they interpret and implement "demand," and sometimes actively shape it, administrators become the active proxies of consumers. In certain institutional locales, their immediate interpretations of service to clientele become controlling: faculty labor trails along, more other- than inner-driven. But in other major settings, the faculty clearly lead, field by field, taking cues from peers and converting administrators to the fiction that "the faculty is the institution." What we find in academic authority in America depends on where we look in the institutional hierarchy.

CHAPTER VII

The Promises of Career

When I was an undergraduate I really enjoyed college and I enjoyed academic pursuits and it seemed to me that being a professor was just the nicest kind of job in the world. I liked time to think about things that really interested you and that you would always work with students and that you would always be at a college or university. I liked all that.

—POLITICAL SCIENCE PROFESSOR, SECOND-
RANK UNIVERSITY

What can one really do if one wants to raise a family and be free and have obligations such that they don't really interfere? . . . Nineteen hours may sound like a lot, but there is a lot of maneuvering time in there to also live and have some kind of a life. That is one reason, maybe not the best. It is one that many women that I know feel. There is a prestige about it, it is a profession, it is respected. It is exciting and there is movement in it . . . it grows.

—BIOLOGY PROFESSOR, COMMUNITY COLLEGE

S INCE ACADEMIC EMPLOYMENT is decided subject by subject, careers of academics are segmented by discipline and fine-tuned by specialty. Typically, in America they begin in graduate school, sometimes in the undergraduate college, when neophytes work their way into one or more specialties within a particular discipline or professional subject. There they assume identities that define and steer them for years and, often, for a lifetime of work. There they begin to see themselves as molecular biologists, political scientists specializing in American government, professors of education deeply immersed in the study of early childhood, while taking an advanced degree in a subject. Though some academics make significant shifts in later years, from one specialty to a neighboring one, or even from one discipline to another, by the time they are credentialed with a doctoral, or even a master's degree, they have made an investment in a subject they do not readily surrender, especially when

187

the accompanying occupational label has become lodged in personal identity. New Ph.D.'s are among the staunchest true-believers in the value of their own disciplines and perspectives; their confidence and commitment lie in newly won mastery of subject.

At the same time that the discipline is so compelling in fashioning academic careers, employment necessarily entails an institutional assignment, thereby placing careers on an institutional axis. Again, later adjustments are possible: American higher education is premised on competitive mobility that allows reputed scientists and scholars to make frequent institutional changes. Academics at various levels of the system may move from one institution to another. But the initial location is an important differentiator: It assigns an academic to a career line in a type of institution that may be hard to shake.

Academic careers thus become locations in a matrix of disciplinary affiliations and institutional assignments, occupancies that are fluid and shifting for some and stable and constant for others. Careers may or may not be a movable feast; they are always a mixture of opportunity and constraint. Career lines operate as tapering tunnels down which academics are beckoned, by whatever rewards, intrinsic and extrinsic, particular specialties in particular types of institutions are able to muster.

Research on academic careers in modern America, always fragmentary and confusing, leaves much to explore.[1] The zigs and zags in hundreds of thousands of individual careers make simple description a mockery. Sociologists of science have spent much time simply probing the careers of those at the highest reaches of the institutional hierarchy, seeking to track how social background, sponsorship, and institutional status influence individual achievement and prestige among "productive" scientists. But such work omits career patterns exhibited by those affiliated with nine-tenths or more of academe. An interesting broader analysis by Neil Smelser and Robin Content observed that there are many quite strongly differentiated, but still overlapping, markets for academic services: Specialists hire their own kind, field by field, and institutional sectors look for different types of services. The principal operative currency in the upper-level sectors of the labor market is prestige rather than monetary compensation, with competition for talent then becoming "simultaneously a competition

188

for individual services and a competition *between* universities trying to advance or solidify their own position in the prestige hierarchy."[2]

We did not set out to track career pathways in depth, a monumental task that would have precluded other topics we wished to pursue. But in the course of long interviews, faculty respondents had many opportunities to convey to us how and why they got into an academic career and what kinds of opportunities and constraints they faced as time went by. In the four sections that follow, I first explore how academics are attracted to their careers, and how they get started in them. The gateways are diverse and loosely guarded; important differences in patterns of attraction and recruitment exist between "hard" and "soft" disciplines. I then pursue four fault lines in the profession's matrix of careers. First, and most important, is the obvious divide between research and teaching, redefined as specialist and generalist careers. The second is the distinction between full- and part-time appointments: In large numbers part-timers, both temporary and permanent, are now part of the American professoriate. The third divide lies between tenured and nontenured personnel, an important matter for the stability of academic employment and the fundamental beliefs of the profession. Last is the pure-applied distinction, a critical issue within professional schools, notably medical schools heavy with clinical tracks, which places some professional schools at odds with letters and science fields. The ultimate peripheral involvement, a virtual noncareer, is the wandering academic gypsy who is only able to find a bit of work here and there. The gypsy—the freeway scholar—exists in a hand-to-mouth fashion a light-year away from regular employment and a steady career.

A third exploration probes movement in rank. Once academics embark on careers in different disciplines in different types of institutions, the vast majority encounter a ladder to climb. That ladder has been widely standardized in the three major levels of assistant, associate, and full professor. A more junior level of instructor and, occasionally, such flexible categories as *lecturer* and *adjunct professor* turn up as supplements. Progress in an academic career is widely associated with movement up the ranks. But, it turns out, the ranks may be subordinated, even eliminated. And what criteria determine progress? The main fault line occurs between merit and seniority; the first goads individual ambition, the other offers the support of equity and community. I explore how institutions weigh and combine the two, and how they influence career lines as they maneuver between the extremes of merit and seniority criteria.

The concluding section looks at the satisfactions and solaces of academic careers. Our faculty respondents offered rich accounts, taking us through a maze of hopes and disappointments, intrinsic as well as extrinsic rewards, which went beyond the identifications and ideologies identified in the earlier chapter on academic culture. Their descriptions point to the stubborn capacity that academic careers still possess to excite and to challenge.

ATTRACTION AND ENTRY

There are so many frontdoors, backdoors, sidedoors, and hidden passageways for entering the vast work force of the American academic profession that no simple picture of attraction and recruitment can be constructed. Some who come to postsecondary teaching enter from the trades, from business, and from the military, especially among community college faculties. Naturally, most recruits come from the educational structure itself, where, somewhere along the line, individuals find themselves attracted to particular subjects and the profession at large. But even here the portals are many.

Interest in certain subjects sometimes follows from early images of science and scholarship. A leading physicist, Richard A. Muller of the University of California, Berkeley, has offered a striking illustration. At a very early age he became intrigued with dinosaurs, read all the books on dinosaurs, saw movies about dinosaurs, made models of dinosaurs for science fairs—but never won any prizes—moved on to playing with telescopes and microscopes, and learned to associate "science with beauty." By the time he was in high school he knew he wanted to be a physicist (see Vignette Three). The career line picked up early under a full head of steam from burning personal interest and was solidly established in graduate school, where, in a short time, he became an active participant in "the center of the physics world"—the physics department at Berkeley and the nearby affiliated Lawrence Radiation Laboratory. For this recruit it was science all the way; a straight-line path of attraction and entry where personal commitment moved from science to physics to a specialty within physics.

Beyond such early, precollege attraction, which depends on childhood

190

VIGNETTE THREE
THE RUNNING START

I loved dinosaurs. I drew a Tyrannosaurus rex fighting a Triceratops nearly every day during recess. I tried to make my sketch look just like the painting in *Life* magazine. My class took a trip to the American Museum of Natural History, and I saw a Tyrannosaurus skeleton fight a Triceratops skeleton. . . . The school library had only one book on the subject, called "The Dinosaur Hunters." I learned that the dinosaurs had all disappeared 65 million years ago, long before humans had appeared. . . . But nobody really knew why they disappeared. Perhaps clever little mammals with a taste for dinosaur eggs had been responsible. It was the first problem I ever heard about in science that was admittedly unsolved.

I saw a copy of the book "Biography of the Earth," by George Gamow, on a rack of pocket books at a drugstore. It had reproductions of dinosaur paintings as well as pictures of the moon and planets, and only cost 35 cents. I convinced my parents to buy it for me. Later I bought "One Two Three . . . Infinity," also by Gamow. These books were full of excitement: discussions of infinity, photographs of molecules, theories about the beginning of time and size of the universe, about continental drift (this in 1941!). It was physicists who did most of this work, and that was what I wanted to be.

In high school, even though I found biology more interesting than physics, I still knew I wanted to be a physicist. From Gamow's books I knew that real physicists didn't spend all their time with pulleys and inclined planes. They tried to solve the riddles of the origin of the universe and the nature of the atom.

In graduate school at the University of California at Berkeley, I chose for my thesis elementary particle physics, the study of the pieces that make up the nucleus of the atom. It was the field that everybody at the time found most interesting, and the Lawrence Berkeley Laboratory near campus seemed to be the center of the physics world. I appeared to have moved as far from the study of dinosaurs as one could imagine. I never would have guessed that my thesis advisor, Luis W. Alvarez, would lead the team that discovered the immediate cause of the destruction of the dinosaurs, and that I would be led from this to a search for the ultimate cause: a "death star" that orbits the sun.[22]

SOURCE: Richard A. Miller, "An Adventure in Science: The Pleasures of Being an Astrophysicist." *The New York Times Magazine*, March 24, 1985. Copyright 1985 by The New York Times Company. Reprinted by permission.

and adolescent interests and images, the academic profession has a stunning advantage over other professions in occupying the main training ground for all advanced fields. Anyone even thinking of becoming a professional worker of one kind or another must pass through academic hands for four years and more, majoring in some subject. At a time of critical career choice for students, the academic life is paraded before them, generally in a positive light. It is well known that professors of biology explicitly, and by unspoken example, attempt to divert undergraduates from medicine to biology; for them, each person "saved" from medicine is a small step for mankind. A biologist at a leading university recounted his own earlier experience:

> I grew up in Washington, D.C., and anyone who liked biology was a doctor. It's interesting because I lived two miles from NIH [National Institutes of Health, Bethesda, Maryland], and I never knew what NIH was until now. When I grew up, it was just another government building. . . . When I was an undergraduate student at Tulane, a professor I was working with there asked, "Why are you applying to medical school?" I thought all people who liked biology applied to medical school. He said, "Well, it's very different to go to graduate school." That was a totally new idea to me—so I went to graduate school. I went to Purdue University and got my Ph.D. in molecular biology there in 1980.

By the early 1980s biology had virtually taken first place among the sciences as the locus of exciting science, laying an array of fascinating and promising specialties before undergraduate and graduate students. As departments of biology spell out specific tracks for taking the Ph.D., students early set their minds on specialties. A professor of biology told us: "I talk to students now, and they know exactly, or think they know, what subdiscipline of molecular biology they want. It's really a big change."

Biology has also become *the* field in which the Ph.D. is not enough for a career in academic research: The "postdoctoral" appointment, often of two years, duration, is more common than unusual—a training option not to be ignored.[3] It showed up repeatedly in biologists' accounting of their training and mobility in early posts:

> After Purdue I went to the University of California at Santa Barbara and did a two-year postdoctoral fellowship, and then I ap-

192

plied for jobs. (*Do most people still go the postdoctoral route?*) Yes, I would say in molecular biology all people do . . . in this kind of university, all candidates, even in ecology. We're interviewing ecologists now, and they go for postdocs.

A biology professor in a small leading liberal arts college told of undergraduate years that took him "back and forth between English and biology." He majored primarily in English but then ended up in biology "because I wanted to go to medical school. I did go to medical school at Yale for a year and became seduced by biochemistry, and so then I transferred to Harvard and got a Ph.D. there. I had a postdoc in the Netherlands for two years. . . ."

In biology the only thing better than one postdoc is two postdocs, as told by yet another respondent:

> Then I did a postdoctoral period at Rockefeller University in New York City. . . . There I left plants for a little while and I worked on lysosomes in cardiovascular disease. After that I did another postdoc at the University of California in Santa Cruz. That was plant biochemistry research stuff. (*Each of the postdocs, how long were they?*) About two and a half years each. (*You went from a Ph.D., then, right into a postdoc, and then another postdoc?*) Yes. I was into postdocs for a total of five years.

This biologist was "on the verge of taking" a third postdoctoral position when his present position at a second-tier university came along. He probably could have gone on to a position in full-time research inside academe. Advanced career lines in biology not only measurably extend the years of formal and semiformal training but also lead into posts in full-time research that are apportioned in the health field between the departments of biological sciences and the professional schools. In this form major universities have a legitimate, regularized "nonteaching faculty."

What gradually emerged from the respondents' discursive descriptions of how they got started in their careers is a difference between "hard" and "soft" disciplines in patterns of recruitment.[4] The disciplines with substantial bodies of well-organized theory and method have relatively straightforward arrangements for entering academic careers. Most undergraduate course work is sequentially ordered; graduate students have clear definitions of alternative specialties; the years between the bachelor's de-

193

gree and the doctorate are more likely four than ten. Subjects that lack well-organized theory and method stand in sharp contrast. Potential recruits may stagger in and out, weaving their way among subjects, often choosing some of this and some of that, even fashioning a liberal education by accident as much as by choice.

Among the six fields in which we interviewed, English stood over against physics and biology in the degree to which students bounced around among subjects. A professor in a second-tier university had taken his bachelor's and master's degrees from two different universities in journalism; he then received a Ph.D. from a third university, in American Studies—"the bulk of it was American literature and American history, but then we also took economics, political science, and art"; finally, he went on to an appointment in an English department. Extremely common were prolonged periods spent in graduate work: The above professor took his bachelor's in 1948; his Ph.D. came eighteen years later, in 1966. And a fuller account offered by a professor of English in a leading liberal arts college spells out the vicious circles of delay and doubt and hedging into which graduate students in soft fields may readily fall:

> I did my undergraduate work at Duke and I got a B.A. in English, and I also took a lot of music. Then I went to Oxford. I got a Marshall scholarship and a Danforth fellowship. . . . I got a second B.A. at Oxford. . . . Then I came back and did my graduate work at Harvard. I went to Harvard in '75 and received my degree in '82, but I was at Harvard physically, I guess, through the 1978–1979 academic year . . . before I had finished my degree I went off to Denmark and taught part-time in two universities in Denmark, and that I did for two and a half years. Then I came back and finished my degree in one semester at Harvard.

> . . . the reason that I spent so long doing my degree at Harvard is that at Harvard you can teach your head off as a graduate student if you want to, because the faculty don't do the real teaching . . . from my second year on, I taught quite a bit at Harvard as a teaching fellow, which, it's not like being a T.A. [teaching assistant], it's really running your own class in [a] number of cases. That's very time-consuming; it's one of those vicious cycles. In order to get money to be there to finish your degree you have to teach, but if you teach you don't have any more time

to finish your degree. . . . I kept up my music the whole time at Harvard, wisely I think, because I didn't want to be in the position where I cut off that option as a profession, so I also did part-time work as an organist. . . . I actually was a full-time organist for one of those semesters.

This young professor had obviously been well thought of (Marshalls and Danforths are prestigious awards) and had been well trained in the best of places, Oxford and Harvard. But the time at Oxford, however educational, was several more years spent obtaining, in effect, a second bachelor's degree; and then graduate work at Harvard took another seven years, with the Ph.D. in hand roughly a decade after completing undergraduate work at an American university. Her graduate work was pursued at no more than half-speed, since she was busy teaching classes entirely on her own and hedging her bet on an academic career by keeping alive an alternative line into music. Lacking the major research funds of the sciences, humanities graduate students clearly are more likely to earn their way by teaching, thereby dragging out completion of course work and especially the dissertation.

The greater number of sharp turns and odd angles between the bachelor's degree and the Ph.D. in softer fields is also more likely, in the case of faculty in intermediate and lower institutions, to entail some public school teaching or other employment outside higher education. A senior professor in English at a second-level university reported:

> [As an undergraduate] I went to a state college in Pennsylvania. I went there to play some basketball and ended up teaching high school English and coaching basketball. Went from there to Bucknell and was in their M.Ed. [Master of Education] program for a while. I decided I wanted to get back into English. . . . I also worked for the Department of Public Instruction in Harrisburg during that time I went to Kent State in 1966. I earned my M.A. in 1967; stayed in the program and earned my Ph.D. in 1969.

Once on the graduate track, he had raced through in three years. But this was after some high school teaching, some time pursuing a master's degree in education, and some outside employment.

Softer fields lend themselves to midcareer or midlife entry in a way hardly possible in scientific fields, which virtually require continuous study at an early age from high school to college to graduate work. Here is the account of a professor of English at a second-level liberal arts college whose elapsed time between taking the bachelor's degree and finishing the Ph.D. was thirty-one years:

> I graduated in 1944 from . . . a small Catholic women's college. Then I taught public school for one year, then was married, and then I didn't resume teaching until 1964. . . . I began teaching here in [a major city] at the high school level in English. After three years or so of high school teaching I decided I needed to get a master's degree, which I did. . . . I had every intention of remaining a high school English teacher but I found that I was quite impatient with the bureaucracy of high school systems. I then decided to try to get a job at the college or community college level. I began teaching part-time here at [her present college], which I did for two years, and then I decided to get my Ph.D. up at [a nearby university]. I was up there for four years, working as a T.A. [teaching assistant] and working on my Ph.D. When I finished my degree in '75, I then taught for two years part-time at the University . . . and part-time [here]. (*I imagine teaching part-time at two places was a fairly rigorous thing?*) I thought that it might be, but there was no committee work involved, which soon becomes the monster that devours all one's time. (*Even so, it still requires a certain kind of commitment and I guess I'm wondering why do that at this stage in your life?*) Because I wanted to teach so badly, and I kept hoping and praying for a full-time position, and I knew that the only way to get a full-time position was by doing this. (*So you came to [her present college] in 1975?*) As a part-time teacher and received a full-time contract in '77.

Occasionally, virtue triumphs: The persistent part-timer, the late career entrant, ends up with a full-time post, even if this happy ending comes not far from retirement.

Early or later, entry to the academic profession is nearly always made by way of entry to a constituent disciplinary profession: The discipline is chosen first, membership in the overall profession follows.[5] And for American students the graduate level is where choices finally become serious. Fateful choices come earlier in the transition from secondary to postsecondary ed-

196

ucation in most other countries, for it is then that one enters the medical faculty or the law school or a disciplinary specialty. For most prospective entrants to the major and minor professions in the United States, the undergraduate realm encourages a spread of attention among the array of courses the faculty have designated as appropriate for a general or liberal education. It is a time to sample subjects; to switch from one major field to another is simple. Save engineering, serious commitment is relegated to the master's and Ph.D. programs, which, in contrast to European advanced levels, are highly structured with course work and term-by-term requirements. Here requisite degrees are obtained and one becomes fully introduced to a disciplinary way of thinking as well as to an essential body of knowledge. Here recruits enter into the neophyte roles of teaching assistant and research assistant. Here they are launched into job hunting and placement. When one has "earned" the doctorate, or, in some cases, the master's degree, the crucial first step in the career ladder has been traversed.

THE DIFFERENTIATION OF CAREER LINES

The academic sector of society demonstrates in extreme form that an advancing division of labor always causes professional careers to be more and more segmented, fine-tuned both in substantive content and institutional location. Academic subfields become career lines: The development of molecular biology has established a special labor market in which credentialed molecular biologists look for jobs appropriate to their training and interest, while at the same time, institutions search for faculty in this particular slice of the biological sciences. Ethnomethodologists develop a career category in sociology, one made active when hiring departments decide to take their chances with those who do research and teach in that particular tunnel. History departments do not go looking for a historian to fill an opening; they go for a European historian rather than an American one. They, in fact, narrow the position in leading institutions with large departments to a historian of France, not to one specializing in Germany, Britain, Scandinavia, or Eastern Europe, and finally, to a specialist in nineteenth-, not eighteenth- or twentieth-century French history. As Neil Smelser and Robin Content commented: "Certainly it is rare for one dis-

197

cipline to hire outside its own ranks, and each discipline is divided into numerous groups of subspecialists who tend to hire their own but not other specialists (for example, econometricians hire econometricians, economic historians hire economic historians, and so on."[6]

Academics understand that this is the way the system works, the way knowledge advances, the way careers are shaped. Indeed, specialization is widely seen as the price of competence:

> I would like to be called a biologist, but I can't in good conscience call myself that anymore because the field is too large. (*Was this the case ten years ago?*) No, I don't think so at all. (*Why? Explain the changes in the discipline.*) Specialization. At least in molecular biology the technology is advancing so fast that to work with it and to understand it, one has to become very specialized.

As they become labeled by specialty, individual biologists become sharply constrained in career choices, making shifts among specialties difficult. An "ecology" type in biology at a second-level university remarked, "They get the idea that you are a squirrel person: It is very hard, for instance, to [become] a wind pollination person [rather than] a squirrel person."

The closer one gets to the top of the institutional hierarchy, the more career specialization takes hold. Such concentration is obvious in biology, chemistry, and physics, but it occurs across all the disciplines and professional areas. Two political scientists in different research universities explained the situation in their field:

> (*Do individuals frequently work in more than one subfield?*) Less and less, simply because to maintain familiarity with the literature over more than one of those subfields, which are very broad, is an incredible responsibility.

> (*Do individuals frequently change subfields?*) I suppose it is rare because it is hard enough to make a name for oneself and make a contribution to gain some visibility in one subfield, without having to do it in more than one.

Matters are no simpler in the humanities, especially in such huge disciplines as English and history. "To gain some visibility," and, "to make a name for oneself and make a contribution," only a few travel the route of

198

the large, integrative effort, with all its dangers of superficiality and error. Here too, the expanding base of knowledge makes specialization the price of perceived competence, the route to visibility, and the way to the rewards that come from making a contribution. When asked to talk about specialization in his field, a professor of English explained at some length:

> There are a number of people in the field of English nowadays— and I suppose this is one of the changes that came about or began chiefly during the sixties—who have never taken what I would tend to think of as a kind of traditional, indispensable background of courses for the study of English. That is, a lot of people have never studied Old English or Middle English or know practically nothing about medieval or Renaissance literature except maybe Shakespeare, and it is like different worlds sometimes. Trying to talk about common values or things common to the discipline of English with such people [is impossible for me], and I am sure that from their point of view my total incomprehension of much contemporary poetry and things of that sort looks just the same way. Clearly the field of English has expanded to the point where it is in danger of just flying apart, I would think. There are a lot of areas within it, subareas, where people spend their lives almost totally out of communication with people in other subareas. . . .

Tunnel vision may well increase over the course of a university career. No matter how conscious of the phenomenon, and even how embarrassed by it, respondents report that the process by which one becomes "almost totally out of communication with people in other subareas" is self-reinforcing. A political scientist at a second-level university explained:

> I am probably more guilty of this than anyone is, the fact that we learn more and more about less and less. Our vision becomes myopic. You asked me if I tend to teach the same courses or are there different preparations. I tend to teach the same course, and I know an awful lot about the presidency. However, I do not know very much about other aspects of American government and very little about international political or comparative governments, and I haven't read theory or philosophy, I am embarrassed to say, in years. I constantly feel extremely narrow and that is the subdiscipline orientation, not discipline. . . . The subfield orientation tends to be very restrictive, and now we have

these little groups within subfields. I was recently president of one of the presidency research groups, and we have our own program at our convention, we go to our seminars, we talk to ourselves, and that is a recipe for isolation; that is a recipe for being very withdrawn from reality.

Specialization varies greatly by type of institution, however. The above respondents are all associated with large discipline-driven universities, where careers are centered in research and advanced graduate training. The accounts shift as soon as we move into undergraduate-centered institutions; there careers cannot be so specialized. In liberal arts colleges small size as well as total concentration on undergraduates discourages specialization. A department of biology may have four faculty members, not twenty or forty. Each member must then stand ready to cover a number of specialties, even as the department narrows the waterfront that it attempts to cover. And undergraduates do not need the advanced instruction reserved for graduate students. General introductory courses are the first compulsion upon teaching, followed by the intermediate-level courses normal in the upper division years. A biologist in a small private college noted how much he had to spread his efforts:

> If you are as small as we are—we only have four people—you have to assume this cutting edge in some aspects you deal with, whether you feel really qualified or not. You have to cope with that. We have to be so flexible because we are small. You teach six or seven totally separate subjects. I guess we are kind of used to this, and I am used to learning new things every week.

Smallness is then seen as a virtue in that it stays the hand of specialization, forcing academics back toward a general posture. Again, a biologist comments:

> (*Is there such a thing anymore as a biologist, or are they biochemists, molecular biologists, etc.?*) Yes, I guess there are, but a biologist will have a specialty if he is real. Very often, after a while, he won't be conversant with other parts of biology. Again, the virtue of a small college is that I have to keep up with a wide area in biology, [especially] since I am in charge of the first semester introductory courses as well, so that forces my hand, and that is

good. I think I am better prepared to ask interesting questions about membrane biochemistry because I am forced to keep up with a pretty wide area.

It was a third biologist in a small college that drew a useful distinction between "horizontal research" and "vertical research." The nature of his institution, he pointed out, led him in the direction of the horizontal, with the advances of breadth seen as compensating somewhat for the lack of depth.

Academics in other disciplines in small colleges also report the same institutional push toward breadth. In the case of a physicist-chemist:

> At the university level . . . individuals become very, very narrowly focused. . . . In smaller schools, where by necessity you have to wear several hats, you tend to branch out. The same is very true for smaller companies, where you might be asked to be both chemist, chemical engineer, and marketing man, and everything at one time. Here my research interests are broad.

A political scientist in a leading small college, taking note of his own interest in breadth alongside the institutional pressure to be a generalist, suggested that self-selection plays an important role:

> Did I find it comfortable to stay here because my interests are broad, relatively speaking, or . . . do I do the things that I do because I can't . . . ? I mean, I certainly would not have been happy here had I been somebody who was concerned to make my name and a major contribution by advancing some new way of studying state courts, for instance. It wouldn't have worked as well.

It is interactive, a professor of English explained: The personal preference for breadth that serves to bring a person to a small college interacts with on-the-job institutional pressures—"I've gotten much more diverse and flexible since I came here, even though I already was, because you're encouraged to do that. You're rewarded for it, and it's encouraged." One must also teach widely in a subject to cover courses when colleagues are on leave and otherwise "to fill in here or there." As told by another English professor:

201

By the time most people have taught here six or eight years, they have probably taught a range of English literature which would cover Tennessee. The bulk of it would be in a much more defined area than that, but you simply find yourself to some extent being called upon to fill in here to there; somebody is on leave or a sabbatical replacement is hard to arrange or various things happen. But I think also that most of us feel a great desire occasionally to teach something that is off the well-worn track for us.

The substantive content of careers at colleges varies decidedly from careers at first-level universities. The difference is virtually epistemological.

Even at the university level, where career specialization is uppermost, a powerful condition promotes a more general regrouping, even a return to the basics. That condition is retrenchment, a narrowing of the resource base, especially at the graduate level, which causes institutions to increase loads and impels departments to shift faculty assignments toward introductory and other general courses. The humanities were hardest hit in this regard in the 1970s and early 1980s. They lost both undergraduates and graduate students. The latter were a double loss, since they both provide the enrollments that justify graduate classes and serve as teachers in undergraduate classes, especially the ones professors prefer not to teach. A professor of English at a second-level university drew a clear picture:

> If you divide English into language and literature, most of us have been trained in literature. We teach composition as graduate students so that we can teach literature as faculty members. . . . The composition courses were always the courses that graduate students taught. . . . There has been a healthy change in the profession . . . composition and rhetoric are receiving more and more attention as fields of study, as fields of scholarly interest. We have within our M.A. [Master of the Arts program] a concentration in rhetoric and composition. . . . It has only been established in the last few years. . . . Over the years, more and more [faculty] have been forced to teach composition. When I came here in 1969, I was told that I would never have to teach composition, that I would teach literature. That's changed. We don't have as many students, we don't have as many literature courses. . . . (*Is it possible then for individuals to move from one subfield to another?*) That is called retrenchment. It is occurring more and more simply because we don't have as many graduate

students as we had several years ago. There aren't as many undergraduate English majors, so people have had to retool. They
have had to reconsider their interests in the profession since
[they] don't get as much of an opportunity to teach in their original subfield as before. . . . They are teaching composition more.

These effects of retrenchment have been deepened by the remedial work
forced on English departments in recent years by the inadequate teaching
of the rudiments of the English language in American elementary and secondary schools.

So there are counterforces to the trend of increasing specialization in the
universities. But generally, the specialist careers are located at the top of
the institutional hierarchy and the generalist careers are found further
down the line. Decade by decade the bulk of institutions move toward the
norms of the top: The steady expansion of knowledge in each discipline
alone insures that the rewards of specialization will dominate. The institutional imperatives of undergraduate teaching, however, act as a major
constraint, especially in small-scale settings. The teaching of introductory
materials to neophytes, including the great mass of students majoring outside of each field, forces courses into more general packages and causes
would-be specialists to operate horizontally rather than vertically, spreading their competence rather than narrowing and intensifying it.

Community colleges are here again positioned at the extreme, offering
settings where it is difficult to achieve even a modest degree of specialized
teaching in the form of sophomore classes: "Second-year classes tend to be
advanced classes of a lower number [smaller enrollment]; one has to fight
to get those kind of classes in the schedule and keep them [since] the
administration is concerned with primarily numbers in classes. . . . Most
of my work in practice has been teaching American government." This
community college instructor in political science had not majored in American government but rather in such other areas as political theory, international relations, and comparative government. He did not now "have
opportunities to utilize my preparation." Long noted by academics who
move into teaching careers, a disjuncture exists between the intense specialization of graduate school preparation and the generalist performance
demanded in job assignments. The wish to lessen this gap is one reason

why, historically, community colleges have sought academics who terminated their studies with the master's degree. The Ph.D.'s are "overeducated."

Academics in specialist careers may well pay the cost of knowing "more and more about less and less." Breadth may be sacrificed to depth: The more focused vision may produce an incapacity to grasp and use other perspectives. But the generalist career, particularly when pushed to the extreme, is a lifetime of introductory and mildly specialized courses in which the spread of attention, relative to the advancing field, means that one knows "less and less about more and more." Out goes depth and the capacity to probe with a finely honed form of analysis. Substantively, each type of career has its benefits and its costs.

The Subsidiary Fault Lines

When viewed in a cross-national perspective, American higher education appears as a market-like system in which competition and institutional initiative insure a relatively high degree of labor mobility. Academics need not come to an institution to stay a lifetime: "Exit" decisions abound. In the course of their careers, some professors move from liberal arts colleges to universities, or from universities to state colleges. What becomes difficult is movement across major fault lines of differentiation; here the difference between specialist and generalist careers is the most important but only the first. Three other differences overlap each other significantly but run on different axes than the primary one. They also have grown to major proportions in the expansion and contraction of employment opportunities since 1960. They are full-time versus part-time academic employment, the divide between tenured and nontenured employment, and the distinction between academic and clinical appointments in professional schools.

Part-timers have become, as one respondent remarked, "the hidden college" of American higher education. They are not new in the academic work force, but they are increasingly numerous and varied. The deeper the American system has plunged into mass higher education, a trend begun long ago, the more have institutions needed the capacity to adjust quickly to shifting numbers of students with part-time staff. Willing hands have been available. Graduate students have long sought short-term as well as

204

part-time employment in their own or nearby institutions; municipal colleges have learned to use them as a reserve army of labor, even calling upon them a few days before classes begin in the fall when student registrations prove to far exceed the expected size. Professional schools have long had a natural interest in outside professional experts who affiliate on a part-time basis. They may hold a full-time position elsewhere or occupy two or more part-time positions or have household responsibilities.[7] Departments of music commonly staff the "performance" side of their operations heavily with part-time faculty who come in one or two days a week to give instrumental or vocal instruction. They are hired year by year, without tenure; the full-time, tenured posts go mainly to those who teach the history and theory of music or otherwise hold down the "academic" side.

Because many part-time faculty flit in and out of the shadows of institutional listings of faculty, they are an elusive group in American higher education. It is highly uncertain whether 3,000 institutions even report their full-time faculty accurately. What is certain is that part-timers slip through the cracks of national statistics in ways that cause them to be underreported. Many are "unrostered." Unless deliberately designed to find them, faculty surveys also largely miss them. When an intensive study of part-time faculty was concluded in 1982, three researchers observed: "We encountered extraordinary problems in defining and measuring who and what part-time faculty are. They are a highly fluid work force, coming and going for short terms, with only evanescent ties to employing institutions. In fact, many colleges and universities have no records on their part-time faculty. Nor were we able to find reliable national, or even statewide, data in other than occasional form."[8] Their research, and that of others, has reasonably established that in the mid-1980s part-timers constitute at least one-third of the academic work force.[9] The institutions at the top of the institutional hierarchy use them relatively lightly, the less selective institutions quite heavily. Community colleges become the extreme case: In sheer numbers of faculty, they now are predominantly staffed by part-timers. In 1968 part-timers were about one-third of the community college faculty; in 1980 they were well over one-half.[10]

We did not allocate a significant amount of time in our study to the pursuit of part-timers. But we did interview some, who had rich stories to tell, and we occasionally asked full-timers about their part-time colleagues.

When asked about "adjuncts" and their involvement, a full-time professor of physics in a community college noted:

> That's an unfortunate thing. . . . We don't have too much contact with the adjuncts. . . . They've [the administrators] started using adjuncts during the day session. Actually, it's saving the administration money to use adjuncts rather than full-time faculty, and there are times when we've had to cover . . . a full-time load, or more than a full-time load, and we do [it] piecemeal with adjuncts. Now that was very bad because an adjunct doesn't spend his time here; he just comes and goes. Well, a full-time person spends a whole day here and has office hours for students and also mixes with the faculty, too, but a part-time adjunct doesn't.

A professor of biology in another community college noted with dismay that "we have many more part-time than we have full-time. . . . We use so many that it's almost like a hidden college. . . . The pay is so bad for part-timers that we've had occasional difficulties, like poor instruction." Among the many types of institutions, community colleges have gone the farthest in the use of part-timers as a disposable faculty that is cheaper as well as highly flexible.

The instructional costs of such heavy use of marginal faculty were well-articulated by a part-time community college instructor in history who was glad to be working even part-time, since "if you fall down on the mall you will be picked up by three unemployed historians":

> One-third of our faculty here is full-time teachers or two-thirds are part-timers. . . . It is very poor pay. I have a daughter who is making more money, and she is an exterminator. . . . (*In what ways are the adjunct faculty members different than the full-time?*) We are not up here as much. . . . Most of the faculty, if they work, they don't even have office hours, and they don't work with the students. . . . What students perceive is that they are just unavailable as far as seeing students. . . . I always put my [home] phone number on the syllabus.

What we heard in our interviews tallied with the summary of research on community college part-timers offered by Arthur Cohen and Florence

206

Brawer: Part-timers have a qualitatively different status. They are re-cruited less carefully, because there is no long-term commitment; they are evaluated less systematically, if at all; they receive little in-service atten-tion; they often have no office space; they rarely participate in campus ac-tivities; they have little contact with students out of class; and they have practically no contact with their peers.[11]

Part-time assignments overlap significantly with those that are nonten-ured (or nontenurable). No reliable estimates are available on what pro-portion of the American academic profession have tenure or are in tenur-able positions. But the proportion of those completely outside the possibility of tenure has clearly been growing and is larger than ordinarily assumed. Nearly all part-timers—one of three academics—fall outside of tenure, since their disposability is second only to their low cost as a reason why they are hired. Only a few achieve some stability by formal means or dependable informal promise. In sheer numbers, then, the nontenured staff of community colleges is larger than the tenured cadre, the ongoing permanent core, around which the two-year units flesh out their changing "manpower needs."

Also nontenured are the many clinicians or practitioners who steadily increase in the professional schools of the universities, particularly those in the health field, and in professional programs of comprehensive col-leges. Medical school deans and faculty report an increased use of "fixed-term appointments," a trend, one medical professor claimed, that will lead to the questioning of tenure in the next decade. Doctors with well-estab-lished practices, serving as clinical professors, see no need for tenure and are hostile to the invidious distinctions it creates. In the vast differentiation of work positions taking place in medical schools, guarantees of "employ-ment without limit of time" are giving way to the realities of high income from private practice in America's best-paying profession as well as to the staffing needs of hospital management. Medical doctors hardly need firm guarantees of university salaried employment.

Beyond part-timers and nontenured professional practitioners there lies a world of "lecturers," "temporary instructors," "fixed-term people," and "full-time temporaries" who have little chance of converting to the ten-urable track in the main structure of ranks. This flexible category of mar-ginal personnel is used virtually everywhere, often quite heavily, with institutions switching to it particularly when retrenchment exacerbates concerns about overtenured staff and high costs of senior faculty. When institutions place a ceiling on the proportion of faculty members that can be tenured—a "sixty-percent rule" in one case—then even "tenure-track" may mean "permanent temporary": "Whether or not you are on a tenure-track position depends upon whether or not a tenured position is available [under the ceiling]. You may still be held on probationary status forever . . . if the places are filled up and these guys simply live forever." Employment is then a matter of being kept on a year at a time. One faculty member pointed out that if some academics in this category turn over rapidly, others may stay on for years: She herself had served continuously in a state college biology department since 1970, a period of fourteen years.

Even compared to a temporary part-time one, a continuous, full-time nontenured appointment sometimes has disadvantages. The full-time lecturer is more likely to commit to one place, putting all of his or her eggs in the one job basket, while many part-timers cope by aggregating two or three jobs or putting together part-time work with domestic responsibilities. For the always temporary lecturer or instructor, the odds are high that he or she will labor in the basement, doing the dirty work: In the English department that often means shoveling coal in composition and remedial writing. In a small liberal arts college it may mean "primarily teaching service-related courses, such as the remedial writing courses and freshman composition. In the case of the two people I mentioned, they also participate in our continuing adult education program." In a second-rank university we were told that the temporary instructors were all "teaching composition."

For the adjuncts who are full-time but never destined to received permanency, status deprivation can show up in a multitude of small ways. The faculty member who had taught in a state college for fourteen years had become an expert in small but telling things, as follows:

> I can't serve on promotion or tenure committees. There are certain college-wide committees that I am not eligible to serve on; there is certain voting that I am not allowed to do. I'm not really assured that I will be rehired every time. I think one of the things that rankles is that my position has to be advertised each summer

and therefore on the fall schedule my name doesn't appear. It just says "staff" after courses I am automatically going to teach.

Viewed as "senior technicians" by a university professor of medicine, the full-time temporary teachers fall readily into a vicious circle. In the English department in a second-rank university:

> It's very difficult because they do come as term appointments, which means they are going to teach more than anyone else, which means they have virtually no opportunity to do any research. Even if they could do research, they are [in] nontenure-track positions anyway. . . . We keep them here for four or five years and then we cut them loose and they have less opportunity for employment when they leave. [As a result] these very fine young people on term appointments . . . form their own collegiality, they have their own problems, they become a faction in the department, and they become frustrated and bitter. . . .

In sum: With varying degrees of willingness and reluctance, one-third to one-half or more of American academics have career lines that distance them from "the regular faculty." The extensive division of labor explored in Chapter IV has given rise to a quite differentiated, if often overlapping, set of careers. The profession is far from having a career line: Beyond the distinction between research-based specialist careers and teaching-based generalist careers, numerous other critical differences help define centrality and marginality. What is developing in the American academic profession is a watershed between a regular faculty that is full-time and tenurable (or *willingly* part-time or nontenured, as in clinical lines in professional schools), and a peripheral work force that is composed of reluctant part-timers and full-time lecturers. In recent years numerous terms have sprung up to characterize the latter academics: migrant laborers of academe, gypsy scholars, displaced academics, academic proletariate, marginal academics, disposable dons, freeway scholars. All serve in a "market for piece work."[12] We know where this marginal professoriate is concentrated: among fields, in the humanities, the arts, and such applied fields as education and business; among institutions, in the community colleges by a large measure and, second, in the comprehensive colleges. The ultimate marginal academic career is one pursued by the nomad who wanders among community colleges teaching English: For him or her the future is occasional part-time instruction in composition classes for mainly remedial students.

THE CONTINUITIES OF RANK

In every country the systems devised by universities and colleges for ranking academic personnel are critical in defining academic careers. Logically, the rank structure may be flat, consisting of a single major grade, but generally, we find a vertical incline of levels the academic professional must climb. After entry at or near the bottom, the recruit must climb or get left behind, and do so over a number of years, since only a few reputed geniuses in fields like mathematics and physics are permitted occasionally to rocket from the Ph.D. launching pad to the uppermost level. The ranks define basic status, including tenure, and apportion monetary rewards. Often, such additional benefits as a larger office, greater access to secretarial help, and more dependable periods of leave are included. In this profession careers are openly and significantly rank-defined.

If some academic rank structures are relatively continuous, others exhibit sharp discontinuities. Cross-national comparison places the common American arrangement as an outstanding case of the incrementally continuous, European systems standing in contrast.[13] In the Federal Republic of Germany, in France, Italy, and the smaller countries of Europe—and to a lesser degree in Britain—the chairholder or single professor occupies a status markedly superior to others and available to only a few. Others serve under "the chair," many as assistants. The chair system has had a long, venerable tradition in Western Europe, with antecedents that stretch back to the status of master in the academic guilds that composed the early universities. Chair organization encountered considerable difficulties after 1960, when expansion in knowledge and clientele overwhelmed the competence of single individuals to control the development of a discipline or a major specialty at a university. It was identified as a source of unresponsive oligarchy in a time of growing pressure for "democratization." Rank-structure reform followed, but a considerable gap between seniors and juniors, the professors and others, remained.[14] Nothing else in European higher education has played a stronger part in patterning academic careers.

210

In the United States in the twentieth century, a continuous, incremental structure of ranks has become firmly institutionalized: usually one progresses from assistant to associate to full professor, with the possible addition of instructor on the front end and the endowed chair at the peak. Major ranks are divided into steps, assistant professor I, II, III, and IV, which offer salary increments and through which academics normally move on a fixed time schedule (usually two years in a step). The University of California "scale" is an example (Table 12). As a public university, its scale is somewhat more systematically defined than that of most private

TABLE 12

RANK STRUCTURE OF THE CONTINUOUS
CAREER

RANK	STEP	ANNUAL SALARY (DOLLARS)
ASSISTANT PROFESSOR	I	27,300
	II	28,100
	III	28,800
	IV	29,700
ASSOCIATE PROFESSOR	I	31,300
	II	33,000
	III	35,200
PROFESSOR	I	37,900
	II	41,600
	III	46,100
	IV	51,100
	V	54,600
	VI	58,700
	VII	63,500
OVER SCALE		(Not fixed)

SOURCE: Graduate School of Education Salary Schedule, University of California, Los Angeles, 1984–85. Ranks and steps shown in the table are identical with those used in the UCLA letters and science departments; the salary figures are slightly higher.

universities. But even in private institutions, similar arrangements define the backbone of academic ranking: Assistant professors know whether they are in their first or sixth year, whether they are joining the faculty at the lowest, intermediate, or highest step of the rank. Successful career progression in this type of rank structure is a steady climb up ten or more steps, with top pay more than doubling the beginning salary. The salary increments become steadily larger: A beginning full professor with a reasonable salary may still have a long upward climb to maximize salary.

How does one move up the steps and climb the ranks? The issue becomes merit versus seniority, assessed competence versus years of service. Both are usually present to some degree, with some movements requiring an assessment of competence and others offering automatic progression based on years of service. Which way the rank structure tilts determines whether an academic is in a merit-dominated or a seniority-based career line.

Common among leading universities and colleges, the University of California scale is heavily merit-based: Ascending across major ranks entails extensive critical review. The ascent from assistant to associate professor is the decisive step, since it includes awarding of tenure. It involves an internal department committee report, many letters of assessment by outside peers, a vote of tenured department faculty, a review by an ad hoc secret committee of the all-campus senate, an approval by the senate's principal standing committee on personnel, and, finally, approval by the campus administration. Statewide university administration and the board of regents also have residual powers to enter in, if they so wish.

The process of major merit review is then repeated for the move from associate to full professor. At leading private institutions where nontenured associate professors are common, this review may well become the most important one. There, a large assemblage of professors asks whether a colleague who may have been associated with the institution for ten or more years is sufficiently worthy of tenure as a full professor. If the answer is negative, the associate professor without tenure must leave, or if already tenured, as in the state universities, he or she remains in grade. Major universities typically have "hung up" associate professors who never make the jump to professor, or who negotiate this critical move on a delayed time table, perhaps after ten, twelve, or fifteen years, or even, as a pension reward for long service, just a few years before retirement.

Other components of merit enter into the common university scheme. Acceleration is possible. Such movement jumps some steps or ranks, or both, a procedure used particularly to retain talented professors who are receiving job offers from other institutions. Promotion to the highest levels of the full professor scale may require another major review that calls for international distinction: The California system, for example, insists upon such a review for anyone wishing to proceed beyond Step V of the professorship. Above the peak of the formal scheme lies the possibility of overscale salaries and appointments to named chairs that may carry unusually high remuneration.

At the same time, seniority plays some role. Within each rank, ascent is relatively automatic; the assistant professor serves two years at each step, for a total of six years as normal time in grade, with Step IV held for occasional use. Time blocks of six years or more may be largely negotiated on the basis of years of service. But the merit decisions are never far away: they control the major moves. The leading universities, private and public, set the competitive standard for toughness of evaluation, a posture highlighted by the expectation, established at Harvard, that assistant professors should *not* expect to be promoted and kept on. Even in a state university, with the leeway of larger staff, half or more of the assistant professors may possibly not make their way to tenure. As upwardly mobile universities seek to be as severe as the institutions ahead of them, institutional hierarchy becomes a major shaper of careers, pushing merit well ahead of seniority.

The balance between merit and seniority shifts toward seniority as we move down the hierarchy into the middle and lower levels, away from the leading private colleges as well as the leading public and private universities. Where teaching, not research, is emphasized, the assessment of merit becomes more difficult. The profession has a moderately reliable means of assessing merit based on research and scholarship, since the results of individual effort are made public in the form of articles and books that can be readily brought into national as well as local councils of peer and administrative review. But similar public and consensual means of assessing merit based on teaching have never been worked out. There is no audience of disciplinary peers, small or large, before whom the results of teaching are laid. "External examiners" who might observe the results of teaching programs as they tested students at the end of course work—a common procedure in Britain—have never been widely adopted in the American system.[15] Professional controls based on merit assessment are then automatically weakened. Standards lose their national, cosmopolitan footing, because judgments on competence are more localized. Professors are less able to use peer acclaim in their disciplines as leverage with administrators and local colleagues. And, at the same time, the institutions are more managerial in character.

The community colleges stand in greatest contrast to the research universities. Evolving mainly out of secondary systems, they have, for the most part, found it a struggle to establish merit principles and merit scales of rank and pay. Because teaching is limited to the first two undergraduate years, and spreads into adult education and community services, *and*, because research plays no role, the conditions for judging merit are at their weakest in these colleges. The tilt to seniority, then, becomes pronounced. Heavily influenced by the lack of ranks at the secondary level, community colleges initially even attempted to operate without the typical rank structure of higher education. Over a third still do, but the majority have adopted the standard pattern of assistant, associate, and full professor.[16] But many crucial features are still shared with the secondary level: Merit judgments are based on assessment of teaching; tenure is achieved early, after one, two, or three years; after tenure, one moves to higher ranks and salary by routine accounting of length of service, educational credits, and degrees earned; acceleration is not offered for especially meritorious effort.

Early tenure is central. Noting from national data that tenure is often awarded after a single year or after a probation of two or three years, Cohen and Brawer concluded that "tenure patterns in community colleges more closely resembled those in the lower schools than they did the procedures in universities. . . . They rarely approximated the seven-year standard common in universities."[17] At the same time, unless countered by union power, administrators have relatively strong veto power. An extended comment from an associate professor in a community college summed up a good share of this picture:

214

Each time I came up for promotion I got the promotion without any hitches. I was never denied promotion. If they keep you on after the second year, you are going to get tenure, so that is no big deal. I will be up for full professor in two years. You have to wait a certain amount of time before you come up. . . . The one thing that is totally inflexible, which I have always objected to, is the length of time that one must wait between associate and full professor—you must wait five years. Now I feel that if somebody is doing super work, publishing and doing all kinds of good things, they should be able to petition for promotion, to send in a letter of intent that they will put themselves up for promotion. You cannot do that here. Here you must wait your time. . . . years ago if you waited the time, it was an automatic thing, and you just got promoted. Now you can still wait the time and be turned down. . . . It is ambiguous, they have a lot of leeway up there and they can play games. . . . [Then you must] smile a lot at administrators and get your name known a little bit.

In the seniority-based career, you "wait your time." Promotion is "an automatic thing," that is, unless financial exigency has been declared. That being so, "they have a lot of leeway up there," an exercise of managerial discretion that encourages sycophancy or the unionization response.

Notable, too, is the bureaucratic detail that adheres to many community college salary schedules, wherein individuals work their way to higher salary by moving down the rows of a basic table by virtue of "years of experience" and by moving across columns according to degrees earned and "points" awarded for additional courses of "college study." A good example is the salary schedule of certified personnel in the Los Angeles Community College District reported in two-page detail in Appendix E. Rank is no longer a critical issue: It exists in the system but does not even appear in the table as a determinant of salary. Minimum preparation can be as little as a bachelor's degree *or* "four years of occupational experience for certain subject fields." Progress down the rows by years served is an automatic thing, but "points" can be manipulated by taking more college courses. A doctor's degree adds so many dollars to each month's salary. "Employees" who are over in the column of maximum return, and progress beyond a certain number of years served, are "eligible" for other "career increments" in pay. The schedule is computed on a monthly basis, not on an annual salary. There are "day-to-day substitute rates" for assignments of "less than three clock hours" or for "three or more clock hours." Everything is quite "objective," bureaucratically, with no suggestion of merit, professionally. Once made permanent, the worst are equal to the best.

In sum, American rank structures provide for continuous careers, with small increments of advancement flowing from one to another. But the structures vary greatly across institutional sectors from research universities to community colleges in how much they emphasize individual merit and how much they reward common advancement by years of service. Where careers are based on research, merit has sturdy footing in peer review within both extended and local disciplinary circles. In careers based on teaching—they are the vast majority—the assessment of merit becomes more localized and more subject to the well-known difficulties of assessing the effectiveness of teaching habits and styles. Small, private colleges apparently offer the conditions where teaching capability can be best assessed, since interpersonal ties among colleagues in a faculty of only 100 to 200 generate considerable informal communication. When a college postpones for six to eight years the crucial decisions on tenure, a standard procedure in private colleges, the teaching quality of younger faculty members is likely to be well known.

Merit decisions are difficult and invidious: Public four-year and especially two-year colleges are in a difficult situation to make them. Such colleges are constrained both internally and externally if they seek to promote one faculty member on merit, while denying the next on the same grounds. As these institutions become larger and more complex, faculty members and administrators develop an interest in standardizing advancement by turning years of service into *the* means of career progress. Union ideals also move faculty in this direction—the greatest good for the greatest number—and operate most powerfully where traditional administrative dominance causes faculty members, as aspiring professionals, to feel relatively powerless.

Predictably, universal higher education thus shifts the bulk of faculty careers from merit to toil. Bureaucratically based careers replace profes-

216

sionally determined ones. Yet, compared to nationalized systems, there are no generalized blockage points. On grounds of merit or seniority, junior academics expect, if not in one institution then in another, to advance eventually to senior levels.

SATISFACTION AND SOLACE
IN THE ACADEMIC CAREER

The 1984 Carnegie survey found that an overwhelming proportion of regular faculty were satisfied with their profession. When asked, "If I had it to do over again, I'd not become a college teacher," only one in five agreed even mildly. Less than one in ten strongly agreed, and they were outnumbered six-fold by those who just as strongly took the opposite view (Table 13). The responses did not vary greatly across types of institutions: With small differences, professors in the best liberal arts colleges were the happiest, those in the second-rank small colleges, the least. When offered the statement, "I feel trapped in a profession with limited opportunities for advancement," only 22 percent strongly agreed, 17 percent agreed with reservations, 22 percent disagreed with reservations, and a flat 50 percent strongly disagreed. Professors in the top universities felt the least confined (Table 14). Or, confronted with the question, "In general, how do you feel about this institution," only one in ten claimed, "It is not the place for me" (Table 15). When four out of ten professors feel their present institution is "a very good place" for them, and another five say it is "a fairly good place," the survey responses at least suggest that the professoriate is not distressed about its lot.

What lies behind these optimistic figures? On the surface there were ample reasons for discontent. Throughout the 1970s and into the early 1980s, salaries had not kept pace with the rate of inflation. Teaching loads had stiffened in institutions largely devoted to teaching. Federal research support was reduced in a number of fields. As of 1984, the higher education system had just undergone an economic recession that helped weaken the financial health of innumerable institutions, forcing some to the wall and others to self-consciously change their orientation to escape bankruptcy. Trustees and administrators openly challenged tenure and sought successfully to employ more part-time faculty. In many quarters—the state col-

217

TABLE 13

UNWILLINGNESS OF FACULTY TO CHOOSE COLLEGE TEACHING AGAIN, BY TYPE OF INSTITUTION

TYPE OF INSTITUTION	STRONGLY AGREE	EXTENT OF AGREEMENT AGREE WITH RESERVATIONS	DISAGREE WITH RESERVATIONS	STRONGLY DISAGREE
		(PERCENT OF FACULTY)		
RESEARCH UNIVERSITIES I	5	13	27	55
RESEARCH UNIVERSITIES II	6	15	24	55
DOCTORAL-GRANTING UNIVERSITIES I	10	13	27	50
DOCTORAL-GRANTING UNIVERSITIES II	8	13	24	55
COMPREHENSIVE UNIVERSITIES AND COLLEGES I	11	13	24	52
COMPREHENSIVE UNIVERSITIES AND COLLEGES II	9	14	23	54
LIBERAL ARTS COLLEGES I	4	9	28	59
LIBERAL ARTS COLLEGES II	7	20	25	48
TWO-YEAR COLLEGES	7	12	26	55
ALL INSTITUTIONS	8	13	25	54

Total respondents, 4,907

QUESTION: "If I had to do it over again, I'd not become a college teacher."

SOURCE: The Carnegie Foundation for the Advancement of Teaching, 1984 Faculty Survey.

TABLE 14

FACULTY FEELINGS OF ENTRAPMENT IN THE PROFESSION, BY TYPE OF INSTITUTION

TYPE OF INSTITUTION	EXTENT OF AGREEMENT			
	STRONGLY AGREE	AGREE WITH RESERVATIONS	DISAGREE WITH RESERVATIONS	STRONGLY DISAGREE
	(PERCENT OF FACULTY)			
RESEARCH UNIVERSITIES I	6	12	18	64
RESEARCH UNIVERSITIES II	8	18	19	55
DOCTORAL-GRANTING UNIVERSITIES I	10	19	22	49
DOCTORAL-GRANTING UNIVERSITIES II	11	15	21	53
COMPREHENSIVE UNIVERSITIES AND COLLEGES I	13	17	24	46
COMPREHENSIVE UNIVERSITIES AND COLLEGES II	13	21	20	46
LIBERAL ARTS COLLEGES I	8	14	25	53
LIBERAL ARTS COLLEGES II	13	20	23	44
TWO-YEAR COLLEGES	13	18	23	46
ALL INSTITUTIONS	11	17	22	50

Total respondents, 4,866

QUESTION: "I feel trapped in a profession with limited opportunities for advancement."

SOURCE: The Carnegie Foundation for the Advancement of Teaching, 1984 Faculty Survey.

TABLE 15

FACULTY FEELING ABOUT THEIR OWN INSTITUTION,
BY TYPE OF INSTITUTION

TYPE OF INSTITUTION	IT IS A VERY GOOD PLACE FOR ME	IT IS FAIRLY GOOD FOR ME	IT IS NOT THE PLACE FOR ME
	(PERCENT OF FACULTY)		
RESEARCH UNIVERSITIES I	49	44	7
RESEARCH UNIVERSITIES II	38	53	9
DOCTORAL-GRANTING UNIVERSITIES I	33	56	11
DOCTORAL-GRANTING UNIVERSITIES II	35	58	7
COMPREHENSIVE UNIVERSITIES AND COLLEGES I	35	51	14
COMPREHENSIVE UNIVERSITIES AND COLLEGES II	36	52	12
LIBERAL ARTS COLLEGES I	56	37	7
LIBERAL ARTS COLLEGES II	42	49	9
TWO-YEAR COLLEGES	47	45	8
ALL INSTITUTIONS	41	49	10

Total respondents, 4,935

QUESTION: "In general, how do you feel about this institution?"

SOURCE: The Carnegie Foundation for the Advancement of Teaching, 1984 Faculty Survey.

leges, the community colleges, the private colleges—there was much about which to worry, even to make academics think their profession was in disrepair.

Certain questions in the national survey did reveal widespread unease, especially those that pointed to material conditions and the availability of jobs for newcomers. When asked if "this is a poor time for any young person to begin an academic career," half of the total faculty agreed; at least four out of ten replied "yes" in each of the institutional categories. When asked, "Thinking about the next ten years, how would you rate the job prospects for graduate students from your department for academic jobs," the "fair," "poor," and "very poor" responses heavily predominated, with only one in six prepared to say "very good." Answers to a question comparing current job prospects for students, with those of five years ago, were more negative than positive. Even departmental morale, compared to the earlier period, was seen as more depressed. (See Appendix E.)

Our field interviews shed much light on what caused dissatisfaction. Near the end of long conversations, faculty were asked what they felt were "the major problems facing the academic profession today." Everywhere comments about (a) money and (b) poorly prepared students were prominent:

> That you have to be so second-class economically when you are so important to society. . . . The biggest problem, then, is [that] the pay is not good enough. (*Professor of physics, research university*)

> That students are not coming in as well prepared as they used to be. . . . They talk about grade inflation, and it's almost forced upon the profession because [of] those students coming out of high schools. Fifteen years ago, at least half of them would have been sent to the writing lab, and now [they] are sent to regular classes. (*Professor of English, second-level university*)

> Students don't come here prepared in the various fundamental things like mathematics and English. (*Professor of English, comprehensive college*)

> I don't feel like students, at least some students, have the academic grounding that they had ten or fifteen years ago. I don't think they are getting it. (*Professor of political science, liberal arts college II*)

> There's always the financial problem. This has become especially acute in biology, because the alternatives have become so lucrative. (*Professor of biology, community college*)

"Lucrative alternatives" naturally heighten concern about salary; hence "pay is not good enough" was a cry heard frequently in medicine and the sciences. Medical school respondents stated that the university cannot

221

"really stay competitive with physicians' salaries"; "serious discrepancies between the salaries of clinical scientists and basic scientists" then develop because the former are raised under pressure of the market place. The laments about poorly prepared students, found in all disciplines in all types of institutions, peaked in the humanities, with departments of English heavily involved in remedial English. There was much about which to worry. The material rewards had not kept pace; secondary schools were providing lower quality-clientele.

How, then, in the face of the grounds for discontent, do we explain the relatively high level of personal satisfaction professors reported overall? Why did they claim that, given the chance to do it over again, they would still be college teachers; that they do not feel trapped; that they are even satisfied with their current institution? The explanation lies in the compensating power of intrinsic rewards.[18] Some clues lurk in the answers to the numerous questions posed in the national survey. Overwhelmingly, in all institutional sectors, faculty members reported a strong belief in education, that "education offers the best hope for improvement of the human condition" (Table 16). Here we find a sustaining myth that can overshadow diminished material rewards. When faculty members believe they are actively engaged in providing man's best hope for improvement, they possess a supreme fiction of great power that echoes with a sense of calling. In response to another question, faculty members noted that they greatly enjoy interacting with young people: As many as nine out of ten professors, from all types of institutions, claim they "enjoy opportunities to interact informally with students outside the classroom," let alone meet them in classes and laboratories. Even in the leading universities, where professors reputedly avoid informal contact with students, the survey respondents took the high road and claimed otherwise. Of course, such responses are relative to the setting and open to various personal interpretations, but taken at face value, they show an impressive willingness to find pleasure in relations with students.

Most important, whenever the intensive field interviews touched the domain of satisfaction, they tapped the strength of intrinsic motivation, the rewards of doing academic work for its own sake, its own challenge and passion.[19] Sometimes immediately manifest, sometimes lying just beneath the surface of comment, respondents moved from the material to the more

222

TABLE 16

FACULTY BELIEF THAT EDUCATION IS BEST HOPE FOR IMPROVING THE HUMAN CONDITION, BY TYPE OF INSTITUTION

TYPE OF INSTITUTION	EXTENT OF AGREEMENT			
	STRONGLY AGREE	AGREE WITH RESERVATIONS	DISAGREE WITH RESERVATIONS	STRONGLY DISAGREE
	(PERCENT OF FACULTY)			
RESEARCH UNIVERSITIES I	51	38	8	3
RESEARCH UNIVERSITIES II	59	32	5	4
DOCTORAL-GRANTING UNIVERSITIES I	57	35	6	2
DOCTORAL-GRANTING UNIVERSITIES II	61	34	3	2
COMPREHENSIVE UNIVERSITIES AND COLLEGES I	60	33	5	2
COMPREHENSIVE UNIVERSITIES AND COLLEGES II	61	31	7	1
LIBERAL ARTS COLLEGES I	54	33	12	1
LIBERAL ARTS COLLEGES II	55	32	9	4
TWO-YEAR COLLEGES	64	31	4	1
ALL INSTITUTIONS	59	33	6	2

Total respondents, 4,947

QUESTION: "I believe that education offers the best hope for the improvement of the human condition."

SOURCE: The Carnegie Foundation for the Advancement of Teaching, 1984 Faculty Survey.

223

intangible, to reasons couched in the shibboleths of academia all tough-minded observers have learned to distrust. But the shibboleths are real: Academic professionals believe them. And a cynical approach by observers is a poor way to capture the intrinsic, the very excitement that many professors find in their teaching or their research. Let us take their formulations seriously as they tell us in some detail why they entered the profession, how it has differed from what they expected, and whether they have considered leaving academia for another line of work. Beginning in the research universities:

> (*What were your reasons for entering the academic profession?*) I discovered that somebody was crazy enough to pay me for what I love doing best. (*Has it differed from what you expected?*) It has been better. What I hadn't imagined was just how exciting the students would be. (*Have you considered or would you consider ever leaving academia?*) No. (*Professor of English*)

> (*Has it differed from what you had expected?*) Oh, yeah. I mean I really had no appreciation for the excitement of research when I decided to go to graduate school. I knew a little bit about research, but it was more the technical experience of getting data and not really the excitement that comes from having some new insights into a problem. (*So basically it sounds like it has fulfilled rather than disappointed your expectations?*) Oh, yeah. (*Would you consider leaving . . . ?*) No. (*Professor of biology and chemistry*)

> (*Would you ever consider leaving . . . ?*) No. I have never been interested in doing anything that might be more lucrative, that would have other applications. I am really interested in solving problems, finding out what makes cells tick. (*Professor of biology*)

The view from the top of the institutional hierarchy can be enormously satisfying, for then the "extrinsic" rewards of high status are blended with the intrinsic motives. A research physicist commenting on the satisfactions of "doing physics" (as reported in Chapter V) indicated how important it was "to be thought about when people think about getting together and having a meeting," to know that you are "good enough to be a part of it," the leading circles, even "if you're not the best." Then "there is noth-

224

ing in the world that will touch it''; others ''don't know what it is to match wits with people whose wits are worth matching.'' Academics love research all the more when national peers applaud and throw garlands of status. The heightened self-esteem that accompanies the applause may help to generate a self-fulfilling prophecy. More applause leads to more research and also to the sense that the accolades that help provide the conditions for advancement are richly deserved. A high cosmopolitanism of this sort in the upper reaches of even the not-so-rich humanities generates an academic jet set that moves around the globe from one conference to another, from one study center in northern New England to another in Italy, a hectic pace hilariously depicted in only somewhat fictional form by David Lodge in *Small World* (see Vignette Four). All in all, in the mid-1980s there are many American academics who never were so well off, and they know it.

When we jump from the research university to the community college, we still hear about rewards that have nothing to do with money, size of office, or job security. Instead, there is the ''good, quick recognition'' you can get ''from dealing with students'':

> (*Why did you become a college professor?*) I like performance, I really do. . . . I think the better I perform at educating, the better students accept it. Accounting, could it be boring? To me it is not boring. To me it is challenging, to me it is fun, it is exciting. . . . I like it so much I feel my enthusiasm conveys. I like to be up front, I like talking in front of people, I like putting an affect on someone. I like the ability to light a spark in someone and see that they like that, and to say that I helped that person make a decision because it was me, because what I gave to them and how I dealt with them, they like what they are doing and maybe they have changed their career because of it. . . . I like the immediate reward that you get from dealing with students—good, quick recognition. (*Professor of business*)

There is a ''psychic gratification'' that makes up for the lack of financial rewards:

> (*Would you ever consider leaving here?*) Right now I'm pretty enthusiastic about teaching. I think it is great. If I didn't feel that it

VIGNETTE FOUR
THE ASCENT TO BELLAGIO

In David Lodge's novel, Small World, *the aggressive American academic, Morris Zapp, a confirmed jet setter, arrives at the Villa Serbelloni in Bellagio, Italy, one of the world's premiere settings for any meeting. Well pleased with his good fortune—richly deserved, he believes—Professor Zapp reviews how one ascends to the highest rung of a merit career.*

Morris was shown into a well-appointed suite on the second floor, and stepped out on to his balcony to inhale the air, scented with the perfume of various spring blossoms, and to enjoy the prospect. Down on the terrace, the other resident scholars were gathering for the prelunch aperitif. . . . He surveyed the scene with complacency. He felt sure he was going to enjoy his stay here. Not the least of its attractions was that it was entirely free. All you had to do, to come and stay in this idyllic retreat, pampered by servants and lavishly provided with food and drink, given every facility for reflection and creation, was to apply.

Of course, you had to be distinguished—by, for instance, having applied successfully for other, similar handouts, grants, fellowships and so on, in the past. That was the beauty of the academic life, as Morris saw it. To them that had, more would be given. All you needed to do to get started was to write one really damned good book—which admittedly wasn't easy when you were a young college teacher just beginning your career, struggling with a heavy teaching load on unfamiliar material, and probably with the demands of a wife and a young growing family as well. But on the strength of that one damned good book you could get a grant to write a second book in more favourable circumstances; with two books you got promotion, a lighter teaching load, and courses of your own devising; you could then use your teaching as a way of doing research for your next book, which you were thus able to produce all the more quickly. This productivity made you eligible for tenure, further promotion, more generous and prestigious grants, more relief from routine teaching and administration. In theory, it was possible to wind up being full professor while doing nothing except to be permanently absent on some kind of sabbatical grant or fellowship. Morris hadn't quite reached that omega point, but he was working on it.[23]

SOURCE: David Lodge, *Small World*, 1984, pp. 151–152. Reprinted by permission of Macmillan Publishing Company.

was fun and that I wasn't getting that feeling of satisfaction out of being part of the community and contributing to the community, then I don't think that it would be worth doing. Obviously, we don't get paid very much, and you have to get psychic gratification to make up for that lack of financial rewards. . . . I can't imagine wanting to go back into a corporation full-time. I didn't find it terribly satisfying. In other words, whether *Time* made $4.25 a share or $4.60, it doesn't really matter to me—I don't really care. The fundamental mission of [that] organization is unimportant to me. And *this* mission is important to me. . . . (*Professor of business*)

And we begin to get broad indications of how academics cope when expectations do not work out:

(*Has it differed from what you expected?*) Yes, it differs in the sense that I originally expected to have more of a mixture of research and teaching. It worked out that being at a community college, the research is very difficult. . . . I simply couldn't do as much research as I'd like to. Also, I would like to teach upper division classes. But, aside from that, I do enjoy my teaching as much as I did at the beginning. I'm very happy it worked out the way it did. (*Professor of biology*)

So, "aside from that"—not being able to do research, not having upper division let alone graduate students—the work of teaching that this community college instructor has makes him "very happy it worked out the way it did."

Another instance of coping, based on prior teaching at the secondary school level and in the face of worry that salary will not be sufficient, was presented:

(*Has it differed from what you expected?*) Doesn't reality always differ? [after explaining that he had taught in secondary schools] I did learn this: The older the student and the more advanced the level . . . the greater I found the appreciation for learning. (*Would you consider leaving the profession . . . ?*) If my salary doesn't improve very quickly, very substantially. There have been times when I've thought about it, not—I don't think that I would willingly do it, unless the opportunity were substantial

227

enough to not just monetarily protect my family but also give me an opportunity to get comparable psychic rewards. (*Professor of political science*)

In the lesser liberal arts colleges, as in the community colleges, some professors reported they were disappointed they were not able to do research. But then they had switched their fulfillment to teaching:

> (*Has it differed from what you expected?*) The second half of it has. I have not been able to do the kind of research I feel I am capable of. Those expectations have not been fulfilled. The personal satisfaction of working with students, and such, has been by and large fulfilled [although] there have been some disappointments, too, in that area. (*Professor of English*)

Avoidance of the business world sometimes arose explicitly, as in the reaction of a professor of political science in a liberal arts college:

> I know you [the interviewer] see a lot of people that really don't have a lot of business sense: I am one of them. I don't mean that everybody in academia has no business sense, but the world of business did not appeal to me, and I know about it because both of my parents had businesses. My mother had a ladies ready-to-wear and my father had a hardware business. It didn't appeal to me. . . .

Better *this* than that!

Then, there is always the free time, especially in summer:

> If you ask me now what it was that did it, I think it was just that I like teaching, and along with that, I should point out, the summer. I could do things in the summer. Sometimes I just had to work, but other times I could travel, and other times I would sit on that porch and lean back and read all the periodicals that I wanted, you know, and it was very nice. It really was, and I realized there are very few people except perhaps the rich who have that much time.

228

Inertia finally seals the bargain:

> (*Would you consider leaving to take a position elsewhere?*) "No, I have already bought my cemetery lot." (*Literally or figuratively?*) "Literally!"

How professors cope in the settings where primary expectations cannot be realized was summed up best by a biology professor in a community college:

> I have different hats, and I wear them at different times. Definitely, I am out of the scholastic end of it, the high-powered end of it. I have given up on that and I have come to terms with it. . . . No, I don't think I would ever change. Most of us here, . . . have come to terms with it, and we live our lives such that we get gratification from various areas. It doesn't all have to come from our profession. It hurt me to go from [a minor university] to here at first, and I felt it was a step down. At [the university] there were always . . . graduate students and professors doing their work, and it was always eight in the morning and ten at night. So I missed that, but I have adjusted to it; and at [the university] I probably could not have thrown myself into teaching as much as I have here, and there are trade-offs, and the trade-off is that I can do my teaching here and look for excitement elsewhere in my life.

Thus there are many ways of coping. If an academic would like to do some research but research time is squeezed out by teaching time, then he or she can seek job satisfaction in the applause of the classroom and informal relations with admiring young people. If teaching becomes routinized and hence too boring, the professor can manipulate the work schedule to have free time for other activities, even second jobs. The free time of summer—one-fourth of the year off—is an attractive bonus. Here again, it cannot be emphasized too strongly that control of time is a central element in the satisfaction of academics. This is true from settings where the teaching load is but a few hours a week to the community colleges with their schedules of fifteen and twenty or more hours.

We were surprised by the many comments made by community college

229

teachers which pointed to the pleasures of free time. Their feelings can be partly attributed to their experiences as high school teachers—they were a sizeable group—or as part of the industrial work force, the military, or some other outside sector of work where nine-to-five, or more, is a normal expectation of time at the job. When community colleges began to develop in the 1920s, as many as four out of five instructors had previous high school experience. The proportion was still over one-half in the 1960s.[20] In 1984, according to the Carnegie survey, over one-third had been teachers or administrators in the schools, one in six had held executive or administrative posts outside of education, one in two had had other outside "professional positions"—probably including the trades—and as high as 7 percent had had careers in the armed forces for six years or more—the latter figure comparing to 2 percent or less in nearly all the other institutional categories (Appendix E). Further, one in seven (14 percent) had been unemployed for two years or more since taking their highest degree, compared to less than 2 percent in the leading universities; and over one-third (37 percent) had been employed part-time for two years or more. Such prior experiences would put a rosy glow on "only" fifteen hours in the classroom. Expectations are adjusted sector by sector.

Further, class preparation is considerably eased when courses are routinized. If professors teach only introductory courses, and do so frequently, they soon know the materials thoroughly. Little or no class preparation is needed: In the 1984 survey two-year college faculty reported virtually no more hours spent preparing for teaching than did faculty in research universities, with three out of four doing their preparation in ten hours a week or less—75 percent compared to 79 percent in the leading universities (Appendix E). And time spent on grading need not be any greater than elsewhere, since introductory contents are relatively easy to assess and can be quickly done, particularly by those who turn to machine-scored objective tests. Most of all, professors located where research is not expected, where the institution is even hostile to it, save a great deal of research time. Thus, as various community college respondents describe in their interviews, a fifteen-to-twenty-hour teaching load—literally backbreaking by the norms of higher education—can be managed so that total work time comes out to less than a forty-hour week, with much of that time, as elsewhere in

230

academia, not requiring one's presence at the college and subject to some personal discretion in daily and weekly calendars.

The extensive differentiation of American higher education plays an important role in promoting satisfaction even though it leads to the unhappiness induced by the invidious distinctions of the institutional hierarchy. The differentiation provides a variety of settings in which individual academics can play to their preferences and strengths. Individuals do not have to attune themselves to one set of incentives and rewards and to fit one set of duties and competencies. By self-selection, researchers drift toward research settings, teachers toward teaching settings; big-city folk toward urban universities, pastoral types toward the small campus in the rolling countryside; those who insist on teaching bright undergraduates toward the better liberal arts colleges, those with the open-access spirit toward the public two-year campuses. The fit of individuals to settings is highly imperfect, leaving many in unwanted locations. When that occurs, the flexibility of personal adjustment that occurs within the dominant duties of the major settings allows academics some meaningful leeway to move toward their preferences and find comfort in their strengths.

We may also conclude that the profession thus provides essentially two main alternative clienteles for recognition and respect: peers and students. For academic researchers who have national and international peers as their primary audience, the importance of that audience deepens with every increase in scientific and academic specialization. To recognize its primacy is to know an essential basic fact of life in modern academia—with the American system, in its upper reaches, an extreme case. This institutionalization of the peer audience as the first basis for recognition and respect continues to escape those observers, intent on reforming undergraduate education in the universities, who believe that by exhortation, or state edict, they can turn university professors from peers to students. Students become the primary audience only when research is essentially removed from the work setting, as in the lesser liberal arts colleges, the state colleges with their twelve-hour loads, and, especially, the community colleges. The fault line is deep between professional peers and student clientele as the first place to which professors turn when thinking about the pleasures and the pains of academic work.

The other principal fault line, we have seen, lies not in clientele but in

231

the very firmness of the academic job, the chance to be a member of the regular faculty, with some security of employment and dependable movement up the ranks. The growth of a peripheral work force is a staggering phenomenon, a massive lump an integrated profession would find hard to swallow. In the vast differentiation of American higher education, the categories of marginal academic labor have multiplied in an uneven, uncontrolled fashion, weak in one discipline but strong in another, hardly to be noticed in the leading small private colleges but qualitatively changing the nature of the professoriate in the public community colleges. It goes without saying that dissatisfaction is extremely high in this secondary work force.[21]

Academic careers now multiply without limit. Mass higher education American style means, from entry to postretirement, a professoriate of endless central and marginal possibilities. And it is a very long way from the core to the periphery.

CHAPTER VIII

The Ties of Association

In every case, at the head of any new undertaking, where in France you would find the government or in England some territorial magnate, in the United States you are sure to find an association.

> —ALEXIS DE TOCQUEVILLE, *DEMOCRACY IN AMERICA*

For what to us is the praise of the ignorant? Let us join together in the bond of our scientific societies, and encourage each other, as we are now doing, in the pursuit of our favorite study; knowing that the world will sometime recognize our services, and knowing, also, that we constitute the most important element in human progress.

> —HENRY A. ROWLAND, ''A PLEA FOR PURE SCIENCE''(1883)

Individuals who are not bound together in associations, whether domestic, economic, religious, political, artistic, or educational are monstrosities.

> —JOHN DEWEY, *INDIVIDUALISM OLD AND NEW* (1930)

AMERICAN ACADEMIC SPECIALISTS do not long remain monstrosities—in John Dewey's vivid imagery—unbound by solid organization that promises to consolidate and further their intellectual effort. They settled a century ago upon the department as their main tool of controlled development inside universities and colleges, a unit primarily centered on individual subjects and devoted to furthering individual disciplines, while it also served as the building block of academic enterprises. But something more was needed to tighten the hold of specialization upon academic life, a device that would serve externally as a carrying mechanism for a discipline at large, a way of furthering specialties without regard to institutional boundaries. By the end of the nineteenth century, American academics en masse found that external arm in the learned society or disciplinary association, a form at once specialized in scope and national in membership and orientation.

Near the end of the twentieth century, we cannot imagine academic life without this type of professional linkage. It serves many interests of academics, idealistic and practical, right down to the "flesh market" realities of job seeking. No academic specialty amounts to anything unless it has a national association, or a section of one—or, as we later see, an "invisible" substitute—to help it develop, spread its influence, and enhance its sense of solidarity. Among the associations operating in 1985, two-thirds had originated since 1940, with 150 starting up after 1960 (Table 4 and Appendix B), clear evidence of the widespread and increasing importance of this form of linkage. Disciplinary associations multiply as fast as specialties develop; they have also begun to reflect the division of academics among institutional sectors.

THE PATTERNS OF ASSOCIATION

The first distinction we need to grasp is between associations of professors and associations of administrators. The duality of disciplines and institutions in American higher education is reflected in the division of national associations into those that center on faculty interests and those that are organized around the interests of college and university administrators. Institutionally tied associations are exemplified and semiofficially capped by the American Council on Education (ACE), a "presidents' club" established in 1918 at the same time as the National Research Council (NRC) and the Social Science Research Council (SSRC). All were voluntary associations established to help link higher education and the national government.[1] While the NRC and the SSRC served as multidiscipline associations organized by and for professors, the ACE became an association of universities and colleges, hence administrator-driven, that was to serve, in part, as an association of associations. Its present locale at One Dupont Circle, an edifice in Washington, D.C., houses the headquarters of many other associations in which institutional members are represented by their top administrators, as in the powerful National Association of State Universities and Land-Grant Colleges (NASULGC) that dates itself in an earlier form as far back as 1887, or in which individuals represent a segment

234

of administration as well as their whole institutions, as in the Council of Graduate Schools (CGS), where graduate school deans, committed primarily to the welfare of graduate education, serve as members. The programs of the annual meetings of these associations do not take up academic subjects, other than, occasionally, the minor specialty known as the study of higher education. They explore not Wittgenstein and Weber, but student personnel services and strains of the college presidency. Representing the interests of administrators in the welfare of whole institutions or major parts thereof—and in personal advancement in administrative careers—an entire set of associations runs on a separate track from the discipline-by-discipline representation we find in the faculty associations.

When graduate deans, business officers, admissions officers, presidents, chancellors, and other clusters of administrators represent institutional concerns, their efforts may well serve faculty interests. They may help to increase financial resources and, generally, to enhance the good name of academia; they may specifically lobby to strengthen the humanities or the sciences. Leaders in these associations may go down two roads simultaneously, running with the faculty hare as well as with the administrator hound. But often they do not: The agendas quite naturally diverge. The administrators tune to governmental actions that would strengthen or adversely affect entire institutions. They are interested in overall institutional leadership and hence in effective administrative controls. They seek counsel on "management." Their agenda stretches from legislative actions on student aid, to relations with universities in other countries, to the never-ending battle to bring big-time collegiate sports under some semblance of control.

In contrast, faculty members operate within disciplines, either individual ones or in combinations of them—the natural sciences, the social sciences, the humanities, the arts—to influence governmental and private-sector actions that will strengthen the research and scholarly base of their own fields. The academicians are particularly strong in science councils, penetrating by means of peer review the ordinary routines of such major agencies as the National Science Foundation and the National Institutes of Health. And, most of the time, their associations turn inward upon periodic meetings in which papers are read and criticized and specialized knowledge is otherwise pursued. Hence it is not surprising that faculty members and administrators from the same campus may go separate ways in representing interests in Washington, D.C., to the point where one does not know what the other is doing, and uncoordinated if not conflicting action is taken, to the surprise of all. Clark Kerr pointed out in the 1960s that the heads of campuses can readily feel things are out of control, and their own authority threatened, when professors strike their own deals in Washington.[2] One story used to illustrate the problem is about the research professor who strolled into the president's office in an Eastern private university to announce that he had just arranged, on a recent trip to Washington, for a research grant that included not only a new laboratory but an entire new building. The professor was sure the president would welcome this good news.

Natural conflict between administrator and faculty associations is exemplified in arguments over the size of "institutional overhead" in the budgeting of federal research grants. Researchers are inclined to see every dollar for overhead as one less dollar for research itself. They strongly prefer to have granting agencies limit the amount allotted to "indirect costs" that goes to the institution as a whole and hence into the hands of central administrators. On the other hand, campus administrators have constantly urged the government to raise the overhead rate. They maintain that big science has long had major hidden costs on university campuses, that "in the early days of indirect costs, everyone was under-recovering."[3] Further, science is steadily becoming more capital intensive, requiring more equipment and buildings that entail significant increased costs in depreciation, maintenance, and administration, which ought to be charged to research projects. At major private universities, the indirect cost rates had climbed by 1984 to between 65 and 70 percent, a very major addition to the allocations made directly for the research itself. Hence, income from this source becomes a major item in the overall budgets of research universities: At Stanford, "indirect cost recovery from government is characteristically the second most important income source, behind tuition but well ahead of all endowment income."[4] A million here and a million there soon add up to real money.

Sharp hostilities broke out over this issue in 1983, when the National Institutes of Health (NIH)—the principal supporter of research in the biological sciences—proposed to withhold 10 percent of indirect cost reim-

236

bursement in order to allocate more money to the research projects themselves. NIH was backed by the Federation of American Societies for Experimental Biology (FASEB), which accused university administrators, in true fighting language, of playing a "four-dimensional shell game" with indirect costs and described them as having made a "triumphant tour de force in evading the issue in the past three years." This serious conflict called out the skills of some of the best academic diplomats, who were soon at work forming another coalition, one of "university associations and scientific groups" that would help to obtain "full funding for both direct and indirect costs." FASEB reversed its position and passed a resolution calling for cooperation.[5] However, the issue is a sore point, a matter on which administrators and professors naturally divide, and on which their associational voices are prone to speak in divergent and often conflicting terms. Administrative associations and faculty associations see the world differently.

Of the disciplinary associations to which faculty members belong, some are almost completely restricted to academics, others center on the outside members, and still others blend the two. The American Historical Association and the American Sociological Association are known as academic associations: Academics heavily predominate, and the organization has a "learned-society" heritage that may have made a simple name change from "society" to "association" a wrenching decision. Such academic organizations are understood to be inside higher education, parts of the academic profession. In contrast, the American Medical Association and the American Bar Association are outside higher education, positioned in major domains of professional practice, with academics a small proportion of their members.

But the lines are rarely hard and fast, and some associations extensively mix academics and others. Academic chemists use the American Chemical Society as their primary association, but they constitute only one-third of its members; membership of the other two-thirds indicates that chemistry is a field in which the Ph.D. degree leads mainly to employment in industry. Founded in 1876, this association has evolved in a century into a complex organization that stretches quite naturally across the boundary between academia and industry. By the standards of wholly academic associations, it is huge, with a membership of 125,000, a budget of over one hundred million dollars, a dozen or more journals, and a fully profession-alized administrative staff of 1,600 people (in a major building of its own in Washington, D.C.) that annually oversees 1,700 local, regional, divi-sional, and other meetings.[6] Academic and nonacademic concerns natu-rally crosshatch, for whatever the differences between the academics and the industrial chemists, they have powerful mutual interests in such spe-cialties as food chemistry, organic chemistry, and physical chemistry. This association epitomizes a longstanding and increasingly more prevalent subject-centered form of organization that bridges between higher educa-tion and other sectors of society, particularly industry. The form is now common in engineering and the sciences, including biology, as a rapidly expanding field in which Ph.D.'s increasingly spread out from the academy to posts in government and private firms.

What gradually emerged in our probing of the associational structure of the profession, particularly in the accounts that respondents provided in field interviews, is the way associations mirror the ongoing contest be-tween centrifugal and centripetal academic forces. "Splinteritis" is every-where. Each academic association finds itself subdividing into numerous major divisions along subject-matter lines, which then divide still further into subsections. As they grow substantively, incorporating more special-ties, associations sow the seed of their own fragmentation. The large as-sociations also tend to divide by institutional sector: One community col-lege president pointed out that in the Modern Language Association and in the National Council of Teachers of English, "there is usually a commu-nity college component or at least a series of workshops dealing with com-munity colleges at these annual meetings." If a major association does not strategically subdivide itself, it faces the constant threat of the loss of au-tonomy-seeking groups of specialists who move to set up their own organ-izations. In the older mainline associations that have managed to remain intact, unitary organization drifts toward a more federative form.

Interests in some fields—preeminently the biological sciences—have been so scattered and diversified from the beginning that no one organi-zation ever established hegemony. Biologists of varying specialties turned to different associations, which then became integrated confederatively from the bottom up by coming together officially in one or more mam-moth umbrella organizations. A well-informed observer of the associa-

238

tions in biology did his best to tell us how a confusing reality was composed:

> The discipline is divided in this country into perhaps a hundred subdisciplinary societies: the ecologists, the physiologists, the microbiologists, the biochemists, and so on. These societies are really independent, but there are two major groups that are umbrellas. One, [the Federation of American Societies for Experimental Biology] has seven societies, and the other group is under the American Institute of Biological Sciences. . . . There are about thirty or forty societies in that group. But, you see, there are many societies that don't belong to either one, and there are some societies that belong to both. The physiologists belong both to AIBS and to FASEB. . . . Now the American Chemical Society, although there are many subdivisions of chemistry, has stuck together as the American Chemical Society. The American Institute of Physics has all of the nine major physics societies in the country under the American Institute of Physics. The biologists are scattered.

> (*Is that because of what biology is, or is it some historical thing that happened?*) That is a very difficult question. It is historical certainly, to a degree. The chemists organized early and stuck together; and the biologists, it seems, as soon as a discipline of biology forms, there are subdisciplines which splinter off. Their jealousies and egos and territorialities become important. For one reason or another, biologists seem to have much more difficulty working together than do the physicists or the chemists or even the engineers, although the engineers are somewhat split, too. There is an American Association of Engineering Societies [total membership, one million!], which has recently been structured to pull together the electrical engineers and the chemical engineers and the mechanical engineers, and so forth, under one umbrella. The point is that in Washington . . . or [in] a national posture, you almost need a strong unified group. . . . The nation simply can't listen to hundreds of little subdisciplines, each one purporting to represent science in their field, because the fields get too small and get too specialized. It's just like medicine. Medicine is also splintered, but somehow the AMA has held together, and the American Association of Medical Colleges has held together. But the biologists probably have the worst case of splinteritis of anyone in the country. . . .

239

You'll find that each individual society feels that it has the key to the future. The ecologists feel that the rest of biology is really not all that important. This is the pinnacle of science. The biochemists, at the other end of the spectrum, say you get anything above the molecule [and] it just becomes hokus-pokus and phenomenological. There is, perhaps, a great deal more sheer arrogance from discipline to discipline in biology than you find anywhere else. I don't understand it completely, and I have been observing it my whole life.

In the set of disciplines known as "the biological sciences," there are numerous associational keys to the kingdom. But a good share of the groups feel they ought to associate loosely with each other in umbrella organizations, just as small individual political states often feel the need to confederate, federate, or band together as a united larger state to exert influence. In biology, however, the larger nation is inherently weak; the individual states have separate historical identities and interests. Still, superimposed upon a resource- and knowledge-rich academic base, umbrella organizations in biology offer impressive credentials. The Federation of American Societies for Experimental Biology, with a combined membership of over 20,000, can rightfully claim it is a powerful and wealthy organization. It publishes over thirty scientific journals, counts over 100 Nobel Prizes earned by its members, and is organized to do massive reports for the federal government and other authorities on food safety and food additives, toxic waste disposal, and other significant, practical issues.[7] Confederative or not, it is a major, busy corner of academia. And its identity and membership blur the lines between the pure and the applied, the private lives of academic disciplines and the public concerns of legislators and public executives.

In efforts to counter splinteritis, multidisciplinary associations interpenetrate one another. Umbrellas are raised over umbrellas. A professor of biology who had been active in the American Zoological Society pointed to the two umbrella organizations mentioned above as larger amalgams, and then noted that he belonged to and had been an officer in yet another wider umbrella organization, the American Association for the Advancement of Science (AAAS), whose interests were very diffuse and included the social sciences and beyond. He continued:

Then, there are global organizations. For example, there is the International Union of Immunological Societies (IUIS), which is the umbrella for all national immunological societies. For example, the American Association of Immunologists holds a seat in IUIS; so does the French Society of Immunologists; so does the British Society of Immunologists. Then there is another one . . . the International Union of Biological Societies. . . .

Umbrella is one metaphor, spider web another, and pyramid yet another that points to the many ways in which proliferating associations constitute a larger maze of linkages. Many relatively small associations do not particularly acknowledge the overtones of shelter and possible subordination inherent in the umbrella concept, yet they weave themselves around a larger national association by holding their annual meeting in the same city, presenting their own programs right before, right after, or during the meeting of the major group. In the social sciences, the Society for the Study of Social Problems (SSSP) has long attached itself in this fashion to the American Sociological Association; most of its members also hold memberships in the ASA, while backing a vehicle for more practical concerns. The Policy Studies Organization, newly sprung largely from political science and public administration, meets with the American Political Science Association, again with an extensive overlap of membership. In turn, the associational networks include pyramids within individual disciplines, as smaller regional associations feed loosely into national associations that, in turn, offer the institutional building blocks plus the members for international associations. In a confusing manner only partially caught in any one metaphor, associations structure the metainstitutional life of the academic profession.

That metastructure has begun to reflect significantly the allocation of academics to types of institutions other than research universities. In at least three major ways, the associational network is adapting to the interests of faculty located in the middle and lower rungs of the institutional hierarchy. For one, national associations themselves have been adjusting their own inner lives, since about 1970, to attract and retain faculty located in state, small private, and community colleges. More attention is paid to teaching the discipline: A teaching specialist is placed in the headquarters staff; a separate budget allocation is made for work on the problems of teaching; a subdivision is organized; and space for discussion of the problems of teaching is inserted in the annual program. Second, regional disciplinary associations take on the character of a home for those who cannot get on the programs of the national associations, and especially for those unable to obtain travel funds to attend distant meetings. Regional associations are also much smaller, and their meetings in most cases seem friendlier as well as more accessible. Coast to coast, lack of travel funds is a major irritant particularly noticeable in the state-college sector. On one coast we heard: "I don't have the money to go. . . . I can't, even if I am invited to present a paper. . . . I couldn't go last year." And on the other coast: "We don't have any money within this system to send people to those things. . . . If they [the meetings] are in the neighborhood, I will go to them." The regional associations are also joined by more localized state and city counterparts, which serve as small worlds attractive to teachers and researchers of less than national renown. Those who serve as officers and as members of the many committees of these associations may receive some local and regional notice in their disciplines in lieu of national accolades.

A third, and most recent, adaptive evolution is the most telling: Disciplinary associations are now forming along sector lines. The more a sector is organizationally set off, the more do associations break off. The community college sector is, therefore, the principal center of this type of proliferation. A community college biology instructor explained how and why a sectoral association was organized in her discipline, in her part of the country, just a few years earlier:

> [We] got a notice that a group of biology professors from various two-year schools were putting together an organization. The purpose of the organization is for communication, [for] exchange of ideas between people who have the same problems, community college biologists that saw a certain type of student, a student that for one reason or another didn't go to a four-year school, either because of money or . . . often because of academic reasons. You know, what textbooks we should use at this level, and how we can use the computer in our courses, and how we can get across this idea at this level. . . . If I go to real high-powered meetings occasionally, and they speak about technologies that I

242

have no idea about anymore, being out of it, [then] I can bring back almost nothing to our students; but from these meetings I bring back a lot because they are geared for the teacher of the two-year institution.

Localization in this case took place on two dimensions simultaneously: The association is statewide instead of national, and it limits itself to the community-college part of the biology professoriate.

Such doubly local associations are both more within reach of the pocketbook, when colleges provide little or no travel funds, and more relevant to substantive interests. A social science instructor in a metropolitan community college told us he wanted to attend disciplinary meetings, but for the last four of five years he had only been able to attend one taking place in his own metropolitan area. He had gotten out of the main national association some time ago:

I used to belong to the American Political Science Association but found in recent years there was such a disparity between what they were doing and what I was doing that I didn't find it to be terribly intellectually stimulating. . . . Given where my students are at and where they are likely to go, given their socioeconomic backgrounds and their language limitations, and their heterogeneity, a lot of things that I see in the journals don't correspond very much to what I can do in class. . . . I mean, reality dictates.

Astute observers have argued cogently that community college faculty are not in a position to follow the cosmopolitan road to professionalism so heavily traveled by university professors: "The community college faculty disciplinary affiliation is too weak, the institutions' demands for scholarship are practically nonexistent, and the teaching loads are too heavy for that form of professionalism to occur." Community college faculty will either undergo more deprofessionalization, slipping further toward the weak professionalism of American schoolteaching, or they will have to bootstrap themselves into a different set of appropriate forms that "reconceptualize the academic disciplines themselves to fit the realities of the community colleges."[8] In this effort, associations and journals are crucial

243

tools. Moves in this direction have included the formation of the Community College Social Science Association and the Community College Humanities Association, together with the establishment of journals directed toward two-year college instructors in such fields as mathematics, journalism, and English.

National surveys have shown clearly that faculty members vary greatly across sectors in attendance at national meetings. In the 1984 Carnegie survey, half of the community college faculty members reported they had not made their way to a meeting during ast year, compared to about 20 percent not having done so in leading liberal arts colleges and 15 percent in leading research universities (Table 17). About one-half of leading liberal arts college faculty members and research university faculty members had attended two or more meetings, with proportions in the other sectors diminishing to one-fourth in the two-year colleges. But the other side of the coin is that, even in the community college sector, one-half of the faculty managed at least one meeting, and one out of four, by personal expense or otherwise, negotiated two or more meetings. Clearly, the urge to meet with other academics outside of one's own institution does not die even in the most adverse settings. Unfortunately, the survey data do not reveal what type of national meeting was attended or how far respondents had to travel. As national associations move their annual meetings from one city to another, a common practice, many faculty members can readily catch a meeting in their region at least every third or fourth year. And, as sector associations develop, principally in the community college area, they can find gatherings appropriate to their own cause.

In short, as the cutting edges of academic specialization become sharply honed, reality dictates that national associations centered on university professors become inappropriate for a good share of the faculty who are so involved in undergraduate teaching that they are "out of it." National meetings replete with papers reporting the latest research results are not relevant to the vast majority of community college teachers and to a large proportion of professors located in four-year institutions. We can predict further proliferation of associations localized by type of institution as well as by geographic area. Only the top third or so of the institutional hierarchy, consisting of the better colleges as well as the research universities, is thoroughly national in interest. Academics in the rest of the system find

244

TABLE 17

FACULTY ATTENDANCE AT NATIONAL MEETINGS, BY TYPE OF INSTITUTION

| | NUMBER OF MEETINGS | | |
TYPE OF INSTITUTION	NONE	ONE	TWO OR MORE
	(PERCENT OF FACULTY)		
RESEARCH UNIVERSITIES I	15	28	57
RESEARCH UNIVERSITIES II	22	29	49
DOCTORAL-GRANTING UNIVERSITIES I	27	32	41
DOCTORAL-GRANTING UNIVERSITIES II	33	27	40
COMPREHENSIVE UNIVERSITIES AND COLLEGES I	31	32	37
COMPREHENSIVE UNIVERSITIES AND COLLEGES II	41	27	32
LIBERAL ARTS COLLEGES I	21	34	45
LIBERAL ARTS COLLEGES II	38	32	30
TWO-YEAR COLLEGES	49	26	25
ALL INSTITUTIONS	33	29	38

Total respondents, 4,863

QUESTION: "During the last year, how many national professional meetings did you attend?"

SOURCE: The Carnegie Foundation for the Advancement of Teaching, Faculty Survey 1984.

their way to types of associations their own realities dictate, including responsiveness to a local undergraduate student clientele in place of responsiveness to a national group of peers. The critical divide between students and peers as primary clientele is increasingly reflected in the associational maze of the professoriate.

A major unanticipated finding that emerged from our interviews is the extent to which university researchers themselves are sometimes finding their major national associations to be empty shells, too general in scope to be relevant to special interests, too large to facilitate interaction among like-minded peers. National associations try to cope with this problem by elaborate sectioning, creating smaller worlds of subject-centered divisions, all with formal names, their own officers and members, perhaps a small budget, and definitely their own piece of the annual programming. The internal life of one association after another in the post-World War II decades has been characterized by a tension between the centrists, who wish to maintain a unitary organization and the section leaders who are busy developing separate parts whose strength and autonomy give the whole organization a confederate cast. History rides with the separatists; there are limits to how much their interests can be appeased by well-integrated generalist organizations.

At the interdisciplinary association level, the problem has struck particularly hard at the American Association for the Advancement of Science, where attendance at annual meetings slipped over 70 percent in a decade and a half, dropping between 1969 and 1985 from 8,000 to 2,300. Association officials have reported a sense of ebbing vitality; they bemoan the lack of announced major new scientific discoveries at their meetings; that "the young scientist who is doing the exciting experiment isn't at this meeting"; that only white-haired veterans, "long past the stage of active scientific work," still come. The cause of the AAAS problem is seen to be that "the increasing specialization of science is ending the popularity of big general meetings that consider scientific and public policy issues of interest to a great range of scientists, not just those from a narrow specialty." As a result, the AAAS, looking to its own vitality and value, has been shifting its center of gravity from the annual meeting, long the flagship activity, into such activities as publishing a science magazine for laymen and programs for improving the quality of precollege science and mathematics education.[9]

At the discipline level, the American Physical Society has seen attendance at its annual meeting slip drastically, from about 7,000 in 1967 to 800 in 1985. The society's executive secretary has concluded that "the general meetings are just disappearing. . . . The only way to have a successful meeting is to have specialized topics," that is, meetings that are themselves limited to such specific topics as basic properties of optical materials or radio-frequency plasma heating. The society has turned to sponsoring two dozen such smaller topical conferences a year, which might be attended by 150 to 300 physicists.[10] University faculty members we interviewed concurred: I do not go "to these gigantic Physical Society meetings, but very often to smaller workshop-things"; "nobody goes to the conferences any more very much. I mean, not the standard APS meetings. I never go; very few of my colleagues go. Instead, we tend to go to special topical meetings, which are set up just for one time only."

Similarly, in biology, where the field is already radically subdivided among national associations, professors speak of seeking smaller networks, some of which can be worked up regionally:

> I tend to go to small, local meetings. There is a guild of population biologists that meets in the Rocky Mountains. There is a prairie states ecology conclave of about five local universities. I find I get to know the people better, and I actually learn more by going to these local meetings, than the big, frustrating national ones.

Another biologist at a leading university viewed meetings of the national associations as "monster meetings." He, too, sought out informal and semiformal "meetings during the year which are smaller and, therefore, more focused. Those are the preferred ones to go to." Where specialization is most advanced, academics have learned to use disposable meetings. They deformalize their networks to better adjust to the shifting contours of research interests.

In the narrowly focused world of topical meetings, we enter a vast underbrush of semiformal and informal linkages characteristic of American academia, ties that also weave, weblike, around the mainline associations. Faculty members speak of going to meet others in their "network" when they go off to attend sessions of their "division" within the national association ("the Business Policy and Planning Division of the Academy of Management is where most of the people in my network are"). Of growing importance also are the ties not dependent on formal associations for their footing, connections that we can view as invisible associations, in line with the fruitful concept of invisible colleges, which has been widely used in the sociology of science. The idea of an invisible college has meant a communication "network of productive scientists" that links "separate groups of collaborators within a research area."[11] We can broaden the idea so that it is not limited to "productive scientists," but instead refers more inclusively to the informal arrangements by which academics connect and communicate on campus and, especially, in the system at large.

Even at top universities, where cosmopolitan ties are strongest, informal associations, for some, may be largely local. A political scientist at a leading university reported that although he often discussed intellectual matters with one important colleague at another university 2,000 miles away, all the others with whom he sought close interaction—a goodly number—he found by roaming his own campus, branching out from his own department to a major campus institute that contained members of several departments and then on to numerous other departments:

> Right now I have just initiated some discussions with a colleague in the linguistics department, and I talked to a colleague in the anthropology department. I have been interested in the evolution of behavior, and I have gotten a lot out of a colleague in the biology department. I have occasional dealings with colleagues in the sociology department and the business school who are also interested in organization theory—and the school of public health—because we have had a group of organization theorists that has gotten together.

This professor felt that he did "a different kind of work," and therefore, did not "feel very strongly identified with any particular group." His own department was satisfactory as "a professional home," but to pursue his own research agenda he needed to fashion his own set of ties, a flexible set of local exchanges.

A major campus is a vast collection of such highly disposable individualized networks, interpersonal ties fashioned by professors with those outside as well as with those within their own departments, as they follow the thrust of their intellectual interests. The social inventions here are

248

many. "Journal clubs," one of them, was described by a professor of biology in a leading university:

> I interact with people in the medical school because there are not other immunologists in this department. . . . Right now, we're not actually connecting on a given project, though we may be starting something like that soon, but we share journal clubs. You know what journal clubs are? That is where you get together with people working in your area and review current papers from the literature that are of interest. So we share a weekly journal club with three other labs in the medical school. . . . This is fairly common in biology, at least.

Two political scientists told us about larger invisible associations of which they were a part; mentor-student ties played an important role here. One, who indicated his closest professional ties were elsewhere, not in his own department, added, "I also have Ph.D.'s all over the place. When you have been at it as long as I have, you are pretty well connected nationally." The informal can stretch to become a whole "school of people" lasting over several academic generations. The second professor spoke of having close friends elsewhere—at Cornell and Harvard and in the government—and went on to describe his main network as an informal and "highly controversial school of people . . . who are identified with a man who taught at Chicago for many years, Leo Strauss, and I am a student of students of Strauss. People who know my work think of me as Straussian."

In all the disciplines, from the humanities to the sciences, the invisible associations have a primary role in self-identity, communication, and the bonding of members of the profession. A humanist declared, "I have better relations with colleagues at other universities simply because they share my interests in Joyce, O'Casey, and Yeats, my interest in Anglo-Irish literature, and it is healthy to meet colleagues." The informal then shades into small-scale associations: "I belong to organizations within my specific field: the Committee for Irish Studies, the James Joyce Society, the O'Casey Society." At the same time, this humanities professor continued his membership in "the major organization in our field. . . . The Modern Language Association."

In the sciences, too, there are extended families that form around a mentor and several generations of students and research associates. In physics: "There are several groups that basically have the same parentage, which sprang from John Wheeler at Princeton University, and he had some great students who spawned some great groups. . . . That family I identify with. I wasn't a student of his, but I was a colleague and a research associate, and that's whom I identify with."

Another physics professor spoke of his professional home as being the "collection of people I sort of professionally grew up with over the last twenty years. . . . My closest collaborators tend to be people immediately around me, but all over there are people who have been close to me and have worked with me in the past." For those struggling to do research in second- and third-level universities, the dominant informal associations were all the more likely to be elsewhere, even abroad, since relevant immediate colleagues are in short supply:

> The persons that I have most contact with in terms of my research goals are not in this department. . . . [They are] people at IBM research labs, or at the Max Planck Institute in Stuttgart, and some other universities.

> [My] closest professional colleagues in the sense of people who do what I do—certainly, they are somewhere else. There is nobody here that does what I do, which is, I guess, typical, at least at a small school.

So segmented is the academic labor market that many specialists in large and small places are hired as one-of-a-kind experts. Their intellectual sustenance then depends largely on associations, informal and formal, which bridge the boundaries of their own institutions.

Weakest in associational ties, of course, are the many reluctant part-time and temporary full-time faculty, whose marginal careers leave them hanging by their fingertips to the edges of academe. They are least likely to have personal or institutional travel funds to attend meetings. They are outside or peripheral to the regular faculty circles that spawn the more informal ties. Associationally, as well as organizationally they get left out. But even here, the drive to associate does not die: Indeed, those in a common weak position have good reason to band together to support one another, to find strength in numbers, to share tips on employment opportunities, and to have intellectual discussions. Thus, in sociology in the 1980s, "independent scholars" became a new network of the unemployed and underemployed, with officers, meetings, a newsletter, and formal affiliation with the mainline national association.

THE ASSOCIATIONAL WEBBING OF ACADEMIC GROUPS

To solve their institutional problems, professors turn to such place-bound tools as departments and senates. To solve their disciplinary problems, they reach for subject-based associations that extend to wherever like-minded peers can be found. The larger the national system, the more academics seem to need to create such ties; they need to bring a cohort of over 500,000 "colleagues," as in the United States, down to the more manageable size of 50,000, or better 5,000 or even better 500 or 50, and sometimes 5. The more a national system is decentralized, the more academics are encouraged to turn to voluntary action, since there are no formal embracing schemes that even pretend to bring them together. Then, too, the individual and small-group autonomies of academia provide the freedom and moral authority to voluntarily associate. Even in the most managerial settings, academics do not have to ask permission from "the boss" before reaching outside their own departments, and then beyond their university or college, to fashion meaningful ties with others. There are virtually no product secrets. Academics communicate with colleagues readily and band together in formations of their own devising as soon as they face new problems or generate new bodies of knowledge. They would rather be association persons than "organization men."

Without any person or group planning it, or even setting the general direction, a division of labor has evolved in America in which postsecondary associations of institutions attend to institutional and student issues while disciplinary associations concentrate, field by field, on issues of research and scholarship. With this division, many issues affecting professors are beyond the bounds of their primary national associations: Organized institutional interests, then, readily predominate over the professional ones. When government officials and legislators, state or national, want advice on "higher education," they turn to institutional heads and their associations. In turn, especially in the national capitol, the presidents' clubs develop a lobbying capacity to represent higher education. But when the state turns directly to "science"—or "the humanities" or "the arts"—do its officials turn to disciplinary groupings. And it is mainly around the needs of scholarship that professor-run associations reciprocally develop a presence as a lobby and learn to penetrate governmental agencies. The many disciplinary associations thereby fashion connections with government that bypass the institutions.

As a class of organizations, American disciplinary associations are more pervasive and powerful than their counterparts in other countries, but their power is narrowly focused. As they concentrate on the research and scholarship of direct interest to their members, they leave other aspects of higher education to administrators. The division of influence parallels the bargain struck within the authority structures of universities and colleges, but the professional base is more dampened. The associational structure reflects the simple fact that the higher the level in the American system, the more pervasive is the sway of management. Senates may be powerful locally, but there are no powerful professor-dominated senates nationally to pull academics together as a professional class.

Since specialization is what counts in the professorial network, right down to professors withdrawing from their own major associations because they view them as too general, all-inclusive associations have a difficult time. They are cast in a secondary role because they deemphasize disciplinary distinctions, swimming against the tide of the proliferating pursuit of such separations. Membership in the American Association of University Professors, for example, then seems relatively costly: One first pays membership dues to a set of regional, national, and possibly international, disciplinary associations and then squeezes the family budget still further to pay the AAUP its annual dues. For those in top places, disciplinary memberships are relatively essential; joining and serving in the AAUP is more in the nature of *noblesse oblige*, done with a sense that less fortunate colleagues in other places need a defense league to protect them against the batterings of politicians, trustees, and administrators.

When the National Education Association and the American Federation of Teachers seriously entered the picture in the late 1960s and the 1970s, in full union dress, they not only deemphasize disciplinary distinctions but also those of status. As we have seen (Chapter VI), they run up against the stubborn fact that successful people in every discipline want the rewards of status. Thus, in a system so much given to diversity, competition, and hierarchy, there are powerful reasons why inclusive bodies in the form of unions are strongest where discipline and status matter least, and weakest where discipline and status count the most. Issues left for unions are then largely economic and managerial in a domain where leadership and stature flow to those who most effectively attend to their focused scholarship and take up the roles of salaried entrepreneurs. For their members, the disciplinary associations, able to build on a substantial consciousness of kind, are often impressive symbols of professional community. The NEA, the AFT, and sometimes the AAUP, in contrast, have only a weak base of common consciousness upon which to operate as vehicles of shared identity. Their base lies in local strains between "workers" and "management."

American higher education is simultaneously underorganized in certain respects and overorganized in others.[12] It has no national ministry and no national formal system of control. Seen in comparative perspective, it is only loosely structured by normal bureaucratic and political tools of state authority. But voluntary association then substitutes for systemwide formal organization. The substitute system is bewildering and hard to capture, quantitatively or qualitatively. It is simultaneously formal, semiformal, and informal; it is visible and invisible. Overall hierarchy is minimal: No peak association or set of ties commands all the rest. Lines of affiliation loop through and around one another, with no regard for unifying principles of order, logic, and accountability. The gaps and redundancies are too numerous to count.

American academics associate voluntarily from the bottom up. Their national network forms from the intellectual and practical interests of thousands of clusters of practicing academics scattered in the vast array of disciplines and institutions that compose the system. What the bottom does not like, the bottom disposes of. More than in other countries, the voluntary lines make for a disposable structure of coordination, thereby promoting system flexibility. Voluntary associating is a good way to have structure follow knowledge, rather than the other way around. Professionals have known for a long time that, as a general form, association is more malleable than bureaucracy. It follows particularly well the many contours of academe. In the American setting, it is deeply a part of the logic of the academic profession.

Paralleling the cultural overlap identified in Chapter V, associational overlap provides some integration in an otherwise chaotic domain. Even in the most narrow specialties, professors face outward from their own campus, joining hands across organizational boundaries. They take up multiple memberships: They join specialty associations and larger disciplinary ones; they belong to a pyramid of regional, national, and international associations; they maneuver in the invisible groupings as well as the formal ones. Specialties in one discipline converge on those in another: Some molecular biologists run some of the time with physicists and chemists. As a biologist put it, "My area of research carries me into other professional societies of which I am also a member." It is hard to distinguish political sociologists from behavioral political scientists; they cross associational lines accordingly, even to occupy high office. The inclusive faculty associations, such as the American Association of University Professors, provide some additional linkage, however secondary its importance. As for liaison among the associations themselves, there are the interdisciplinary umbrella associations and the councils of the umbrella organizations.

In American academic life, where scholars are so scattered by type of institution as well as discipline, reasons for singularity and division abound. Following the division of labor, fragmentation is necessarily—as emphasized throughout this study—the dominant theme. But if there are reasons to isolate, there are reasons to associate. Academics who occupy a common corner in fields of knowledge coalesce so they will not be monstrosities of individualized isolation. As their limited associations, formal and informal, overlap one another, a larger network emerges. In a profession of professions, overlapping voluntary linkages are the nearest thing to a social structure that provides order and integration.

PART III

The Logic of the Profession

CHAPTER IX

The Logic of the Profession

Culture and the institutions that sustain it have always depended on enlightened patronage. That is as true for the modern, sophisticated research university as it was for Michelan-
gelo and Mozart. It is a somewhat more recent truth,
however, one born out of the rise of modern organizations,
that their fate lies largely in the hands of those who work in
them.

—ROBERT M. ROSENZWEIG, *THE RESEARCH
UNIVERSITIES AND THEIR PATRONS* (1982)

Our thesis is that the human coefficient of intellectual activity
is of the utmost importance . . . the producers are an essential
part of the product.

—LOGAN WILSON, *THE ACADEMIC MAN*
(1942)

The shape of American higher education is largely a response
to the assumptions and demands of the academic professions.

—CHRISTOPHER JENCKS AND DAVID RIESMAN,
THE ACADEMIC REVOLUTION (1968)

THE MARCH OF KNOWLEDGE across the world of work has created
tribes of professionals whose manners and mores intensely affect
human affairs. Behind every set of desks there lurks a would-be
profession, knowledge specialists who devise ideologies, certificates, and
associations to back their claims. As they cultivate their own social systems
and cultures, these carriers of intellectual activity perpetuate distinctive
human coefficients, special styles that spring readily to mind when we
think about each profession or encounter doctors, lawyers, psychothera-
pists, and interior designers. Each group develops strange patterns as it
goes about isolating and commanding a domain of work. Mystification is
routine: "We" cannot know what "they" know unless we are willing to
undergo their training and join their circle. Given the difficulties they
cause and the powers they acquire, "we" would undoubtedly, if we could,

do without them, or at least supervise them closely. But we cannot do either. Across the endless array of traditional professions, latter-day professions, semiprofessions, and would-be professions, those who seek particular products and services have to take the producers, and largely on faith.

Among these mystifying occupations that elaborate powerful identities for individuals and groups, the academic profession is at once the easiest to approach and the most difficult to understand. Many individuals, as students, were once within its walls; many serious observers, as faculty, are part of it. Penetration is no problem, participant-observers are abundant. But the two-way differentiation on which we have concentrated erects major screens. Exacting internal specialization spells mutual ignorance, striking everyone somewhat dumb on the spot. Any specific way of knowing is also a way of not knowing. The individualization of many types of institutions further removes academics from one another and presents a confusing and contradictory organizational maze to outside observers. The pattern of mystification we find in professions generally is repeated within this omnibus profession, making it strange to insiders and outsiders alike.

THE THIRD MOVEMENT

It was not always so, since the profession was simple before it became complex. Along the road of elaboration in America, we can distinguish three stages. As noted in Part I, the professional origins of academia were much weaker in the United States than in Europe. Though faculty on the Continent and in Britain from the beginning clung to their own guilds, hunkering down within them when under assault from church or state, American academics began as little groups of hired hands. Throughout the long colonial period and well into the nineteenth century, they were clearly predisciplinary and preprofessional, not yet given to specialization. Attempting to impart a common culture of the more educated classes, their relatively fixed body of common knowledge robbed them of the authority of expertise. Looking back, we see them as amateurs. Many stayed in academic work only for a few years before moving on. Substantively and organizationally, their defenses were weak. The academic occupation had little chance to mystify.

258

Distinctive academic ways developed gradually over the course of the two centuries that stretched from the establishment of Harvard in 1636 to the Civil War years. In the first half of the nineteenth century, specialists were already hard at work elaborating particular subjects. Scientific knowledge was beginning to move beyond the ken of amateurs and generalists. The academic specialist then fully triumphed over the generalist when major disciplines became separate professions in themselves. From the 1870s onward, in a second state of occupational development, the departments of universities and colleges increasingly took charge. They positioned the influence of academics on a firm base of expertise.[1] Joined by many outside fields that set up shop in new professional schools, the disciplinary specialties gave muscle it did not have before to the embracing profession. At the same time, the scale of academia, although many times larger than in the first stage, allowed a lingering sense of oneness. Commonalities could be found in the myths of "the professor," the sense of calling that we now associate with "the old days" of the small campuses of the decades before World War II, and the unifying leadership of the leading scholars who graced the halls of the American Association of University Professors. Modern professionalism had arrived, but it was still enveloped in strong pretenses of community.

For those desiring a strong, unified profession, moment two was the golden age, reflected locally in the growing privileges of the department and the senate and nationally in the unities of the disciplinary associations and the AAUP. Faculty appeared to have crawled out from under the dominance of trustees and administrators, seizing control of the basic operating units and manning an all-campus professional structure that had primary influence in many local matters. In institutions of any substantial standing, the president increasingly had to spend his or her capital of residual power prudently, for, if squandered, stern votes of "no confidence" issuing from the senate would speed departure. A much-used rhetoric of "shared authority" recognized that the faculty knew best in such central matters as selecting staff and deciding curriculum. Their doctrines of freedom of research and freedom of teaching were now undergirded with the privileges of personal autonomy.

The quarter-century since 1960 has seen the full flowering of a third professionalization moment. A "postmodern" complexity has evolved, a startling cross hatching in which segmentation of sectors has interacted with the fragmentation of subjects to give differentiation a quantum leap. Professional school faculties have grown and solidified in universities, establishing large and powerful domains that are out of control as well as out of sight of the letters and science departments; English has little sway over engineering and none over medicine. Within the letters and science core of the universities, general education and liberal education—long on the defensive—have become causes for the saving remnant, so distant are the realities of departmental separation from the pieties of curricular integration. Up and down the hierarchy of institutions, as well as across each type, innumerable nonprofessions, semiprofessions, and newly legitimated professions present their subjects and have them dignified, right down to the trades of hair styling and auto mechanics. It has become virtually impossible to name a subject that someone, somewhere, will not teach; "the profession" is in no position to take responsibility for it, especially to prohibit it. In a radically fractured profession, the less respectable operations are marginalized rather than outlawed. Degree mills come and go, chased by a few state investigators who in no way come from the ranks or represent professional self-control. In a national system composed to do all things for all people, even to repeat the work of the elementary school, the profession is far from a controlled sector of employment. In the third moment the academic profession has no boundaries. It steadily diffuses; the stretch goes on.

We only understand the contemporary American academic profession if we grasp the magnitude of its dispersion into parts that whirl off in different directions. There still are small components, religious and secular, which are gloriously old-fashioned. Some operate as presidential autocracies as others approximate a community of scholars. A few faculties still exist in the form of fellowships where sherry precedes dinner on Thursday night, a collective habit that favors rumination on the eternal verities. But other parts take radically different shapes: The cancer ward is a place where clinical faculty interact intensively with many levels of auxiliary personnel and practice an applied art of great immediacy. The expansion of nominal universities, state colleges, and especially community colleges during the last quarter-century has notably put the majority of academics in locales far from the fellowships of the old-time colleges and the special worlds of the top private universities. Organizationally, those academics may have a champagne taste, but what they get is bottled beer.

In this latter period, though disciplinarians remain much in charge at the top of the hierarchy of institutions, consuming students and responding managers take charge in the non- and slightly selective institutions.[2] The triumph of clientele has been institutionalized in the administrative (and faculty) responses that have put one-third of the professoriate on part-time assignment. A large share of the profession has crawled back under the control of trustees and administrators, with the unionization response adopted as the new road to an adversarial unity of academic workers. Largely created in the 1960s and 1970s, the deprofessionalized bottom of the professoriate leads off into the camps of the gypsy scholars, the new nomads who personally pay the price for consumer-driven flexibility. In the organized tools of mass higher education that assign faculty to the lower one-third to one-half of the clientele in ability and resources, the third moment is a major regression. For the professoriate as a whole, the costs of mass higher education have been high.

Thus, over the long course of three centuries, the character of the intellectual moment in American academic life has changed remarkably. What academics could seize at the beginning was only short-term work as generalists. They then developed posts that turned jobs into lifelong careers that could be taken on their own terms but that still centered on undergraduate residential life. A qualitative shift occurred only when research and specialized scholarship measurably enhanced prestige and power. Academics then had a world of their own: What they thought and what they did became peer oriented and discipline-driven. But this condition was not to be a permanent answer for everyone: In a twentieth-century evolution, centrifugal forces have qualitatively diversified academic conditions. If research settings became always more esoteric, operating as configurations of rare expertise that the laity cannot fathom, other settings have adapted to the imperatives of general teaching for an open-access clientele.

Powering the shift from the first to the second to the third intellectual moment have been the substantive and reactive forms of growth set forth in Chapter II, which operated under the special conditions of intense competition and emerging institutional hierarchy established in Chapter III. In the insight offered by Walter Metzger, substantive growth drove the evolution into the second stage. It was not demands of clientele, but, rather, demands of expanding knowledge that most caused generalists to be replaced by specialists. The clients, especially in the undergraduate classroom, would have preferred to keep teachers who were centered on students' interests and who spoke a general language. But self-amplifying science and scholarship had other designs for higher education. Since expanding knowledge could only be handled by greater specialization, graduate students soon became more important than undergraduates, the Ph.D. more weighty than the bachelor's degree.

In the third stage the full weight of reactive growth has come into play. There could well be sizable assemblies of academics who served "elite" functions, but there had to be even larger congregations who served "mass" functions, academics who would carry the burdens, while facing the challenges, of the open door. There could be institutions that competed nationally for the highest prestige, the best faculty, and the best students, but there had to be many more institutions that would adjust to the demands of unselected students within the limits of local and regional catchments. Faculty growth that followed student growth, in a system characterized by competition and hierarchy, shifted faculty toward another-directed posture in which clients replaced peers.

THE PROFESSION AND THE ORGANIZATION

In the evolution of intellectual moments, professors changed their interests and caused universities and colleges to adapt accordingly. Persuasive is the observation offered by Christopher Jencks and David Riesman that American higher education has been mainly shaped by its resident professional groups. But this conditioning of system by profession has occurred primarily in the uppermost levels of the institutional hierarchy, where a central institutional interest forms around the faculty interest in substantive growth. The organization as a whole then becomes tremendously supportive of the disciplinary commitments of academics. Presidents as well as peers prod professors to become more productive in research and scholarship, thereby competitively enhancing the organization while ostensibly serving the nation and the world.

But as we have seen in abundant detail, other organizational settings of the profession march to quite different drummers. They have not been fashioned to express substantive growth. Major institutional sectors provide different tasks and conditions of work, different institutional identities and histories, different covering authorities, different career paths, and different associational networks. Crucial in the shaping of the profession is the organizational determination of the mix of the two primary tasks, research and teaching. That mix comes close to determining everything else about academic life. Where the combination tilts heavily toward research, it follows that disciplines will be powerful and departments strong; freedom of research will be the reigning ideology; research-centered professors will associate formally and informally in research-defined circles; careers will be defined by recognized scholarly prowess; and administrators will speak lovingly of the faculty as the core of the university and will walk carefully around the plenitude of faculty prerogatives. But when the mix is all teaching and no research, then disciplines will fade in importance and departmental nationhood will be weaker. Freedom of research will no longer be a relevant ideology. Professors will form associational links relevant to their type and level of teaching and will pull away from research circles. Careers will be defined locally, sharply limited in mobility, and rooted in seniority rights. Administrators will be more managerial and, law permitting, will precipitate a unionization response that moves faculty-administration relations into contractual formalities.

Academics know what wins the day in their disciplines. Hence the vast majority want to do some research, and publish a little, even if teaching is their first love. The ideal of combining research and teaching is deeply fixed in American academic consciousness. Field by field, it burns bright. But for a half or more of the professoriate, organizational restraints on research are heavy to the point of near-prohibition, particularly when we count the swollen ranks of the part-timers. As we move down the status hierarchy, organizational imperatives increasingly dominate faculty preferences. The faculty role is specified as only undergraduate teaching, then becomes teaching only in the first two undergraduate years. Academics then maneuver in a sharply limited occupational space that is organizationally defined.

What is so attractive about the university setting for so many faculty members is the reduction of those kinds of organizational constraints. As "teaching load" is lightened, the organization liberates academic time. But it does so only to turn it over to the full might of research expectations that are set and monitored more by the faculty than by the administration. The research university reeks of professional dominance, with professors constantly sliding from the role of employee into that of salaried entrepreneur, going largely their own way in managing their time, their research, and their teaching. They develop a strong sense of nationhood in their own department, ruling it by collective decision making and holding administrators at arm's length from the core tasks. Since trustees have ultimate authority and make occasional large decisions, and since the administrative staff steadily elaborates bureaucratic controls, the setting is far from innocent of contrary forces. But the greater power lies in subjects, the stuff of academic work itself. Those most directly involved in the evolution of the subjects are the beneficiaries of the constant widening and deepening of the knowledge base of academic life.

The interaction between profession and organization produces a fundamental divide among professors that appears in the many dimensions of professionalism. As we ascend the institutional hierarchy, we find professors facing peers for recognition and reward. As we descend, we encounter professors facing students for direct satisfaction and long-term viability and legitimacy. Major segments of the foremost universities function much like think tanks. The more a university moves in this direction, the better its competitive advantage in recruiting faculty. Only the financial need for tuition income, or state allocation based on number of students, acts as a major brake on this tendency. Students are not the point: What counts is recognition afforded by peers. In sharp contrast, the two-year college teacher finds that students are nearly everything, *the* source of daily satisfaction, *the* basis for a successful career. A community college has no chance to become a think tank. Instead, the nature of its work moves it toward the character of a comprehensive secondary school.

Opposing forces thus tend to split the academic profession in two. The upper part in a hierarchy of prestige becomes more professionalized: It is more fully based on arcane knowledge, more involved in peer judgment, more independent of clientele demands and related market forces. The bottom half, especially the bottom one-quarter, becomes less professionalized: It is committed to introductory materials that many can teach, more dependent on student reaction than peer approval, and heavily driven by market demands. Not far from the "shopping mall high school" we find the shopping mall community college.[3] Up the hierarchy we find inner-directed organizations in the hands of professionals; down the line we observe other-directed organizations that are client-driven. Perhaps it cannot be otherwise in a system of higher education that simultaneously seeks to function under a populist definition of equality, where all are admitted, and also tries to serve the gods of excellence in the creation and transmission of all rarefied bodies of knowledge.

In this odd occupation, professionals who primarily answer to peers are certain to be fundamentally different from professionals who are heavily dependent on consumer clientele.[4] The first group have to prove they are producing knowledge, the second that they are making enrollment.

Benefits have costs, strengths have weaknesses. Operating as a professors' medium, the university has difficulty in being responsive to undergraduate students. As professors turn to their research and their graduate students, freshman and sophomore students get the short end. Since the turn of the century, and especially in the post-1945 decades, the task of teaching beginning students has drifted toward the margin of reward and interest. Year in and year out, major universities, including private ones, send away brilliant young teachers, rather than give them tenure when their scholarship does not measure up. Such action often precipitates howls of protest from undergraduates and a march across campus to the president's or chancellor's office, where the loss is duly noted but allowed to stand. Such repetitive professional behavior on the part of the evaluating academics results not from personal willfulness but from the underlying structure of commitments and related rewards. Noting that "administrators give lip service to teaching excellence, whereas major universities promote staff members primarily on the basis of distinction in research and conspicuousness of publication," Logan Wilson remarked four decades ago that "the most critical problem confronted in the social organization of any university is the proper evaluation of faculty services, and giving due recognition through the impartial assignment of status."[5] This underlying problem has not and will not go away. In the inability to reward undergraduate teaching, we find the Achilles heel of the American research university.

In contrast, operating as a students' medium, the community college has difficulty in being responsive to the faculty's need for engagement in scholarship. Disciplinary involvement drifts toward the margin, attenuating scholarly competence and all the intrinsic satisfactions and extrinsic rewards that come with it. In the academic profession it is more blessed to produce than to distribute. When academics are denied all possibilities of engaging in research or scholarly practices, they are removed from the profession's central system of rewards. Then the Achilles heel is found in a winding-down of the scholarly model and a loss of academic respect. The central problems of one sector are virtually opposite the central problems of the other.

Serious reform that seeks to reduce weaknesses while retaining strengths has to address different conditions and effects. Reforms at the university level have to seek a substructuring of the undergraduate function that, in addition to the departmental structure, breaks up the large campus into more personal and more tangible parts: honors programs, subcolleges formed around residences or broad fields of study, special sets of seminars for freshmen and sophomores. The "college" has to be given strong symbolic definition within the university, as it is at Yale College within Yale University. Such changes are somewhere on the drawing board in virtually every major university, challenging administrators and faculty to creatively alter rewards for the professoriate, even at the risk of creating a division between a teaching faculty and a research faculty. Some small gains are made in stiffening the teaching criterion in promotion decisions. But with competition for scholarly status powerfully concentrating the institutional mind, the tides run strong in the opposite direction.

Reforms in the all-teaching settings have an even more difficult time. They have to strengthen the incentives for scholarship, to maintain faculty competence in one field after another in which knowledge and technique change at a rapid rate. Many four-year college faculties sense the danger of residing in the backwaters of academia. Community college staffs are worse off. They are pushed toward a marginality that virtually cuts them out of the academic profession. Heavy teaching loads are at the heart of the problem. Here, small gains can be observed as faculty manipulate their twelve- and fifteen-hour loads to gain more time for keeping up with their fields. The lesser liberal arts colleges are able to look to the leading colleges

266

as models of how to combine some research and scholarship with a primary commitment to undergraduate teaching. But the tides run strong in the other direction. The institutional need for students and the costs of lighter teaching loads powerfully set the institutional bias.

THE LOGIC OF THE PROFESSION

What is finally most useful to grasp are the inherent propensities of this profession, the drives that task and context set for the long term. Primary in the profession's logic is the hegemony of subjects, a characteristic of professions that is magnified in the academy. From the tyranny of subjects there follows the duality of commitment to discipline and institution that is the organizational heart of higher education. And from the liberating force of subjects there follows the intrinsic motivations that turn academic work into a calling.

The Hegemony of Knowledge

Lord Eric Ashby once postulated three main environmental forces acting on systems of higher education: consumer demand, manpower needs, and the patron's influence.[6] All external to the system itself, they enter mainly by means of reactions and translations that take place in the channels of system organization and institutional administration. Consumer demands for access, for example, operate through admission requirements and procedures that are defined by government or are set by the competition of institutions in a market in which applicants and institutions freely interact; labor market demands penetrate the system through the employment anticipations of students, the lures offered graduates by employers and occupational sectors, and placement linkages that have been established between higher education and employment. Professors and administrators are involved in the transactions that bring these external forces to bear internally. Academics may shape decisively the one or the other: when their own committees guard the doors of admission or their internal interests perpetuate certain occupational programs at the expense of others. In both cases they interact with the outside world. They essentially operate much like administrators, even observe an administrative rationality. Frequently

267

they leave such matters to administrators—those in admissions and placement offices—or hand the work to committees on which a few serve in the name of the many. The forces are external; the reactions are "organizational."

A fourth force of knowledge internal to the system and around which reactions are "professional" stands in sharp contrast. As Ashby noted, any higher education system has "its own articles of faith by which its practitioners live," or prefer to live, producing an "inner logic." That inner logic "does for higher education systems what genes do for biological systems: it preserves identity; it is a built-in gyroscope." The articles of faith are closely rooted in the very materials on which academic subunits center their work. As knowledge is newly created by research, and is reformulated and repeatedly transmitted in teaching and service, its force continuously bubbles up from within daily operations, right in the palm of the professional hand. The logic, the identity, the very rationality of the academic profession is thereby rooted in the evolving organization of those categories of knowledge that disciplines and professional fields of study have established historically and carried into the present, producing an inertia that powerfully prefigures the future. This rationality changes everything. If consumer demands, job placements, and the interests of patrons were the only imperatives, academic organization would more nearly resemble standard bureaucratic organization. It is the primacy of cognitive materials and their internal shaping influence that make the difference, turning so many universities and colleges into knowledge-driven organizations possessed by a bottom-up bias. Viability does not depend on the capacity of top-down commands to integrate parts into an organizational whole. Instead, it depends on the quality of the performance of the basic units as nearly self-sufficient entities that do the work of disciplines and reflect their concerns.

In knowledge-driven organizations, where knowledge is the end as well as the means, a fragmented but intense professionalism is the only effective guarantor of standards. Covering authorities cannot offer a guarantee: They are too remote from the laboratory and classroom, too lacking in control of subject to effect useful control over persons. The better universities and colleges are the ones that have adapted their organization to the logic

268

of subject dominion. They then become organizations that are inherently more centrifugal than centripetal.[7]

In the rationality of academic professionalism, peer surveillance serves as the main corrective for error, poor performance, and deviance. Such surveillance is most powerful in the task of research, for then it can be done on relatively visible products and by national and international observers as well as by local colleagues. Virtually cut loose from administrative chiefs, research professors answer to disciplinary sets of judges who effect controls in their judgmental reactions to preprints, articles, conference presentations, books, and a five- or ten-year body of work. However, the surveillance is much less powerful in the task of teaching, for then it must be done almost entirely by local observers and over classroom performances not typically in the public domain. As teaching takes over from research, the thrust of disciplinary controls is lessened, opening the way to the power of external demands, especially consumer satisfaction. The inner logic is muted.

In contradistinction to the more nationalized systems of higher education in Europe, and generally elsewhere in the world, the American system also operates, as I have stressed, at the more macro level by the rationality of competition within a status hierarchy. Institutions that are in or anywhere near the upper quarter of the institutional hierarchy compete sharply for those academics considered to be the primary producers in creating knowledge. The effective institution is one most effective in this competition, working by the simple rule that faculty are the central resource. The effective institutions trumpet their successes: The ambitious ones renew their bids. State governments even enter the competitive picture by awarding chairs and other special resources to their flagship public institutions to help them increase their bidding power and their chance of garnering faculty whose aggregate prowess and prestige will lift the institution another notch in research capability and national renown. Deeply entrenched in the commanding heights of the American professoriate, this competitive ethic drives the academic profession, segment by segment, as much as it does the institutions. The competition goads individual academics, their departments, and their invisible colleges.

But, as with subject domination, the rationality of competition shifts significantly from settings controlled by research to ones possessed by teaching. In the lower-status sectors of the hierarchy, the absence of research means that institutions are no longer competing for the status that follows from the reputation of scholars. If they compete to any degree, all-teaching institutions contend for control of student catchments or directly for individual students, making students rather than faculty the central resource. Financing is more strictly student-driven, and prestige of faculty as scholars adds little to the equations of viability and success. Rational behavior then dictates a shift from the disciplinary game to the institutional one. The rationality of the commanding heights of the many subject fields gives way to one, centered on the character of the student body, which is more subject to administration and hierarchy. Professionally, the situation is problematic: The centrality of faculty is sharply questioned, even strongly denied with the shift to temporary and part-time employment. The unionization response, as in elementary and secondary education, then entangles professionalism with unionism.

The Dualities of Commitment

Given its disciplinary base and its grand diffusion of primary loyalties, this particular profession is more federative than any other. Subjects become states; disciplinary involvements are set off from institutional affiliations, and the two commitments frequently operate at cross purposes. The old distinction between "cosmopolitans" and "locals" pointed to the extremes in which either the discipline or the enterprise emerges as the commitment that subordinates the other. Always belonging to both specialty and locational groups, the academic professional has to work out a balance between the ways of each.

This primary duality becomes ambiguously elaborated in the American system. The radical decentralization of public authority in fifty states and the separation of a private sphere of authority composed of 1,500 autonomous institutions further fragments disciplines and types of institutions as it blocks all the formal integration provided by common civil service status in nationalized systems. It is then not a case of simple polarities between discipline and institution, but of types of disciplinary ties differing from one another as memberships in types of institutions differentiate academics.

270

We also have taken note of the growing unboundedness of this maverick profession, particularly in the form of temporary and part-time personnel whose certification is only weakly controlled if at all, and who perforce wander in and out of the system at the will of institutional administrators and sometimes personal desire. As boundaries are erased, the simple matter of counting the number of academics becomes a tortured exercise in arbitrary, ambiguous definitions. Now adding to the lowered boundaries between inside and outside is the growth of academic-like work external to the academy, occurring somewhat in the military establishment but most strongly in the world of business. "Scholars in corporations" is not a make-believe term.[8] For over a quarter of a century, Bell Laboratories have served as the prototype of the research facility in the business world whose collection of Ph.D. talent in the sciences is equal to that of the leading universities. Other firms have joined in; they also teach and provide for the creation of new knowledge. They produce Ph.D.-level scholars along with recruiting the university's products. The research and development division of many firms takes on a structure and develops a culture resembling that of the research university. Inside business, formal "schools" and "colleges" have now arrived; their privilege of granting degrees is a clear indication the academic profession has found yet another home.

Sociologists who paint on large canvases have had good reason to depict professions as major standardizing and unifying forces in modern society, on a par with, and even replacing, bureaucracies in producing "isomorphism"—similarities in structure and process.[9] Such observers see both patriots and mercenaries in particular occupations capturing territories of work as they grant membership only to those who enter through controlled gates, subscribe to sanctioned procedures, obey a common code—however loose its definition—and establish a common dominance over clients and auxiliary personnel. But the idea of isomorphism ill-fits the academic profession. A profession of professions is inherently centrifugal, especially when each of its subprofessions is driven by a research imperative that constantly enlarges and otherwise unsettles its own knowledge foundations. Polymorphism is the dominant trend; differentiation is more prized than commonality. The academic profession is qualitatively different in its extreme pluralism of contents and commitments.

Any dependable integration that comes about across the multitudinous commitments of the American profession is a product of overlapping connections among differences. From the hardest of the sciences to the softest of the humanities, from the purest fields to the most applied, adjacent fields overlap and even interpenetrate. In the institutional chain the many types of universities and colleges do not operate as watertight compartments but rather border upon and overlap one another, often to the point of heavily confusing the efforts of classifiers to draw lines between them. The fish-scale model of integration is an appropriate one. Hence disciplines and institutions are not only isolating tunnels. They are also mediating institutions that tie individual and small groups into larger wholes of system and profession.

In its extreme heterogeneity the American academic profession is virtually a miniature of the extended diversity of groups that make up American society. Integration is largely unity in diversity, with slight family ties among the resilient and often unmeltable separate groups. Such plurality is dependent on broad respect for differences and on trust in the choices of others.

The Absorbing Errand

Henry James once wrote that true happiness "consists of getting out of oneself, but the point is not only to get out, you must stay out, and to stay out, you must have some absorbing errand."[10] Professions provide such errands, offering serious long-term assignments that captivate and motivate. They take on the coloration of secular religions that inculcate hope, promote a sense of service, and hold out the promise of earthly rewards. Professionals get out and stay out of themselves most fully when they make their tasks a part of themselves. In its many embodiments, the American academic profession exhibits the capacity to engage individuals on such absorbing errands, providing long careers that have a moral life of their own. Professors in a wide range of institutions and disciplines in America find motivation and satisfaction in the very thing itself—in research, or in teaching, or in both.

But the errands are always heavily conditioned by organization, sometimes to the point of descending spiral. Schoolteaching is the clear case in American education. It has endured a critical loss of spirit; its "professionalization project" became stalled, even reversed.[11] Under adverse organizational conditions, elementary and secondary school teachers have had their autonomy and authority subordinated to administrative controls, trustee supervision, and preferences of laymen. In a long downward slide propelled in part by defensive reactions of teachers themselves, careerism has considerably replaced calling. The bargain between teachers and students frequently becomes: I will not bother you if you do not bother me. In the "shopping mall high school," the resident profession has great difficulty in maintaining an absorbing errand.

American higher education is not immune to the conditions that lead to a loss of errand. This volume has pointed to the conditions in colleges and universities that slowly but surely deprofessionalize the professoriate. Most perilous are the sectors where open access and the search for clientele has turned purpose into all things for all people. Then the administrative need to adjust flexibly to floating clienteles becomes more important than the need to have faculty define dominant duties and develop in-house cultures rich in professional meaning. Only true missionaries—always in short supply—can maintain an absorbing errand when the promise of career is reduced to a lifetime of teaching largely remedial composition or remedial mathematics for a revolving-door clientele that is easy in and quickly out.

A generalization of academic work that empties it of advanced contents has become a greater threat to the vitality and standing of the academic profession than all the intense specialization about which American reformers have routinely complained. From an extensive study of faculty in community colleges based on in-depth interviewing, Earl Seidman cogently concluded that "the community college as an institution has eroded the essential intellectual core of faculty work."[12] The perils of student-centeredness are greater that the dangers of professional dominance. In the shopping mall college, intellectual stagnation is a clear and present danger. For sure, the intellectual core runs down.

At the end of his classic essay on science as a vocation, published in 1919, Max Weber offered a set of striking observations that highlighted the richness, actual and potential, of the academic life.[13] Concentrating on "the inward calling" for science, "the personal experience" of science, he pointed to the passion that often lies behind the apparent coldness of strict special-

273

ization. Noting that enthusiasm is a prerequisite of inspiration, he spoke of the "strange intoxication" of the scientist when he feels that "the fate of his soul depends upon whether or not he makes the correct conjecture at this point of this manuscript." Dramatizing that rational thought can be and should be pursued with passionate devotion, he ended his observations with a ringing affirmation of the fulfillment that the scientific-cum-academic calling can bring. Against those who "tarry for new prophets and saviors," he held up the duty of intellectual honesty, insisting that "in the lecture-rooms of the university no other virtue holds but plain intellectual integrity." Hence: "We shall act differently. We shall set to work and meet the 'demands of the day,' in human relations as well as in our vocation. This, however, is plain and simple, if each finds and obeys the demon who holds the fibers of his very life."[14]

Under all the strengths and weaknesses, the autonomies and vulnerabilities, of American academic life, we can sense the problem of calling. When academic work is just a job and a routine career, then such material rewards as salary are front and center. Academics stay at their work or leave for other pursuits according to how much they are paid. They come to work "on time" because they must; they leave on time because satisfactions are to be found after work is concluded. But when academic work is a calling, it "constitutes a practical ideal of activity and character that makes a person's work morally inseparable from his or her life. It subsumes the self into a community of disciplined practice and sound judgment whose activity has meaning and value in itself, not just in the output or profit that results from it."[15] A calling transmutes narrow self-interest into other-regarding and ideal-regarding interests: One is linked to fellow workers and to a version of a larger common good. It has moral content, contributing to civic virtue.

Professionalization projects aim to provide chariots by which multitudes of workers wend their way to a calling, there to find motivating demons as well as the glories of high status and the trappings of power. The academic profession has demons in abundance in the fascinations of research and the enchantments of teaching. Many academic contexts offer a workaday existence rich in content and consequence: As a confederate gathering, the academic profession's continuing promise lies in the provision of a variety of such contexts. In that promise lies the best hope in the long term for the

274

recruitment and retention of talent. But when organization and profession fail one another, the errands run down, the demons disappear, and talented persons search for other fascinations and enchantments.

Near the end of the twentieth century, American higher education is a varied story of success and failure that has only begun to be disentangled by those willing not just to yearn for lost virtues but to take seriously its contradictory complexities. One cannot understand America's 3,000 institutions of higher education without grasping how they are variously conditioned by the divergent ranks of the academic profession. And one cannot understand the profession without grasping the enormous differences exacted by different institutional frameworks. The American academic profession has become different worlds. The miracle is that organization and profession between them still often provide the errands that offer the rewards of personal fulfillment and a sense of societal service.

Bureaucracy is needed in academia, since formal organization is compellingly necessary if researchers are to do research, teachers are to teach, and students are to learn. But if the tools of professionalism are to be put to good use in the promotion of academic activity, the supporting organizations must be essentially profession-driven, offering conditions that heighten the intrinsic rewards of teaching and research and the intrinsic satisfactions of the academic life. Only professional norms and practices are positioned, person by person, in everyday activity to constructively shape motivation and steer behavior. Grasping this point, academic statesmen seek to create the conditions of professional inspiration and self-regulation. Failing to grasp the logic of the profession, indeed the very requirements of an effective modern system of higher education, narrow management attempts to substitute the nuts and bolts of bureaucratic regulation. Then the calling is reduced, the errand loses its fascination.

The third moment of professionalization has fragmented American academia into a thousand parts. But inside the many ranks and beneath the weariness of hurried toil, something extraordinary often resides. In our cultural world the academy is still the place where the devotion to knowledge remains most central, where it not merely survives but has great power. Many academic men and women know that power and still believe in it. They glow with that belief. In devotion to intellectual integrity, they find a demon who holds the fibers of their very lives.

275

APPENDICES

APPENDIX A

Research Focus and Procedures

FROM ITS INCEPTION in mid-1983, the UCLA Study of the Academic Profession focused on academics as professionals located simultaneously in disciplines, going concerns in their own right, and in universities and colleges, the employing institutions. We posed the basic question of how, separately and together, these social structures shape the nature of the profession. Behind this question was a theoretical interest in the relative strength of opposing forces of fragmentation and integration, a vein of thought in sociology associated with the classic work of Emile Durkheim on social order in increasingly differentiated societies.[1] We wanted to sense the ways in which academics diverged in a fragmented domain and how, at the same time, they might still resemble one another and hang together. If near the end of the twentieth century the American academic profession is both the one and the many, what is the nature of the one and the character of the many? Just how far apart from one another are academics in two-year colleges, four-year colleges, and universities—and in physics, English, and business—in the nature of their work, professional beliefs, and patterns of authority? What bonds seem to unite them?

Thus we felt that disciplinarians should be taken seriously, rather than to be quickly blurred together under such general rubrics as "academic man"; that institutional locations should be given full respect, not overlooked, as when "the university" or "the liberal arts college" is mistaken for the whole or allowed to preempt attention. We also wanted to avoid the myopia of the view from the top that has transformed much research on American "higher education" into research on "the university," much work on science into an avoidance of science as it is practiced in the four-fifths of academia that lies outside the most active research sites. Insisting that analysis should dig deeply inside the system, we also wanted to roam

279

widely across the academic landscape in a large country. How else could we possibly reach some of the deep, hidden currents of the profession unless we penetrated its extended and changeable surface? Context matters, and immediate context matters a great deal. For an advanced occupation thoroughly embedded in formal instruments, in an age of bureaucracy and profession, an internalist orientation has great merit.

We purposely did not attempt to scout society in pursuit of demographic trends, the changing state of the economy, and other external "forces" that might shape the academic profession. Other observers pursue these matters, commonly with little or no attention to the imperatives of disciplines, the response tendencies of institutions, and the capacity of academics to stay the course, filtering and reshaping outside forces as they play upon the system. We were also aware that another major study of the professoriate was already under way in 1983 that would explore such economic issues as the impact of remuneration on the quality of academic labor.[2] Further, we largely ignored the play of social background in the lives of American academics, subordinating stratification issues posed by students of class and race, and put to one side the question of political, economic, and religious identification often posed by political sociologists. Hence we did not set out to ask who had been poor or rich, was born in the city or the countryside, was Catholic, Jewish, or Protestant, white, or black, voted Democratic or Republican in the last election, drove a foreign car or one manufactured in Detroit.[3]

We also held a tight rein on the indulgent impulse in sociology to speculate freely on the "functions" of the academic profession in society. To think intelligently about larger connections and effects, we first need to understand more thoroughly the nature of different segments of the higher education system, especially the disciplines and the main institutional sectors; involvement in different sets of tasks means different relations to the outside world. Large views of this profession in society will be better informed when they take into account the differences among such academic types as physicists in universities, classicists in small private colleges, and business instructors in public community colleges.

To pursue disciplines, we fixed on six: physics, to represent the physical sciences; biology, to enter the second major arena of science; political science, as a toss-up among the social sciences; English, as a central, large field in the humanities. Under limits established by time, resources, and the wish to work intensively, this minimal coverage of letters and science fields allowed us to delve into two major professional areas: medicine, as a veritable organizational monster in its capacity to absorb personnel and money but a field limited to university settings; and business, as a major and fast-growing "applied" domain stretching from universities to community colleges. To pursue types of institutions, we settled on six categories fashioned from the Carnegie classifications of 1973 and 1976, selecting three institutions in each of four major sectors and two in each of two liberal arts college groupings that together now have only about 5 percent of the professoriate. The sixteen institutions were selected with an eye for the public-private distinction as well as for geographic spread. Table A–1 identifies the specific institutions.

Aiming wherever feasible for two or more interviews in each field in each institution, our matrix, as shown in Table A–2, provided approximately thirty interviews in each field, except medicine, spread throughout the types of institutions, and offered some nine to fourteen primary interviews in each institution, or approximately thirty to forty interviews for the larger institutional categories and twenty for the smaller ones. In each department or professional school, we sought to interview a junior nontenured member and a senior tenured professor. This basic faculty sample was supplemented by an additional sixty-seven interviews, conducted for background purposes, with administrators, associated faculty, union representatives, and faculty leaders. These secondary interviews were particularly helpful in penetrating the mysteries of medical school structures and faculty procedures, a particularly tangled terrain that deserves much fuller analysis.

Working from faculty rosters of the selected institutions, we generally reached potential interviewees by telephone in advance of a campus visit. The individuals we approached were promised anonymity and were told during the tape-recorded interviews that they would be identified only by type of institution and discipline, for example, "a political scientist at a research university." Refusals to be interviewed were rare; generally they were made on the grounds of inconvenient time. Only three individuals refused because they did not wish to participate; two others did not allow

TABLE A–1

THE SIXTEEN INSTITUTIONS OF THE STUDY

INSTITUTION AND TYPE	PUBLIC/ PRIVATE	STATE
RESEARCH UNIVERSITY I		
Stanford University	Private	California
University of Michigan	Public	Michigan
University of North Carolina at Chapel Hill	Public	North Carolina
RESEARCH UNIVERSITY II AND DOCTORAL-GRANTING UNIVERSITIES		
George Washington University	Private	Washington, D.C.
Kansas State University	Public	Kansas
Southern Illinois University at Carbondale	Public	Illinois
COMPREHENSIVE UNIVERSITIES AND COLLEGES		
California State University, Hayward	Public	California
Glassboro State College	Public	New Jersey
University of New Orleans	Public	Louisiana
LIBERAL ARTS COLLEGES I		
Bowdoin College	Private	Maine
Carleton College	Private	Minnesota
LIBERAL ARTS COLLEGES II		
High Point College	Private	North Carolina
Regis College	Private	Colorado
COMMUNITY COLLEGES		
East Los Angeles Community College	Public	California
Piedmont Valley Community College	Public	Virginia
Suffolk County Community College	Public	New York

NOTE: In each of the first three categories of institutions, 75 percent or more of enrollment is in public institutions. In the two liberal arts categories, enrollment is over 95 percent private. In the community colleges, it is 95 percent public. Definitions of the above categories and a full listing of institutions by type and state may be found in The Carnegie Foundation for the Advancement of Teaching, *A Classification of Institutions of Higher Education* (1976).

TABLE A–2

THE MATRIX OF INTERVIEWS

INSTITUTIONS	DISCIPLINE						
	PHYSICS	BIOLOGY	POLITICAL SCIENCE	ENGLISH	BUSINESS	MEDICINE	TOTAL
RESEARCH UNIVERSITY I							
Stanford University	2	2	2	2	2	3	13
University of Michigan	2	2	2	2	2	4	14
University of North Carolina	2	3	2	2	2	3	14
RESEARCH UNIVERSITY II AND DOCTORAL-GRANTING UNIVERSITIES							
George Washington University	2	1	1	2	2	4	12
Kansas State University	2	2	2	2	2	2	12
Southern Illinois University	2	2	2	2	2	2	12
COMPREHENSIVE UNIVERSITIES AND COLLEGES							
California State University, Hayward	2	2	2	2	2	—	10
Glassboro State College	2	2	2	2	2	—	10
University of New Orleans	2	2	2	2	2	—	10

TABLE A–2 (*cont.*)

INSTITUTIONS	PHYSICS	BIOLOGY	POLITICAL SCIENCE	ENGLISH	BUSINESS	MEDICINE	TOTAL
LIBERAL ARTS COLLEGES I							
Bowdoin College	2	2	2	3	–	–	8
Carleton College	2	2	2	2	2	–	10
LIBERAL ARTS COLLEGES II							
High Point College	1	2	2	2	1	–	9
Regis College	1	2	2	2	2	–	9
COMMUNITY COLLEGES							
East Los Angeles	2	2	2	2	2	–	10
Piedmont Valley	2	2	2	2	2	–	10
Suffolk County	2	2	2	1	2	–	9
TOTALS	30	32	31	32	29	18	172

DISCIPLINE

NOTE: An Additional 67 background interviews were conducted, 36 in medical schools and 31 in the other fields, for a total of 236 interviews.

us to tape their conversations. The interviews were carried out mainly during 1984.

In the interviews we aimed for structured flexibility. Questions were carefully prepared and pretested in ten major categories: personal background, work activities and conditions, commitment to institution, disciplinary structure and commitment, departmental affairs, academic and vocational orientations, general academic values, the reward structure of promotion and tenure, authority, and major problems of the profession.[4] The questions were often broad and necessitated more than simple responses. Answers in one category frequently shaded into other topics, and beyond: Professors are trained to talk, to conceptualize, and to direct the flow of conversations. The interviews often departed from the sequence of the schedule of questions while attempting to remain faithful in coverage.

Two postdoctoral research associates carried out most of the interviews, with some help from three graduate-student research assistants, all working with the Comparative Higher Education Research Group in the Graduate School of Education, UCLA. The ability of the interviewers to digress from the sequence of questions to follow where the interviewees wanted to go in the flow of discussion, but still hue to the main scheme, was critical to the success of the fieldwork. Originally targeted for a little over an hour, the interviews commonly lasted between one and one and one-half hours, with a few extending to two hours. One-half of the taped interviews were transcribed into protocols that averaged fifteen single-spaced pages; the others remained on tape. The transcriptions represented about half the interviews from each field and about half from each institution.

The academics and officials approached for the secondary interviews were chosen on a case-by-case basis. The dean of the faculty or someone in an equivalent position was always interviewed, as was the head of the union, if there was one, or a campus faculty representative. With much variation from one type of institution to another, we sought out administrators with specific responsibilities, for example, a vice-president for research, and part-time or temporary faculty. Seeking information on the broader institutional context, these quite unstructured interviews pursued such topics as the recent historical development of the institution, faculty rules and regulations, basic faculty statistics, tenure policies, campuswide governance, and the use of part-time and temporary faculty.

285

Mid-stream in the research, we decided to mount a small effort to explore the nature of faculty associations by extending our interviewing and data gathering to the headquarters of national associations and to a few professors located on campuses who had had a major role in one or more of the associations we contacted. By interview and by written materials supplied to us, work carried out largely by Kenneth P. Ruscio, we were able to gain useful information on a number of associations—the American Physical Society, the American Chemical Society, the Federation of American Societies for Experimental Biology, the American Political Science Association, the American Historical Association were included—to supplement what we were learning from the faculty interviews and the journal literature about the fascinating yet vastly understudied world of academic associations.

Serving somewhat as a quantitative counterpart to our qualitative field research, the national survey of faculty conducted by The Carnegie Foundation for the Advancement of Teaching and the Opinion Research Corporation in spring 1984 was a welcomed additional source of information.[5] With 5,000 respondents in over 300 institutions, the 1984 survey covered a wide range of topics, including questions used in earlier Carnegie surveys in 1969 and 1975. The data obtained in this survey will be a resource for researchers for years to come, permitting analysis over time and the use of various multivariant techniques. With the survey data added to the great mass of material obtained in the field visits, the UCLA research group had an overload of information. We limited our use of the survey to a few rudimentary analyses of such "objective" matters as hours spent teaching, and, secondarily, to the results of a few queries in the more "subjective" domain of expressed attitudes and declared values. In short, we went with the interviews, emphasizing intensive exploration rather than extensive coverage, fully aware that ethnographic materials on their face appear to be less compelling than statistical data. But all survey analyses of any value are also selective and interpretative, with results that are heavily affected by the wording of questions and the superficiality inherent in set responses that cannot be probed or clarified. In either case, what finally counts is the interpretative and explanatory power that analysts can muster as they put mind and material together.

In writing this volume I was torn between the immensity of the specific and the historical and the desire to elaborate a good idea or two and to fashion some generalizations. At numerous points I have sought to err on the side of the particular, even at the risk of boring readers, in order to stress how much we must disaggregate American academia to avoid misleading myths and to grasp significant differences. In part, this approach is a reaction to the generalizing literature that has refused to pursue particulars. An instructive case in point is Talcott Parsons and Gerald M. Platt's *The American University*, a major statement considerably emptied of valuable substance because it draws largely upon personal experience, readily brushes aside the undergraduate realm, ignores four-fifths of American higher education, and treats of "cultural functions" to the virtual exclusion of the arrangements of work, interest, and authority. Too much of the flux, perversity, and sheer dirtiness of real life is left out.[6] An unnecessarily abstract picture emerges, with the normative heavily clothed in the analytical. A useful corrective is to roam around in one fashion or another, listen closely and read attentively, and pick up the particulars. When the analyst then returns to the large ideas, the particulars instruct the interpretative choices.

General points have been made in each chapter as I have attempted to highlight systematic patterns among the multitudes of variations. Weaving among the complexities, the generalizations are not necessarily consistent. But the broadest interpretations are brought together in the concluding chapter on the logic of the academic profession in its American settings. My hope is that these explanations are at worst appropriate supplements to the visions of others, and, at best, are superior in explaining this profession in this particular country near the end of the twentieth century. In the normal course of social inquiry, time and critical assessment will tell.

APPENDIX B

American Disciplinary Associations, 1985

NAME OF ASSOCIATION	FOUNDING DATE
Academy of Applied Science	1962
Academy of Management	1936
Academy of Marketing Science	1971
Academy of Political Science	1880
Accounting Researchers International Organization	1973
Afghanistan Studies Association	1971
American Association of Slavic and East European Languages	1940
American Council of Teachers of Uncommonly Taught Asian Languages	1973
American Society for German Literature of the 16th and 17th Centuries	1970
American Academy of Advertising	1956
American Academy of Arts and Sciences	1780
American Academy of the History of Dentistry	1951
American Academy of Political and Social Science	1889
American Agricultural Law Association	1980
American Anthropological Association	1902
American Association for the Advancement of Slavic Studies	1948
American Association for Applied Linguistics	1977
American Association for the Comparative Study of Law	1951
American Association for Social Psychiatry	1971
American Association for the Advancement of Science	1848
American Association of Anatomists	1888
American Association of Bioanalysts	1956
American Association of Evangelical Students	1945
American Association of Housing Educators	1965
American Association of Immunologists	1913
American Association of Phonetic Sciences	1973
American Association of Physical Anthropologists	1930

American Association of Physics Teachers	1930
American Association of Professors of Yiddish	1974
American Association of Teacher Education in Agriculture	1959
American Association of Teachers of French	1927
American Association of Teachers of German	1926
American Association of Teachers of Italian	1924
American Association of Teachers of Spanish and Portuguese	1917
American Astronomical Society	1899
American Biological Society	1978
American Catholic Historical Association	1919
American Catholic Philosophical Association	1926
American Catholic Sociological Society	1938
American Chemical Society	1876
American Classical League	1919
American Comparative Literature Association	1960
American Council of Learned Societies	1919
American Council on Education for Journalism	1929
American Council on Pharmaceutical Education	1932
American Economic Association	1885
American Educational Research Association	1915
American Educational Studies Association	1968
American Entomological Society	1859
American Epidemiological Soviet	1927
American Ethnological Society	1842
American Eugenics Society	1926
American Federation of Information Processing Societies	1961
American Folklore Society	1888
American Genetic Society	1903
American Geographical Society	1852
American Geological Institute	1948
American Geophysical Union	1919
American Historical Association	1884
American Home Economics Association	1909
American Humor Studies Association	1974
American Institute of Aeronautics and Astronautics	1963
American Institute of Biological Sciences	1947
American Institute of the History of Pharmacy	1941
American Institute of Indian Studies	1961
American Institute of Musicology	1945
American Institute of Physics	1931
American Law Institute	1923
American Law Student Association	1949
American Legal Studies Association	1975
American Mathematical Association of Two Year Colleges	1974
American Mathematical Society	1888

American Microchemical Society	1935
American Name Society	1951
American Ornithological Union	1883
American Philological Association	1869
American Philosophical Association	1900
American Philosophical Society	1743
American Physical Society	1899
American Physiological Society	1887
American Phytophalological Society	1908
American Political Science Association	1903
American Psychiatric Association	1844
American Psychological Association	1892
American Psychopathological Association	1912
American Society for Eighteenth Century Studies	1969
American Society for Engineering Education	1893
American Society for Legal History	1956
American Society for Neurochemistry	1969
American Society for Pharmacology and Experimental Therapeutics	1908
American Society for Political and Legal Philosophy	1955
American Society for Public Administration	1939
American Society for the Study of Religion	1960
American Society for Theatre Research	1959
American Society for Value Inquiry	1970
American Society of Adlerian Psychology	1951
American Society of Biological Chemists	1906
American Society of Christian Ethics	1959
American Society of Ethnohistory	1953
American Society of Human Genetics	1948
American Society of Ichthyologists and Herpetologists	1913
American Society of Landscape Architects	1899
American Society of Mammalogists	1919
American Society of Mechanical Engineers	1880
American Society of Microbiology	1899
American Society of Naturalists	1883
American Society of Parasitologists	1924
American Society of Primatologists	1976
American Society of Professional Biologists	1947
American Society of University Composers	1966
American Society of Zoologists	1890
American Sociological Association	1905
American Statistical Association	1839
American Studies Association	1951
American Theological Society	1927
American Vacuum Society	1953

Animal Behavior Society	1964
Archaeological Institute of America	1879
Associated Organizations for Teacher Education	1959
Associated University Bureaus of Business and Economic Research	1947
Association for the Advancement of Baltic Studies	1968
Association for Arid Lands Studies	1977
Association for Comparative Economics	1972
Association for Computers and the Humanities	1978
Association for Cooperative Economic Studies	1972
Association for Correctional Research and Information Management	1971
Association for Counselor Education and Supervision	1964
Association for Education in International Business	1959
Association for Education in Journalism	1912
The Association for the Anthropological Study of Play	1973
Association for the Education of Teachers in Science	1933
Association for Evolutionary Economics	1963
Association for General and Liberal Studies	1961
Association for Informal Logic and Critical Thinking	1983
Association for Jewish Studies	1969
Association for Korean Studies	1974
Association for Measurement and Evaluation In Guidance	1965
Association for Politics and Life Sciences	1980
Association for Professional Broadcasting Education	1955
Association for Research in Ophthalmology	1928
Association for Student Teaching	1921
Association for Symbolic Logic	1936
Association for the Sociological Study of Jewry	1971
Association for the Study of the Nationalities	1972
Association for the Study of Soviet-Type Economics	1972
Association of American Geographers	1904
Association of American Rhodes Scholars	1907
Association of Ancient Historians	1974
Association of Caribbean Studies	1978
Association of Existential Psychology and Psychiatry	1960
Association of Health Occupations	1978
Association of Marshal Scholars and Alumni	1959
Association of Professors of Medicine	1954
Association of Social Science Teachers	1935
Association of Student International Law Societies	1961
Association of Teachers of Japanese	1962
Association of Teachers of Latin American Studies	1970
Association of Teachers of Maternal and Child Health	1968
Association of Teachers of Preventive Medicine	1942

Association of Teachers of Technical Writing	1973
Association of Universities for Research in Astronomy	1957
Association of University Anesthetists	1953
Association of University Radiologists	1953
Behavior Genetics Association	1972
Bioelectromagnetics Society	1978
Biophysical Society	1957
Business Education Research Foundation	1927
Byron Society	1971
C. G. Jung Foundation for Analytical Psychology	1963
Caribbean Studies Association	1974
Catecholamine Club	1969
Catholic Economic Association	1941
Cell Kinetics Society	1977
Charles Ives Society	1973
Children's Literature Association	1972
College Art Association of America	1912
College Language Association	1937
College Music Society	1947
Comparative Education Society	1956
Conference Board of the Mathematical Sciences	1960
Conference for the Study of Political Thought	1968
Conference Group on French Politics and Society	1974
Conference Group on German Politics	1968
Conference Group on Italian Politics	1975
Conference on British Studies	1951
Conference on College Composition and Communication	1949
Conference on Latin American History/Hispanic Foundation	1926
Cooper Ornithological Society	1893
Council for Distributive Teacher Education	1960
Council for Philosophical Studies	1965
Council for Professional Education for Business	1916
Council of Social Work Education	1952
Council on Hotel, Restaurant and Institutional Education	1946
Council on Optometric Education	1930
D. H. Lawrence Society of North America	1975
Dickens Society	1970
Ecological Society of America	1915
Econometric Society	1930
Economic History Association	1941
Electrochemical Society	1902
Endocrine Society	1918
Engineers Council for Professional Development	1932
English Institute	1938
Entomological Society of America	1953

Eugene O'Neill Society	1978
Ezra Pound Society	1978
Federation of American Societies for Experimental Biology	1913
Genetics Society of America	1932
Geochemical Society	1955
Geological Society of America	1888
Goethe Society of North America	1979
Great Plains Historical Association	1960
Group for the Use of Psychology in History	1972
Gypsy Lore Society, North American Chapter	1977
Hegel Society of America	1968
Hemingway Society	1980
Hispanic Society of America	1904
History of Economics Society	1972
History of Education Society	1960
History of Science Society	1924
Institute for Intercultural Studies	1943
Institute of International Education	1919
Institute of Mathematical Statistics	1930
Intercollegiate Society of Individualists	1966
International Association for Philosophy and Literature	1976
International Association for Philosophy of Law and Social Philosophy	1963
International Association of Buddhist Studies	1976
International Courtly Literature Society	1973
International Dostoevsky Society	1971
International Galdos Association	1979
International Organization for the Study of Human Development	1969
International Society for Human Ethology	1973
International Society for Metaphysics	1973
International Society for Neoplatonic Studies	1973
International Society for Research on Aggression	1970
International Studies Association	1959
Inter-University Consortium for Political Research	1962
Jane Austen Society of North America	1979
Jaspers Society of North America	1981
Jean Piaget Society	1970
Jesuit Seismological Association	1925
Jewish Academy of Arts and Sciences	1927
John Dewey Society	1935
Joint Committee on Continuing Legal Education	1947
Joint Council on Economic Education	1948
Joseph Conrad Society of America	1974
Journalism Association of Junior Colleges	1957

Kafka Society of America	1975
Kroeber Anthropological Society	1949
Law Student Civil Rights Research Council	1963
Linguistics Society of America	1924
Mark Twain Society	1970
Mathematics Association of America	1915
Medieval Academy of America	1925
Metaphysical Society of America	1950
Modern Humanities Research Association	1918
Modern Language Association of America	1883
Mongolian Society	1961
Mycological Society of America	1931
Nathaniel Hawthorne Society	1974
National Academy of Education	1965
National Academy of Engineering	1964
National Academy of Sciences–National Research Council	1916
National Association for Physical Education of College Women	1897
National Association for Practical Nurse Education and Service	1941
National Association for Research in Science Teaching	1928
National Association of College Wind and Percussion Instructors	1952
National Association of Dramatic and Speech Arts	1936
National Association of Geology Teachers	1938
National Association of Industrial Teacher Education	1937
National Association of Teacher Educators for Business Education	1970
National College Physical Education Association for Men	1897
National Collegiate Association for Secretaries	1962
National Conference on Research on English	1937
National Council on Measurement in Education	1938
National Federation of Modern Language Teachers' Associations	1916
National Institute for Architectural Education	1894
National Institute of Social Science	1912
National Organization on Legal Problems of Education	1954
National Society for the Study of Communications	1950
National Society for the Study of Education	1901
National Society of College Teachers of Education	1902
National Student Nurses' Association	1953
Nietzsche Society	1979
North American Dostoevsky Society	1970
North American Society for the Sociology of Sport	1980
Nuttall Ornithological Club	1873

Operations Research Society of America	1952
Organization of American Historians	1907
Parapsychological Association	1957
Paul Claudel Society	1968
Philosophic Society for the Study of Sport	1972
Philosophy of Education Society	1941
Philosophy of Science Association	1934
Phychological Society of America	1946
Poe Studies Association	1972
Psychometric Society	1935
Psychonomic Society	1959
Radiation Research Society	1952
Rural Sociological Society	1937
Scientific Research Society of America	1886
Seismological Society of America	1906
Shakespeare Association of America	1972
Sherwood Anderson Society	1975
Society for the Advancement of American Philosophy	1972
Society for the Advancement of Education	1939
Society for Ancient Greek Philosophy	1953
Society for the Anthropology of Visual Communication	1972
Society for Applied Anthropology	1941
Society for Armenian Studies	1974
Society for Asian and Comparative Philosophy	1968
Society for Developmental Biology	1939
Society for Ethnomusicology	1955
Society for Experimental Biology and Medicine	1903
Society for French Historical Studies	1955
Society for General Systems Research	1954
Society for Historians of the Early American Republic	1978
Society for the History of Discoveries	1960
Society for the History of Technology	1958
Society for Latin American Anthropology	1969
Society for Medical Anthropology	1971
Society for Medieval and Renaissance Philosophy	1979
Society for Neuroscience	1969
Society for Nursing History	1979
Society for Phenomenology and Existential Philosophy	1962
Society for Projective Techniques and Personality Assessment	1938
Society for the Psychological Study of Social Issues	1936
Society for Psychophysiological Research	1960
Society for the Scientific Study of Sex	1957
Society for Slovene Studies	1973
Society for South India Studies	1968

Society for the Study of Early China	1975
Society for the Study of Evolution	1946
Society for the Study of Male Psychology and Physiology	1975
Society for the Study of Southern Literature	1968
Society for the Study of Symbolic Interaction	1975
Society for the Study of Women in Legal History	1979
Society of American Archivists	1936
Society of American Forestry	1900
Society of American Historians	1939
Society of American Law Teachers	1974
Society of Architectural Historians	1940
Society of General Physiologists	1946
Society of Multivariate Experimental Psychology	1960
Society of Spanish and Spanish-American Studies	1976
Society of University Surgeons	1939
Society of Women Geographers	1925
Sociological Research Association	1905
Sociology of Education Association	1972
Southern Historical Association	1934
Speech Association of America	1914
Standards Engineers Society	1947
Student American Medical Association	1950
Student National Education Association	1957
Student Personnel Association for Teacher Education	1951
Thomas Hardy Society of America	1979
Thomas Wolfe Society	1979
Tissue Culture Association	1946
Ukrainian Political Science Association in the U.S.	1970
University Association for Emergency Medicine	1970
University Aviation Association	1948
Urban Affairs Association	1969
Virginia Woolf Society	1975
Vladimir Nabokov Society	1978
Western Humor and Irony Membership	1980
Wilson Ornithological Society	1888
Wordsworth-Coleridge Association	1970

SOURCE: Disciplinary associations and their dates of origin are from the *Encyclopedia of Associations*, 1985. Four additional associations did not report founding dates. Analysis by Ronald Opp.

APPENDIX C

Supplementary Tables for Chapter IV: The Imperatives of Academic Work

TABLE C-1

WORK LOAD: TIME SPENT ON TEACHING GRADUATE OR PROFESSIONAL COURSES, BY TYPE OF INSTITUTION

TYPE OF INSTITUTION	NONE	HOURS PER WEEK			
		1–4	5–10	11–20	OVER 20
		(PERCENT OF FACULTY)			
RESEARCH UNIVERSITIES I	30	50	16	3	1
RESEARCH UNIVERSITIES II	36	42	19	2	1
DOCTORAL-GRANTING UNIVERSITIES I	39	41	16	4	0
DOCTORAL-GRANTING UNIVERSITIES II	44	34	19	3	0
COMPREHENSIVE UNIVERSITIES AND COLLEGES I	56	30	12	2	0
COMPREHENSIVE UNIVERSITIES AND COLLEGES II	64	23	11	1	1
LIBERAL ARTS COLLEGES I	92	2	5	0	1
LIBERAL ARTS COLLEGES II	76	13	7	3	1
TWO-YEAR COLLEGES	93	3	1	2	1
ALL INSTITUTIONS	58	28	11	2	1

TOTAL RESPONDENTS, 3,925

QUESTION: "How many hours per week on the average are you spending on normal classroom instruction in graduate or professional courses?"

SOURCE: The Carnegie Foundation for the Advancement of Teaching, 1984 Faculty Survey.

TABLE C–2

TIME SPENT ON WORK ACTIVITIES, OTHER THAN RESEARCH OR CLASSROOM TEACHING, BY TYPE OF INSTITUTION

TYPE OF INSTITUTION	NONE	1–4	5–10	11–20	OVER 20
			HOURS PER WEEK		
	(PERCENT OF FACULTY)				
RESEARCH UNIVERSITIES I					
Advising/counseling	10	63	22	3	2
Professional practice	75	12	9	2	2
Teaching preparation	6	30	43	16	5
RESEARCH UNIVERSITIES II					
Advising/counseling	8	65	23	2	2
Professional practice	71	14	8	5	3
Teaching preparation	5	26	45	19	5
DOCTORAL-GRANTING UNIVERSITIES I					
Advising/counseling	12	67	18	2	1
Professional practice	71	13	10	3	3
Teaching preparation	4	24	50	19	3
DOCTORAL-GRANTING UNIVERSITIES II					
Advising/counseling	10	62	24	3	1
Professional practice	66	19	9	5	5
Teaching preparation	3	22	52	18	5
COMPREHENSIVE COLLEGES AND UNIVERSITIES I					
Advising/counseling	11	63	22	3	1
Professional practice	69	13	10	5	3
Teaching preparation	3	21	48	23	5
COMPREHENSIVE COLLEGES AND UNIVERSITIES II					
Advising/counseling	8	66	22	4	0
Professional practice	67	14	13	2	4
Teaching preparation	2	30	41	23	4

TABLE C-2 (*cont.*)

TYPE OF INSTITUTION	NONE	HOURS PER WEEK			
		1–4	5–10	11–20	OVER 20
		(PERCENT OF FACULTY)			
LIBERAL ARTS COLLEGES I					
Advising/counseling	5	68	23	3	1
Professional practice	68	16	11	3	2
Teaching preparation	2	14	42	33	9
LIBERAL ARTS COLLEGES II					
Advising/counseling	9	68	21	1	1
Professional practice	67	16	10	2	4
Teaching preparation	4	16	51	26	3
TWO-YEAR COLLEGES					
Advising/counseling	15	68	14	2	1
Professional practice	68	11	12	4	5
Teaching preparation	6	23	46	21	4
TOTAL					
Advising/counseling	11	65	20	3	1
Professional practice	70	13	10	4	3
Teaching preparation	4	24	46	21	5

TOTAL RESPONDENTS, 4,742

QUESTION: "How many hours per week on the average are you spending on work other than research or classroom teaching?"

SOURCE: The Carnegie Foundation for the Advancement of Teaching, 1984 Faculty Survey.

Supplementary Tables for Chapter V:
The Enclosures of Culture

TABLE D–1

FACULTY SELF-CHARACTERIZATION AS INTELLECTUALS, BY TYPE OF INSTITUTION

TYPE OF INSTITUTION	STRONGLY AGREE	AGREE WITH RESERVATIONS	DISAGREE WITH RESERVATIONS	STRONGLY DISAGREE
	(PERCENT OF FACULTY)			
RESEARCH UNIVERSITIES I	30	52	15	3
RESEARCH UNIVERSITIES II	28	51	15	6
DOCTORAL-GRANTING UNIVERSITIES I	31	49	15	5
DOCTORAL-GRANTING UNIVERSITIES II	27	50	17	6
COMPREHENSIVE UNIVERSITIES AND COLLEGES I	29	48	16	7
COMPREHENSIVE UNIVERSITIES AND COLLEGES II	38	45	12	5
LIBERAL ARTS COLLEGES I	38	44	15	3
LIBERAL ARTS COLLEGES II	25	52	17	6
TWO-YEAR COLLEGES	23	53	16	8
ALL INSTITUTIONS	28	50	16	6

TOTAL RESPONDENTS, 4,863

QUESTION: "I consider myself an intellectual."

SOURCE: The Carnegie Foundation for the Advancement of Teaching, 1984 Faculty Survey.

TABLE D–2

FACULTY BELIEF THAT THEY SHARE COMMON PROFESSIONAL VALUES, BY TYPE OF INSTITUTION

TYPE OF INSTITUTION	STRONGLY AGREE	AGREE WITH RESERVATIONS	DISAGREE WITH RESERVATIONS	STRONGLY DISAGREE
	(PERCENT OF FACULTY)			
RESEARCH UNIVERSITIES I	17	53	22	8
RESEARCH UNIVERSITIES II	16	46	28	10
DOCTORAL-GRANTING UNIVERSITIES I	16	51	24	9
DOCTORAL-GRANTING UNIVERSITIES II	15	57	19	9
COMPREHENSIVE UNIVERSITIES AND COLLEGES I	17	50	22	11
COMPREHENSIVE UNIVERSITIES AND COLLEGES II	16	46	23	15
LIBERAL ARTS COLLEGES I	15	50	26	9
LIBERAL ARTS COLLEGES II	19	50	23	8
TWO-YEAR COLLEGES	18	48	25	9
ALL INSTITUTIONS	17	49	24	10

TOTAL RESPONDENTS, 4,947

QUESTION: "Despite the differences among institutions of higher education, members of the academic profession share a common set of professional values."

SOURCE: The Carnegie Foundation for the Advancement of Teaching, 1984 Faculty Survey.

305

APPENDIX E

*Supplementary Information and Tables
for Chapter VII: The Promises of Career*

TABLE E–1

FACULTY BELIEF THAT NOW IS A POOR TIME TO BEGIN AN ACADEMIC CAREER, BY TYPE OF INSTITUTION

TYPE OF INSTITUTION	STRONGLY AGREE	AGREE WITH RESERVATIONS	DISAGREE WITH RESERVATIONS	STRONGLY DISAGREE
	(PERCENT OF FACULTY)			
RESEARCH UNIVERSITIES I	13	29	38	20
RESEARCH UNIVERSITIES II	15	36	31	18
DOCTORAL-GRANTING UNIVERSITIES I	15	35	31	19
DOCTORAL-GRANTING UNIVERSITIES II	17	36	32	15
COMPREHENSIVE UNIVERSITIES AND COLLEGES I	18	36	31	15
COMPREHENSIVE UNIVERSITIES AND COLLEGES II	27	34	24	15
LIBERAL ARTS COLLEGES I	14	44	31	11
LIBERAL ARTS COLLEGES II	18	34	31	17
TWO-YEAR COLLEGES	14	31	30	25
ALL INSTITUTIONS	16	34	31	19

TOTAL RESPONDENTS, 4,915

QUESTION: "This is a poor time for any young person to begin an academic career."

SOURCE: The Carnegie Foundation for the Advancement of Teaching, 1984 Faculty Survey.

TABLE E-2

FACULTY RATINGS OF JOB PROSPECTS FOR GRADUATE STUDENTS FOR THE NEXT TEN YEARS, BY TYPE OF INSTITUTION

TYPE OF INSTITUTION	VERY GOOD	FAIRLY GOOD	FAIR	POOR	VERY POOR
	(PERCENT OF FACULTY)				
RESEARCH UNIVERSITIES I	20	33	30	14	3
RESEARCH UNIVERSITIES II	16	21	35	20	8
DOCTORAL-GRANTING UNIVERSITIES I	18	24	29	19	10
DOCTORAL-GRANTING UNIVERSITIES II	16	19	37	17	11
COMPREHENSIVE UNIVERSITIES AND COLLEGES I	14	20	32	22	12
COMPREHENSIVE UNIVERSITIES AND COLLEGES II	14	20	27	22	17
LIBERAL ARTS COLLEGES I	8	30	26	29	7
LIBERAL ARTS COLLEGES II	14	26	33	18	9
TWO-YEAR COLLEGES	14	17	34	22	13
ALL INSTITUTIONS	15	23	32	20	10

TOTAL RESPONDENTS, 4,315

QUESTION: "Thinking about the next ten years, how would you rate the job prospects for graduate students from your department?"

SOURCE: The Carnegie Foundation for the Advancement of Teaching, 1984 Faculty Survey.

TABLE E-3

FACULTY COMPARISON OF JOB PROSPECTS FOR GRADUATE STUDENTS TODAY WITH THOSE OF FIVE YEARS AGO, BY TYPE OF INSTITUTION

TYPE OF INSTITUTION	MUCH BETTER	SOMEWHAT BETTER	ABOUT THE SAME	SOMEWHAT SAME	MUCH WORSE
		(PERCENT OF FACULTY)			
RESEARCH UNIVERSITIES I	5	17	43	29	6
RESEARCH UNIVERSITIES II	5	19	36	30	10
DOCTORAL-GRANTING UNIVERSITIES I	3	21	39	28	9
DOCTORAL-GRANTING UNIVERSITIES II	4	16	42	25	13
COMPREHENSIVE UNIVERSITIES AND COLLEGES I	5	17	40	31	7
COMPREHENSIVE UNIVERSITIES AND COLLEGES II	3	23	32	34	8
LIBERAL ARTS COLLEGES I	4	16	47	27	6
LIBERAL ARTS COLLEGES II	1	20	40	35	4
TWO-YEAR COLLEGES	6	20	35	33	6
ALL INSTITUTIONS	4	19	39	31	7

TOTAL RESPONDENTS, 4,673

QUESTION: "How would you compare these aspects of your work situation today with the situation five years ago . . . job prospects for students?"

SOURCE: The Carnegie Foundation for the Advancement of Teaching, 1984 Faculty Survey.

TABLE E-4

FACULTY COMPARISON OF DEPARTMENTAL MORALE TODAY WITH THAT FIVE YEARS AGO, BY TYPE OF INSTITUTION

TYPE OF INSTITUTION	MUCH BETTER	SOMEWHAT BETTER	ABOUT THE SAME	SOMEWHAT SAME	MUCH WORSE
	(PERCENT OF FACULTY)				
RESEARCH UNIVERSITIES I	7	22	36	23	12
RESEARCH UNIVERSITIES II	6	17	35	27	15
DOCTORAL-GRANTING UNIVERSITIES I	6	20	33	26	15
DOCTORAL-GRANTING UNIVERSITIES II	10	17	27	32	14
COMPREHENSIVE UNIVERSITIES AND COLLEGES I	6	17	35	27	15
COMPREHENSIVE UNIVERSITIES AND COLLEGES II	8	18	32	29	13
LIBERAL ARTS COLLEGES I	9	25	39	23	4
LIBERAL ARTS COLLEGES II	7	20	37	30	6
TWO-YEAR COLLEGES	7	15	38	27	13
ALL INSTITUTIONS	7	18	35	27	13

TOTAL RESPONDENTS, 4,692

QUESTION: "How would you compare these aspects of your work situation today with the situation five years ago . . . departmental morale?"

SOURCE: The Carnegie Foundation for the Advancement of Teaching, 1984 Faculty Survey.

TABLE E-5

FACULTY ENJOYMENT OF INTERACTION WITH STUDENTS OUTSIDE THE CLASSROOM, BY TYPE OF INSTITUTION

TYPE OF INSTITUTION	STRONGLY AGREE	AGREE WITH RESERVATIONS	DISAGREE WITH RESERVATIONS	STRONGLY DISAGREE
	(PERCENT OF FACULTY)			
RESEARCH UNIVERSITIES I	47	44	7	2
RESEARCH UNIVERSITIES II	45	44	10	1
DOCTORAL-GRANTING UNIVERSITIES I	46	43	9	2
DOCTORAL-GRANTING UNIVERSITIES II	48	44	7	1
COMPREHENSIVE UNIVERSITIES AND COLLEGES I	50	40	8	2
COMPREHENSIVE UNIVERSITIES AND COLLEGES II	49	41	9	1
LIBERAL ARTS COLLEGES I	51	44	5	0
LIBERAL ARTS COLLEGES II	64	31	4	1
TWO-YEAR COLLEGES	44	45	9	2
ALL INSTITUTIONS	48	42	8	2

TOTAL RESPONDENTS, 4,964

QUESTION: "I enjoy opportunities to interact informally with students outside the class-room."

SOURCE: The Carnegie Foundation for the Advancement of Teaching, 1984 Faculty Survey.

TABLE E-6

TIME SPENT BY FACULTY IN ELEMENTARY OR SECONDARY TEACHING OR ADMINISTRATION SINCE OBTAINING HIGHEST DEGREE, BY TYPE OF INSTITUTION

TYPE OF INSTITUTION	NEVER	1 YEAR OR LESS	2–5 YEARS	6 YEARS OR MORE
		(PERCENT OF FACULTY)		
RESEARCH UNIVERSITIES I	91	3	3	3
RESEARCH UNIVERSITIES II	88	3	5	4
DOCTORAL-GRANTING UNIVERSITIES I	88	2	5	5
DOCTORAL-GRANTING UNIVERSITIES II	71	6	15	8
COMPREHENSIVE UNIVERSITIES AND COLLEGES I	80	4	8	8
COMPREHENSIVE UNIVERSITIES AND COLLEGES II	79	6	7	8
LIBERAL ARTS COLLEGES I	84	4	7	5
LIBERAL ARTS COLLEGES II	65	8	15	12
TWO-YEAR COLLEGES	62	9	14	15
ALL INSTITUTIONS	78	5	9	8

TOTAL RESPONDENTS, 3,832

QUESTION: "Since obtaining your highest degree, how long have you spent in . . . teaching or administration in an elementary or secondary school?"

SOURCE: The Carnegie Foundation for the Advancement of Teaching, 1984 Faculty Survey.

TABLE E-7

TIME SPENT BY FACULTY IN ADMINISTRATIVE POSTS OUTSIDE EDUCATIONAL INSTITUTIONS SINCE OBTAINING HIGHEST DEGREE, BY TYPE OF INSTITUTION

TYPE OF INSTITUTION	NEVER	1 YEAR OR LESS	2–5 YEARS	6 YEARS OR MORE
	(PERCENT OF FACULTY)			
RESEARCH UNIVERSITIES I	90	4	4	2
RESEARCH UNIVERSITIES II	88	2	5	5
DOCTORAL-GRANTING UNIVERSITIES I	89	1	7	3
DOCTORAL-GRANTING UNIVERSITIES II	87	3	5	5
COMPREHENSIVE UNIVERSITIES AND COLLEGES I	85	3	7	5
COMPREHENSIVE UNIVERSITIES AND COLLEGES II	84	3	5	8
LIBERAL ARTS COLLEGES I	94	1	4	1
LIBERAL ARTS COLLEGES II	87	3	7	3
TWO-YEAR COLLEGES	82	3	6	9
ALL INSTITUTIONS	86	3	5	6

TOTAL RESPONDENTS, 3,756

QUESTION: "Since obtaining your highest degree, how long have you spent in . . . an executive or administrative post outside educational institutions?"

SOURCE: The Carnegie Foundation for the Advancement of Teaching, 1984 Faculty Survey.

TABLE E–8

TIME SPENT BY FACULTY IN ANOTHER PROFESSIONAL POSITION SINCE OBTAINING HIGHEST DEGREE, BY TYPE OF INSTITUTION

TYPE OF INSTITUTION	NEVER	1 YEAR OR LESS	2–5 YEARS	6 YEARS OR MORE
	(PERCENT OF FACULTY)			
RESEARCH UNIVERSITIES I	77	5	10	8
RESEARCH UNIVERSITIES II	75	6	11	8
DOCTORAL-GRANTING UNIVERSITIES I	73	6	11	10
DOCTORAL-GRANTING UNIVERSITIES II	62	11	15	12
COMPREHENSIVE UNIVERSITIES AND COLLEGES I	69	6	13	12
COMPREHENSIVE UNIVERSITIES AND COLLEGES II	63	10	15	12
LIBERAL ARTS COLLEGES I	83	6	4	7
LIBERAL ARTS COLLEGES II	71	9	11	9
TWO-YEAR COLLEGES	54	9	18	19
ALL INSTITUTIONS	68	7	13	12

TOTAL RESPONDENTS, 3,774

QUESTION: "Since obtaining your highest degree, how long have you spent in . . . other professional positions?"

SOURCE: The Carnegie Foundation for the Advancement of Teaching, 1984 Faculty Survey.

TABLE E–9

TIME SPENT BY FACULTY IN THE ARMED FORCES SINCE OBTAINING HIGHEST DEGREE, BY TYPE OF INSTITUTION

TYPE OF INSTITUTION	NEVER	1 YEAR OR LESS	2–5 YEARS	6 YEARS OR MORE
	(PERCENT OF FACULTY)			
RESEARCH UNIVERSITIES I	77	4	17	2
RESEARCH UNIVERSITIES II	80	3	15	2
DOCTORAL-GRANTING UNIVERSITIES I	80	4	13	3
DOCTORAL-GRANTING UNIVERSITIES II	83	3	13	1
COMPREHENSIVE UNIVERSITIES AND COLLEGES I	81	3	12	4
COMPREHENSIVE UNIVERSITIES AND COLLEGES II	79	3	17	1
LIBERAL ARTS COLLEGES I	87	3	8	2
LIBERAL ARTS COLLEGES II	86	1	11	2
TWO-YEAR COLLEGES	74	2	17	7
ALL INSTITUTIONS	79	3	14	4

TOTAL RESPONDENTS, 3,715

QUESTION: "Since obtaining your highest degree, how much time have you spent in . . . the armed forces?"

SOURCE: The Carnegie Foundation for the Advancement of Teaching, 1984 Faculty Survey.

TABLE E–10

FACULTY UNEMPLOYMENT SINCE OBTAINING HIGHEST DEGREE, BY TYPE OF INSTITUTION

TYPE OF INSTITUTION	1 YEAR OR LESS	2–5 YEARS	6 YEARS OR MORE
	(PERCENT OF FACULTY)		
RESEARCH UNIVERSITIES I	8	1	1
RESEARCH UNIVERSITIES II	9	3	2
DOCTORAL-GRANTING UNIVERSITIES I	14	3	2
DOCTORAL-GRANTING UNIVERSITIES II	13	5	4
COMPREHENSIVE UNIVERSITIES AND COLLEGES I	18	3	3
COMPREHENSIVE UNIVERSITIES AND COLLEGES II	15	2	4
LIBERAL ARTS COLLEGES I	13	1	2
LIBERAL ARTS COLLEGES II	21	5	5
TWO-YEAR COLLEGES	23	9	5
ALL INSTITUTIONS	16	4	3

TOTAL RESPONDENTS, 4,325

QUESTION: "Since obtaining your highest degree, how many years have you spent *not* in employment?"

SOURCE: The Carnegie Foundation for the Advancement of Teaching, 1984 Faculty Survey.

317

TABLE E-11

PART-TIME FACULTY EMPLOYMENT SINCE OBTAINING HIGHEST DEGREE, BY TYPE OF INSTITUTION

TYPE OF INSTITUTION	NEVER	1 YEAR OR LESS	2–5 YEARS	6 YEARS OR MORE
	(PERCENT OF FACULTY)			
RESEARCH UNIVERSITIES I	82	7	6	5
RESEARCH UNIVERSITIES II	73	11	7	9
DOCTORAL-GRANTING UNIVERSITIES I	71	13	9	7
DOCTORAL-GRANTING UNIVERSITIES II	67	12	13	8
COMPREHENSIVE UNIVERSITIES AND COLLEGES I	64	14	13	9
COMPREHENSIVE UNIVERSITIES AND COLLEGES II	63	13	17	7
LIBERAL ARTS COLLEGES I	66	12	13	9
LIBERAL ARTS COLLEGES II	58	15	16	11
TWO-YEAR COLLEGES	48	15	24	13
ALL INSTITUTIONS	64	13	14	9

TOTAL RESPONDENTS, 4,312

QUESTION: ''Since obtaining your highest degree, for how many years in total have you been employed part-time?''

SOURCE: The Carnegie Foundation for the Advancement of Teaching, 1984 Faculty Survey.

AN ACADEMIC NON-MERIT SALARY SCHEDULE

The two pages that follow are verbatim copies of pages in the "Personnel Guide" of the Los Angeles Community College District. The salary schedule is modeled after those used for secondary schools: Salary is determined by years of experience ("step placement" in rows of the schedule) and by educational degree level and credit for college courses or occupational experience outside of employment in the district ("column placement"). Academic rank does not enter in as a determinant of salary and does not appear in the table. "Minimum preparation" may be less than a bachelor's degree; a "doctor's degree" is worth $81 more a month. Advancement in salary by years on the job is automatic; advancement by educational preparation and "points" can be manipulated by taking more college courses, or by taking in-service courses, or by claiming relevant travel—the latter two possibilities are not mentioned in these two pages.

The schedule and its accompanying rules exhibit a high degree of bureaucratic standardization. The standardization is enhanced by union preference for uniformity that promises fair treatment for union members.

LOS ANGELES COMMUNITY COLLEGES PERSONNEL GUIDE		

ISSUE DATE:
12-12-84
 	
REPLACES:
  PG B320
  (6-20-84)
	SERVICE:
	Certificated
	
	DISTRIBUTION: General
	(See PG B339 for
	  decoding)
	Issued By: Pers Oper Br
		CHANGES: New rates authorized
		by Board of Trustees, 11-21-84
		Effective 7/1/84.

1984-85 Salary Schedules. (Monthly rate instructors, counselors, instructor-advisors, librarians, department chairs, and consulting instructors).

Rates indicated are basic rates for a four-week month (10 months a year). "Pts" refers to points; a point is equivalent to one semester unit or 1.5 quarter units.

1.   Preparation Salary Schedule. (Probationary, Permanent, Temporary Contract, and Long-term Substitutes).
     NOTE: To the rates below add $81 for a doctor's degree or $68 for a certificate differential.

RATING IN Years Exp	STEP	COL. A Min Prepa- ration	COL. B Min + 30 Pts or MA	COL. C Min+50 Pts or MA+ 20 Pts	COL. D Min+70 Pts or MA+ 40 Pts	COL. E Min+90 P or MA+ 60 P
0-1	1	$2,059	$2,169	$2,281	$2,402	$2,525
2-3	2	2,142	2,256	2,374	2,497	2,626
4-5	3	2,232	2,348	2,470	2,597	2,736
6-7	4	2,325	2,441	2,568	2,705	2,841
8-9	5	2,418	2,542	2,675	2,813	2,957
10-11	6	2,520	2,646	2,785	2,926	3,076
12-13	7	2,623	2,759	2,896	3,043	3,194
14 or more*	8	2,736	2,870	3,014	3,164	3,320
	9	2,846	2,990	3,135	3,291	3,452
	10	2,964	3,109	3,263	3,423	3,586
	11				3,558	3,726
	12					3,869

Maximum rate with one career increment	3,937
Maximum rate with two career increments	4,003
Maximum rate with one career increment and doctorate differential	4,018
Maximum rate with two career increments and doctorate differential	4,084

*Limit for initial allocation on schedule

2. <u>Monthly Rates</u>.

    a.   <u>Step Placement</u>. New employees are placed on the first step of the first column of the schedule until evidence of experience is submitted and evaluated. (See PG B358 for information concerning acceptable experience.) Credit for experience as a faculty member in an accredited college or university shall be granted on the basis of one year of experience for each step on the salary schedule. All other applicable experience shall be granted on the basis of two years of experience for each step on the salary schedule. New employees may be allocated up to and including Step 8.

    b.   <u>Column Placement</u>. New employees are placed on the first column of the schedule until evidence of preparation (training) is submitted and evaluated. New employees may be allocated up to and including Column E. Minimum preparation requirements are: 120 college semester units or 180 quarter units included in a bachelor's degree from an accredited college or university; or four years of occupational experience for certain subject fields as indicated on PG B358a. A "point" is the equivalent of one semester unit or 1.5 quarter units of college study completed since the date of meeting minimum preparation requirements.

    c.   <u>Degree and Certificate Differentials</u>. At any monthly rate on the preparation schedule an additional $81 per month is paid for an earned doctor's degree or $68 per month for a specified professional certificate.

    d.   <u>Career Increment</u>. Employees who have received pay at Column E, Step 10 or higher on the preparation schedule for the equivalent of 130 full-time days in each of five years are eligible to receive an increment of $68 per month. Employees who have been so paid for eight years are eligible to receive an increment of $134.

    e.   <u>Employees in Service</u>. After initial allocation to the salary schedule, employees are limited to one column advance per year (See PG B350).

        Employees may earn one step advance per year either at the beginning of the first pay period within their regular assignment basis or at the beginning of their first pay period which commences on or after the beginning of the spring semester. Active service for 130 days is required for step advance (See PG B350).

3. <u>Differential Salary Rates</u>. Regular, temporary, and substitute employees serving in the classes of counselor, instructor-advisor and consulting instructor shall receive the salary rates to which they are entitled on the preparation schedule plus a salary differential of $204 per pay period. A department chair shall receive the $204 differential if eligible according to the provisions of the collective bargaining unit agreement.

4. <u>Hourly Rates</u>. For hourly rate salary, see PG B364.

5. <u>Day-to-Day Substitute Rates</u>. Day-to-day substitute employees who serve in the place of employees paid on the preparation salary schedule will be paid a "flat" rate of $112.85 a day for each day's assignment of three or more clock hours, and $58.20 for each day's assignment of less than three clock hours.

NOTES

INTRODUCTION

1. For an outstanding explanation of the historical perspective as applied to higher education, see Perkin, Harold, "The Historical Perspective," in Clark, Burton R., ed. *Perspectives on Higher Education: Eight Disciplinary and Comparative Views* (Berkeley, Los Angeles, London: University of California Press, 1984), pp. 17–55.
2. Clark, Burton R., *The Higher Education System: Academic Organization in Cross-National Perspective* (Berkeley, Los Angeles, London: University of California Press, 1983), especially chapter 2.
3. Clark, Burton R. (ed.), *The Academic Profession: National, Disciplinary, and Institutional Settings* (Berkeley, Los Angeles, London: University of California Press, 1987). On Japan, see Cummings, William K., Ikuo Amano, and Kazuyuki Kitamura, eds., *Changes in the Japanese University: A Comparative Perspective* (New York: Praeger, 1979).
4. Early attempts to state the essence of professionalism include Tawney, R. H., *The Acquisitive Society* (New York: Harcourt Brace, 1948), and Carr-Saunders, A. M., and P. A. Wilson, *The Professions* (Oxford: Oxford University Press, 1933). A wide-ranging collection of articles and selections assembled in the mid-1960s may be found in Vollmer, Howard M., and Donald L. Mills, eds., *Professionalization* (Englewood Cliffs, N.J.: Prentice-Hall, 1966). A recent collection is available in Dingwall, Robert, and Philip Lewis (eds.), *The Sociology of the Professions: Lawyers, Doctors and Others* (London: Macmillan, 1983).
5. As primary sources on professions see Parsons, Talcott, "Professions" in *International Encyclopedia of the Social Sciences* (New York: Macmillan, Free Press, 1968); Freidson, Eliot, *Professional Dominance* (New York: Atherton Press, 1970); Larson, Magali Sarfatti, *The Rise of Professionalism* (Berkeley, Los Angeles, London: University of California Press, 1977).
6. Starr, Paul, *The Social Transformation of American Medicine* (New York: Basic Books, 1982), p. 15.
7. Ibid., p. 16.
8. DiMaggio, Paul J., and Walter W. Powell, "The Iron Cage Revisited: Institutional Isomorphism and Collective Rationality in Organizational Fields," *American Sociological Review*, April, 1985, pp. 147–160.
9. For a cross-national comparison of academic systems that portrays work, belief, and authority as the three primary elements, see Clark, Burton R., *The Higher Education System: Academic Organization in Cross-National Perspective* (Berkeley, Los Angeles, London: University of California Press, 1983).

323

CHAPTER I

1. "The teaching staff at Harvard throughout the [seventeenth] century consisted of the president and young inexperienced tutors waiting for a pulpit. Tutors usually supervised particular classes through the entire three- (later four-) year curriculum. There were no academic departments and often not very competent tutors." Guralnick, Stanley, *Science and the Ante-Bellum College* (Philadelphia: American Philosophical Society, 1975), p. 4.

2. Hofstadter, Richard, and Walter P. Metzger, *Development of Academic Freedom in the United States* (New York: Columbia University Press, 1955); Rudolph, Frederick, *The American College and University* (New York: Knopf, 1962).

3. Whitehead, John, *The Separation of College and State: Columbia, Dartmouth, Harvard and Yale, 1776–1876* (New Haven: Yale University Press, 1975).

4. Clark, Burton R., *The Higher Education System: Academic Organization in Cross-National Perspective* (Berkeley, Los Angeles, London: University of California Press, 1983), ch. 4, "Authority."

5. Metzger, Walter P., "The Academic Profession in the United States," in Clark, Burton R. (ed.), *The Academic Profession: National, Disciplinary, and Institutional Settings* (Berkeley, Los Angeles, London: University of California Press, 1987).

6. Tewksbury, Donald G., *The Founding of American Colleges and Universities Before the Civil War* (New York: Teachers College Press, 1932), p. 28. Useful reinterpretations of the Tewksbury analysis may be found in Naylor, Natalie A., "The Ante-Bellum College Movement: A Reappraisal of Tewksbury's The Founding of American Colleges and Universities," *History of Education Quarterly*, Fall, 1973, pp. 261–274; and Burke, Colin B. *American Collegiate Populations: A Test of the Traditional View* (New York: New York University Press, 1982).

7. Hofstadter, Richard, and Walter P. Metzger, *Development of Academic Freedom in the United States* (New York: Columbia University Press, 1955), Part 2, "Age of the University"; Storr, Richard J., *The Beginnings of Graduate Education in America* (Chicago: University of Chicago Press, 1953).

8. Rudolph, Frederick, *The American College and University* (New York: Knopf, 1962), ch. 13; Curti, Merle, *The Growth of American Thought* (New Brunswick, N.J.: Transaction Books, 1981), pp. 456–457.

9. Ben-David, Joseph, *Centers of Learning: Britain, France, Germany, United States* (New York: McGraw-Hill, 1977), p. 61.

10. See the two-age division made by Richard Hofstadter and Walter P. Metzger—"the age of the college" and "the age of the university"—in *Development of Academic Freedom in the United States* (New York: Columbia University Press, 1955). On the rise of administration, see Veysey, Laurence R., *The Emergence of the American University* (Chicago: University of Chicago Press, 1965), pp. 302–317. On the development of the universities into major research establishments in the twentieth century, see Geiger, Roger L., *To Advance Knowledge: The Growth of American Research Universities, 1900–1940* (New York: Oxford University Press, 1986).

11. Pangburn, Jesse M., *The Evolution of the American Teachers College* (New York: Columbia University, 1932).

324

12. Riesman, David, *Constraint and Variety in American Education* (Lincoln, Neb.: University of Nebraska Press, 1956), p. 49.

13. Walter P. Metzger, "The Academic Profession in the United States" in Clark, Burton R. (ed.), *The Academic Profession: National, Disciplinary, and Institutional Settings* (Berkeley, Los Angeles, London: University of California Press, 1987), p. 167.

14. Carnegie Council on Policy Studies in Higher Education, *A Classification of Institutions of Higher Education, 1973; revised edition,* 1976.

15. Useful reviews of institutional rankings may be found in Webster, David, *Academic Quality Rankings of American Colleges and Universities* (Springfield, Illinois: Charles C. Thomas, 1986); and Lawrence, Judith, and Kenneth C. Green, *A Question of Quality: The Higher Education Ratings Game.* AAHE-ERIC Higher Education Research Report no. 5 (Washington, D.C.: American Association for Higher Education, 1980). Published assessments of the status of universities go back as far as James McKeen Cattell's efforts between 1903 and 1910 to establish academic quality ratings. See Webster, David, "James McKeen Cattell and the Invention of Academic Quality Ratings, 1903–1910," *The Review of Higher Education,* 1985, pp. 107–121. The best-known ranking, one that has served as a benchmark in recent decades, is Cartter, Allan M., *An Assessment of Quality in Graduate Education* (Washington, D.C.: American Council on Education, 1966).

16. See Riesman, David, Joseph Gusfield, and Zelda Gamson, *Academic Values and Mass Education: The Early Years of Oakland and Monteith* (Garden City, N.Y.: Doubleday, 1970); and Grant, Gerald, and David Riesman, *The Perpetual Dream: Reform and Experiment in the American College* (Chicago: University of Chicago Press, 1978).

17. Zammuto, Raymond F., "Are the Liberal Arts an Endangered Species?" *Journal of Higher Education,* March-April, 1984, pp. 184–211.

18. Shea, John R., "Design and Function," in Pifer, Alan, John Shea, David Henry, and Lyman Glenny, *Systems of Higher Education: United States* (New York: International Council for Educational Development, 1978), pp. 27, 28.

19. Zammuto, "Are the Liberal Arts An Endangered Species?" pp. 192–193.

CHAPTER II

1. Robert K. Merton's original distinction of locals and cosmopolitans was first applied to higher education by Gouldner. See Gouldner, Alvin W., "Cosmopolitans and Locals—I," *Administrative Science Quarterly,* vol. 2, Dec., 1957, pp. 281–306; "Cosmopolitans and Locals: Toward an Analysis of Latent Social Roles—II," *Administrative Science Quarterly,* vol. 2, March, 1958, pp. 444–480.

2. Cipolla, Carlo M., "The Professions: A Long View," *The Journal of European Economic History,* Spring, 1973, pp. 37–52.

3. This section is heavily indebted to Walter Metzger. Beyond the attributed quotations, I have drawn extensively upon his organization of historical data and especially his conceptualization of growth. See his "The Academic Profession in the United States" in Clark, Burton R., ed., *The Academic Profession: National, Disciplinary, and Institutional Settings* (Berkeley, Los Angeles, London: University of California Press, 1987).

4. Albers, Donald J., and G. L. Alexanderson (eds.), *Mathematical People: Profiles and Interviews* (Boston: Birkhauser, 1985), p. vii.

5. Guralnick, Stanley, *Science and the Ante-Bellum College* (Philadelphia: American Philosophical Society, 1975), p. ix.

6. Ibid., p. 157.

7. Haber, Samuel, "The Professions and Higher Education: A Historical View," in Gordon, Margaret S., ed. *Higher Education and the Labor Market* (New York: McGraw-Hill, 1974), pp. 237–280.

8. Wiebe, Robert H., *The Search for Order, 1877–1920* (New York: Hill and Wang, 1967), p. 121.

9. Metzger, Walter P., "The Academic Profession in the United States," in Clark, Burton R., ed. *The Academic Profession: National, Disciplinary, and Institutional Settings* (Berkeley, Los Angeles, London: University of California Press, 1987), p. 13.

10. Guralnick, pp. 16–17.

11. Geiger, Roger, "The Conditions of University Research, 1900–1920," *History of Higher Education Annual*, vol. 4 (1984), p. 4.

12. Ibid., p. 5; the quotation is from a 1922 report of the American Association of University Professors.

13. See Ben-David, Joseph, *Centers of Learning: Britain, France, Germany, United States* (New York: McGraw-Hill, 1977), chap. 5, and Clark, Burton R., *The Higher Education System: Academic Organization in Cross-National Perspective* (Berkeley, Los Angeles, London: University of California Press, 1983), pp. 49–53.

14. On the growing dominance of university graduate schools, see Jencks, Christopher, and David Riesman, *The Academic Revolution* (Garden City, N.Y.: Doubleday, 1968). Laurence R. Veysey and the authors of papers in Oleson, Alexandra, and John Voss, eds., *The Organization of Knowledge in Modern America, 1860–1920* (Baltimore, Md.: The Johns Hopkins University Press, 1979) place the time of greatest change in the late nineteenth and early twentieth centuries when the modern organization of knowledge came into being. See also Veysey, Laurence R. *The Emergence of the American University* (Chicago: University of Chicago Press, 1965); and Geiger, Roger L., *To Advance Knowledge: The Growth of American Research Universities, 1900–1940* (New York: Oxford University Press, 1986).

15. Oleson and Voss, eds., *Organization of Knowledge in Modern America*, p. xii.

16. Ibid.

17. Metzger, "The Academic Profession in the United States," p. 136.

18. Ibid., pp. 19–20 (original ms).

19. *UCLA Graduate Catalog, 1981–82.*

CHAPTER III

1. Jencks, Christopher, and David Riesman, *The Academic Revolution* (Garden City, N.Y.: Doubleday, 1968), p. 2.

2. Quoted in Rudolph, Frederick, *The American College and University* (New York: Knopf, 1962), p. 210.

3. Clark, Burton R., *The Distinctive College: Antioch, Reed, and Swarthmore* (Chicago: Aldine, 1970), pp. 13–15.

4. Rowland, Henry A., "A Plea for Pure Science" (an 1883 address to the American Association for the Advancement of Science), in *The Physical Papers of Henry Augustus Rowland* (Baltimore, Md.: The Johns Hopkins University Press, 1902), pp. 599–600.

5. Hawkins, Hugh, *Between Harvard and America: The Educational Leadership of Charles W. Eliot* (New York: Oxford, 1972), pp. 64–67.

6. Metzger, Walter P., "The Academic Profession in the United States," in Clark, Burton R., ed., *The Academic Profession: National, Disciplinary, and Institutional Settings* (Berkeley, Los Angeles, London: University of California Press, 1987), pp. 145–146.

7. Rudolph, Frederick, *The American College and University* (New York: Knopf, 1962).

8. Babbidge, Homer D., and Robert Rosenzweig, *The Federal Interest in Higher Education* (New York: McGraw-Hill, 1962), p. 158.

9. Clark, Burton R., ed., *The School and the University: An International Perspective* (Berkeley, Los Angeles, London: University of California Press, 1985), ch. 11.

10. Sykes, Gary, "Teacher Education in the United States" in Burton R. Clark, ed., *The School and the University: An International Perspective* (Berkeley, Los Angeles, London: University of California Press, 1985), ch. 10.

11. These data were obtained from diverse noncomparable sources. On Sweden: National Board of Universities and Colleges, *Higher Education and Research in Sweden, 1984–85* (Stockholm: 1985). On the Federal Republic of Germany: Peisert, Hansgert, and Gerhild Framhein, *Systems of Higher Education: Federal Republic of Germany* (New York: International Council for Educational Development, 1978), and *UNESCO Statistical Yearbook, 1984* (Paris: 1984). On France: Alain Bienaymé, *Systems of Higher Education: France* (New York: International Council on Educational Development, 1978) and Friedberg, Erhard, and Christine Musselin, "The Academic Profession in France," in Clark, Burton R., ed., *The Academic Profession: National, Disciplinary, and Institutional Settings* (Berkeley, Los Angeles, London: University of California Press, 1987); on Great Britain: Scott, Peter, "Has the Binary Policy Failed?" in *The Structure and Governance of Higher Education at the University* (Guildford, Surrey, England: The Society for Research into Higher Education, 1983), pp. 166–196; and Perkin, Harold, "The Academic Profession in Great Britain," in Clark, Burton R., ed., *The Academic Profession: National, Disciplinary, and Institutional Settings* (Berkeley, Los Angeles, London: University of California Press, 1987).

12. *Education Week*, vol. 4, no. 22, February 20, 1985, p. 28.

13. Neave, Guy R., "Elite and Mass Higher Education in Britain: A Regressive Model?" *Comparative Education Review*, vol. 29, no. 3, August, 1985, pp. 347–361.

14. On the capacity of the American system of higher education to support so-called "elite functions," see Trow, Martin, " 'Elite Higher Education': An Endangered Species?" *Minerva*, vol. 14, no. 3, Autumn, 1976, pp. 355–376; Kerr, Clark, "Higher Education: Paradise Lost?" *Higher Education*, vol. 7, no. 3, August, 1978, pp. 261–278, and Clark, Burton R., *The Higher Education System: Academic Organization in Cross-National Perspective* (Berkeley, Los Angeles, London: University of California Press, 1985), pp. 155–157.

15. Hoch, Paul K., "The Reception of Central European Refugee Physicists of the 1930s: U.S.S.R., U.K., U.S.A." *Annals of Science*, vol. 40, 1983, pp. 217–246. Quotation, pp. 222–223 (emphasis in the original).

16. Fermi, Laura, *Illustrious Immigrants*, second edition (Chicago and London: University of Chicago Press, 1971), p. 96.

17. Hoch, Paul K., "The Reception of Central European Refugee Physicists of the 1930s: U.S.S.R., U.K., U.S.A." *Annals of Science*, vol. 40, 1983, p. 223.

18. Ibid., p. 244.

19. Hughes, H. Stuart, *The Sea Change: The Migration of Social Thought, 1930–65* (New York: Harper & Row, 1975).

20. For cross-national comparison of institutional hierarchies, see Clark, Burton R., *The Higher Education System*, pp. 63–69, 255–257; and Trow, Martin, "The Analysis of Status," in Clark, Burton R., ed., *Perspectives on Higher Education: Eight Disciplinary and Comparative Views* (Berkeley, Los Angeles, London: University of California Press, 1984), pp. 132–164.

21. The more noted, comprehensive rankings have included: Keniston, Hayward, *Graduate Study and Research in the Arts and Sciences at the University of Pennsylvania* (Philadelphia, University of Pennsylvania Press, 1959); Cartter, Allan M., *An Assessment of Quality in Graduate Education* (Washington, D.C.: American Council on Education, 1966); Roose, Kenneth D., and Charles J. Andersen, *A Rating of Graduate Programs* (Washington, D.C.: American Council on Education, 1970); and The Conference Board of Associated Research Councils, *An Assessment of Research-Doctorate Programs in the United States* (Washington, D.C.: National Academy Press, 1982). The latter assessment presented five volumes on mathematical and physical sciences, humanities, biological sciences, engineering, and social and behavioral sciences. A major review of the many rankings made since the turn of the century may be found in Webster, David, *Academic Quality Rankings of American Colleges and Universities* (Springfield, Ill.: Charles C. Thomas, 1986).

22. Rowland, Henry A., "A Plea for Pure Science," in *The Physical Papers of Henry Augustus Rowland* (Baltimore: The Johns Hopkins University Press, 1902), pp. 593–619. Quotation, p. 610.

23. In his outstanding assessment of the basic structure of secondary schooling in Japan, with its strength contrasting to the weakness of the American arrangement, Thomas P. Rohlen offered the telling observation that "the merit principle and hierarchical differentiation are inseparable in public education." Rohlen, Thomas P., *Japan's High Schools* (Berkeley, Los Angeles, London: University of California Press, 1983), p. 313.

24. Rhoades, Gary, "Higher Education in a Consumer Society," unpublished manuscript, p. 33.

25. Neave, Guy, and Gary Rhoades, "The Academic Estate in Western Europe," in Clark, Burton R., ed., *The Academic Profession: National, Disciplinary, and Institutional Settings* (Berkeley, Los Angeles, London: University of California Press, 1987); Mommsen, Wolfgang, "The Academic Profession in the Federal Republic of Germany" and Friedberg, Erhard, and Christine Musselin, "The Academic Profession in France," in Clark, Burton R., ed., *The Academic Profession*, 1987.

26. See Perkin, Harold, "The Academic Profession in the United Kingdom," in Clark, Bur-

ton R., ed., *The Academic Profession* (1987) and Metzger, Walter P., "The Academic Profession in the United States," in Clark, *The Academic Profession*.

27. Rosenberg, Charles, "Toward an Ecology of Knowledge: On Discipline, Contexts, and History," in Oleson, Alexandra, and John Voss eds., *The Organization of Knowledge in Modern America, 1860–1920* (Baltimore, Md.: The Johns Hopkins University Press, 1979), p. 444.
28. Geiger, Roger, "The Conditions of University Research, 1900–1920," in *History of Higher Education Annual*, vol. 4 (1984), p. 10.
29. A particular research project offered as an example by Holton involved researchers at four American universities and the University of Bologna, with a roster of names that read like a United Nations of ethnicities and nationalities—Leitnev, Gessaroli, Cohn, Kovacs, Bugg, and so on. Holton, Gerald, "Scientific Research and Scholarship: Notes Toward the Design of Proper Scales," *Daedalus*, vol. 91, part I (1962), p. 362–399. Quotation from p. 375. Emphasis in the original.
30. See Metzger, Walter P., "The Academic Profession in the United States," in Clark, Burton R., ed., *The Academic Profession*, pp. 153–156.

CHAPTER IV

1. See epigraph at the beginning of the chapter.
2. A useful summary of the literature on faculty work may be found in Austin, Ann E., and Zelda F. Gamson, *Academic Workplace: New Demands, Heightened Tensions*. ASHE-ERIC Higher Education Research Report, no. 10 (Washington, D.C.: Association for the Study of Higher Education, 1983). Major earlier studies and statements include: Blau, Peter M., *The Organization of Academic Work* (New York: John Wiley, 1973); Fulton, Oliver, and Martin Trow, eds., "Research Activity in American Higher Education," in Trow, Martin, ed., *Teachers and Students: Aspects of American Higher Education* (New York: McGraw-Hill, 1975), pp. 39–83; Light, Donald R., "Introduction: The Structure of the Academic Profession," *Sociology of Education*, vol. 47 (Winter, 1964), pp. 2–28; Ladd, Everett Carll, Jr., and Seymour Martin Lipset, *Survey of the Social, Political, and Educational Perspectives of American College and University Faculty*. Final Report. 2 volumes. Storrs, Conn.: Connecticut University Press), 1976; Cohen, Arthur M., and Florence B. Brawer, *The Two-Year College Instructor Today* (New York, London: Praeger, 1977); and Finkelstein, Martin J., *The American Academic Profession* (Columbus, Ohio: Ohio State University Press, 1983).
3. Coleman, James S., "The University and Society's New Demands Upon It," in Kaysen, Carl, ed., *Content and Context: Essays on College Education* (New York: McGraw-Hill, 1973), p. 370.
4. Fulton, Oliver, and Martin Trow, "Research Activity in American Higher Education," in Trow, Martin, ed., *Teachers and Students*, p. 47 (emphasis added).
5. Cohen, Arthur M., and Florence B. Brawer, *The American Community College* (San Francisco: Jossey-Bass, 1982), pp. 33–36.
6. Ruscio, Kenneth P., "The Distinctive Scholarship of the Selective Liberal Arts College," *Journal of Higher Education*, vol. 58, no. 2, March-April, 1987.
7. Cohen and Brawer, *The American Community College*, p. 77.

8. Cohen, Arthur M., "Student Access and the Collegiate Function in Community Colleges," *Higher Education*, vol. 14, no. 2, April, 1985, pp. 149–163. Data on mean, median, and modal age, p. 161.

9. Ibid., p. 156.

10. Richardson, Richard C., Jr., Elizabeth C. Fisk, and Morris A. Okun, *Literacy in the Open Access College* (San Francisco: Jossey-Bass, 1983). Chapter 3, "Teaching and Learning in the Classroom," and Chapter 4, "Reading and Writing Requirements."

11. Cohen and Brawer, *The American Community College*, p. 156.

12. Cohen, Arthur M., "Student Access and the Collegiate Function in Community Colleges," *Higher Education*, vol. 14, no. 2, April, 1985, p. 157.

13. Cohen and Brawer, *The American Community College*, pp. 69–72.

14. See Becher, Tony, "The Cultural View," in Clark, Burton R., ed., *Perspectives on Higher Education: Eight Disciplinary and Comparative Views* (Berkeley, Los Angeles, London: University of California Press, 1984), and Becher, Tony, "The Disciplinary Shaping of the Profession," in Clark, Burton R., ed., *The Academic Profession: National, Disciplinary, and Institutional Settings* (Berkeley, Los Angeles, London: University of California Press, 1987).

15. Such major statements as those offered by Logan Wilson, even when centered on top universities, generally push the professional schools aside. See Wilson, Logan, *The Academic Man* (London: Oxford University Press, 1942), and Wilson, Logan, *American Academics: Then and Now* (New York: Oxford University Press, 1979). Parsons, Talcott, and Gerald M. Platt, *The American University* (Cambridge, Mass.: Harvard University Press, 1973) devoted chapter 5 to university professional schools but their entirely "theoretical" discussion avoided the empirical reality of what professors in those schools actually do.

16. Halpern, Sydney Ann, "Professional Schools in the American University" in Clark, Burton R., ed., *The Academic Profession: National, Disciplinary, and Institutional Settings* (Berkeley, Los Angeles, London: University of California Press, 1987). The information and four quotations that follow have been drawn from Halpern's paper.

17. Ruscio, Kenneth P., "The Links Between Specializations: The Cases of Biology and Political Science," *The Review of Higher Education*, forthcoming; and Ladd, Everett Carll, Jr., "The Work Experience of American College Professors: Some Data and an Argument," *Current Issues in Higher Education, 1979* (Washington, D.C.: American Association for Higher Education, 1979), pp. 3–12.

18. A somewhat similar distinction has been drawn by Jane Jacobs in her depiction of cities that stay alive because they concentrate on "development work," and others that stagnate because they become monopolized by "production work." See Jacobs, *The Economy of Cities* (New York: Vintage Books, 1970).

19. Ibid., pp. 87–88.

20. Glazer, Nathan, "The Schools of the Minor Professions," *Minerva*, vol. 10, July, 1974, pp. 346–364; and Sykes, Gary, "Teacher Education in the United States" in Clark, Burton R., ed., *The School and the University: An International Perspective* (Berkeley, Los Angeles, London: University of California Press, 1985), pp. 264–289.

21. Becher, Tony and Maurice Kogan, *Process and Structure in Higher Education* (London: Heineman, 1980), p. 110.

1. Polanyi, Michael, *The Logic of Liberty: Reflections and Rejoiners* (Chicago: University of Chicago Press, 1980), reprint, p. 23.

2. Mansbridge, Jane J., *Beyond Adversary Democracy* (Chicago: University of Chicago Press, 1983), p. 26.

3. For a review of the literature on academic culture that stresses the disciplinary and institutional lines of affiliation and division, see Clark, Burton R., *The Higher Education System: Academic Organization in Cross-National Perspective*, ch. 3, "Belief." The concept of culture, as applied to academic life, is clarified in Becher, Tony, "The Cultural View," in Clark, Burton R., ed., *Perspectives on Higher Education: Eight Disciplinary and Comparative Views* (Berkeley, Los Angeles, London: University of California Press, 1984).

4. See Neave, Guy, and Gary Rhoades, "The Academic Estate in Western Europe," in Clark, Burton R., ed., *The Academic Profession: National, Disciplinary, and Institutional Settings* (Berkeley, Los Angeles, London: University of California Press, 1987).

5. On the impact of general secularization and the growing weight of graduate schools and research universities in diminishing the importance of religious beliefs in colleges and universities, see Jencks, Christopher, and David Riesman, *The Academic Revolution* (Garden City, N.Y.: Doubleday, 1968), esp. ch. 8 and 9.

6. Ladd, Everett Carll, Jr., and Seymour Martin Lipset, *The Divided Academy: Professors and Politics* (New York: McGraw-Hill, 1975), particularly ch. 3 and 5; and S. M. Lipset, "The Academic Mind at the Top: The Political Behavior and Values of Academic Elites." *Public Opinion Quarterly*, 46 (1982), pp. 143–168.

7. ". . . gross national differences between men and women in higher education mask an important fact: *within* institutional groups the gap narrows substantially. That is, women act quite similarly to men in similar settings. Women in elite institutions act more like men in elite institutions, women at community colleges act more like men at community colleges . . . [most] of the gross national difference is due to the *concentration* of women in less prestigious institutions—where they act quite similar to the men in those same institutions." Baldridge, J. Victor, David V. Curtis, George Ecker, and Gary L. Riley, *Policy Making and Effective Leadership* (San Francisco: Jossey-Bass, 1978), p. 203. Emphasis in the original.

8. Hofstadter, Richard, and Wilson Smith, eds., *American Higher Education: A Documentary History* (Chicago: University of Chicago Press, 1968), vol. I, pp. 212–213.

9. Merton, Robert K., "The Normative Structure of Science," in Storer, Norman W., ed., *The Sociology of Science: Theoretical and Empirical Investigations* (Chicago: University of Chicago Press, 1973), pp. 267–278.

10. Crane, Diana, "Cultural Differentiation, Cultural Integration, and Social Control," in Gibbs, Jack P., ed., *Social Control: Views from the Social Sciences* (Beverly Hills, California: Sage Publications, 1982), p. 239.

11. Campbell, Donald T., "Ethnocentrism of Disciplines and the Fish-Scale Model of Omniscience," in Sherif, M., and C. Sherif, eds., *Interdisciplinary Relationships in the Social Sciences* (Chicago: Aldine, 1969), pp. 328, 330.

12. Ibid., pp. 328, 331.

13. Polanyi, Michael, *The Tacit Dimension* (Garden City, N.Y.: Doubleday, 1967), p. 72.

CHAPTER VI

1. Cohen, Michael D., and James G. March, *Leadership and Ambiguity: The American College President* (New York: McGraw-Hill, 1974), and March, James G., and Johan P. Olsen, *Ambiguity and Choice in Organizations* (Bergen, Norway: Universitetsforlaget, 1976).
2. Lane, Jan-Eric, "Academic Profession in Academic Organization," *Higher Education*, vol. 14, no. 3, June, 1985, pp. 241–268. Quotation, p. 256.
3. *The United States Law Week*, vol. 54, no. 23, December 10, 1985. Extra Edition no. 2, Supreme Court Opinions, p. 4058.
4. Freidson, Eliot, *Profession of Medicine: A Study of the Sociology of Applied Knowledge* (New York: Dodd, Mead, 1970), p. 71.
5. On professionals in organizations, see particularly Vollmer, Howard M., and Donald L. Mills, eds., *Professionalization* (Englewood Cliffs, N.J.: Prentice-Hall, 1966), ch. 8, "Professionals and Complex Organizations"; Larson, Magali Sarfatti, *The Rise of Professionalism* (Berkeley, Los Angeles, London: University of California Press, 1977) chap. 11, "Profession and Bureaucracy"; Dingwall, Robert and Philip Lewis, eds., *The Sociology of the Professions* (London: Macmillan, 1983).
6. On the nature and power of the scientific estate in modern-day America, see Price, Don K., *The Scientific Estate* (Cambridge, Mass.: Harvard University Press, 1973).
7. For insightful statements on the relations between science and higher education, especially the legitimacy that the first adds to the second, see: Polanyi, Michael, *The Logic of Liberty: Reflections and Rejoinders* (Chicago: University of Chicago Press, reprint, 1980); Ben-David, Joseph, *The Scientist's Role in Society: A Comparative Study* (Englewood Cliffs, N.J.: Prentice-Hall, 1971); and Schwartzman, Simon, "The Focus on Scientific Activity," in Clark, Burton R., ed., *Perspectives on Higher Education: Eight Disciplinary and Comparative Views* (Berkeley, Los Angeles, London: University of California Press, 1984), pp. 199–225.
8. See Clark, Burton R., *The Higher Education System: Academic Organization in Cross-National Perspective* (Berkeley, Los Angeles, London: University of California Press, 1983), ch. 4, "Authority," pp. 107–134.
9. For analytical perspectives particularly sensitive to *levels* of work and control in systems of higher education, see Van De Graaff, John H., Burton R. Clark, Dorotea Furth, Dietrich Goldschmidt, and Donald Wheeler, *Academic Power: Patterns of Authority in Seven National Systems* (New York: Praeger, 1978); Becher, Tony, and Maurice Kogan, *Process and Structures in Higher Education* (London: Heineman, 1980); and Kogan, Maurice, "The Political View," in Clark, Burton R., ed., *Perspectives on Higher Education: Eight Disciplinary and Comparative Views* (Berkeley, Los Angeles, London: University of California Press, 1984), pp. 56–78.
10. For extensive discussion of guild organization in the academic life, see Clark, Burton R., *Academic Power in Italy: Bureaucracy and Oligarchy in a National University System* (Chicago: University of Chicago Press, 1977), ch. 5, "Guild"; and Clark, Burton R., *The Higher Education System: Academic Organization in Cross-National Perspective* (Berkeley, Los Angeles, London: University of California Press, 1983), pp. 110–116.

11. Caplow, Theodore, and Reece J. McGee, *The Academic Marketplace* (New York: Basic Books, 1958), pp. 206–207.

12. Drawing upon the work of Hughes and Durkheim, Gary Rhoades suggested to me the idea that academic work is impermeable. In his classic study, *Men and Their Work* (1958), Edward Cherrington Hughes noted that "the ability of laymen to see a professional relationship involving the things and people dear to them is always somewhat limited. Durkheim referred to something which he called the impermeability of professions to outside view and intervention." See *Men and Their Work* (Glencoe, Ill.: Free Press, 1958), p. 86.

13. See Clark, Burton R., ed., *The Academic Profession: National, Disciplinary, and Institutional Settings* (Berkeley, Los Angeles, London: University of California Press, 1987), particularly chapters on France by Erhard Friedberg and Christine Musselin; on the Federal Republic of Germany by Wolfgang Mommsen; and "The Academic Estate in Western Europe" by Guy Neave and Gary Rhoades. See also Daalder, Hans, and Edward Shils, eds., *Universities, Politicians and Bureaucrats* (Cambridge, England: Cambridge University Press, 1982).

14. I am indebted to Kenneth P. Ruscio and Gary Rhoades for the concept of authority environments.

15. Lodahl, Janice Beyer, and Gerald Gordon, "The Structure of Scientific Fields and the Functioning of University Graduate Departments," *American Sociological Review*, vol. 37, February, 1972, pp. 57–72. Quotation, p. 70. On the impact of knowledge contents on disciplinary cultures and the academic profession at large, see Becher, Tony, "The Cultural View" in Clark, Burton R., ed., *Perspectives on Higher Education: Eight Disciplinary and Comparative Views* (Berkeley, Los Angeles, London: University of California Press, 1984), and Becher, Tony, "The Disciplinary Shaping of the Professions," in Clark, Burton R., ed., *The Academic Profession: National, Disciplinary, and Institutional Settings* (Berkeley, Los Angeles, London: University of California Press, 1987).

16. Biglan, Anthony, "Relationships Between Subject Matter Characteristics and the Structure and Output of University Departments," *Journal of Applied Psychology*, vol. 57, 1973, pp. 204–213. Quotation, p. 213.

17. Kemerer, Frank R., and J. Victor Baldridge, *Unions on Campus* (San Francisco: Jossey-Bass, 1975), p. 1.

18. Douglas, Joel M., and Elizabeth A. Kotch, *Directory of Faculty Contracts and Bargaining Agents in Institutions of Higher Education* (New York: The National Center for the Study of Collective Bargaining in Higher Education and the Professions, Baruch College, City University of New York, 1985), vol. 11, pp. 1–7.

19. Kemerer and Baldridge, *Unions on Campus*.

20. Ladd, Everett Carll, Jr., and Seymour Martin Lipset, *Professors, Unions and American Higher Education* (Berkeley: The Carnegie Commission on Higher Education, 1973), ch. 3.

21. Garbarino, Joseph W., *Faculty Bargaining: Change and Conflict* (New York: McGraw-Hill, 1975), ch. 3.

22. Riesman, David, in David Riesman and Verne A. Stadtman, eds., *Academic Transformation: Seventeen Institutions Under Pressure* (New York: McGraw-Hill, 1973), p. 426.

23. Riesman, David, *On Higher Education: The Academic Enterprise in an Era of Rising Student Consumerism* (San Francisco: Jossey-Bass, 1980).

24. See Rhoades, Gary, "The Profession and the Laity," unpublished manuscript.

25. See Rueschemeyer, Dietrich, "Professional Autonomy and the Social Control of Expertise," in Dingwall, Robert, and Philip Lewis, eds., *The Sociology of the Professions: Lawyers, Doctors, and Others* (London: Macmillan, 1983), pp. 38–58, especially pp. 45–48.

CHAPTER VII

1. See the review of the literature by Finkelstein, Martin J., in *The American Academic Profession* (Columbus, Ohio: Ohio State University Press, 1983), ch. 4, "Academic Career." Also, Youn, Ted I. K., and Daniel Zelterman, "Academic Career Mobility in Multiple Academic Labor Markets," paper presented at the annual meeting of the American Sociological Association, Washington, D.C., 1985; Breneman, David W., and Ted I. K. Youn, eds., *Academic Labor Markets and Academic Careers in American Higher Education*, in press; and McPherson, Michael S., "The State of Academic Labor Markets," in Smith, Bruce L. R., ed., *The State of Graduate Education* (Washington, D.C.: The Brookings Institution, 1985), pp. 57–83.

2. Smelser, Neil J., and Robin Content, *The Changing Academic Market: General Trends and a Berkeley Case Study* (Berkeley, Los Angeles, London: University of California Press, 1980), ch. 1, "General Contours of an Academic Market." Quotation, p. 7, emphasis in the original.

3. On the lengthening of training into postdoctoral years and all it implies for the competitive definition of expertise, see Zumeta, William, *Extending the Educational Ladder: The Changing Quality and Value of Postdoctoral Study* (Lexington, Mass.: D.C. Heath, 1985).

4. On the value of distinguishing between hard and soft disciplines (and also between the pure and the applied), see Becher, Tony, "The Disciplinary Shaping of the Profession," in Clark, Burton R., ed., *The Academic Profession: National, Disciplinary, and Institutional Settings* (Berkeley, Los Angeles, London: University of California Press, 1987).

5. See Finkelstein, *American Academic Profession*, pp. 45–47.

6. Smelser and Content, *Changing Academic Market*, p. 3.

7. From a national 1977 survey of part-timers, Tuckman and Tuckman distinguished four types: "full-mooners," those holding a full-time position elsewhere; "part-mooners," those holding two or more part-time positions; "hopeful full-timers," those holding full-time academic positions; and "homeworkers," women with household responsibilities who teach part-time. See Tuckman, R. H., and H. P. Tuckman, "Women as Part-Time Faculty Members," *Higher Education*, March, 1981, pp. 169–179.

8. Leslie, David W., Samuel E. Kellams, and G. Manny Gunne, *Part-Time Faculty in American Higher Education* (New York: Praeger, 1982), p. vi.

9. For a useful review of research on part-time faculty, see Gappa, Judith M., *Part-Time Faculty: Higher Education at a Crossroads*, ASHE-ERIC Higher Education Research Report No. 3, 1984 (Washington, D.C.: Association for the Study of Higher Education, 1984).

10. Cohen, Arthur M., and Florence B. Brawer, *The American Community College* (San Francisco: Jossey-Bass, 1982), pp. 69–72.

11. Ibid., p. 72.

12. Abel, Emily, *Terminal Degrees: The Job Crisis in Higher Education* (New York: Praeger, 1984), passim.

13. See Clark, Burton R., ed., *The Academic Profession: National, Disciplinary, and Institutional Settings* (Berkeley, Los Angeles, London: University of California Press, 1987).

14. Neave, Guy, and Gary Rhoades, "The Academic Estate in Western Europe," in Clark, Burton R., ed., *The Academic Profession: National, Disciplinary, and Institutional Settings* (Berkeley, Los Angeles, London: University of California Press, 1987).

15. *The* model of the use of outside examiners in the United States since the 1920s has been the Honors track at Swarthmore College. See Clark, Burton R., *The Distinctive College: Antioch, Reed, and Swarthmore* (Chicago: Aldine, 1970), ch. 7–9.

16. Data supplied by Maryse Eymonerie Associates, August, 1985, based on analysis of information provided by the AAUP Annual Reports on the Economic Status of the Profession.

17. Cohen and Brawer, *The American Community College*, p. 73.

18. On intrinsic and extrinsic rewards, see the summary of the literature in Finkelstein, *American Academic Profession*, pp. 79–80.

19. The responses from the field interviews, rich in their depiction of the intrinsic and extrinsic bases for satisfaction and discontent, have encouraged me to read the results of the 1964 Carnegie faculty survey in a relatively optimistic vein. I do not think that the American professoriate in the mid-1980s is a "national resource imperiled," nor that "the faculty" has a sense of being "deeply troubled." The professoriate's pleasures and discomforts are greatly disaggregated; coping behaviors are many and vigorous; and over the long term the system is a self-correcting one. For other interpretations, see Bowen, Howard R., and Jack H. Schuster, *American Professors: A National Resource Imperiled* (New York: Oxford University Press, 1986); and The Carnegie Foundation for the Advancement of Teaching, "The Faculty: Deeply Troubled," *Change* (Sept.-Oct., 1985), pp. 31–33.

20. Cohen and Brawer, *American Community College*, p. 76.

21. For an ethnographic documentation of this dissatisfaction, see Abel, *Terminal Degrees*.

CHAPTER VIII

1. Bloland, Harland G., *Higher Education Associations in a Decentralized Education System* (Berkeley: Center for Research and Development in Higher Education, University of California, 1969), pp. 77–99.

2. Kerr, Clark, *The Uses of the University* (Cambridge, Mass., Harvard University Press, 1963), pp. 56–60.

335

3. Kennedy, Donald, "Government Policies and the Cost of Doing Research," *Science*, February 1, 1985, pp. 480–484. Quotation, p. 482.
4. Ibid., p. 483.
5. Ibid., pp. 480, 483.
6. American Chemical Society, *Programs and Activities of the American Chemical Society* (Washington, D.C., 1983).
7. Federation of American Societies for Experimental Biology, *Annual Report, 1982* (Washington, D.C., 1982).
8. Cohen, Arthur M., and Florence B. Brawer, *The American Community College* (San Francisco: Jossey-Bass, 1982), pp. 88–90.
9. Boffey, Philip M., "Prestigious Forum Slides into a Troubling Decline," *New York Times*, June 4, 1985, pp. C1–C2.
10. Ibid.
11. Crane, Diana, *Invisible Colleges: Diffusion of Knowledge in Scientific Communities* (Chicago: University of Chicago Press, 1972), pp. 54, 35.
12. Wilson, Logan, *American Academics: Then and Now* (New York: Oxford University Press, 1979), pp. 155–159.

CHAPTER IX

1. Metzger, Walter P., "The Academic Profession in the United States," in Clark, Burton R., ed., *The Academic Profession: National, Disciplinary, and Institutional Settings* (Berkeley, Los Angeles, London: University of California Press, 1987); Jencks, Christopher, and David Riesman, *The Academic Revolution* (Garden City, N.Y.: Doubleday, 1968); and Veysey, Laurence R., *The Emergence of the American University* (Chicago: University of Chicago Press, 1965).
2. Riesman, David, *On Higher Education: The Academic Enterprise in an Era of Rising Student Consumerism* (San Francisco: Jossey-Bass, 1980).
3. On the similarity of American schools to shopping malls, see Powell, Arthur G., Eleanor Farrar, and David K. Cohen, *Shopping Mall High School* (Boston: Houghton-Mifflin, 1985).
4. John P. Heinz, and Edward O. Laumann have portrayed the American legal profession as divided primarily by the character of the clients served: The distinction between corporate and individual clients divides the bar into two separate "hemispheres." See Heinz, John P., and Laumann, Edward O., *Chicago Lawyers: The Social Structure of the Bar* (New York: Russell Sage, 1982). The distinction between peer and consumer clienteles that we have observed in the academic profession may be applicable to a number of other professions, where the orientation to research and innovation is stronger than it is in law: e.g., medicine—now a part of "the health sciences"—architecture, and engineering.
5. Wilson, Logan, *The Academic Man* (London: Oxford University Press, 1942), pp. 219, 112.
6. Ashby, Eric, "The Structure of Higher Education: A World View," Occasional Paper no. 6 (New York: International Council for Educational Development, 1973).

336

7. Lane, Jan-Eric, "Academic Profession in Academic Organization," *Higher Education*, vol. 14, no. 3, June, 1985, pp. 241–268.

8. Eurich, Nell P., *Corporate Classrooms: The Learning Business* (Princeton: The Carnegie Foundation for the Advancement of Teaching, 1985).

9. DiMaggio, Paul J., and Walter W. Powell, "The Iron Cage Revisited: Institutional Isomorphism and Collective Rationality in Organizational Fields," *American Sociological Review*, vol. 48, April, 1985, pp. 147–160.

10. Comment attributed to Henry James: exact reference unknown.

11. Sykes, Gary, "Teacher Education in the United States," in Clark, Burton R., ed., *The School and the University: An International Perspective* (Berkeley, Los Angeles, London: University of California Press, 1953).

12. Seidman, Earl, *In the Words of the Faculty: Pespectives on Improving Teaching and Educational Quality in Community Colleges* (San Francisco: Jossey-Bass, 1985), p. 275.

13. Weber, Max, "Science as a Vocation," in H. H. Gerth and C. Wright Mills, eds., *From Max Weber: Essays in Sociology* (New York: Oxford University Press, 1946), pp. 129–156.

14. Ibid., p. 156.

15. Bellah, Robert N., Richard Madsen, William M. Sullivan, Ann Swidler, and Steven M. Tipton, *Habits of the Heart: Individualism and Commitment in American Life* (Berkeley, Los Angeles, London: University of California Press, 1985), p. 66. In exploring individualism and commitment in American life, Bellah and his associates, in four research projects, mainly pursued love and marriage, therapy, and several forms of civic or political participation among upper-middle-class people. Unfortunately, they concentrate for only a few pages on the world of work, where, especially for upper-middle-class professionals, much commitment is centered. See pages 65–71 and pages 287–290, where the call for reform centers on "a reappropriation of the idea of vocation or calling."

APPENDIX A

1. For the Durkheimian literature on differentiation and integration, see: Durkheim, Emile, *The Division of Labor in Society* (New York: Free Press, 1947); *Emile Durkheim on Morality and Society*, edited by Robert N. Bellah (Chicago: University of Chicago Press, 1973); Rueschemeyer, Dietrich, "Structural Differentiation, Efficiency, and Power," *American Journal of Sociology*, vol. 83, no. 1, July, 1977, pp. 1–25; and Jonathan H. Turner, "Emile Durkheim's Theory of Integration in Differentiated Social Systems," *Pacific Sociological Review*, vol. 24, no. 4, Oct., 1981, pp. 379–391. For application to higher education, see Clark, Burton R., *The Higher Education System: Academic Organization in Cross-National Perspective* (Berkeley, Los Angeles, London: University of California Press, 1983), section on "The Process of Differentiation," pp. 214–227.

2. See Bowen, Howard R., and Jack H. Schuster, *American Professors: A National Resource Imperiled* (New York: Oxford University Press, 1986).

3. For major surveys done by mail questionnaire or large-scale interviewing that have tapped such matters, see Lazarsfeld, Paul F., and Wagner Thielens, Jr., *The Academic*

Mind: Social Scientists in a Time of Crisis (Glencoe, Ill.: Free Press, 1958); Ladd, Everett Carll, Jr., and Seymour Martin Lipset, *The Divided Academy: Professors and Politics* (New York: McGraw-Hill, 1975); and, Fulton, Oliver, and Martin Trow, "Research Activity in American Higher Education," in Trow, Martin, ed., *Teachers and Students: Aspects of American Higher Education* (New York: McGraw-Hill, 1975), pp. 39–83.

4. Copies of the interview guide may be obtained by writing the Comparative Higher Education Research Group, Department of Education, University of California, Los Angeles, California 90024.

5. The Carnegie Foundation for the Advancement of Teaching, *1984 Faculty Survey*; and Opinion Research Corporation, *Technical Report: 1984 Carnegie Foundation National Surveys of Higher Education* (Princeton: 1984).

6. Parsons, Talcott, and Gerald M. Platt, *The American University* (Cambridge, Mass.: Harvard University, 1973). For an insightful review of this book, see Gusfield, Joseph R., "Review Symposium on *The American University* by Talcott Parsons and Gerald M. Platt," *Contemporary Sociology*, vol. 3, no. 4 (July, 1974), pp. 291–295.

BIBLIOGRAPHY

Abel, Emily, *Terminal Degrees: The Job Crisis in Higher Education* (New York: Praeger, 1984).

Albers, Donald J., and G. L. Alexanderson, eds., *Mathematical People: Profiles and Interviews* (Boston: Birkhauser, 1985).

American Chemical Society, *Programs and Activities of the American Chemical Society* (Washington, D.C., 1983).

Ashby, Eric, "The Structure of Higher Education: A World View," Occasional Paper no. 6 (New York: International Council for Educational Development, 1973).

Austin, Ann E., and Zelda F. Gamson, *Academic Workplace: New Demands, Heightened Tensions*, ASHE-ERIC Higher Education Research Report no. 10 (Washington, D.C.: Association for the Study of Higher Education, 1983).

Babbidge, Homer D., and Robert Rosenzweig, *The Federal Interest in Higher Education* (New York: McGraw-Hill, 1962).

Baldridge, J. Victor, David V. Curtis, George Ecker, and Gary L. Riley, *Policy Making and Effective Leadership* (San Francisco: Jossey-Bass, 1978).

Becher, Tony, "The Cultural View," in Clark, Burton R., ed., *Perspectives on Higher Education: Eight Disciplinary and Comparative Views* (Berkeley, Los Angeles, London: University of California Press, 1984).

Becher, Tony, and Maurice Kogan, *Process and Structure in Higher Education* (London: Heineman, 1980).

————, "The Disciplinary Shaping of the Profession," in Clark, Burton R., ed., *The Academic Profession: National, Disciplinary, and Institutional Settings* (Berkeley, Los Angeles, London: University of California Press, 1987).

Bellah, Robert N., Richard Madsen, William M. Sullivan, Ann Swidler, and Steven M. Tipton, *Habits of the Heart: Individualism and Commitment in American Life* (Berkeley, Los Angeles, London: University of California Press, 1985).

Ben-David, Joseph, *Centers of Learning: Britain, France, Germany, United States* (New York: McGraw-Hill, 1977).

————, *The Scientist's Role in Society: A Comparative Study* (Englewood Cliffs, N.J.: Prentice-Hall, 1971).

339

Bienaymé, Alain, "Systems of Higher Education: France" (New York: International Council on Educational Development, 1978).

Biglan, Anthony, "Relationships between Subject Matter Characteristics and the Structure and Output of University Departments," *Journal of Applied Psychology*, vol. 57, 1973, pp. 204–213.

Blau, Peter M., *The Organization of Academic Work* (New York: John Wiley, 1973).

Bloland, Harland G., *Higher Education Associations in a Decentralized Education System* (Berkeley: Center for Research and Development in Higher Education, University of California, 1969).

Bowen, Howard R., and Jack H. Schuster, *American Professors: A National Resource Imperiled* (New York: Oxford University Press, 1986).

Breneman, David W., and Ted I. K. Youn, eds., *Academic Labor Markets and Academic Careers in American Higher Education*, in press.

Burke, Colin B., *American Collegiate Populations: A Test of the Traditional View* (New York: New York University Press, 1982).

Campbell, Donald T., "Ethnocentrism of Disciplines and the Fish Scale Model of Omniscience," in Sherif, M., and C. Sherif, eds., *Interdisciplinary Relationships in the Social Sciences* (Chicago: Aldine, 1969), pp. 328–348.

Caplow, Theodore, and Reece J. McGee, *The Academic Marketplace* (New York: Basic Books, 1958).

Carnegie Council on Policy Studies in Higher Education, *A Classification of Institutions of Higher Education* (rev. ed.) (Berkeley, California, 1976).

The Carnegie Foundation for the Advancement of Teaching, *1984 Faculty Survey* (Princeton, 1984).

———, "The Faculty: Deeply Troubled," *Change*, September-October 1985, pp. 31–33.

Carr-Saunders, A. M., and P. A. Wilson, *The Professors* (Oxford: Oxford University Press, 1933).

Cartter, Allan M., *An Assessment of Quality in Graduate Education* (Washington, D.C.: American Council on Education, 1966).

Cipolla, Carlo M., "The Professions: A Long View," *The Journal of European Economic History* 2, Spring, 1973, pp. 37–52.

Clark, Burton R., *The Distinctive College: Antioch, Reed, and Swarthmore* (Chicago: Aldine, 1970).

———, *Academic Power in Italy: Bureaucracy and Oligarchy in a National University System* (Chicago: University of Chicago Press, 1977).

———, *The Higher Education System: Academic Organization in Cross-National Perspective* (Berkeley, Los Angeles, London: University of California Press, 1983).

340

Clark, Burton R., ed., *The School and the University: An International Perspective* (Berkeley, Los Angeles, London: University of California Press, 1985).

————, *The Academic Profession: National, Disciplinary, and Institutional Settings* (Berkeley, Los Angeles, London: University of California Press, 1987).

Cohen, Arthur M., "Student Access and the Collegiate Function in Community Colleges," *Higher Education*, vol. 14, no. 2, April, 1985, pp. 149–163.

Cohen, Arthur M., and Florence B. Brawer, *The Two-Year College Instructor Today* (New York, London: Praeger, 1977).

————, *The American Community College* (San Francisco: Jossey-Bass, 1982).

Cohen, Michael D., and James G. March, *Leadership and Ambiguity: The American College President* (New York: McGraw-Hill, 1974).

Coleman, James S., "The University and Society's New Demands Upon It," in Kaysen, Carl, ed., *Content and Context: Essays on College Education* (New York: McGraw-Hill, 1973).

The Conference Board of Associated Research Councils, *An Assessment of Research-Doctorate Programs in the United States*, 5 vols. (Washington, D.C.: National Academy Press, 1982).

Crane, Diana, *Invisible Colleges: Diffusion of Knowledge in Scientific Communities* (Chicago: University of Chicago Press, 1972).

————, "Cultural Differentiation, Cultural Integration, and Social Control," in Gibbs, Jack P., ed., *Social Control: Views from the Social Sciences* (Beverly Hills, California: Sage Publications, 1982).

Cummings, William K., Ikuo Amano, and Kazuyuki Kitamura, eds., *Changes in the Japanese University: A Comparative Perspective* (New York: Praeger, 1979).

Curti, Merle, *The Growth of American Thought* (3d. ed.) (New Brunswick, N.J.: Transaction Books, 1981).

Daalder, Hans, and Edward Shils, eds., *Universities, Politicians and Bureaucrats* (Cambridge, England: Cambridge University Press, 1982).

Dewey, John, *Individualism Old and New* (New York: Minton, Balch, 1930).

Dill, David, "The Structure of the Academic Profession," *Journal of Higher Education*, vol. 53, no. 3, 1982, pp. 255–267.

DiMaggio, Paul J., and Walter W. Powell, "The Iron Cage Revisited: Institutional Isomorphism and Collective Rationality in Organizational Fields," *American Sociological Review*, vol. 48, April, 1985, pp. 147–160.

Dingwall, Robert, and Philip Lewis, eds., *The Sociology of the Professions* (London: Macmillan, 1983).

Douglas, Joel M., and Elizabeth A. Kotch, *Directory of Faculty Contracts and Bargaining Agents in Institutions of Higher Education*, vol. 11 (New York: The National Center for the Study of Collective Bargaining in Higher Education and the Professions, Baruch College, City University of New York, 1985).

Durkheim, Emile, *The Division of Labor in Society* (New York: Free Press, 1947).

————, *Emile Durkheim on Morality and Society*, Robert N. Bellah, ed. (Chicago: University of Chicago Press, 1973).

Eurich, Nell P., *Corporate Classrooms: The Learning Business* (Princeton: The Carnegie Foundation for the Advancement of Teaching, 1985).

Federation of American Societies for Experimental Biology, *Annual Report* (Washington, D.C., 1982).

Fermi, Laura, *Illustrious Immigrants* (2nd ed.) (Chicago and London: University of Chicago Press, 1971).

Finkelstein, Martin J., *The American Academic Profession: A Synthesis of Social Scientific Inquiry Since World War II* (Columbus, Ohio: Ohio State University Press, 1984).

Freidson, Eliot, *Profession of Medicine: A Study of the Sociology of Applied Knowledge* (New York: Dodd, Mead, 1970).

————, *Professional Dominance* (New York: Atherton Press, 1970).

Friedberg, Erhard, and Christine Musselin. "The Academic Profession in France," in *The Academic Profession: National, Disciplinary, and Institutional Settings*, Burton R. Clark, ed. (Berkeley, Los Angeles, London: University of California Press, 1987).

Fulton, Oliver, and Martin Trow, "Research Activity in American Higher Education," in *Teachers and Students: Aspects of American Higher Education*, Martin Trow, ed. (New York: McGraw-Hill, 1975), pp. 39–83.

Gappa, Judith M., *Part-Time Faculty: Higher Education at a Crossroads*, ASHE-ERIC Higher Education Research Report no. 3 (Washington, D.C.: Association for the Study of Higher Education, 1984).

Garbarino, Joseph W., *Faculty Bargaining: Change and Conflict* (New York: McGraw-Hill, 1975).

Geiger, Roger, "The Conditions of University Research, 1900–1920," *History of Higher Education Annual*, no. 4, 1984, pp. 3–29.

————, *To Advance Knowledge: The Growth of American Research Universities, 1900–1940* (New York: Oxford University Press, 1986).

Glazer, Nathan, "The Schools of the Minor Professions," *Minerva*, vol. 10, July, 1974, pp. 346–364.

Gouldner, Alvin W., "Cosmopolitans and Locals—I," *Administrative Science Quarterly*, vol. 2, Dec., 1957, pp. 281–306; "Cosmopolitans and Locals: Toward an Analysis of Latent Social Roles—II," *Administrative Science Quarterly*, vol. 2, March, 1958, pp. 444–480.

Grant, Gerald, and David Riesman, *The Perpetual Dream: Reform and Experiment in the American College* (Chicago: University of Chicago Press, 1978).

Guralnick, Stanley, *Science and the Antebellum College* (Philadelphia: American Philosophical Society, 1975).

Gusfield, Joseph R., "Review Symposium on *The American University* by Talcott Parsons and Gerald M. Platt," *Contemporary Sociology*, vol. 3, no. 4, July 1974, pp. 291–295.

Haber, Samuel, "The Professions and Higher Education in America: A Historical View," in Gordon, Margaret S., ed., *Higher Education and the Labor Market* (New York: McGraw-Hill, 1974), pp. 237–280.

Halpern, Sydney A., "Professional Schools in the American University," in Clark, Burton, R. ed., *The Academic Profession: National, Disciplinary, and Institutional Settings* (Berkeley, Los Angeles, London: University of California Press, 1987).

Hawkins, Hugh, *Between Harvard and America: The Educational Leadership of Charles W. Eliot* (New York: Oxford, 1972).

Heinz, John P., and Edward O. Laumann, *Chicago Lawyers: The Social Structure of the Bar* (New York: Russell Sage, 1982).

Higham, John, "The Matrix of Specialization," in Oleson, Alexandra and John Voss, eds., *The Organization of Knowledge in Modern America, 1860–1920* (Baltimore, Md.: The Johns Hopkins University Press, 1979), pp. 3–18.

Hoch, Paul K, "The Reception of Central European Refugee Physicists of the 1930s: U.S.S.R., U.K., U.S.A.," *Annals of Science*, vol. 40, no. 3, May, 1983, pp. 217–246.

Hofstadter, Richard, and Walter P. Metzger, *Development of Academic Freedom in the United States* (New York: Columbia University Press, 1955).

Hofstadter, Richard, and Wilson Smith, eds., *American Higher Education: A Documentary History* (Chicago: University of Chicago Press, 1968), vol. 1.

Holton, Gerald, "Scientific Research and Scholarship: Notes Toward the Design of Proper Scales," *Daedalus*, vol. 91, 1962, part 1, pp. 362–399.

Hughes, Edward Cherrington, *Men and Their Work* (Glencoe, Ill.: Free Press, 1958).

———, *Students' Culture and Perspectives: Lectures on Medical and General Education* (Lawrence, Kansas: University of Kansas School of Law, 1961).

Hughes, H. Stuart, *The Sea Change: The Migration of Social Thought, 1930–65* (New York: Harper and Row, 1975).

Jacobs, Jane, *The Economy of Cities* (New York: Vintage Books, 1970).

Jencks, Christopher, and David Riesman, *The Academic Revolution* (Garden City, N.Y.: Doubleday, 1968).

343

Kemerer, Frank R., and J. Victor Baldridge, *Unions on Campus* (San Francisco: Jossey-Bass, 1975).

Kennedy, Donald, "Government Policies and The Cost of Doing Research," *Science*, vol. 227, February 1, 1985, pp. 480–484.

Keniston, Hayward, *Graduate Study and Research in the Arts and Sciences at the University of Pennsylvania* (Philadelphia: University of Pennsylvania Press, 1959).

Kerr, Clark, *The Uses of the University* (Cambridge, Mass.: Harvard University Press, 1963).

———, "Higher Education: Paradise Lost?" *Higher Education*, vol. 7, no. 3, August, 1978, pp. 261–278.

Kogan, Maurice, "The Political View," in Clark, Burton R., ed., *Perspectives on Higher Education: Eight Disciplinary and Comparative Views* (Berkeley, Los Angeles, London: University of California Press, 1984), pp. 56–78.

Ladd, Everett Carll, Jr., "The Work Experience of American College Professors: Some Data and an Argument," in *Current Issues in Higher Education 1979* (Washington, D.C.: American Association for Higher Education, 1979), pp. 3–12.

Ladd, Everett Carll, Jr., and Seymour Martin Lipset, *Professors, Unions and American Higher Education* (Berkeley: The Carnegie Commission on Higher Education, 1973).

———, *Survey of the Social, Political, and Educational Perspectives of American College and University Faculty*, final report, 2 vols. (Storrs, Conn.: University of Connecticut, 1976).

———, *The Divided Academy: Professors and Politics* (New York: McGraw-Hill, 1975).

Lane, Jan-Eric, "Academic Profession in Academic Organization," *Higher Education*, vol. 14, no. 3, June, 1985, pp. 241–268.

Larson, Magali Sarfatti, *The Rise of Professionalism* (Berkeley, Los Angeles, London: University of California Press, 1977).

Lawrence, Judith, and Kenneth C. Green, *A Question of Quality: The Higher Education Ratings Game*, AAHE-ERIC Higher Education Research Report no. 5 (Washington, D.C.: American Association for Higher Education, 1980).

Lax, Eric, *Life and Death on 10 West* (New York: Dell, 1984).

Lazarsfeld, Paul F., and Wagner Thielens, Jr., *The Academic Mind: Social Scientists in a Time of Crisis* (Glencoe, Ill.: Free Press, 1958).

Leslie, David W., Samuel E. Kellams, and G. Manny Gunne, *Part-Time Faculty in American Higher Education* (New York: Praeger, 1982).

Light, Donald R., "Introduction: The Structure of the Academic Profession," *Sociology of Education*, vol. 47, Winter, 1974, pp. 2–28.

Lipset, Seymour M., "The Academic Mind at the Top: The Political Behavior and Values of Faculty Elites," *Public Opinion Quarterly*, vol. 46, 1982, pp. 143–168.

Lodahl, Janice B., and Gerald Gordon, "The Structure of Scientific Fields and the Functioning of University Graduate Departments," *American Sociological Review*, vol. 37, 1972, pp. 57–72.

Lodge, David, *Small World: An Academic Romance* (London: Secker and Warburg, 1984).

McPherson, Michael S., "The State of Academic Labor Markets," in Smith, Bruce L. R., ed., *The State of Graduate Education* (Washington, D. C.: The Brookings Institution, 1985), pp. 57–83.

Mansbridge, Jane J., *Beyond Adversary Democracy* (Chicago: University of Chicago Press, 1983).

March, James G., and Johan P. Olsen, *Ambiguity and Choice in Organizations* (Bergen, Norway: Universitetsforlaget, 1976).

Merton, Robert K., "The Normative Structure of Science," in Stover, Norman W., ed., *The Sociology of Science: Theoretical and Empirical Investigations* (Chicago: University of Chicago Press, 1973), pp. 267–278.

Metzger, Walter P., "The Academic Profession in the United States," in Clark, Burton R., ed., *The Academic Profession: National, Disciplinary, and Institutional Settings* (Berkeley, Los Angeles, London: University of California Press, 1987).

Mommsen, Wolfgang, "The Academic Profession in the Federal Republic of Germany," in Clark, Burton R., ed., *The Academic Profession: National, Disciplinary, and Institutional Settings* (Berkeley, Los Angeles, London: University of California Press, 1987).

National Board of Universities and Colleges, *Higher Education and Research in Sweden 1984–85: Some Facts and Figures* (Stockholm, 1985).

Naylor, Natalie A., "The Ante-Bellum College Movement: A Reappraisal of Tewksbury's 'The Founding of American Colleges and Universities,' " *History of Education Quarterly*, vol. 13, Fall, 1973, pp. 261–274.

Neave, Guy R., "Elite and Mass Higher Education in Britain: A Regressive Model?" *Comparative Education Review*, vol. 29, no. 3, August, 1985, pp. 347–361.

Neave, Guy, and Gary Rhoades, "The Academic Estate in Western Europe," in Clark, Burton R., ed., *The Academic Profession: National, Disciplinary, and Institutional Settings* (Berkeley, Los Angeles, London: The University of California Press, 1987).

Neumann, Franz, *The Cultural Migration: The European Scholar in America* (Philadelphia: University of Pennsylvania Press, 1953).

Oleson, Alexandra, and John Voss, eds., *The Organization of Knowledge in Modern America, 1860–1920* (Baltimore, Md.: The Johns Hopkins University Press, 1979).

345

Opinion Research Corporation, *Technical Report: 1984 Carnegie Foundation National Surveys of Higher Education* (Princeton, 1984).

Pangburn, Jessie M., *The Evolution of the American Teachers College* (New York: Columbia University, 1932).

Parsons, Talcott, "Professions," in *International Encyclopedia of the Social Sciences*, vol. 12 (New York: Free Press, 1968).

Parsons, Talcott, and Gerald M. Platt, *The American University* (Cambridge, Mass.: Harvard University, 1973).

Peisert, Hansgert, and Gerhild Framhein, *Systems of Higher Education: Federal Republic of Germany* (New York: International Council for Educational Development, 1978).

Perkin, Harold, "The Historical Perspective," in Clark, Burton R., ed., *Perspectives on Higher Education: Eight Disciplinary and Comparative Views* (Berkeley, Los Angeles, London: University of California Press, 1984), pp. 17–55.

————, "The Academic Profession in the United Kingdom," in Clark, Burton R., ed., *The Academic Profession: National, Disciplinary, and Institutional Settings* (Berkeley, Los Angeles, London: University of California Press, 1987).

Polanyi, Michael, *The Tacit Dimension* (Garden City, N.Y.: Doubleday, 1967).

————, *The Logic of Liberty: Reflections and Rejoinders*, reprint (Chicago: University of Chicago Press, 1980).

Powell, Arthur G., Eleanor Farrar, and David K. Cohen, *Shopping Mall High School* (Boston: Houghton-Mifflin, 1985).

Price, Don K., *The Scientific Estate* (Cambridge, Mass.: Harvard University Press, 1973).

Rhoades, Gary, "Higher Education in a Consumer Society," *The Journal of Higher Education*, vol. 58, no. 1, January-February, 1987, pp. 1–24.

————, "The Profession and the Laity," unpublished ms.

Richardson, Richard C., Jr., Elizabeth C. Fisk, and Morris A. Okun, *Literacy in the Open-Access College* (San Francisco: Jossey-Bass, 1983).

Riesman, David, *Constraint and Variety in American Education* (Lincoln, Neb.: University of Nebraska Press, 1956).

————, in Riesman, David, and Verne A. Stadtman, eds., *Academic Transformation: Seventeen Institutions Under Pressure* (New York: McGraw-Hill, 1973).

————, *On Higher Education: The Academic Enterprise in an Era of Rising Student Consumerism* (San Francisco: Jossey-Bass, 1980).

Riesman, David, Joseph Gusfield, and Zelda Gamson, *Academic Values and Mass Education: The Early Years of Oakland and Montheith* (Garden City, N.Y.: Doubleday, 1970).

Rohlen, Thomas P., *Japan's High Schools* (Berkeley, Los Angeles, London: University of California Press, 1983).

Roose, Kenneth D., and Charles J. Andersen, *A Rating of Graduate Programs* (Washington, D.C.: American Council on Education, 1970).

Rosenberg, Charles, "Toward an Ecology of Knowledge: On Discipline, Contexts, and History," in Oleson, Alexandra, and John Voss, eds., *The Organization of Knowledge in Modern America, 1860–1920* (Baltimore, Md.: The Johns Hopkins University Press, 1979).

Rosenzweig, Robert M., *The Universities and Their Patrons* (Berkeley, Los Angeles, London: University of California Press, 1982).

Rowland, Henry A., "A Plea for Pure Science" (an 1883 address to the American Association for the Advancement of Science), in *The Physical Papers of Henry Augustus Rowland* (Baltimore, Md.: The Johns Hopkins Press, 1902), pp. 593–619.

Rudolph, Frederick, *The American College and University* (New York: Knopf, 1962).

Rueschemeyer, Dietrich, "Structural Differentiation, Efficiency, and Power," *American Journal of Sociology*, vol. 83, 1977, pp. 1–25.

———, "Professional Autonomy and the Social Control of Expertise," in Dingwall, Robert, and Philip Lewis, eds., *The Sociology of the Professions: Lawyers, Doctors, and Others* (London: Macmillan, 1983), pp. 38–58.

Ruscio, Kenneth P., "The Distinctive Scholarship of the Selective Liberal Arts College," *Journal of Higher Education*, vol. 58, no. 2, March-April, 1987, pp. 205–222.

———, "The Links Between Specializations: The Cases of Biology and Political Science," *The Review of Higher Education*, forthcoming.

Schwartzman, Simon, "The Focus on Scientific Activity," in Clark, Burton R., ed., *Perspectives on Higher Education: Eight Disciplinary and Comparative Views* (Berkeley, Los Angeles, London: University of California Press, 1984), pp. 199–225.

Scott, Peter, "Has the Binary Policy Failed?" in *The Structure and Governance of Higher Education at the University* (Guildford, Surrey, England: The Society for Research into Higher Education, 1983), pp. 166–196.

Seidman, Earl, *In the Words of the Faculty: Perspectives on Improving Teaching and Educational Quality in Community Colleges* (San Francisco: Jossey-Bass, 1985).

Shea, John R., "Design and Function," in Pifer, Alan, John Shea, David Henry, and Lyman Glenny, *Systems of Higher Education: United States* (New York: International Council for Educational Development, 1978).

Smelser, Neil J., and Robin Content, *The Changing Academic Market: General Trends and a Berkeley Case Study* (Berkeley, Los Angeles, London: University of California Press, 1980).

Starr, Paul, *The Social Transformation of American Medicine* (New York: Basic Books, 1982).

Storr, Richard J., *The Beginnings of Graduate Education in America* (Chicago: University of Chicago Press, 1953).

Sykes, Gary, "Teacher Education in the United States," in Clark, Burton R., ed., *The School and the University: An International Perspective* (Berkeley, Los Angeles, London: University of California Press, 1985), pp. 264–289.

Tawney, R. H., *The Acquisitive Society* (New York: Harcourt Brace, 1948).

Tewksbury, Donald G., *The Founding of American Colleges and Universities Before the Civil War* (New York: Teachers College Press, 1932).

Tocqueville, Alexis de, *Democracy in America*, ed. by Phillips Bradley (New York: Knopf, 1944).

Trow, Martin, " 'Elite Higher Education': An Endangered Species?" *Minerva*, vol. 14, no. 3, Autumn, 1976, pp. 355–376.

————, "The Analysis of Status," in Clark, Burton R., ed., *Perspectives on Higher Education: Eight Disciplinary and Comparative Views* (Berkeley, Los Angeles, and London: University of California Press, 1984), pp. 132–164.

Tuckman, R. H., and H. P. Tuckman, "Women as Part-Time Faculty Members," *Higher Education*, vol. 10, March, 1981, pp. 169–179.

Turner, Jonathan H., "Emile Durkheim's Theory of Integration in Differentiated Social Systems," *Pacific Sociological Review*, vol. 24, 1981, pp. 379–391.

UNESCO, *UNESCO Statistical Yearbook 1984* (Paris, 1984).

U.S. Department of Education, National Center for Education Statistics, *Digest of Education Statistics: 1982*, Washington, D.C.: 1983.

Van De Graaff, John H., Burton R. Clark, Dorotea Furth, Dietrich Goldschmidt, and Donald Wheeler, *Academic Power: Patterns of Authority in Seven National Systems* (New York: Praeger, 1978).

Veblen, Thorstein, *The Higher Learning in America* (Stanford, Calif.: Academic Reprints, 1954). Originally published in 1918 by B. W. Huebsch.

Veysey, Laurence R., *The Emergence of the American University* (Chicago: University of Chicago Press, 1965).

Vollmer, Howard M., and Donald L. Mills, eds., *Professionalization* (Englewood Cliffs, N.J.: Prentice-Hall, 1966).

Wayland, Francis, A discourse in commemoration of the life and character of the Hon. Nicholas Brown, Brown University, November 3, 1841 (Boston: Gould, Kendall and Lincoln, 1841).

Weber, Max, "Science as a Vocation," in Gerth, H. H., and C. Wright Mills, eds., *From Max Weber: Essays in Sociology* (New York: Oxford University Press, 1946), pp. 129–156.

Webster, Daniel, "Daniel Webster and the Saga of Dartmouth College," in Hofstadter, Richard, and Wilson, Smith, eds., *American Higher Education: A Documentary History* (Chicago: University of Chicago Press, 1970).

Webster, David, "James McKeen Cattell and the Invention of Quality Ratings 1903–1910," *The Review of Higher Education*, vol. 8, 1985, pp. 107–121.

———, *Academic Quality Rankings of American Colleges and Universities* (Springfield, Ill.: Charles C. Thomas, 1986).

Whitehead, Alfred North, "Universities and Their Functions," *Atlantic Monthly*, vol. 141, no. 5, 1928, pp. 638–644.

Whitehead, John, *The Separation of College and State: Columbia, Dartmouth, Harvard and Yale, 1776–1876* (New Haven: Yale University Press, 1975).

Wiebe, Robert H., *The Search for Order, 1877–1920* (New York: Hill and Wang, 1967).

Wilson, Logan, *The Academic Man* (London: Oxford University Press, 1942).

———, *American Academics: Then and Now* (New York: Oxford University Press, 1979).

Youn, Ted I. K., and Daniel Zelterman, "Academic Career Mobility in Multiple Academic Labor Markets," paper presented at the annual meeting of the American Sociological Association, Washington, D.C., 1985.

Zammuto, Raymond F., "Are the Liberal Arts an Endangered Species?" *Journal of Higher Education*, vol. 55, no. 2, March/April, 1984, pp. 184–211.

Zumeta, William, *Extending the Educational Ladder: The Changing Quality and Value of Postdoctoral Study* (Lexington, Mass.: D. C. Heath, 1985).

INDEX

Absorbing Errand of professoriate, 272–75
Academic drift, 143
Academic freedom, 134–40, 142–43
Academic man ideal, 109, 123–29
Academic work: blending of, 70–71; and control of higher education, 101, 184–85; as a cottage industry, 71–72; definition of, 72, 73–80; and disciplines, 89–98; and hierarchy, 99, 101; paradox of, 98–102; rewards in, 72, 98–102; types of, 70–71, 79–80, 92, 102–4. *See also* Administration; Institution, types of; Research; Teaching; Teaching load; specific type of institution
Academy of Management, 247
Access, 56
Activists, 117–18
Adjuncts. *See* Part-time faculty
Administration. *See* Academic work; Authority; Bureaucracy; Control of higher education; Governance; Institutions; Unions
Adult education, 22
Advising/counseling. *See* Academic work: types of
Albany State College [Georgia], 19
Alumni, 7–8
American Academy of Arts and Sciences, 36
American Association for the Advancement of Science [AAAS], 36, 240, 246
American Association of Engineering Societies, 239
American Association of Immunologists, 240–41
American Association of Medical Colleges, 239
American Association of University

Professors [AAUP], 16–17, 252, 253, 254, 259
American Bar Association, 237
American Chemical Society, 237–38, 239
American Council of Education [ACE], 234
American Economic Association, 36
American Federation of Teachers, 252–53
American Geographical Society, 36
American Historical Association, 36, 237
American Institute of Biological Sciences, 239
American Institute of Physics, 239
American Medical Association, 237, 239
American Philosophical Society, 36
American Physical Society, 36, 246–47
American Political Science Association, 241, 243
American Society of Zoologists, 36
American Sociological Association, 237, 241
American Statistical Association, 36
American Zoological Society, 240
Amherst College, 14
Anthropology, 31, 36–37
Antioch College, 47
Applied disciplines, 170–72, 189 *See also* name of specific discipline
Appointments, faculty, 189, 204–9. *See also* Part-time faculty
Artom, Camillo, 57
Arts, 41, 209
Ashby, Eric, 267, 268
Association of American Medical Colleges [AAMC], 98
Association of American Universities [AAU], 19, 32

351

Guralnick, Stanley M., 27–28
Gypsy scholars, 189, 209–10, 261

Halpern, Sydney Ann, 97
Hard/soft disciplines, 193–96
Harper, William Rainey, 8
Hartford Graduate Center, 21
Harvard University: careers at, 213; disciplines at, 27, 30; dissidents at, 46; early history of, 3, 4, 5; prestige/quality of, 19, 47–48, 179, 195
Hierarchy: and academic work, 99, 101; and authority, 161–62; and culture, 120, 142–43; and open system of higher education, 58–62; and unions, 182–83. *See also* Institutions, types of
Higher education, American: access to, 56; as an organized anarchy, 147–48, 152, 183–84; and commitment, 270–75; compared with elementary/secondary education, 53–54; and competition, 46–58, 188–89, 204, 269–70; contemporary division of, 17–23; control of, 51, 52–53, 62–63, 101; diversity in, 4–17; dynamic aspects of, 45–46, 100–101; growth of, 4–7, 22–23, 50–51, 69–70, 258–63; hierarchy in, 58–62; institutional role in, 51–52, 262–65; and knowledge, 267–70; and logic of profession, 267–75; open system of, 45–66; organization of, 64–65; quality control in, 61; reforms needed in, 266–67; research/teaching impacts on, 263–64; retrenchment in, 202–3; and rewards, 263–65; size of system of, 54–56; state coordination of, 51; weaknesses of, 265–66. *See also* Early American colleges; Graduate education; Institutions; Institutions, types of; Liberal arts colleges; Private higher education; Professional education; Public higher education; Undergraduate education; Universities; specific type of institution

Higher education, European: access to, 56; authority/control in, 52, 62–63, 153–54; careers in, 197, 210
Higher education, European, and competition, 269
Higher education, European: and disciplines, 26, 31; and graduate education, 33; organizational patterns of, 6; professoriate in, 56–58, 258; size of system in, 55. *See also* name of specific institution or country
History, 30–31, 36–37, 41, 198–99, 237
Hoch, Paul K., 57
Holton, Gerald, 65
Humanities, 38, 41, 93, 143, 183, 195–96, 198–99, 202, 209. *See also* name of specific association; name of specific discipline

Idaho State University, 17
Ideal of academic man, 109, 123–29
Identification with disciplines/institution, 106–8, 109–22, 141, 143–45
Independent scholars, 250–51. *See also* Gypsy scholars
Influence. *See* Power
Institutional definition of academic work, 73–80
Institutional initiative, 51–52
Institutional overhead, 236–37
Institutions: associations of, 234–37, 251–52; and careers, 188–89; role in American higher education of, 262–65. *See also* Institutions, types of
Institutions, types of: and academic freedom, 134–36, 139–40, 142–43; and academic work, 70–71, 79–80, 92, 102–4; and associations, 238, 241, 242–44, 245; and authority, 155–68, 174, 184, 186; and logic of profession, 269–70; and teaching load, 73–75, 83–84, 89. *See also* specific type of institution
Integration of academic culture, 105–6, 109, 140–45

357

358

Top-down management, 159–66
Trenton State College, 19
Trow, Martin, 73–74
Trust, 151
Trustees, 5, 15, 179–80. *See also* Authority; Control of higher education; Governance

Umbrella associations, 238–41
Unaccredited institutions, 22
Undergraduate education, 10–11, 20, 74–76, 265. *See also* Careers; Research; Teaching; Teaching load; specific type of institution
Unions, 16, 80, 174–83, 184, 214, 216
United Kingdom. *See* Great Britain
Universities: and academic man ideal, 123–25, 129; and academic work, 89; and associations, 244–45; and authority, 156–58, 174; and bureaucratic administrations, 11; and careers, 193, 200, 202, 208, 212, 213, 217, 222, 224–25; and competition, 53; and culture, 109–12, 113–15; and faculty, 17–20; German influence on, 8; growth of, 8, 10; and hierarchy of higher education, 59; hybrid nature of, 10–11; land-grant, 8, 10; and presidential leadership, 8; private, 8, 11, 13–14; and professional education, 29, 94; public, 8, 10–12, 14–15; reforms needed in, 266; specialized, 11–13; and teaching/teaching load, 32–33, 73, 74, 76, 89; and unions, 175, 178, 182; weaknesses of, 265

Values, 122–40, 142–43
Veblen, Thorstein, 70, 104
Virginia Woolf Society, 36–37
Vocational programs, 21–22
Voss, John, 34

Weber, Max, 273–74
Webster, Daniel, 7–8, 46, 113
Weisskopf, Victor, 57
Western Kentucky University, 14
Westminster College, 14
Wheeler, John, 250
Whitehead, Alfred North, 147–48
Wiebe, Robert H., 29
William and Mary, 4, 46
Williams College, 20
Wilson, Logan, 265
Winthrop College, 57
Wisconsin, University of, 19

Yale University, 4, 8, 14, 19, 27, 32, 46, 49, 266
Yeshiva University, 182

Zest of professoriate, 82–85, 102, 272–75
Zoology, 36